Wisdom and Psalms

A Feminist Companion to the Bible
(Second Series)

edited by Athalya Brenner and Carole R. Fontaine

The Feminist Companion to the Bible (Second Series)

2

Editors
Athalya Brenner and
Carole R. Fontaine

Sheffield Academic Press

Copyright © 1998 Sheffield Academic Press

Published by Sheffield Academic Press Ltd
Mansion House
19 Kingfield Road
Sheffield, S11 9AS
England

Printed on acid-free paper in Great Britain
by The Cromwell Press
Trowbridge, Wiltshire

British Library Cataloguing in Publication Data

A catalogue record for this book is available
from the British Library

ISBN 1-85075-917-0

To the memory of

Fokkelien van Dijk-Hemmes

תַּנְצְבָה

CONTENTS

Part I
IN GENERAL

Part II
WISDOM LITERATURE

Part III
FEMINISTS READ THE PSALMS

ABBREVIATIONS

AB	Anchor Bible
ABD	David Noel Freedman (ed.), *The Anchor Bible Dictionary* (New York: Doubleday, 1992)
AGJU	Arbeiten zur Geschichte des antiken Judentums und des Urchristentums
ANET	James B. Pritchard (ed.), *Ancient Near Eastern Texts Relating to the Old Testament* (Princeton: Princeton University Press, 1950)
AOAT	Alter Orient und Altes Testament
ATANT	Abhandlungen zur Theologie des Alten und Neuen Testaments
BEATAJ	Beitrage zur Erforschung des Alten Testament und des antiken Judentums
BBB	Bonner biblische Beiträge
BEFAR	Bibliothèque des écoles francaises d'Athènes et de Rome
BETL	Bibliotheca ephemeridum theologicarum lovaniensium
BEvT	Beiträge zur evangelischen Theologie
BHS	*Biblia hebraica stuttgartensia*
BHT	Beiträge zur historischen Theologie
Bib	*Biblica*
BibInt	*Biblical Interpretation*
BIS	Biblical Interpretation Series
BJS	Brown Judaic Studies
BK	*Bibel und Kirche*
BKAT	Biblischer Kommentar: Altes Testament
BN	*Biblische Notizen*
BZAW	Beihefte zur *ZAW*
CBQ	*Catholic Biblical Quarterly*
CBQMS	*Catholic Biblical Quarterly*, Monograph Series
ConBOT	Coniectanea biblica, Old Testament
CRBS	*Currents in Research: Biblical Studies*
CTR	*Criswell Theological Review*
EHS.T	Europäische Hochschuylschriften Reihe XXIII, Theologie
EvQ	*Evangelical Quarterly*
FAT	Forschungen zum Alten Testament

FCB	The Feminist Companion to the Bible
FOTL	The Forms of the Old Testament Literature
FThSt	Freiburger Theologische Studien
HS	*Hebrew Studies*
HSM	Harvard Semitic Monographs
HTR	*Harvard Theological Review*
ICC	International Critical Commentary
Int	*Interpretation*
JAAR	*Journal of the American Academy of Religion*
JBL	*Journal of Biblical Literature*
JSOT	*Journal for the Study of the Old Testament*
JSOTSup	*Journal for the Study of the Old Testament*, Supplement Series
JSPSup	*Journal for the Study of the Pseudepigrapha*, Supplement Series
KAT	Kommentar zum Alten Testament
LÄ	Lexikon der Ägyptologie
NCB	New Century Bible
NEB	Neue Echter Bibel, Kommentar zum Alten Testament
NedTTs	*Nederlands theologisch tijdschrift*
NICOT	New International Commentary on the Old Testament
NSKÄT	Neuer Stuttgarter Kommentar Altes Testament
NTG	New Testament Guides
OBO	Orbis biblicus et orientalis
OTG	Old Testament Guides
OTL	Old Testament Library
OTS	*Oudtestamentische Studiën*
ResQ	*Restoration Quarterly*
RTP	*Revue de théologie et de philosophie*
SBL	Society of Biblical Literature
SBLDS	SBL Dissertation Series
SBS	Stuttgarter Bibelstudien
SEA	*Svensk exegetisk årsbok*
ThWAT	G.J. Botterweck and H. Ringgren (eds.), *Theologisches Wörterbuch zum Alten Testament* (Stuttgart: W. Kohlhammer, 1970–95)
TOTC	Tyndale Old Testament Commentaries
VT	*Vetus Testamentun*
VTSup	*Vetus Testamentum*, Supplements
WBC	Word Biblical Commentary
WMANT	Wissenschaftliche Monographien zum Alten und Neuen Testament
WO	*Die Welt des Orients*
ZAW	*Zeitschrift für die alttestamentliche Wissenschaft*
ZBKAT	Zürcher Bibelkommentar zum Alten Testament

| ZDPV | *Zeitschrift des deutschen Palästina-Vereins* |
| ZTK | *Zeitschrift für Theologie und Kirche* |

LIST OF CONTRIBUTORS

Ulrike Bail, Faculty of Theology, Ruhr-University-Bochum, Universitätstr. 150/GA8, 44780 Bochum, Germany

Gerlinde Baumann, Fachgebiet Altes Testament, Fachbereich Ev. Theologie, Philipps-Universität, Marburg, Lahntor 3, D-35037 Marburg, Germany

Alice Ogden Bellis, Howard Divinity School, 1400 Shepherd St. NE, Washington DC 20017, USA

Athalya Brenner, Department of Theology and Religious Studies, University of Amsterdam, Oude Turfmarkt 147, 1012 GC Amsterdam, The Netherlands

Eric Christianson, Department of Theology and Religious Studies, University College Chester, Parkgate Road, Chester CH1 4BJ, England

Sidnie White Crawford, Classics and Religious Studies, University of Nebraska-Lincoln, Lincoln, NE 68588, USA

Carole Fontaine, Andover Newton Theological School, Newton Centre, MA 02159, USA

Ross Kraemer, Department of Religious Studies, University of Pennsylvania, Philadelphia, PA 19104, USA

Christl Maier, Faculty of Theology, OT Seminar, Humboldt University, Waisenstr. 28, 10179 Berlin, Germany

Roland Murphy, Whitefriars Hall, 1600 Webster St. NE, Washington DC 20017, USA

Brian Noonan, 47 Gaster St., New Haven, CT 06511, USA

Silvia Schroer, Feldeggstr. 28, CH-3098 Köniz, Switzerland

Beth LaNeel Tanner, SBN 7, Princeton Theological Seminary, Box 5204, Princeton, NJ 08543, USA

Job's Wife in the Etchings of William Blake

In 1825, English mystical poet and artist William Blake published *Illustrations of the Book of Job*, which on his title page, are said to be 'invented and engraved' by the artist. The process by which Blake was able to make his engravings directly on the etching plate, without any use of acid (as is customary), had direct impact in producing the exquisite quality of these line engravings, and the secret of his method died with him in 1827. The effects of this process are, however, fully available to the modern viewer, and they make a fitting introduction to this second volume on Wisdom Literature (and Psalms) making its appearance in the *Feminist Companion to the Bible* series.

Blake's main characters are all portrayed as we might expect by this unruly 'child of his time': God is clearly the great patriarch in the sky. The Satan is winged, and beautiful, but accompanied by deep shadows in which lurk creatures and wings. Job's children and friends are all healthy and sleek, well-dressed and well-fed in their 'before' and 'after' poses that represent Job's life before the demonic rupture caused by the test initiated in Heaven, and Job's exit from the liminal zone of his public suffering. But Ms Job, variously named Dinah or Rahmat by later midrashim, is something of a puzzle. We do not always see her where we might expect her, but we find her in Blake's 'reading' in places from which the biblical text and its interpreters have routinely excluded this co-victim, so readily castigated under patriarchy as one who 'talks as foolish women do' (Job 2.10). She is the paradigmatic feminist critic in Blake's vision: forced into the margins, assigned the role of onlooker to her own life, destined to be a 'hearer' rather than an 'interlocutor'. Yet she is still directly caught up, through 'corporate responsibility' and patriarchal ideology, in action which plainly affects her, but permits her a voice only so it can be silenced. But Blake found a way to let this character 'speak': the key to interpreting Dinah-Rahmat in Blake is to be found in the work of her hands.[1]

Clasped in prayerful attitude of worship in the 'before' scenes, Ms Job is also found there holding an open book upon her lap, suggesting that she, too, is an avid and faithful student of her received tradition (see Fig. 1). Blake's placement of her on 'Stage Right' (the viewers' left) already tells us that the artist views her in a better light than does scripture: in Blake's Joban iconography, the 'right' represents intuition, the spiritual imagination, and growth while the left (where Job is placed!) signifies received tradition, bodily life, reason, and that which impedes spiritual understanding.[2] By her placement, critics have taken Blake to mean that she is 'closer', even in the beginning, to understanding the problem of external works and their relation to integrity than is Job with his reliance upon past deeds. She raises her folded hands above her head in—shock? distress? horror? disbelief?— when the bad news of the destruction of wealth is delivered to her husband, and we note that she continues along side Job in Blake's vision, for her life, too, is being tested. During the afflictions of Job she is seen first, bowed in grief, her head in her hands, and next, cradling Job's head and shoulders in a manner very similar to the classic 'pieta' style: we sense that she plays the role of Job's comforting mother, as much as his companion in trouble. While friends accuse Job, she sits next to him, consternation and confusion on her troubled face, with her hands crossed as though bound at the wrist. She is given no place in wisdom's dialogues about divine justice, though conceivably as a woman, she might have a different point of view to con-

---

1.   Blake's 'vocabulary' of striking hand gestures was influenced by his work in the engraving studio of Henry Fuseli, an older artist who supported the younger artist's work in the early years, saying that Blake was 'damn good to steal from'; in turn, Blake characterized Fuseli as 'The only Man that e'er I knew / Who did not make me almost spew' (Morton D. Paley, *William Blake* [New York: Greenwich House, 1983], p. 18).

2.   John H. Wicksteed, *Blake's Vision of the Book of Job* (London: J.M. Dent & Sons, 1910), pp. 18-23.

tribute…as Naomi angrily does, when her own children die unexpectedly (Ruth 1.13). But at least Blake imagines her as an interested and engaged on-looker of men's discourse in ways few commentators have ever ventured to suggest.

Figure 1. 'Thus Did Job Continually'

By the time of Elihu's speech,[3] she has, like her husband, given up any attempt to wade through the victim-blaming retribution theology of the friends. Once again she sits, with her head

---

3. The turning point for Blake, if not for commentators.

bowed in grief, hands together but nearly formed into fists, face hidden. It is part of Blake's brilliance that what the character of Job conveyed through words in the Third Dialogue his wife embodies in posture, evoking wordless solidarity with her man. God's address from the whirlwind finds Ms Job with eyes open and praying hands, like her husband, while the voices of patriarchy—those friends—cringe abjectly, muzzled at last by theophany that contradicts their words of tradition (42.7-8). She opens her hands as if to clap in unison with the Bene elohim who celebrate creation, and along with Job, she views the mysteries of the creatures Behemoth and Leviathan. In Blake's Job, God blesses directly both marriage partners in the final illustrations for scenes from chapter 42. Ms Job is displaced by the beauty of her progeny when Job's three daughters are praised,[4] but in the final illustration of a restored and whole life (Fig. 2), her hands have finally abandoned the text to take up a lute and…what? Sing her own song, or once again form the accompaniment for her husband's?[5] Both Blake and the text leave us uncertain as to what Ms. Job's song will be in her 'latter days', but the tool of voice in her hands must give pause to readers of this variant.

The Present Volume

It is the way of wisdom to pose questions, to search the cosmos and the human heart with the best abilities of reason and experience. As the 'intellectual tradition' of scribes and bureaucrats of the Hebrew Bible, wisdom literature has often been home to the kind of 'problem literature' familiar from Egypt and Mesopotamia, a literary heritage which challenges traditional theological teachings made hoary by long adherence and unquestioning compliance. It is only with an inner fight that feminist critics in wisdom face up to the painful exclusions felt in Job and

---

4.   In fact, the design for this illustration is one of Blake's early works, executed in about 1785 in egg tempura (Paley, *Blake*, p. 69).

5.   The entire family has taken up musical instruments in the restoration scene, the same instruments that hung unused in the background in the first episode (compare Figs. 1 and 2).

Figure 2. 'So the Lord Blesses the Latter End of Job'

Qoheleth, or the ideological constructs about 'own' and 'foreign' women constructed by Proverbs. It is hard to let wisdom go without a blessing, because it has so much insight into the world of the private, the family quarters, the instructions of parents— all places where scant evidence of women's lives might be traced. Yet, the essays in this volume—the work of many hands—may leave the reader feeling decidedly 'unblessed'— perhaps feeling a bit like Job's friends as they hear him move through the phase of not 'sinning with his lips' to opening his mouth in biting lament.

As Murphy's essay in this volume suggests, wisdom is as much at home in the world of daily village life as in the schools and courts of Jerusalem, and more comfortably calls out to the God of Israel in the dress of creator rather than as historical redeemer. If women under ancient patriarchies knew little of redemption, at least as modern women might see it, they are nevertheless sites of family wisdom and tradition, especially during the oral stages of village wisdom, or when postexilic writers sit down to laud the authority of parental instructions, including the 'torah of your mother.' (Prov. 1.8; 6.20).

The first volume of this series dealing with wisdom investigated multiple aspects of the characterizations of women found in wisdom literature; the second takes up questions of voice, exclusion, and construction and reinforcement of world views which, while perhaps necessary to the survival of the postexilic community as a whole, nevertheless had a legacy of continued gender asymmetry in Judaism and Christianity. Are we any better off, some of our authors wonder, if the highly exalted and loquacious female character of Lady Wisdom speaks primarily to men and reinforces stereotypes about women which cannot be considered helpful? Even if there is an F voice to be found among the voices of Proverbs, where does that get us if it only speaks in the dialect of the M idiom which silences any contradictory views?

This volume represents an attempt to move beyond the study of the characterization of females which formed one of the first steps of modern feminist criticism, the recovery of what had been ignored or trivialized by androcentric readings dominant through the centuries. It may be that in wisdom literature, the task is ultimately to study not women but men; to focus, not as ancient scribes did, on the character of God's justice but rather on his character as a patriarchal God. If criticism can breach this gap, it will have deconstructed the false dualisms of retribution theology and the world of proverbs, dualisms which force hearers into believing there are but two contrasting ways to live in the world, only one of which can be correct and chosen. In a world of grey, the black and white world view portrayed by wisdom literature at its worst must yield to the 'grey-scale' that Job and Qoheleth struggle with. Perhaps, when this happens, we shall see a new story, alongside the old ones, as clearly etched as Blake's lost process could allow[6], of women and their way with wisdom. Like Ms Job, we may exchange our texts for better instruments, ones that offer us not just the possibility for speech, but an invitation to song.

Finally, some acknowledgments. I would like to thank, first of all, our authors for their bright and thoughtful contributions to this volume. I would also like to acknowledge the consistently industrious work of my research assistants Jean Sangster, Mary Jane Jenson and Margaret Tabor for their help in the preparation of this manuscript. The essay '"Many Devices": Qoheleth, Misogyny and the *Malleus Maleficarum*' was written during a sabbatical made possible by Andover Newton Theological School.

Figure 3. Job 38.7: 'Anatyahu Rejoicing with the Bene-elohim

6. It should be remembered here that all Blake's lettering appearing on the engravings had to be etched *backwards* in order to print properly.

INTRODUCTION

Athalya Brenner

In General

What is biblical 'Wisdom'? What is the place of those 'W/wisdom[s]' and the so-called wisdom literature in biblical literature in general? These much-debated questions surely precede the main issue of this volume, namely, recent developments in feminist thinking about biblical 'Wisdom' and specific cases thereof. We have therefore chosen to begin this collection with Roland Murphy's non-feminist, non-gender specific 'Wisdom and Creation', an article which stands outside the evolving trends of feminist criticism. Murphy's essay, originally the address for his term as president of the American Society of Biblical Literature (1984), proceeds from work done by von Rad, Westermann and Zimmerli to view creation and wisdom as 'mirror images', since 'creation' not only refers to 'beginnings' but also to the experience of the world, its mysteries, its hopes, its gifts and its creator-god. When moving on to assess Wisdom as self-reflection and theology, Murphy defines the female wisdom figure of Prov. 8.22-36, for instance, as 'the revelation of God, not merely the self-revelation of creation. She is the divine summons issued in and through creation, sounding through the vast realm of the created world and heard on the level of human experience'. In other words, the phenomenology of the wisdom figure is given attention and significance from all perspectives (is 'she' a goddess, a queen, a teacher?), apart from those of gender and its implications. Furthermore, Murphy states that 'Wisdom is largely a postexilic phenomenon, at least as a literature (Ecclesiastes, Sirach, Wisdom of Solomon, parts of Proverbs and Job). In this period it was tied in closely to the Torah, but without losing its distinctive lineage.' Again, the historical and theological considerations are certainly valid; however, no sociological considerations—including gender perspectives—are present. This omission of gender from otherwise enlightening, definitive discussions of biblical wisdom literature is precisely the niche feminist Bible criticism is concerned with, be its particular ideological hue as it will. However, ignoring previous scholarship on the same subject simply because it pays no heed to gender issues is unhelpful. Feminist Bible criticism, as we hope, learns from non-feminist scholarship positive as well as negative lessons.

Feminists Read Wisdom Literature

Proverbs: On Teachers, Parents, Wisdom and Woman
The three essays in this section are discussions of passages from Proverbs 1–9: 'On A Figure with Many Facets: The Literary and Theological Functions of Personified Wisdom in Proverbs 1–9', by Gerlinde Baumann; 'The Gender and Motives of the Wisdom Teacher in Proverbs 7', together with an 'Appendix: A Letter to my Daughters', by Alice Ogden Bellis; and 'Conflicting Attractions: Parental Wisdom and the Strange Woman in Proverbs 1–9', by Christl Maier.

Baumann's frame of reference, unlike Murphy's, is recent work by feminist scholars such as Camp, Schroer, Cady, Newsom and Ronan. She states that 'The *Sitz im Leben* of the Wisdom Figure in Prov. 1–9…may give more information about the function of the Wisdom Figure regarding its context, the Book of Proverbs, and also with regard to Israelite wisdom literature.' She then compares the literary function with a theological model of the development of the Egyptian *Ma'at* and *Personal Piety*. On the basis of these results she tries to determine the literary and theological function of the Wisdom Figure and then interpret it from a feminist perspective. Baumann soon opts for dealing with the *Sitz im Buch* of Proverbs 1–9 within the whole of Proverbs, including the figures of personified wisdom and the *zārâ* woman, rather than guess about the actual *Sitz im Leben*. After making contributions to the historical, religious and theological understanding of Proverbs 1–9, she concludes by assessing the significance of this collection's female, 'metaphorical' and otherwise, figures for contemporary feminist theology.

It has been noticed by many feminist critics that the negative *zārâ* figure, so prominent and recurrent in Proverbs 1–5, bears an uncanny resemblance to the positive Wisdom figure. Both are attractive, both have considerable rhetorical prowess, both are described in erotic terms, both advertise their offerings, both appeal to (young, inexperienced?) males, and so on. Paradoxically, nowhere does the *zārâ* figure seem as seductive as in the chapter devoted to a hyperbolic warning against 'her' (Prov. 7). One of the issues concerning this chapter, and Proverbs 1–9 as a whole, is its gender provenance: is it the product of female or male authorship? Does it contain at least implied F voices, in addition to the obvious M voices? Bellis warns us against both gynocentrism in reading the Bible (a timely warning, perhaps), and against forcing our own western standards on biblical texts. Proceeding from this double warning, Bellis agrees that the wisdom teacher of Proverbs 7 is a woman. She disagrees, however, that this female teacher's standards are internalized androcentric ones: rather, she views those as motivated by the wish to restrict male sexual freedom and prevent pre- and non-marital sex in favour of monogamy, future offspring and social stability. Bellis views the *zārâ* figure as a prostitute, and the address of the female teacher to 'sons' as a correct tactic in an androcentric world, designed to influence the sexual behaviour of both genders but not emanating from woman-hatred. Finally, admitting that her readerly position is conditioned by being a mother to daughters, Bellis 'redresses' the biblical balance by appending to her essay a letter to her daughters.

Maier's discussion of the *zārâ* woman is considerably different. Maier tries to differentiate the text's rhetoric from a discussion of its authors and socio-historical setting in order to, ultimately, focus on the role women played in formulating the multifaceted characterization of the *zārâ* woman and on modern feminist interpretations that respond to such forms of textual rhetoric. Maier agreesthat Israel's sapiential tradition in its present form is late and leans on the Torah (see Murphy). However, she objects to the use of power structures and the social and textual authority invoked against the various levels of female 'strangeness' and

Otherness the *zārâ* woman has come to symbolize. Finally, she too raises the issue of reading as a feminist from a certain place.

Qoheleth and Socio-Religious Misogynism
Three essays are discussions of Qoheleth, in relation to women and feminist concerns: 'Qoheleth the "Old Boy" and Qoheleth the "New Man": Misogynism, the Womb and a Paradox in Ecclesiastes', by Eric S. Christianson; '"Many Devices" (Qoheleth 7.23–8.1): Qoheleth, Misogyny and the *Malleus Maleficarum*', by Carole R. Fontaine; and an Appendix to Fontaine's essay, 'Wisdom Literature among the Witchmongers', by Brian B. Noonan.

Christianson's primary questions are: Is 'Qoheleth' a woman-hater? Do we ask or answer this question, however we do, in a manner that suits our readerly concerns, whatever they may be? And what were and are the implications of our answers? Focusing on Qoh. 7.25-29, Christianson first reviews scholars' interpretations about Qoheleth, women and the womb, then discusses their implications for gender relations. This particular passage is a difficult one textually and linguistically. Does it mean that 'Qoheleth' is a misogynist, the opposite, or simply a realist, something in between? Scholars have variously given all three answers. Christianson's next step is to review other Qoheleth passages that bear on this issue of attitudes to woman and womanhood, especially 9.9. Then follows a discussion of the 'womb' in this obviously M text: 'The place of the womb, and the acknowledgment of its mystery, is chosen to convey one of Qoheleth's most fundamental tenets: the inscrutability of the divine will', especially as it is linked to women and birthing. Qoheleth's motives remain unclear and mixed, its messages contradictory: hence the paradox of conflicting understandings. Finally, Christianson mentions how this text was used in the Inquisitor's witch-hunting manual, *Malleus Maleficarum* ('Witches' Hammer'), 'to sanction torture of women accused of witchcraft' .

Fontaine and Noonan take off from this point. Fontaine recounts a Christian seminary *Sitz im Leben* for *teaching* Qoheleth. Even in that setting , and in spite of scholarly objections and socio-historical explanations, there is no getting away from the understanding, in her view, that in wisdom literature 'Though I might offer many ways of understanding the background of these misogynist passages, I could not displace the "plain sense" being conveyed by the anti-female sentiments expressed'. Unlike Christianson, Fontaine defines her passage as Qoh. 7.25–8.1a rather than 7.26-29. Like Christianson, she proceeds from establishing the 'plain sense' of the passage by linguistic inquiry; but also adds a short review of contextual attitudes to woman, such as in Proverbs and in related extrabiblical materials. Fontaine then moves to examine Qoheleth in general and the passage under discussion in particular, in traditional Jewish literature (Talmud, Midrash and so on), *en route* to dealing with traditional Christian sources—from the New Testament onwards—and especially the *Malleus Maleficarum*. A short history of witch-hunting in western Europe, and the role the *Malleus* played in it, follows. Fontaine analyses the use made of Qoh. 7.26 here to justify woman-hating and baiting, in keeping with previous Christian opinions, before moving on to modern commentators. Ultimately, this exercise in tracing religious and theo-cultural reception of a canonized text shows how misogynist—or, at the very least, ambivalent (see Christianson)—attitudes are exploited to buttress and advance the social *status quo*.

Noonan examines the use made of Qoheleth as anti-woman/witch propaganda in the *Malleus*. He undertakes quantified analysis to answer the basic question, Does Qoheleth serve to advance witch-hunting more than other biblical books or passages? His findings are set out in diagram and list forms. Not surprisingly perhaps, Noonan's statistical findings can be read in their turn as ambivalent—in keeping with the ambivalence residing (read into?) the Qoheleth text itself.

On Reading Job
'What about Job? Questioning the Book of the "Righteous Sufferer" ', by Christl Maier and Silvia Schroer, raises some general issues, in keeping with recent feminist tendencies not to be restricted to biblical texts about woman figures or family life. This book, in which men talk excessively and from which women are almost altogether absent, is difficult fare for feminist critics on many counts. Maier and Schroer begin, therefore, by

setting out a framework for critical feminist readings of it. The main issues for them are the figure of the righteous sufferer in the ANE (a comparative approach); Job as a sufferer; reward and punishment; the dialogues and the frame narrative; social, historical, religio-theological questions (*Sitz im Leben*). Of these topics, they choose to focus on the dialogues first, then on the frame story and the book's history of interpretation in both Judaism and Christianity. In the dialogue section, Maier and Schroer attempt to foreground the little material there is about woman, women and woman figures (including 'wisdom' in Job 28); in the frame story, the figures of Job's wife and daughters. The reception and history section includes a survey of Qur'ān materials and Job reception in art in addition to the usual Judeo-Christian surveys. Other welcome sections discuss post-*Shoah* Jewish and Christian liberation theology interpretations of the book. Finally 'keys' to feminist exegesis of Job are suggested: working from textual gaps, multifocality and an emphasis on 'wisdom' and questioning.

Two Examples of Wisdom's Postbiblical Career
'Wisdom', as is well known, has a marvelous postbiblical career in both Jewish and Christian sources. Two discussions of this personified figure's *nachleben* are: 'Lady Wisdom and Dame Folly at Qumran', by Sidnie White Crawford; and 'Aseneth as Wisdom', by Ross Kraemer.

The example of 'wisdom' or 'sapiential' texts found at Qumran are now easily accessible. They can be read, in the original Hebrew, on the CD-ROM published by E.J. Brill (Leiden); or in English translation, conveniently, in García Martínez's edition.[1] Some of these (like 4Q184, 4Q185, 4Q298) show similarities, correspondences and dependence on biblical wisdom texts, including the anti-woman bias that apparently informs some of the Proverbs and Qoheleth texts (see especially 4Q184). In that sense, the Qumran texts are part and parcel of an ongoing tradition to which Ben Sira belongs too, among others. Crawford White's essay is a preliminary investigation of such texts.

Kraemer shows how a *zārâ* woman in an extrabiblical text is

---

1.   F. García Martínez, *The Dead Sea Scrolls Translated: The Qumran Texts in English* (trans. Wilfred G.E. Watson; Leiden: E.J. Brill, 1994), pp. 379-98.

converted, or converts herself, into a 'wisdom' figure. Aseneth is a foreigner from Joseph's perspective: she is an Other culturally, religiously, ethnically. Yet, through an internal journey, she manages to transform her cultural and religious Otherness in keeping with 'wisdom' precepts. By so doing, she manages to change her erotic otherness as well: she and Joseph fall in love and are able to marry. Consequently she is not a *zārâ* any more. Thus Kraemer makes a convincing case for reading (*Joseph and*) *Aseneth* as influenced by the relevant passages in Proverbs 1–9 and other biblical 'wisdom' texts.

Feminists Read the Psalms

Until recently, not many feminist Bible scholars studied the Psalms. This was very much in keeping with the notion that feminists chose to study texts in which female figures featured, or which could be linked to traditional female areas of interest. When I was gathering materials for the *Feminist Companion* first series it was impossible for me to edit a volume on the Psalms. A whole volume is still difficult to put together. Hence, we chose to include the three articles we have in the volume about biblical wisdom literature. Since much work has been done in recent decades about the connections between Hebrew psaltery and 'wisdom', we feel that the decision can be defended on theoretical and methodological grounds too.

The three articles are ' "O God, hear my prayer": Psalm 55 and Violence against Women', by Ulrike Bail; ' "Under the Shadow of your Wings": The Metaphor of God's Wings in the Psalms, Exodus 19.4, Deuteronomy 32.11 and Malachi 3.20, as Seen through the Perspectives of Feminism and the History of Religion', by Silvia Schroer; and 'Hearing the Cries Unspoken: An Intertextual-Feminist Reading of Psalm 109', by Beth LaNeel Tanner.

Bail reads Psalm 55 *as if* it were the lament of a woman who has suffered violence and is required, in addition, to keep silent about it—a situation well recognized by survivors of rape and battering. A translation and discussion of this textually difficult psalm is followed by noting that a contrast obtains in it between (symbolical) 'city' and 'desert'. This topographic symbolism can be read also in the sense that the 'city' is the woman's body. The woman, the implied speaker-in-the-psalm, trusts in God and finds healing and a new identity against the violence committed against her, and its perpetrators, by talking and praying. Since the psalm's lament is non-specific it lends itself to such a reading, thus acquiring new value for contemporary women's situations.

Schroer looks at the metaphor of the biblical god's 'wings': mainly in the Psalms, but also in passages from the Torah and Malachi. Like other metaphors, the 'wings' refer first and foremost to a concrete image or concrete images. Whose 'wings' are they, then, and what is their theological significance in general and for feminists in particular? Schroer moves from language to ancient art to show that, in the psalms, the 'wings' signify God's protection and shelter-giving properties, and they are the wings of the '*cherubim*'. In the Torah they are vultures' 'wings' and, in Malachi, the sun's 'wings'. The discussion is accompanied by references to and illustrations from artistic representation of 'wings' from cognate ancient cultures. An assessment of the image/symbol/representation's theological-religious contents is concluded by an appeal to feminists to take up this type of investigation.

Tanner begins by considering questions of methodology: intertextuality, 'text', readerly production of meaning, readerly ideology. Placing herself firmly within a feminist intertextual hermeneutics, she then proceeds to retitle Psalm 109 as 'A Prayer for Leah and Rachel when their Father forced them to marry Jacob', with the intention to 'illustrate how reading a psalm with a narrative concerning women can provide a new feminist reading of both texts; and highlight new images in the metaphorical poetry of the psalms that are not dependent on the temple cult for an explanation'. This act of appropriation—or is it reappropriation?—through scholarship (wisdom?) is a fitting conclusion, we hope, for this volume.

Part I

IN GENERAL

WISDOM AND CREATION[*]

Roland E. Murphy, O. Carm.

Wisdom is no stranger to the presidential addresses delivered at the Society's annual meeting. This is not to say that an outgoing president increases wisdom, biblical or otherwise, much less increases in wisdom. In 1960 R.B.Y. Scott presented wisdom in a triad of priests, prophets, and sages, who contributed 'something indispensable to the Bible as the Book of the Knowledge of God'.[1] In 1966 John L. McKenzie pushed wisdom as far as it can conceivably go: 'Evidently I have identified the wise men of Israel with the historians and thus effectively designated the historical books as wisdom literature.'[2] In 1984 the present incumbent continues the presidential tradition by proposing reflections about wisdom and creation.

We begin with a broader contextual question: How has the biblical data on creation been integrated into Old Testament theology? The answer to this question is usually guided by a fateful presupposition: theology has to do with something called 'Yahwism', which may be described as a religion of salvation focused upon the patriarchal promises, the Exodus experience, Sinai, and the prophetic development of this heritage. In this view, creation doctrine has to be justified as genuinely 'Yahwistic' or pertinent to Old Testament theology.

[*] The Presidential Address delivered 8 December 1984 at the annual meeting of the Society of Biblical Literature held at the Palmer House, Chicago, IL. Originally published in *JBL* 104.1 (1985), pp. 3-11. Reprinted by permission.

1. R.B.Y. Scott, 'Priesthood, Prophecy, Wisdom, and the Knowledge of God', *JBL* 80 (1961), pp. 1-15 (14).

2. John L. McKenzie, S.J., 'Reflections on Wisdom', *JBL* 86 (1967), pp. 1-9; see p. 8.

Various ingenious solutions have been provided. Gerhard von Rad found a place for creation in the Decalogue: the prohibition of images of the Lord pointed to a transcendence that issued into an understanding of the world and creation.[3] Further theological support was derived from the biblical positioning of Genesis 1–11 in such a way as to constitute the beginning of salvation history. The final touch to this theological systematization (where creation is 'swallowed up' in redemption), is seen in the use of the creation theme in tandem with salvation in Deutero-Isaiah (Isa. 40.28; 42.5; 44.24; 45.12; 49.24-28; 51.9-10) and in Psalms (Pss. 33, 136, 148).

The view of C. Westermann is somewhat different. The theological justification of creation is secured by subsuming it under the category of blessing, the benign outreach of the creator Lord of Genesis. However, it remains pretty much of a bastard, by making it a child of blessing. Creation is not an item of belief, a credendum. Again, the saving experience is essential: 'the history established by God's saving deed was expanded to include the beginning of everything that happens'.[4]

Like his colleagues, Walther Zimmerli sought to 'legitimate' wisdom theology, which he correctly characterized as 'creation theology'. He anchored it in Gen. 1.28. Thus the Lord authorizes human dominion over (better, harmony with?) creation—wisdom's task.[5] Zimmerli also raised the question whether the creation doctrine and wisdom lore might be considered as possibly a 'second source of revelation'. He denied this and claimed that 'what happened was that Israel opened the entire world of

---

3. G. von Rad, *The Problem of the Hexateuch and Other Essays* (New York: McGraw–Hill, 1966), pp. 130-65, comprehending his two essays on creation and on world-view; see especially pp. 142, 150.

4. Claus Westermann, *Elements of Old Testament Theology* (Atlanta: John Knox Press, 1982), p. 86; this is set in a chapter entitled 'The Blessing God and Creation'. Westermann's understanding of belief is based on a narrow analysis of *he'ĕmîn b-* which must necessarily allow of an 'alternative' (p. 72). His view of creation reflects his understanding of wisdom, whose purpose 'requires neither revelation nor theological reflection. Wisdom is secular or profane' (p. 100).

5. W. Zimmerli, 'The Place and the Limit of the Wisdom in the Framework of the Old Testament Theology', *SSJT* 17 (1964), pp. 146-58.

creation and entered it with its faith in Yahweh, by subordinating the realms it discovered there to Yahweh. This is the locus of wisdom lore, whose international character...was well known to Israel.'[6] Again, wisdom and creation are felt to be foreign to a true Israelite.

For all three of these scholars, creation and wisdom turn out to be mirror images. In their methodological treatment of Old Testament theology creation has found an insecure, if necessary, home. Wisdom too is treated as marginal. Although both are obvious components of the Hebrew Bible, they have to be tacked onto the 'real' faith of Yahwism.

One may surely agree that Israel's encounter with the Lord has historical roots, whether one locates them in the patriarchal promises, the revelation to Moses, or elsewhere. Israel became a people under the ineffable name YHWH. It was by this name that they identified with the God of creation and the God of wisdom. There was in fact no other alternative for the 'true believer'.[7] There is no evidence that they regarded creation wisdom as outside their faith. They were obviously aware of the wisdom and the creation stories of their neighbors, and their understanding of the Lord permeated whatever they assimilated from their neighbors. But the Israelites did not hold creation/wisdom apart from their belief at a secondary level. In fact, they developed their own theology of wisdom/creation, and it should be accepted as a genuine heritage from the Bible. They did not advert to the 'tension' that modern theologians find between salvation and creation. They created a canon that embraced both.

6.   W. Zimmerli, *Old Testament Theology in Outline* (Atlanta: John Knox Press, 1978), p. 158; see also p. 40. One should note also the nuanced conclusion of B.W. Anderson in the introduction to the volume he edited, *Creation in the Old Testament* (Issues in Religion and Theology, 6; Philadelphia: Fortress Press, 1981), that the 'cosmic view of creation was probably introduced into the mainstream of Israelite life and thought by interpreters who stood in the royal covenant tradition' (p. 8).

7.   The dilemma created by wisdom literature was most obvious in G.E. Wright, *God Who Acts* (SET, 8; Chicago: Regnery, 1952), pp. 102-105. G. von Rad's final location of wisdom seems adequate: 'The wisdom practised in Israel was a response made by a Yahwism confronted with specific experiences of the world' (*Wisdom in Israel* [Nashville: Abingdon Press, 1972]), p. 307.

One need not therefore justify wisdom and creation from the standpoint of an alleged 'Yahwism' with a relatively narrow track of encounter in salvation history. Rather, the concept, as well as the development of creation in wisdom theology, can be accepted as a genuine element (and not merely an importation) of the faith of the Israelites as they encountered the Lord in the created world.

The implications of this are significant on two counts: creation as the story of 'beginnings', and creation as the arena of human experience where people live out their lives. Considerable attention has always been given to creation as the doctrine of 'beginnings'. The current debate on creationism shows how lively a topic that is. On the other hand, the role of creation in human experience has been somewhat glossed over. I wish to comment briefly on both aspects of creation from the viewpoint of wisdom.

1. Creation as 'beginnings'. The contribution of wisdom on this score has been ambiguous, because of the uncertainty of the translation of '*āmôn* (craftsman or nursling?) in Prov. 8.30.[8] Lady Wisdom has received great press by reason of her association with creation, but her precise role remains unclear. The Wisdom of Solomon solved the ambiguity by calling her a *technitis*, or crafts(wo)man (Wis. 7.22; 8.6; 14.2). The common interpretation of the pedantic statement in Prov. 3.19 'reduces' her to the status of a divine attribute, lost among the other attributes of divinity. For the most part theology has not been able to do much with the role of Lady Wisdom in the act of creation, but we shall return to her at a later point.[9]

2. Creation as an arena of experience. This aspect of wisdom/

8.   See H.P. Ruger, '"Amôn-Pflegekind: Zur Auslegungsgeschichte von Prov. 8:30a', in *Übersetzung und Deutung: Studien zu dem AT und seiner Umwelt A.R. Hulst gewidmet von Freunden und Kollegen* (Nijkerk: F. Callenbach, 1977), pp. 154-63, for a survey of opinions; he concludes that '*āmôn* 'can be well translated as "favorite" or "foster-child"'.

9.   We prescind here from the use of personified wisdom as the background of New Testament Christology. On this see H. Gese, 'Wisdom, Son of Man, and the Origins of Christology: The Consistent Development of Biblical Theology', *Horizons in Biblical Theology* 3 (1981), pp. 23-57; and the essay by S. Terrien, 'The Play of Wisdom: Turning Point in Biblical Theology', in the same issue, pp. 125-53.

creation deserves greater elaboration. We are considering creation here as continuous and ongoing, providing the fundamental parameters within which humans live and die. In comparison
with the prophetic experience, which is unique and then shared
with the community, or the liturgical experience, which recalls
and re-presents primarily the saving acts of history, the dialogue
with creation may be termed the 'wisdom experience':[10] It lives
in the present and reacts to the variety of creation, experience of
which a human being is part. The wisdom experience is not
something necessarily apart from a faith experience. In the
concrete it involves an attitude to God that can be described as
faith. In the case of Israel, von Rad expressed this reality very
clearly: 'The experiences of the world were for her always divine
experiences as well, and the experiences of God were for her
experiences of the world.'[11]

By creation the Bible understands the whole range of existing
things, from humans to ants, not excluding the abyss and
Leviathan. This is the world open to human experience (or to
human imagination, in the case of Leviathan). And this world
was not dumb.

Job admonishes the three friends to learn from beasts and
birds, from reptiles and fish, the agency of the Almighty in all
that happens (Job 12.78). Similarly, the sage draws on the animal
world to underline the lessons (Prov. 6.6-8; 30.15-31). Creation
speaks, but its language is peculiar (Ps. 19). It is not verbal, but
it is steady, and it is heard (Ps. 19.2). It is parallel to the
Torah, which 'gives wisdom to the simple' (Ps. 19.8).[12] With fine

10. See R.E. Murphy, 'Israel's Wisdom: A Biblical Model of Salvation',
Studia Missionalia 30 (1981), pp. 1-33, esp. 39-42.

11. *Wisdom in Israel*, p. 62.

12. Not all would interpret Ps. 19 in this fashion. In contrast to his earlier
view (*The Problem of the Hexateuch*, p. 157), G. von Rad later recognized this
as a language heard by humans (*Wisdom in Israel*, p. 162). H.-J. Kraus explicitly denies that creation has anything to say to human beings because Ps.
145.10 supposedly indicates that the works of creation direct their message
to the creator; see H.-J. Kraus, 'Logos und Sophia', in *Karl Barths Lichterlehre*
(TS, 123; Zürich: Theologischer Verlag, 1978), p. 24. The implications of this
language of the world have been developed by O. H. Steck, *World and Environment* (Nashville: Abingdon Press, 1978), pp. 113-227; and C. Link, *Welt
als Geichnis* (BEvT, 73: Munich: Chr. Kaiser Verlag, 1976), pp. 268-310.

perception both Karl Barth and Gerhard von Rad concur that the Lord allowed creation to do the speaking for him in Job 38–41 ('will [the lightnings] say to you, "Here we are?"', 38.35).[13] Creation had a voice which spoke differently to Job than the chorus of the three friends.

These examples suggest that wisdom is more than a set of rules. It is not to be reduced to a teaching—and certainly not to an optimistic doctrine of retribution. It is as much an attitude, a dialogue with the created world, as it is a set of admonitions or insights concerning various types of conduct. We must distinguish between doctrine and style, just as Qohelet did. He dissented from traditional wisdom at several points, but he never ceased to be a sage. He constantly employed the experiential tests of wisdom (Eccl. 2.1-3; 7.23). The approach of the sage turns out to be a model for living, a style of operation that aimed at life, the gift of the Lord.

Von Rad described the style in the following words: 'The most characteristic feature of her (Israel's) understanding lay, in the first instance, in the fact that she believed man to stand in a quite specific, highly dynamic, existential relationship with his environment.'[14] This relationship extended far beyond events in Israel's history such as the Exodus or the Sinai covenant. It was a relationship to well-being and suffering, life and non-life, as the psalmists portrayed in their complaints. They clamored for deliverance from Sheol, for the presence of the Lord, for life. Their interpretation of their experience, whether beneficent or evil, was an interpretation of their relationship to the divinity. While the liturgy indeed represented the saving events of Israel's history, it was also a telling witness of the high points and troughs of daily life, in which God hid his face (Ps. 13.2; 104.29) but also showed it (Ps. 31.17; 80.20).

The wisdom experience was reenacted not only in the limited situations recorded in Job and Ecclesiastes. It was found also in the jejune events of everyday life. These were not unambiguous. Silence, a wisdom ideal, cut both ways (Prov. 17.27-28): it could signal folly as well as understanding. Poverty might be the result of laziness (Prov. 6.9-11), but not always: 'Better a little with fear

13. *Wisdom in Israel*, p. 225.
14. *Wisdom in Israel*, p. 301.

of the Lord...' (Prov. 15.16; cf. 16.8). Kindness to the poor is frequently emphasized (Prov. 14.21, 31; 17.5). The uncertainty of the meaning of riches did not go unnoticed; they could be a temptation (14.28). Although one could conclude from appearances (Prov. 6.13), these were often deceptive; a bitter thing could turn out to be sweet (Prov. 27.7), and a soft tongue could break a bone (Prov. 25.15). The most delicate area is that of personal motivations and judgments (Prov. 16.2; 21.2): 'Sometimes a way seems right to a man, but the end of it leads to death' (Prov. 16.25).

It is important to underscore the uncertainties that the sages entertained, because so often they are accused of being simplistic. This judgment may be derived from the lapidary style in which they expressed their conclusions. Such is the style of many teachers! But this should not blind the interpreter to the tentativeness of wisdom. Experience spoke with a forked tongue many times. Above all, the greatest limitation on wisdom was the Lord himself (Prov. 16.9; 21.30). An appreciation of the divine mystery, God's being beyond wisdom, underlies the entire enterprise. The most dogmatic expression of the triumph of wisdom as opposed to folly, with its guarantee of life and prosperity, must be taken more as a matter of trust and hope than of experience. What the Lord had guaranteed through similar teaching in Deuteronomy and the prophets could not be without effect—even when the claims of certain sayings seem to be opposed by facts. Hence the sage advised the youth to trust in the Lord (Prov. 3.5; 16.3, 20).

The wisdom experience is further characterized as gift (even as much as any event in salvation history is gift). Wisdom is a gift of the Lord (Prov. 2.5-6), for it is the reverential fear of God that leads to wisdom (Prov. 1.7). The gift character of wisdom is in tension with the obvious pedagogical ploys of the sage, who makes use of discipline and even coercion. The sayings are directed to making wisdom obvious and hence available to any who will listen. But if it is true that 'what the tongue utters is from the Lord' (Prov. 16.1), wisdom is unattainable without the divine activity.

Thus far we have tried to exemplify the role played by wisdom/creation in the experience and faith of the Israelite. We may now turn to the topic of Wisdom's personification and assess its contribution to our understanding of wisdom/creation. Biblical theologians generally regard this development as a later stage in wisdom thinking, when wisdom reflects on itself or becomes 'theologized'.[15]

As we have already seen, the particular role of Lady Wisdom in the creative activity described in Prov. 8.22-31 is not clear. But there can be no doubt about her divine origin, and it is certain that she is somehow associated with creation. Indeed, a specific role in the created world is clearly stated: her delight is to be with human beings (Prov. 8.31). Her intercourse with humans is to be gleaned from her preaching to them (Prov. 1, 8, 9). She threatens, cajoles and issues a promise of life that is identified with the divine favor (Prov. 8.35). She is a divine gift (Prov. 2.16; Wis. 9.4) to all who will listen (Prov. 1.20-22; 8.4-5, 32; 9.4).

Who is Lady Wisdom? Current biblical scholarship has excelled in providing more her pedigree than her identity. She is variously interpreted as goddess (Ishtar? Ma'at? Isis?), queen (Prov. 8.12-16), and teacher (or 'personified school-wisdom').[16] It is hard to deny that these elements have entered into the portrait that emerges from the Bible. They constitute, as it were, her literary prehistory, but they fail to answer the question of identity. The most profound answer to date seems to be that of G. von Rad: Lady Wisdom is the 'self-revelation of creation'.[17] This bold conceptualization of von Rad appears in his interpretation of Prov. 3.19: 'the Lord by wisdom founded the earth, established the heavens by understanding'. This means that God established the earth into wisdom, not by wisdom. Wisdom was somehow outside of God, not merely a divine attribute. To the desperate question of Job 28.12, 20 ('Where is wisdom to be found?'), von Rad pointed to the order implicit in creation. Wisdom is a

15. So H.H. Schmid, *Wesen und Geschichte der Weisheit* (BZAW, 101; Berlin: Alfred Töpelmann, 1966), p. 144; and earlier G. von Rad, *Old Testament Theology* (New York: Harper & Row, 1962), I, p. 441.

16. See the helpful study of Bernhard Lang, *Frau Weisheit: Deutung einer biblischen Gestalt* (Düsseldorf: Patmos, 1975), especially pp. 174-84. Lang takes Lady Wisdom to be personified school-wisdom.

17. See the title of a chapter in G. von Rad, *Wisdom in Israel*, pp. 148-76; on this see also R.E. Murphy, 'What and Where is Wisdom?', *Currents in Theology and Mission* 4 (1977), pp. 283-87.

mystery, distinct from the works of creation, yet somehow present. Ben Sira put it best: 'He has poured her [wisdom] forth upon all his works...he has lavished her upon his friends' (Sir. 1.9-10; Job 28.27).

Just at this point one may ask if von Rad has gone far enough. For him Wisdom turns out to be an 'order', a mysterious order truly, but rather abstract all the same.[18] The concept of order is widely accepted in the current understanding of biblical wisdom.[19] One need not deny that the presumption of regularity underlies the observations of the sages, but it is another thing to say they were searching for order, or that the lyrical description of Proverbs 8 is adequately captured by the term 'order'. The biblical metaphors portraying Lady Wisdom indicate a wooing, indeed an eventual marriage. Who has ever sued for, or been pursued by, order, even in the surrogate form of a woman? The very symbol of Lady Wisdom suggests that order is not the correct correlation. Rather, she is to be somehow identified with the Lord, as indicated by her very origins and her authority. The call of Lady Wisdom is the voice of the Lord. She is, then, the revelation of God, not merely the self-revelation of creation. She is the divine summons issued in and through creation, sounding through the vast realm of the created world and heard on the

18. Perhaps it can be inferred that von Rad himself was not satisfied with the concept of 'order', which at the same time addresses human beings. Cf. *Wisdom in Israel*, contrasting p. 151 with pp. 107, 109. And on p. 95 there is the tantalizing question, 'Is it faith in the orders or faith in Yahweh?' That should not be hard to answer. See also S. Terrien, *The Elusive Presence* (New York: Harper & Row, 1978), p. 384 n. 38.

19. A standard presentation of wisdom as 'Ordnung' can be found in H.H. Schmid, *Wesen und Geschichte der Weisheit*. In a giant leveling process Egyptian *ma'at*, Sumerian *me*, and Israelite *ḥokmâ* are subsumed under this concept (e.g., pp. 17, 116, 196). He has gone on to make the concept of order (= justice) the basis for a new program in biblical theology. Order is the basic ingredient in the world-view of the ancient Near East, and applicable as well to the notion of salvation: 'Creation-faith, that is, the belief that God has created and maintained the world with its manifold orders, is not a marginal theme of biblical theology, it is basically the theme.' Cf. H. Schmid *Altorientalische Welt in der alttestamentlichen Theologie* (Zürich: Theologische Verlag, 1974), p. 25. For Schmid 'creation theology', based on the concept of world order, constitutes the total horizon (*Gesamthorizont*) of Old Testament theological statements (p. 31).

level of human experience. Thus she carries out her function with human beings (Prov. 8.31).

If this assessment of Lady Wisdom is correct, there are serious implications here for systematic theology. The classical disciplines of philosophy and theology have separated out rational knowledge of God (or 'natural theology') from revealed knowledge. But this distinction, a valid enterprise in itself, does not square with the experience of Israel. It should not be imposed on biblical literature in such a way as to separate out documents of faith as opposed to rational knowledge. The simple fact of the matter is that Israel did not distinguish between faith and reason.[20]

The further description of Lady Wisdom in Sirach 24 is in harmony with what has been said thus far, even if Ben Sira goes beyond it.[21] Her speech is now described as uttered before the

20. This fundamental observation has been made by such different scholars as G. von Rad and Karl Rahner. See *Wisdom in Israel*, p. 64: 'We hold fast to the fact that in the case of the wise men's search for knowledge, even when they expressed their results in a completely secular form, there was never any question of what we would call absolute knowledge functioning independently of their faith in Yahweh'. Compare K. Rahner, who speaks from the point of view of a systematic theologian in *Foundations of Christian Faith* (New York: Seabury, 1978), p. 57: 'From a theological point of view, the concrete process of the so-called natural knowledge of God in either its acceptance or its rejection is always more than a merely natural knowledge of God... The knowledge of God we are concerned with, then, is that concrete, original, historically constituted and transcendental knowledge of God which either in the mode of acceptance or of rejection is inevitably present in the depths of existence in the most ordinary human life. It is at once both natural knowledge and knowledge in grace, it is at once both knowledge and revelation-faith...' For a differing point of view, see John J. Collins, ('The Biblical Precedent for Natural Theology', *JAAR* 45.1 Supplement [March 1977], B: pp. 35-67, esp. p. 42) and also A. De Pury ('Sagesse et révélation dans l'ancien testament', *RTP* 27 [1977], pp. 1-50), who considers wisdom the realm of the rational, as opposed to revelation, which is an encounter.

21. For the textual relationship between Prov. 8 and Sir. 24, see P.W. Skehan, 'Structures in Poems on Wisdom: Proverbs 8 and Sirach 24', *CBQ* 41 (1979), pp. 365-79. See also J. Marböck, *Weisheit im Wandel* (BBB, 37; Bonn: Hanstein, 1977), pp. 34-96; O. Rickenbacher, *Weisheitsperikopen bei Ben Sira* (OBO, 1; Freiburg: Universitätsverlag, 1973), pp. 111-72.

heavenly court (24.2), but nonetheless she issues an invitation to all who desire her (24.19). She describes her divine origin, but also her restlessness, making the circuit of the vault of heaven and walking in the depths of the abyss (24.5) until finally she follows the recommendation of the creator to make her dwelling in Jacob, where she will perform a liturgical service (24.8-10). The truly new move of Ben Sira is to identify Lady Wisdom with the Torah, an identification prepared for by Psalm 19 and derived from the idea that wisdom is somehow a communication of God. It matters not whether one terms this the divine will or any other divine attribute. There is movement here, a divine communication, which is also necessarily a revelation of some kind. This view of wisdom suggests (again?) how insufficient is the conceptualization of wisdom as 'order'.

Finally, we should admit that it is hazardous to make conclusions about wisdom because of the serious gaps in our knowledge. Wisdom is largely a postexilic phenomenon, at least as a literature (Ecclesiastes, Sirach, Wisdom of Solomon, parts of Proverbs and Job). In this period it was tied in closely to the Torah, but without losing its distinctive lineage. We may see in this identification an effort to magnify the previously humble status of wisdom in Israel's life, an attempt that was also aided by the mysterious figure of Lady Wisdom. It is astonishing that there is no other personification of such magnitude and depth in the Old Testament as this, and it succeeded in correlating the wisdom heritage most intimately with the Lord. Such also was the insight that the fear of the Lord was the beginning of wisdom, that it led to wisdom (Prov. 1.7; 9.10).

In the obscure period of the postexilic age, in *gurgite vasto*, Lady Wisdom claimed to have walked 'in the depths of the abyss, in the waves of the sea' (Sir. 24.4-5), until she found a resting place in Israel. Any attempt to find her and to identify her is difficult, as we are reminded:

> The first man never finished comprehending wisdom, nor will the last succeed in fathoming her (Sir. 24.28).

personified Wisdom as 'Israel's God in the imagery of a woman and the language of goddesses'.[3] While Susan Cady, Marian Ronan and Hal Taussig[4] also describe the function of the Wisdom Figure as part of the postexilic Israel imagery of God in positive terms, Carol A. Newsom's examination of the Wisdom Figure is more critical. At the end of her literary deconstruction of Proverbs 1–9, personified Wisdom appears as the cultural voice of the fathers and other patriarchal authorities.[5] Athalya Brenner and Fokkelien van Dijk-Hemmes characterize personified Wisdom in similar ways. Brenner states that Wisdom in Proverbs 8 'is God's possession, consort…and then child—both normal positions of dependence for a socially adjusted female'.[6] Van Dijk-Hemmes goes a step further and calls personified Wisdom an 'advertiser for the dominant male culture'.[7]

3.   S. Schroer, 'Weise Frauen und Ratgeberinnen in Israel—literarische und historische Vorbilder der personifizierten Chokmah', *BN* 51 (1990), pp. 41-60 (reprinted in Schroer, *Die Weisheit hat ihr Haus gebaut: Studien zur Gestalt der Sophia in den biblischen Schriften* [Mainz: Grünewald, 1996], pp. 63-79); 'Die göttliche Weisheit und der nachexilische Monotheismus', in M.-Th. Wacker and E. Zenger (eds.), *Der eine Gott und die Göttin: Gottesvorstellungen des biblischen Israel im Horizont feministischer Theologie* (QD, 135; Freiburg: Herder, 1991), pp. 151-82 (reprinted in Schroer, *Die Weisheit hat ihr Haus gebaut*, pp. 27-62).

4.   S. Cady, M. Ronan and H. Taussig, *Sophia: The Future of Feminist Spirituality* (San Francisco: Harper & Row, 1986), analyze 'Sophia' not only in Prov. 1–9, but also in her further development in Sir. and Wisdom: 'Sophia is a new kind of figure within the Hebrew world view. She encourages or rather demands reflection on the meaning of a wide variety of happenings in the world. In this she runs counter to tendencies (particularly among the priestly class of Israel) in later Hebrew tradition to withdraw Hebrew faith into a nostalgia for the earlier, "holier" times. Sophia calls on humans to think about what is happening in their world' (p. 36).

5.   C.A. Newsom, 'Woman and the Discourse of Patriarchal Wisdom: A Study of Proverbs 1–9', in Peggy L. Day (ed.), *Gender and Difference in Ancient Israel* (Minneapolis: Augsburg–Fortress, 1989), pp. 142-60, esp. pp. 155-57.

6.   A. Brenner in A. Brenner and F. van Dijk-Hemmes, *On Gendering Texts: Female and Male Voices in the Hebrew Bible* (BIS, 1; Leiden: E.J. Brill, 1993), p. 127.

7.   Van Dijk-Hemmes in Brenner and van Dijk-Hemmes, *Gendering Texts*, p. 54.

In this essay I will deal with aspects of the Wisdom Figure on which feminist research has not yet focused. I will follow feminist, historical and religious approaches that may contribute some insight. The *Sitz im Leben* of the Wisdom Figure in Proverbs 1–9 is one issue where there are still some unresolved questions. An examination of the *Sitz im Leben*, however, may give more information about the function of the Wisdom Figure regarding its context, the book of Proverbs, and also with regard to Israelite wisdom literature. Then I will compare the literary function with a theological model of the development of the Egyptian *Ma'at* and *Personal Piety*. On the basis of these results, I will try to determine the literary and theological function of the Wisdom Figure and then interpret it from a feminist perspective. Who and what is personified Wisdom if it is analyzed with the help of a wider range of methods, and how can its role be described for feminist theology?

The Sitz im Leben *of Proverbs 1–9*

In the methodology of historical criticism the so-called *Sitz im Leben* is deduced from literary types or text genres. There are a number of different genres in Proverbs 1–9. Whereas the first speech of the Wisdom Figure in Proverbs 1.22-33 contains prophetic elements and Prov. 8.22-31 is a hymn, the comprehensive text genre in Proverbs 1–9 is written in a didactic style. It starts with an 'appeal for attention' ('listen…'), which can also be found in prophetic texts of the Old Testament.[8]

It is not likely, however, that the instructions of the teacher or the Wisdom Figure in Proverbs 1–9 are primarily situated in a prophetic context. This can be concluded from the speaker's and listener's names. A parental teacher (a mother in 1.8 and 6.20 or a father in 1.8; 4.1 and 6.20) speaks in ten didactic lectures to an adolescent.[9] At first glance this points to the family as the forum

---

8.   E.g. frequently in the book of Amos: Amos 3.1, 13; 4.1; 5.1; 8.4.
9.   This adolescent is defined as a male in some of the texts in Prov. 1–9, whereas no woman is addressed in particular. Even words which potentially address both sexes (נפשׁ as personal or reflexive pronoun, בן/בנים; as 'child/children', בני אדם as 'human beings' and אדם as 'man/woman')

where education takes place in Proverbs 1–9.

On the other hand, expressions like 'father'(אב) and 'child' or 'son' (בן) not only describe actual blood relations in the Old Testament, but also the relationship between teacher and pupils, as is the case in the ancient Near East.[10] This leads to the assumption that the *school* might be the *Sitz im Leben* of Proverbs 1–9.

From the beginning, the discussion about the existence of an ancient Israelite school has been connected with the assumption that parts of the book of Proverbs serve as a textbook[11]—but it has not yet been proven that such a school ever existed. Krispenz makes a critical comment on the attempts to prove the existence of an Israelite school:

> …who learned what for how long from whom and in which manner remains obscure. We only know that there were pupils who were being taught to write in the area and time in question. We can infer from the written remains in the Old Testament that those responsible for passing on the Israelite tradition were able to write. This scarce inventory should draw attention to the fact that we don't have much information about the Israelite school and that accordingly every reconstruction must be speculative.[12]

actually address in every third case only men, who are warned against committing adultery with other men's wives.

10. Apart from the natural father, grandfather, or ancestor אב also means 'the founder of a profession or a way of life,' commonly 'a particularly honourable man,' a protector, counselor, or originator; H. Ringgren, 'אב *ʾāḇ*' *ThWAT*, I, cols. 1-19 (from col. 7).

11. For a survey of the discussion see B. Lang, *Die weisheitliche Lehrrede: Eine Untersuchung von Sprüche 1-7* (SBS, 54; Stuttgart: Katholisches Bibelwerk, 1972), pp. 11-30; 'Schule und Unterricht im alten Israel', in M. Gilbert, (ed.), *La sagesse de l'ancien Testament* (BETL, 51; Gembloux: Duculot, 1979), pp. 186-201, esp. 186-92; N. Shupak, *Where can Wisdom be found? The Sage's Language in the Bible and in Ancient Egyptian Literature* (OBO, 130; Göttingen: Vandenhoeck & Ruprecht, 1993), p. 349; and R. Liwak, '"Was wir gehört und kennengelernt und unsere Väter uns erzählt haben" (Ps 78,3): Überlegungen zum Schulbetrieb im Alten Israel', in E. Axmacher and K. Schwarzwäller (eds.), *Belehrter Glaube: Festschrift für J. Wirsching zum 65. Geb.* (Frankfurt/M.: Peter Lang, 1994), pp. 175-93.

12. J. Krispenz, *Spruchkompositionen im Buch Proverbia* (EHS.T, 349; Frankfurt/M.: Peter Lang, 1989), p. 20; translation of all German quotations: G.B.

This fact has consequences for the determination of form in Proverbs 1–9. Krispenz points to the circular effect produced by the connection of the research of the Israelite school with the search for a *Sitz im Leben* of the Proverbs. The Proverbs are 'normally classified as school texts, and as a result of this classification the question of the school arises, because the school is the *Sitz im Leben* of the genre 'school text'.[13] This raises the problem that there is no such thing as a 'school text', as Krispenz demonstrates with the use of log tables, textbooks and Goethe's 'Faust', 'because there is no unity of form'.[14] Comparable practice texts do not exist in the Old Testament, and as a consequence there is no basis for classifying Proverbs as school texts within the methodology of historical criticism. Furthermore, the classification of Proverbs as school texts has often been a way 'of explaining the apparent or seeming triviality and the lack of a systematic order: they were just practice material'.[15] The book of Proverbs, however, has been more than just practice material for ancient Israel; this is evidenced by the fact that it has been included in a canon of holy scriptures.

It does not seem to be very helpful in our search for a *Sitz im Leben* to simply classify Proverbs as school texts or didactic speech. Obviously, a different approach is needed. Let me first point out that the speeches in Proverbs 1–9 address an audience; they are designed to be listened to rather than read or copied. The chapters contain theologically commented instructions or rules of life that must be heard. In addition, these texts are written in a poetic style.[16]

It has sometimes escaped notice that Proverbs 1–9 is not an independent book but the introduction to the book of Proverbs. Whether parts of Proverbs 1–9 ever existed separately can only be speculated. In the Masoretic version of the book of Proverbs, however, they obviously have a literary function. Although it is difficult to determine a *Sitz im Leben* for Proverbs 1–9, an approach to a *Sitz im Buch*—meaning a literary setting in the

---

13. Krispenz, *Spruchkompositionen*, p. 22.
14. Krispenz, *Spruchkompositionen*, p. 22.
15. Krispenz, *Spruchkompositionen*, p. 22.
16. So, e.g., R. Alter, *The Art of Biblical Poetry* (San Francisco: Harper Collins, 1985), p. 163.

book of Proverbs—might be possible.

I would like to start the search for such a *Sitz im Buch* with some thoughts on how the meaning of an event can be changed through the process of being written down. For this I will refer to Jan Assmann[17] and Carol A. Newsom,[18] who have developed a different perspective from that of Camp,[19] who has also dealt with this question. Using Egyptian wisdom texts, Assmann illustrates what may also be significant for the book of Proverbs: 'Wisdom literature can only depict wisdom in a literal way, because the pragmatic or performative dimension is omitted.'[20] Wisdom teachings were originally connected to concrete situations. Written down, they are deprived of their original context and application. Any literate person can read the Proverbs, but the original didactic situation no longer exists. At the same time, the transcription broadens the possible 'time of application'. What is written down can be updated as long as the carrier material, for example papyrus, exists. 'Transcription artificially stretches the situation of sapiential education from primeval times until the last days; it creates a horizon of eternity.'[21] The element of primeval time in Proverbs 1–9 can also be found in the pre-existence of personified Wisdom, for example her presence at the creation of the world in 8.22-31, and also the teacher's reference back to the father and grandfather in 4.1-4. An eternal horizon is created through the teaching situation: Young people are called upon to listen—up to this day.

The form of instruction in Proverbs 1–9 is the parental didactic speech. This situation given in the text has lead to the assumption that Proverbs 1–9 is a text of education for school or at home in the family. Proverbs 1–9, however, is a literary text and not a

17. J. Assmann, 'Weisheit, Schrift und Literatur im Alten Ägypten', in A. Assmann (ed.), *Weisheit: Archäologie der literarischen Kommunikation, III* (Munich: Fink, 1991), pp. 475-500.

18. Newsom, 'Discourse', pp. 142-60.

19. Camp describes the consequences of the decontextualization of the older Proverbs sayings (Prov. 10–30) as the loss of their function as cultural models, which leads to the appearance of dogmatism and creates the appearance of a split between the sacred and the profane; see *Wisdom*, pp. 165-78.

20. Assmann, 'Weisheit', p. 492.

21. Assmann, 'Weisheit', p. 493.

live recording of a school lesson. What Assmann describes with regard to Egyptian wisdom texts, therefore, is relevant: 'It is correct that they are all couched in the form of paternal instruction. They are, however, anything else but accurate reports of a common way of speaking. They are, in fact, highly literary texts.'[22] In this context, Assmann speaks of literary fiction[23] or 'staged form'.[24] The staged discourse regarding Wisdom and YHWH, the 'Strange Woman', and sinners occurs in Proverbs 1–9 in the form of parental teachings. These teachings appear as 'upbringing' (מוסר; 1.8) or 'rule' (מצוה; 6.20) from the father and as 'education' (תורה; 1.8; 6.20) from the mother. They are connected to both parents who are mentioned together 12 times in Proverbs as well as in the Decalogue (Exod. 20.12; Deut. 5.16).[25] When parents are honoured (כבד; hi.), YHWH's commandment is obeyed (Deut. 5.16) and long life will be the reward. In a similar way, the didactic speeches in Proverbs 1–9 promise that listening to them will bring long life, happiness and welfare (Prov. 3.2). The appreciation of parental authority is not at all an unusual feature of Proverbs 1–9. Unlike Egyptian wisdom teachings, however, Proverbs 1–9 mentions the mother. It is improbable that she is only invented for the stylistic reasons of balancing out the father's person in the *parallelismus membrorum*, as Bernhard Lang claims.[26] Lang does not take into account that the teacher is created as literary fiction in the same manner as the parents are. If the mother had not been a person of authority, mentioning her would not have strengthened but, rather, undermined the teacher's authority.

Indeed, the mother in Prov. 1.8, 6.20 has to be regarded as a teacher in the family. If she had not had the 'cultural prestige' which Assmann claims for the Egyptian paternal figure,[27] and if the mother as a literary fiction had not had an 'equivalent in

---

22. Assmann, 'Weisheit', p. 492.
23. Assmann, 'Weisheit', p. 493.
24. Assmann, 'Weisheit', p. 479.
25. Cf. Brenner, in Brenner and van Dijk-Hemmes, *Gendering Texts*, p. 118 n. 3.
26. Lang, 'Schule', pp. 186-201 (194).
27. Assmann, 'Weisheit', p. 494.

reality',[28] this fiction would not have been plausible. 'Without the social roles of the father [and the mother] as teachers, the fundamental esteem of old age and the authority of experience, …this literary fiction would not have functioned over thousands of years.'[29] That it works or has been regarded as working in those times is both an indication that father *and* *mother* were teaching authorities, and that the texts of Proverbs 1–9 stage the family as their educational forum.[30] Because of the imagined situation and the direct address of the readers by a teaching authority, the didactic speeches in Proverbs 1–9 have a less apodeictic but a more reflective and discursive character.[31] The situation of family discussions is constructed as a literary fiction, and during these conversations the experienced parents teach their 'wisdom' to the child. In this fiction, the readers appear as children or adolescents who still have to learn the fundamental principles of life, its possibilities and danger.[32] In effect, the readers find themselves in a 'deficit-situation'.[33] It is not only the texts of Proverbs 1–9 that claim to remedy this situation, but the book of Proverbs as a whole. The sayings or statements in the central part of the book (chs. 10–29) do not have a 'staged form' for themselves which would make their understanding easier, give reasons for the necessity of learning them, or provide a summary of their contents. The headings of this central part just give the authors (10.1; 17.1; 24.23; 25.1) and, unlike the introduction in 1.1-7 and the final framework in 31.1, do not contain any indication regarding the purpose or use of the sayings collected in it. All of this, however, is supplied in Proverbs 1–9: Instead of confronting the readers, who are interested in orientation for their lives, with a simple collection of single sayings, there is a short description of purpose in 1.1-7 together with a staged context which constructs a situation for

28. Assmann, 'Weisheit', p. 493.

29. Assmann, 'Weisheit', p. 493.

30. Similarly Camp, *Wisdom*, pp. 251-53.

31. So Assmann, 'Weisheit', p. 493, about the Egyptian wisdom instructions.

32. The same situation is taken as a basis for the king's mother's instructions to her son Lemuel in the final framework in Prov. 31.1.

33. Assmann, 'Weisheit', p. 488.

learning. Not only with the help of arguments should the readers be convinced to study the book of Proverbs (1.1-7); they are also addressed directly as children who stand in need of education. Newsom explains that it is probably more difficult to resist such an address and such an integration into a teaching situation than simply to refuse an argument.[34] It will not be easy to find yourself in the situation of a minor or of someone who is inexperienced and to reject the wisdom offered right then and there. In this way, Proverbs 1–9 assigns a role to the readers which nearly forces them to read and to learn the proverbs. The concentration in Proverbs 1–9 on a few themes also makes it possible for the readers to survey the following chapters and not to lose track. Furthermore, the concentration on certain topics helps to emphasize the different degrees of importance[35] or unimportance[36] of particular subjects in Proverbs 1–9 in contrast to those of chs. 10–30. In this context, together with the parents, personified Wisdom teaches the inexperienced. Why, then, has she been invented, and what does she stand for?

What Kind of 'Wisdom' is Represented by the Wisdom Figure?

Georg Fohrer gives an important outline of the phenomenology of wisdom in the Old Testament.[37] He describes the phenomenon 'wisdom' with the help of the following aspects:

34. Newsom, 'Discourse', p. 147, illustrates it with the help of ideological theory.

35. Prov. 1–9 emphasizes, e.g., the 'Strange Woman' and the sinners.

36. E.g. the kings; within Prov. 1–9 they are mentioned only together with other rulers in 8.15-16.

37. G. Fohrer, 'Die Weisheit im Alten Testament', in G. Fohrer, *Studien zur alttestamentlichen Theologie und Geschichte (1949-1966)* (BZAW, 115; Berlin: W. de Gruyter, 1969), pp. 242-74 (the text is identical with G. Fohrer's article 'σοφία' in *TWNT*, VII, pp. 483-96), gives a detailed description of the phenomenon 'wisdom' in the Old Testament. Alternative outline, e.g., by H.-P. Müller (in Müller and M. Krause, 'חכם *ḥākam*', *ThWAT*, II, cols. 920-44 [929-39]), which he bases upon G. Fohrer, and adds an assignment of wisdom to certain life contexts (court, trade); but this makes the classification more hypothetical and the model more confusing because of the different levels in question.

(III) human intelligence and knowledge:
   (1) magic and mantic,
   (2) skill and ability,
   (3) prudence, cleverness and cunning,
   (4) common sense,
   (5) education,
   (6) rules of behaviour,
   (7) ethical conduct,
   (8) religious conduct,
   (9) didactic wisdom teachings,
   (10) eschatological salvation
   and the gifts of the apocalyptic seers,

(IV) divine intelligence and knowledge:
   (1) God possesses 'wisdom',
   (2) God gains and creates 'wisdom'.[38]

While some aspects of human intelligence and knowledge can be found in older texts of the Old Testament, the aspects of God's wisdom in Fohrer's point IV occur only in younger, postexilic texts at the time when Proverbs 1–9 was being written.

Which aspects of this extensive concept of wisdom are combined in the Wisdom Figure, and what are the consequences?

Among the aspects mentioned above, the Wisdom figure in Proverbs 1–9 represents first of all skill and ability (2), as can be seen from the semantic parallels in Prov. 8.12-14 and Exod. 31.3, 35.10. Prudence (3) and common sense (4) are also contained in the Wisdom Figure in Prov. 8.12-14. 'Education' (5) occurs only in a small number of places in the Old Testament.[39] Together with the aspects of rules of behaviour (6), ethical (7) and religious conduct (8), it is present in Proverbs 1–9 as a subject that has to be studied. Because of the parallelism of Prov. 8.15-16 and Isa. 11.2-3 which I have outlined elsewhere,[40] the Wisdom Figure also represents the eschatological salvation and the gifts of the apocalyptic seers.

In contrast, personified Wisdom does not represent the aspects of magic and mantic (1). These are usually mentioned in the Old Testament in narrations about neighbouring cultures, describing

38. So Fohrer, 'Die Weisheit', pp. 242-74.
39. Fohrer, 'Die Weisheit', p. 257.
40. See Baumann, *Die Weisheitsgestalt*, pp. 91-93.

prediction and related phenomena such as astrology and the consulting of oracles.[41] Wisdom does, however, constitute one facet of mantic wisdom when speaking as a prophetess in Prov. 1.22-33.[42] Personified Wisdom differs, though, from cleverness and cunning (3), that is, the use of intelligence to harm others. Neither is Wisdom to be seen as a canon of didactic wisdom instruction (9). Such an aspect is created in Proverbs 1–9: After their completion, these texts serve as a canon of wisdom facets that can be referred to from this point forward.

Thus, in personified Wisdom, all aspects with an ethically dubious character are omitted: The Wisdom Figure embodies neither magic, which partly contradicts the faith in YHWH, nor cunning wisdom, which can be harmful to others. On the other hand, both aspects can be found in Proverbs 1–9. They are connected to the 'Strange Woman', who tries to seduce the young man in Prov. 7.10-27 by means of tricks and promises.

In Proverbs 1–9, therefore, only the positive aspects of wisdom are assigned to the Wisdom Figure. At the same time, this works as a reformulation of the phenomenon of wisdom. For the first time in the Old Testament, through the personification of Wisdom and creation of the Wisdom Figure, the concept of wisdom is comprised and unified. Aspects which are not mentioned here are no longer part of the wisdom phenomenon. This might be in reply to some critical tendencies towards particular 'wisdoms' which can be found, for example, in Isa. 47.10. Israelite wisdom, which from now on is represented and unified in the Wisdom Figure, is no longer the object of such criticism.

How, then, is this Wisdom Figure related to wisdom as God's intelligence and knowledge? 'It is remarkable and must be specifically addressed that in the Old Testament, the term "wisdom" is seldom related to God and then only in special idioms and quite late. That God is "wise" is only mentioned once in the Old Testament, and in fact in a passage (Isa. 21.2) where this statement is obviously meant ironically'.[43]

41. Fohrer, 'Die Weisheit', p. 254; with regard to mantic wisdom and its further development see Müller, 'חכם *ḥākam*', esp. pp. 292-93.

42. For prophecy as a branch of mantic see K. Koch, *Die Profeten*. I. *Assyrische Zeit* (Stuttgart: Kohlhammer, 3rd edn, 1995), p. 53.

43. M. Noth, 'Die Bewährung von Salomos "göttlicher Weisheit"', in

To go beyond this observation by Martin Noth, we have to ask how the Wisdom Figure in Proverbs 1–9 is related to divine wisdom. Personified Wisdom represents a concept of wisdom that, especially in Prov. 8.22-31, is associated with YHWH as his creation. In Prov. 2.6 the most certainly non-personified wisdom is called a gift of YHWH. This character is also attributed to the Wisdom Figure in Prov. 8.15–21 as the power to rule, as can be seen from texts like 1 Kgs. 3.9, 12 which form the background of this idea.

Other concepts of wisdom were formulated at the same time, mainly in connection with YHWH's creation of the world.[44] The main difference between those concepts and Proverbs 1–9 is that even though Job 28 acknowledges a 'wisdom' present in Creation or underlying it like a building plan, this wisdom is nei-ther personified nor does it represent the wisdom phenomenon like the Wisdom Figure in Proverbs 1–9. Personified Wisdom as an original 'being' and a creation of YHWH is quite unique for its time. The models developed alternatively do not claim to give such a complete description of wisdom personified, because they are normally reduced to the aspect of the creation of the world. Additionally, the Wisdom Figure in Proverbs 1–9 is described as a figure close to YHWH, because her words and idioms resemble YHWH-speech.[45] The closeness between YHWH and Wisdom is thus noticeable in what is said but is hardly ever explicitly discussed.

With regard to its theological content, the Wisdom Figure unifies the complex phenomenon of wisdom. Except for the neg-ative aspects of cunning and magic, it embodies all aspects of Old Testament's human and divine wisdom. One consequence

M. Noth and D.W. Thomas (eds.), *Wisdom in Israel and in the Ancient Near East* (VT Sup, 3; Leiden: E.J. Brill, 1955), pp. 225-37 (232).

44. See Fohrer, 'Die Weisheit', pp. 262-67.

45. Such parallels can, e.g., be found in Prov. 8.17 in the field of love imagery (see G. Baumann, *Die Weisheitsgestalt*, pp. 98-102) and in the explanation for the macarism of personified Wisdom in 8.35-6 (*Die Weisheitsgestalt*, pp. 163-70). In 1.20-33 Wisdom partly speaks like YHWH himself (*Die Weisheitsgestalt*, p. 198). Either the qualification of Wisdom's speech in 8.6-9 (*Die Weisheitsgestalt*, pp. 78-81) or the parallel terms for Wisdom in 8.12-14 (pp. 86-93) point to an authority of Wisdom similar to that of YHWH.

of excluding the negative aspects is that the new summary of
wisdom in the Wisdom Figure appears as purified and exclusively positive. The Wisdom Figure establishes her authority as a
teacher by modeling her speech on YHWH-speech and by
emphasizing her pre-existence (8.22-31). It is not likely that this
authority, as in the case of the parents' authority, existed previously as a specific cultural value that she could use. It seems
more plausible that the Wisdom Figure had not been invented
until Proverbs 1–9. The Wisdom Figure strengthens the authority
of the parental teaching by speaking in a way similar to the parents, and at the same time she awards a nearly divine position to
the phenomenon of wisdom with all its facets. Because of this,
she demands obedience, and at the same time expects obedience
of the wisdom sayings from ch. 10 onwards.

In various ways Proverbs 1–9 functions as an introduction to
the book of Proverbs. The *Sitz im Buch* can be sufficiently outlined, whereas the *Sitz im Leben* of an imprecise 'genre' of didactic speech or teaching can only be described hypothetically. The
situation of family teaching, in the newly proposed perspective
on the text, serves to emphasize the necessity of a profound
study of the book of Proverbs. Therefore it is plausible to outline
the *Sitz im Leben* of Proverbs 1–9 based upon the *Sitz im Buch*,
especially its introductory function. This means that Proverbs 1–
9 has to be looked at as a product of literature with a literary
purpose. Its imagined didactic situation serves as a 'staged form'
for the book. At the same time, the complex phenomenon of
wisdom is unified in the personification of Wisdom; it is
redefined and memorizing it is made easier.

Having outlined the literary function of the Wisdom Figure,
we now have to look at the theological function.

The Image of God in the Book of Proverbs

For a more detailed description of the theological function of the
Wisdom Figure in Proverbs 1–9, it is at first necessary to outline
the image of God. What is new about Israelite wisdom theology
becomes clearer when we compare the ideas about YHWH and
wisdom in the older and newer parts of the Book of Proverbs.

Lennart Boström has written an extensive work about the

concept of God in the book of Proverbs.[46] He characterizes the main topics of the concept of God as follows: YHWH as the creator of the world is presupposed rather than explicated. YHWH is thought of as a universal God. With respect to world order, YHWH is a supreme God. The anthropocentric perspective of the proverbs connects this concept of God with the human freedom to choose one's own way of life: a way pleasing to God or the way of the sinner.[47] Seen in the perspective of religious history, YHWH is a sovereign God. He is situated above his creation, and he is responsible for justice and retribution. His main characteristics are transcendence, incomparability, freedom and justice.[48] At the same time YHWH also functions as a personal God who cares, in particular, for the weak and disadvantaged members of society.[49]

YHWH, therefore, shows two sides of himself: On one hand, he appears as the universal, creating, sovereign and supreme God; and, on the other hand, he is personally interested in specific human needs.

Does this picture change when only Proverbs 1–9 is taken into account? Indeed, YHWH is portrayed differently in these chapters than in the older Proverbs of chs. 10–30.

First of all, the concept of YHWH seems to be changed by the appearance of the Wisdom Figure, who belongs to the divine sphere together with YHWH.[50] Another difference pointed out by Boström is the lack of concern on YHWH's part for society's underprivileged members, as it is illustrated by the fact that 'dishonest weights and measures' are an abomination in the eyes of YHWH. They are mentioned in Prov. 11.1, 16.11 and 20.10, 23, but not in Proverbs 1–9. This subject is closely connected with the question of social justice. It also presupposes that YHWH is deeply involved in human affairs, particularly caring for the poor and the weak that are hit hardest by fraud in the market

46. L. Boström, *The God of the Sages: The Portrayal of God in the Book of Proverbs* (ConBOT, 29; Stockholm: Almqvist & Wiksell, 1990), from p. 88.

47. Boström, *Sages*, pp. 139-40.

48. Boström, *Sages*, pp. 190-92.

49. Boström, *Sages*, pp. 236-38.

50. Boström, *Sages*, pp. 190-91.

place.[51] In this regard, YHWH in Proverbs 1–9 is not named explicitly as the spokesman for the weak, the poor and the defenseless. On the contrary, poverty is seen as the result of laziness in 6.11. This attitude of Proverbs 1–9 is probably embedded in an ethos of justice[52] that grants a minimum of care for the poor. The solidarity of YHWH with the victims of everyday injustice is, however, not mentioned further, and is therefore not integrated into the theology of Proverbs 1–9.

There are other differences regarding the concept of YHWH in the older and the newer sections of the book of Proverbs: In Proverbs 1–9, YHWH is no longer called the God who looks into a person's heart like in Prov. 15.11; 16.2, and 17.3. This points to a partial loss of the personal relationship between YHWH and his people.

Another point is that the king who is mentioned in Prov. 21.1, 24.21 and 29.25 in connection with YHWH is not mentioned in Proverbs 1–9. Instead, 'the kings' are referred to in 8.15 only among other rulers in the speech of the Wisdom figure. The kings' high rank[53] is abandoned; he is just one among several groups of rulers. Their guiding principle shall be justice (צדק, 8.16b), for only in the case of just governing practices will rulers appear as having the gift of wisdom. Since the poor mentioned above are not of interest here, the rulers are the only social group of which Wisdom *explicitly* speaks. In the perspective of Proverbs 1–9, only this group enjoys the privilege of having their own wisdom.

Unlike in the older Proverbs, in Proverbs 1–9 YHWH is more clearly visible as the creator of the world. World order as a theme closely connected to the creation of the world is brought home to the readers in Proverbs 1–9 by the direct address of the teacher and the Wisdom Figure. From Proverbs 10, world order is touched on in several sayings, but it is not directly related to YHWH or taught as a concept or way of life.

In contrast to the older Proverbs, therefore, in chs. 1–9 a

51. So Boström, *Sages*, pp. 200-201.
52. For the attitude of Prov. 1–9 toward rich and poor also see Baumann, *Die Weisheitsgestalt*, pp. 102-107.
53. For this see Camp, *Wisdom*, pp. 272-80; Schroer, 'Die göttliche Weisheit', pp. 173-76 and Baumann, *Die Weisheitsgestalt*, pp. 300-303.

different relationship between YHWH and his people is established: in the field of personal relationship, YHWH is still a God
that is close to them; this is explicitly restricted, however, to
those who seek wisdom (3.1-12, 26, 32-34). YHWH's special relationship to the problems of everyday life of the underprivileged
is not mentioned any more in Proverbs 1–9, nor is the usual
response to God's care, that is, the care for one's neighbour.[54]
This aspect may be implied in several formulas, for example in
that of the choice of the right way of life (3.6, 32). Only the rulers,
however, are explicitly mentioned as those endowed with wisdom. Additionally, characteristic features of YHWH which are
only indirectly related to everyday life are emphasized in Proverbs 1–9: the creation of the world and world order. The text's
explicit evidence reserves YHWH's closeness to the wise or to
those who seek wisdom.

Now, on the basis of this differing concept of God, the difference between older and newer Proverbs concerning YHWH's
relation to wisdom can be examined. According to Boström,
YHWH's relation to wisdom in the older Proverbs is expressed
only in Prov. 21.30—as some kind of opposition:

> 21.30. No wisdom, no understanding, no counsel against the Lord

> It is not necessary to interpret this sentence as maintaining a pejo-
> rative stance towards wisdom. Its limitations and subordinations
> to Yahweh should be considered together with similar sentences
> which lay special stress on God's sovereignty. But it is notewor-
> thy that this one instance where wisdom and the Lord are directly
> related to each other in a sentence, points to a gap between
> wisdom and God.[55]

The concept of wisdom described by Boström fits the חכמה of the
older Proverbs, without exception a desirable human competence that can be achieved by observing what happens in the

54. A. Meinhold, 'Gott und Mensch in Proverbien iii,' *VT* 37 (1987), pp.
468-77, comments on Prov. 3: 'Human piety's double relationship to both
God and neighbour in the traditional Old Testament law compendiums,
and especially in the decalogue, is applied in Prov. iii in this ranking only to
the individual'(pp. 474-75).

55. Boström, *Sages,* p. 40; elsewhere in the Old Testament the relationship between wisdom and YHWH is explained rarely and only in late texts;
see Baumann, *Die Weisheitsgestalt,* pp. 279-80.

world. Such a competence, which in the sapiential perspective leads to a good and successful life, must be closely related to YHWH's world order.[56]

The idea of order existing behind the visible world is also expressed in Proverbs 1–9. Men and women are warned especially in 3.5, 7 against overestimating the possibilities of human insight instead of relying on YHWH. But the relationship between חכמה and YHWH has changed in comparison to the older Proverbs: Here Wisdom is a gift from YHWH (2.6); together with her YHWH founded the world (3.19-20), and he gave life to Wisdom before creating the world (8.22).

The close relationship between wisdom and theology and between the human world and God's creation is expressed in Proverbs 1–9 *figuratively*—in Prov. 2.6; 3.19-20 and 8.22-31, for example. The most detailed picture (8.22-31) translates the implicit presuppositions of sapiential theology into a kind of 'metaphorical theology'. The underlying axiom of sapiential reflections is not only couched in a theoretical statement as it is in Prov. 3.19-20. Proverbs 8.22-31 demonstrates with the help of a *metaphor* that YHWH gave a good and wise order to the world. This is guaranteed by the Wisdom Figure as a pre-existing being and witness of primeval creation. Thus חכמה in these texts is a theologumenon turned into an image, a metaphor for something that before could only be expressed argumentatively and theoretically.

---

56. H. Gese, 'Die Weisheit, der Menschensohn und die Ursprünge der Christologie als konsequente Entfaltung der biblischen Theologie', *SEA* 44 (1979), pp. 77-114. P. 81 qualifies sapiential education as follows: 'Man, having learned to be independent through an understanding of the world and by being able to judge, had found standards of human thought and deed which were not covered by the traditional collective rules of cult, law and ethics. The difference can be explained in terms of rule and counsel. The rule of the decalogue stands under divine authority of Israel's revelation and belongs to the elementary priestly tradition which is binding for the whole of Israel. Counsel, on the other hand, is what a sage gives to an individual. Whether the individual follows it or not is his or her own responsibility. Therefore, the difference found in this example is no reason to overlook the final authority of divine world order which is the background of counsel.'

This type of metaphorization of theology[57] in the Wisdom Figure in Proverbs 1–9 can, upon examination, also be discovered in other points of view.[58] Boström writes about the Proverbs' theology as regards retribution and world order: 'This approach emphasizes the freedom of man to choose his way of life while at the same time making it crystal clear that he will be held responsible for this choice.'[59] This fundamental theological topic is represented in Proverbs 1–9 in the Wisdom Figure: As the personification of sapiential theology she calls men and women to make a free choice regarding their way of life (Prov. 1.20-33; 8.4-21), and at the same time announces the consequences of this choice (1.24-33; 8.32-36).

Wisdom as a gift from YHWH bestowed upon rulers (Prov. 8.15-16) can also be explained in this manner: This gift of YHWH is manifested in the Wisdom Figure. There is no theoretical statement that wisdom is a prerequisite talent for just rule; rather, Wisdom herself explains that only 'through her' are rulers enabled to rule.

Up to this point, wisdom has been the human ability to understand regularities in the order of the world. Now this wisdom becomes YHWH's *creation*. According to this view, human understanding is something made possible by YHWH.

In Proverbs 1–9, the Wisdom Figure, in a metaphorical way, brings about an understanding of the wisdom that is closely connected to YHWH. How can this connection be described more precisely? I would like to suggest a model that allows a distanced look at postexilic Israel's theology.

---

57. A phenomenon that resembles the outlined 'metaphorical theology' is described in the context of Egyptian theology as an 'icon' by J. Assmann, *Ägypten: Theologie und Frömmigkeit einer frühen Hochkultur* (Stuttgart: Kohlhammer, 1984), p. 130: 'Icons are pictures of the imagination, figurative illustrations of processes, actions, and events of the divine world which can be concretely expressed in texts and pictures. What the implicit theology of traditional Egyptian polytheism makes of the sun's course is 'icons', modeled illustrations of the sense of salvation which interpret the phases of cosmic events; icons are timeless or related to a 'timeless presence', for they are prototypes of processes in the divine world which are constantly performed in cult and in the cosmos' (p. 135).

58. I only mention the most obvious aspects here.

59. Boström, *Sages*, p. 139.

The Development of Egyptian Ma'at-Thought and the
Transition to Personal Piety: A Heuristic Model

In the field of religious history scholars involved with research into the Wisdom Figure of Proverbs 1–9 have sometimes regarded the Old Egyptian Ma'at as a prototype or parallel figure.[60] The Egyptian development of Ma'at-thought in relation to Personal Piety, therefore, might be useful as a model for explaining the formulation of the Israelite Wisdom Figure.[61]

Ma'at in Egypt is both a goddess and an intellectual concept represented by the goddess. 'Ma'at stands in the middle between morality and religion.'[62] The moral aspect originates, according to Assmann, in the 'group moral of tribal associations integrated by family ties',[63] whereas the religious aspect is rooted in the divine world order which is represented in a corresponding 'rule over creation'. A similar connection between religion and ethics can also be observed in the Wisdom Figure of Proverbs 1–9. If we look at the theological implications we find that there is a parallel between the Egyptian idea of Ma'at and the Israelite concept of the so-called *Tun-Ergehen-Zusammenhang*,[64] that is the

60. See Chr. Kayatz, *Studien zu Prov. 1–9. Eine form- und motivge-schichtliche Untersuchung unter Einbeziehung ägyptischen Vergleichsmaterials* (WMANT, 22; Neukirchen–Vluyn: Neukirchener, 1966), pp. 135-39.

61. The following outline is based on the work of H. Brunner, 'Der freie Wille Gottes in der ägyptischen Weisheit', in *Les sagesses du proche-orient ancien: Colloque de Strasbourg 17-19 mai 1962*, Bibliothèque des centres d'études supérieures spécialisés. Travaux du centre d'études supérieures spécialisés d'histoire des religions de Strasbourg (Paris: Presses Universitaires de France, 1963), pp. 103-20; 'Persönliche Frömmigkeit', *LÄ*, IV (1982), pp. 951-63; also J. Assmann, 'Weisheit, Loyalismus und Frömmigkeit', in E. Hornung and O. Keel (eds.), *Studien zu altägyptischen Lebenslehren* (OBO, 28; Freiburg: Universitätsverlag; Göttingen: Vandenhoeck & Ruprecht, 1979), pp. 11-72; J. Assmann, *Ma'at: Gerechtigkeit und Unsterblichkeit im Alten Ägypten* (Munich: Beck, 1990); and M. Lichtheim, *Maat in Egyptian Autobiographies and Related Studies* (OBO, 120; Freiburg: Universitätsverlag; Göttingen: Vandenhoeck & Ruprecht, 1992). Partly they differ in their view on the topic.

62. Assmann, *Ma'at*, p. 243.

63. Assmann, *Ma'at*, p. 243.

64. The discussion behind this term in Old Testament research cannot be

notion that one's ethical choices determine one's welfare or 'illfare', as the case may be, behind the terms צדקה and צדק.[65] The meaning of Egyptian Ma'at reaches even further. Ma'at is

> ...the program of political order which not only intends to establish social justice among the people but actually intends to bring the whole world of men and gods into accord and keep it going.[66] In order to establish the Ma'at-sphere in the state—and without Ma'at, without the basic trust and agreement it brings about, no communication is possible—a superior institution is needed, i.e. the institution of kingship.[67]

This notion prevailed in Egypt until the Late Period, although, according to Assmann,[68] it had been undermined since the Eighteenth Dynasty by a new school of thought called 'Personal Piety'[69] or 'theology of [God's] will'.[70] This theological trend probably occurred in the political crisis of the Second Transition Period and in the theological disruption of the Amarna-Period. Its characteristic feature is 'a feeling of total dependence on God on the part of the individual'.[71] The main difference between these two theological concepts is the role of the king. Whereas the Ma'at-idea requires him as a mediator, Personal Piety is able to do without the king or any other mediator.

With regard to the Israelite Wisdom Figure, it is interesting that in certain statements of Personal Piety, older, loyalistic

---

repeated here. Suffice it to say that I do not believe that YHWH 'completes' the *Tun-Ergehen-Zusammenhang* in a nearly automatic way. The parallel between Ma'at-thought and the *Tun-Ergehen-Zusammenhang* is drawn by Assmann, *Ma'at*, e.g., p. 66.

65. Kayatz does not think that the aspect of world order embodied in Ma'at is represented in the Wisdom Figure (Assmann, *Ma'at*, p. 138). Especially regarding the work of H.H. Schmid (*Gerechtigkeit als Weltordnung: Hintergrund und Geschichte des alttestamentlichen Gerechtigkeitsbegriffes* [BHT, 40; Tübingen: J.C.B. Mohr, 1968], p. 61), the Egyptian concept of Ma'at is, for the Israelites, connected with the terms צדקה and צדק.

66. Assmann, *Ma'at*, p. 34.

67. So according to Assmann, *Ma'at*, p. 201.

68. Assmann, *Ma'at*, pp. 252-72.

69. So, e.g., H. Brunner, 'Der freie Wille', p. 108; 'Frömmigkeit', 1982; also Assmann, 'Weisheit, Loyalismus', p. 15 n. 9.

70. Assmann, *Ma'at*, p. 252.

71. Brunner, 'Frömmigkeit', p. 951.

teachings have been assimilated and transformed.[72] In some literary genres the king is replaced by a god or goddess. According to Assmann, this means that the king gradually loses his role as mediator between God and man.[73]

Ma'at was not suddenly replaced by Personal Piety; rather, both trends coexisted for quite a long time in Egyptian theology. This was made possible by the fact that Personal Piety presupposed and supported the same rules of social existence basically outlined in the Ma'at-concept.

> The texts affirm over and over that a man *knew* what the god wished him to do. A man's heart taught him to distinguish right from wrong, and taught him that right-doing was what the god desired... Wisdom and piety were partners in the endeavour to formulate and teach the right kind of living.[74]

There are parallels to both Ma'at and Personal Piety in the Israelite Wisdom Figure, and they can mainly be seen in following aspects:[75]

Personal piety, as well as the Wisdom Figure, owe their invention to a time of crisis. In both cases the times are characterized by the loss or questioning of kingship.[76] Camp has shown the postexilic Israelite Wisdom Figure in a mediating role; the figure replaces the king as mediator.[77]

Both Personal Piety and the Wisdom Figure have to be seen as phenomena together with other forms of religion and theology; there is no evidence for open conflict in the source material.[78] In both cases the sources are ethical instructions. Both concepts occur in aretalogies, macarisms and hymns.[79] It has to be noted that in the texts of Personal Piety, men and women turn to a god

---

72. This is shown by Assmann, 'Weisheit, Loyalismus'.

73. Assmann, 'Weisheit, Loyalismus', p. 50.

74. Lichtheim, *Maat in Egyptian Autobiographies*, p. 100.

75. The outline of Personal Piety given here is based upon Brunner's article ('Frömmigkeit'). The following notes in my text only refer to parallel aspects in regard to Personal Piety.

76. Brunner, 'Frömmigkeit', 1982, p. 951.

77. Camp, *Wisdom*, pp. 272-80; similarly Schroer, 'Die göttliche Weisheit', pp. 173-76; cf. also Baumann, *Die Weisheitsgestalt*, pp. 300-303.

78. So Brunner, 'Frömmigkeit', p. 951.

79. In regard to Personal Piety, see Brunner, 'Frömmigkeit', p. 952.

or goddess. In Proverbs 1–9, however, nobody actually approaches the Wisdom Figure. It is the Wisdom Figure alone who gives out information about herself.

The most striking terminological concurrence concerns the giving and accepting of love through the god or goddess and through the Wisdom Figure. In both contexts, it is not possible to reverse the order of human and divine love. 'As far as the texts speak of a mutual relationship between God and man [woman], human acts or qualities come first, and God's love is the answer ... there is no evidence of the opposite, i.e. of a man [woman] returning the love that first came from God.'[80] Other parallels of both transcendent figures are their fairness of judgment and their great power.[81] Evidence of their benevolence toward an individual may manifest itself, for example in long life.[82] The human ideal is that of a pious person (*m3'ti* or צַדִּיק).[83] This person walks in the ways of the god, goddess or the Wisdom Figure (Prov. 3.17; 8.20, 32), calls upon them (1.28),and receives them into the heart.[84]

In addition to these parallels there are also some differences between the Egyptian Personal Piety and the Israelite Wisdom Figure. In Egypt, a person is called a 'servant' (*b3k*) of the personal god,[85] for which there is no parallel in Proverbs 1–9. No prayers are addressed to the Wisdom Figure,[86] nor sacrifices offered to her, nor is she worshipped in the temple.[87]

In conclusion we can say that there are not only parallels between the Wisdom Figure in Proverbs 1–9 and the Egyptian Ma'at-concept, but also between Wisdom and the concept of Personal Piety. This leads to the assumption that personified Wisdom in postexilic Israel was formulated in a situation similar

80. Brunner, 'Frömmigkeit', pp. 957-58.
81. Brunner, 'Frömmigkeit', pp. 953-54.
82. Brunner, 'Frömmigkeit', pp. 953-54; and also Assmann, *Ma'at*, p. 263.
83. Brunner, 'Frömmigkeit', p. 955.
84. Brunner, 'Frömmigkeit', p. 955; cf. the approach to Wisdom (Prov. 2.2), the coming of Wisdom into a person's heart (Prov. 2.10) or similarly the binding of the teacher's rule onto the heart (6.21).
85. Brunner, 'Frömmigkeit', p. 956.
86. Possibly the passage in Prov. 1.28 can be interpreted this way.
87. Brunner, 'Frömmigkeit', p. 958.

to that which accompanied the transition in Egypt from Ma'at-thought to Personal Piety. I would like to combine this result with my conclusion concerning the literary and theological function of personified Wisdom in order to give it a place in postexilic Israelite theology.

The Theological Function of the Wisdom Figure in
Proverbs 1–9 in Postexilic Israel

The Wisdom Figure emerged within a specific framework that shaped it and influenced its formulation. One factor was the apparent need for a summary of the 'wisdom' phenomenon to be used in the introduction to the collection of older Proverbs. Another factor was the specific facet of Israelite theology which found its expression in the *Tun-Ergehen-Zusammenhang*; this can be understood as the 'Ma'at-element' in Israel. A third factor is that, at the time when personified Wisdom emerged, a partial reorientation of Israelite theology was necessary because the kingship and its institutions had been lost. In addition to this problem, the economic situation was difficult for many people,[88] even though they remained faithful to YHWH and had no reason to reproach themselves for alleged sinful behaviour. Therefore, the relevance of pre-exilic and exilic theological concepts was limited. The theological task in postexilic Israel, where the Wisdom Figure emerged, is to develop a theological concept

88. See the results of socio-historical research of the Judaean postexilic community in the sixth–fourth centuries BCE: C. Maier, *Die 'fremde Frau' in Proverbien 1-9: Eine exegetische und sozialgeschichtliche Studie* (OBO, 144; Freiburg: Universitätsverlag; Göttingen: Vandenhoeck & Ruprecht, 1995), pp. 25-68, esp. p. 67: 'In the middle of the 5th century an "agricultural crisis" occurred among the peasants which lead to a "social crisis" in the community. The starting point was the tax burden that had to be obtained by forced agricultural production. Moneylenders from society's upper strata aggravated the situation by demanding high interest. During the recruitment of all family tribes for the building of the wall, the peasants, heavily in debt, complained and together with parts of the priesthood and Nehemiah formed a coalition against the creditors. If there really was a single waiving of the debts cannot be proved. An increasing gap between rich and poor was probably a consequence of this crisis.' See also Maier, 'Conflicting Attractions', in this volume.

that both takes into account the experience of the fragility of the
Tun-Ergehen-Zusammenhang but does not abandon God's sover-
eignty, nor his closeness to Israel, or his care for the people.

The loss of the kingship led to a transfer of the king's theological functions onto other figureheads, as can be seen in the idea of
the Messiah. The Wisdom Figure is one of these new figureheads. The recommended loving relationship with her resembles
the Egyptian theology of Personal Piety. People do not only refer
(Prov. 3) in terms of religious admiration or love to YHWH, but
also to the Wisdom Figure. She is, however, more than just a
transcendent figure. She also represents the positive aspects
of what Israel knew to be wisdom. This includes a knowledge
of God's world order which makes orientation in the world possible. In part, this order is identical with the *Tun-Ergehen-Zusammenhang* that, in the postexilic period, had now become questionable. How can Wisdom, as a figure of the divine sphere, be
convincing when the world is perceived as a place of disorder
rather than order, where people are so utterly miserable?

In some ways the Israelite situation resembles that of Egypt
during the Eighteenth Dynasty. The synthesis found there of
worshipping a personal Deity while simultaneously holding on
to the principle of 'connective justice'[89] could have been a model
for postexilic Israel. This is all the more the case since Egyptian
literature from this period was known in Israel, as can be seen
from the strong resemblance[90] between verses in Prov. 22.17-
24.22 and the Egyptian instruction of Amenemope, an early representative of Personal Piety. While parts of Amenemope served
as a model for the older Proverbs, this more recent concept was
not adopted in Israel.[91] Similar phrases as in the theology

89. Assmann, *Ma'at*, p. 283.

90. F.-J. Steiert, *Die Weisheit Israels—ein Fremdkörper im Alten Testament?
Eine Untersuchung zum Buch der Sprüche auf dem Hintergrund der ägyptischen
Weisheitslehren* (FThSt, 143; Freiburg: Herder, 1990), pp. 196-200, gives a
synopsis of Prov. 22.17-23.11 and Amenemope. For a more detailed
comparison of Amenemope and Prov. 22.11-24.22, see K.F.D. Römheld,
Wege der Weisheit: Die Lehren Amenemopes und Proverbien 22,17-24,22
(BZAW, 184; Berlin: W. de Gruyter, 1989), pp. 151-81.

91. 'The biblical instruction [in Prov. 22.17–24.22] depends on
Amenemope and is therefore historically younger than its model, but
within the framework of Egyptian Wisdom history it appears as being

of Personal Piety can be found in other Old Testament texts, for
example, the mutual love between YHWH and Israel in
Deuteronomy or the love between Wisdom and the people in
Proverbs 1–9. The Egyptian symbiosis shows that it was possible
for different theological concepts to coexist. For postexilic Israel a
similar coexistence can be assumed. I believe that in Proverbs 1–9
we have a synthesis of the old concept of world order and
elements of Personal Piety. YHWH's deeds, according to older
sections in Proverbs, follow

> the same principle of mutuality which is the basis of social inter-
> action—with the crucial difference that YHWH's intervention can
> be expected, but is not at man's disposal...YHWH is related to
> the Tun-Ergehen-Zusammenhang, but the freedom of his will
> remains untouched.[92]

A combination of both the experience of deficient social interaction and the freedom of YHWH's will lead to a certain distance
between YHWH and humankind. The postexilic period also
allows for a more sceptical and less pious interpretation of
YHWH's free will. Every human effort to understand YHWH's
plans is either looked upon as impossible and therefore useless
(Qohelet), or the consequences of YHWH's free will are presented in a way which comes close to despotism or tyranny (Job).

Proverbs 1–9 proposes a different way out of this dilemma. In
order to understand this solution it should be remembered that
the texts function as an introduction to the older sayings of
Proverbs 10 onwards. A person who 'edits' theological texts like
the older Proverbs in a period where there are completely different economic and theological problems than in the time during
which the old Proverbs originated will display a somewhat
conservative attitude. Texts from the past appear to provide at
least some outlines for a solution to today's crises, possibly even
a way out of today's problems. This lies at the basis of Proverbs
1–9: Neither does the older concept of the *Tun-Ergehen-
Zusammenhang* come into question, nor does the belief in a world

older!', Steiert, *Die Weisheit Israels*, p. 183.
    92. B. Janowski, 'Die Tat kehrt zum Täter zurück: Offene Fragen im
Umkreis des "Tun-Ergehen-Zusammenhangs"', *ZTK* 91 (1994), pp. 247-71
(269).

order which people could understand if they really tried. As far as this notion is concerned there are no significant differences between older Proverbs and Proverbs 1–9.[93]

What the Wisdom Figure and the teacher in Proverbs 1–9 announce is rendered 'new' by the direct address and the underlying urgency, but in essence it has been known for centuries. The new element within these teachings is the Wisdom Figure as a teacher. Still, most of her facets are well known from older Israelite traditions.[94] In this way, Wisdom may appear as a new phenomenon, as a female, personified synthesis of the Old Testament's wisdom, but she is nothing new or alien. At a time of crisis, she shows people a way that follows traditional patterns and gives them a sense of confidence in the world's good order. This confidence had vanished when the *Tun-Ergehen-Zusammen-hang* became questionable due to the problems of everyday life in the postexilic period. Elements from YHWH-speeches are used to show that the way recommended by Wisdom is in fact theologically the right way. The main theological problem in postexilic Israel, the question of how YHWH's world order can still be valid in times of injustice, is solved by the testimony of a trustworthy witness: the Wisdom Figure was present when YHWH created the world in its order. Thus she can bear witness that there was a primeval order in the world which was so good that she, Wisdom, and humankind rejoiced about it (Prov. 8.31). In the course of history, however, man's actions disturbed the world order.[95] Nevertheless, the destiny of men and women can take a turn for the better if they live according to the teachings of the Wisdom Figure which correspond to the world order.

The Wisdom Figure affirms the possibility of change, the ability of people to mend their ways, because she embodies both human and divine wisdom. As a heavenly being close to

93. This hypothesis is supported by Gerhard von Rad's denial of a substantial break between Prov. 10–30 and 1–9; see G. von Rad, *Weisheit in Israel* (Neukirchen–Vluyn: Neukirchener, 3rd edn, 1985), p. 201. In von Rad's opinion, Prov. 1–9 was written at the end of Israel's Monarchic Period; von Rad, *Weisheit in Israel*, pp. 214-15.

94. So the result of my research on the history of traditions used in the text; see Baumann, *Die Weisheitsgestalt*, pp. 66-251.

95. Baumann, *Die Weisheitsgestalt*, pp. 152-73.

YHWH, she enhances the theological value of human wisdom
that is based upon experience. Until then, human experience had
not enjoyed such theological value. Thus the *Tun-Ergehen-
Zusammenhang* is beyond human criticism which arose during
the times of hardship. On the other hand, the Wisdom Figure
turns to men and women as a close, trustworthy, and loving
figure. Both aspects are therefore represented by personified
Wisdom: the 'old' concept of the world order with its *Tun-
Ergehen-Zusammenhang* as well as the loving care of Personal
Piety. Thus, taking into account the historical situation, the call
of personified Wisdom in Proverbs 1–9 is an appeal to believe in
the good order which YHWH wove into his creation before all
times—even though the present situation seems to contradict it.

The question is now, How such an important theological
figure was integrated into Israelite belief.

The Wisdom Figure within the Context of
Postexilic Israelite Monotheism

There are a number of aspects of the Wisdom Figure which
allow it to be placed within postexilic theology. Personified
Wisdom combines in herself divine and human wisdom. She is a
heavenly, transcendent being. Her speech resembles YHWH's
speech in several points; she speaks with an authority that comes
close to YHWH's own.[96] These aspects identify her as something
close to a goddess. The speeches of the Wisdom Figure, however,
evade a precise determination of her relationship with YHWH.
Proverbs 8.22-31—the text which comes closest to such a determination—uses three verbs regarding YHWH's creation of personified Wisdom for which a precise meaning cannot be found:
קנה ('to acquire/to create'), סכך ('to weave/to form') and חיל ('to
be in labour/to give birth to'). The Wisdom Figure is called
ראשית ('beginning/first child') of YHWH's path, and as his אמון
(probably, but not exclusively: 'pet child, darling') she dwells by
his side.[97] Such an accumulation of ambiguous terms cannot be
accidental. This choice of words presumably indicates that the

96. See above, n. 45.
97. I have shown the ambiguity of the listed terms in Baumann, *Die
Weisheitsgestalt*, pp. 116-22 and 131-38.

text's authors intended *not to determine* YHWH's relationship to
the Wisdom Figure in an unambiguous way. What *is* said is that
personified Wisdom is YHWH's transcendent creation. Whether
their subsequent relationship is hierarchical or egalitarian
remains open.

One problem that appears in the context of YHWH's relationship to the Wisdom Figure is the image of YHWH himself. It is
not clear which characteristic features can be ascribed to YHWH.
Can YHWH's image be reduced to the features mentioned in
Proverbs 1–9 and especially Proverbs 3? Perhaps there was no
need for YHWH's image to be pictured more precisely in
Proverbs 1–9 because it could be safely assumed that everyone
was familiar with other religious writings, worship or the law.
Which of these sources to choose, and which of the potential
aspects of YHWH to select, is unclear.

What is certain about Proverbs 1–9, however, is that חכמה
exists as a transcendent being of goddess-like rank at YHWH's
side. She is his transcendent creation. Because of her knowledge
about the world's order she is able to teach an ethos to men and
women that resembles YHWH's commandments in its consequences.[98] People are to love the Wisdom Figure like a 'personal
goddess' and walk in her ways. Nothing is said about a cult of
the Wisdom Figure or about the possibility of addressing prayers
to her. Her call is for a spiritual relationship of individuals
towards her, which manifests itself by keeping the Torah.

One reason for the invention of the Wisdom Figure—so as to
reduce the diverse elements within wisdom personified—was to
find a common denominator for the introductory figure to the
older Proverbs collection. Additionally, she acquired the theological function of reassuring men and women of the existence of a
functioning world order and of YHWH as a benevolent God;
maybe this was because YHWH was no longer able or supposed
to give this assurance himself or guarantee a good world order.
The reasons for this development of YHWH's image can only
be hypothetical. Does YHWH distance himself from his people
so that a mediator becomes necessary, or was something like
the Wisdom Figure invented in order to allow for a more

---

98. For an outline of this thesis see Baumann, *Die Weisheitsgestalt*,
pp. 294-99.

transcendent image of YHWH, which could be distinguished more easily from his creation and its history? Does the Wisdom Figure in this way compensate for a deficit in the image of YHWH, or does she enhance specific aspects of YHWH? Both seem possible.

Throughout this essay the Old Testament is presented as the Wisdom Figure's background. The figure is firmly set in its context. Even though it is possible that goddess imagery from the ancient Near East may also have influenced the formulation of the Wisdom Figure, all the important motifs and aspects are Israelite.[99] This means that contemporary postexilic theology and faith in YHWH tolerated or even required a transcendent figure in addition to YHWH. That this figure is female can not only be explained by the feminine *genus* of חכמה.[100] In the postexilic period the cultural prestige and authority of women must have been considerable, as Camp and Schroer have shown;[101] otherwise a female personification like the Wisdom Figure would not have made sense. The texts of Proverbs 1–9 show no resistance against the Wisdom Figure. These texts, however, allow a certain range of interpretation of the Wisdom Figure: She can be seen as a goddess on a similar level to YHWH, or only as his subordinate creature. There are a number of parallels to YHWH-speech which support the first explanation, but the texts do not commit themselves to it, nor dictate it to their readers. It seems possible that the authors of Proverbs 1–9 intend to go beyond the contemporary boundaries of faith in YHWH in a somehow playful manner. Chapters 1–9 do not explicitly say anything that would not be acceptable to those who worship YHWH alone; to those who want to see it differently, though, the texts speak about a

99. Another reason for the invention of the Wisdom Figure might have been that she could be used as a defense against the goddesses of Israel's neighbouring countries who were in competition with YHWH. In this case, the Wisdom Figure would have been given some outstanding attributes of these goddesses. There are some indications of this; cf. Schroer, 'Die göttliche Weisheit', pp. 166-68.

100. A noun with a similar meaning, but of masculine *genus* is e.g. טעם, which could be personified in the image of a man if a female personification had not been plausible.

101. Camp, *Wisdom*, pp. 255-82; and Schroer, 'Weise Frauen', pp. 53-56.

goddess-like figure at YHWH's side.

The period during which Proverbs 1–9 was written must therefore have been open for some transcendent figure apart from YHWH. The standing of this figure, however, is not exactly determined in Proverbs 1–9. In any case, YHWH is no longer the only transcendent being which was important for the Israelites in the postexilic period. Therefore, there was no exclusive mono-theism in Israel when Proverbs 1–9 was written. But how then can this faith be characterized?

I will follow Lang, who has briefly outlined some models of understanding the monotheism of postexilic Israel.[102] He thinks that there are several types of monotheism to be found in the Old Testament: On one hand, there is the absolute, exclusive monotheism of the radical, exilic Judaism which outright denies the existence of other deities. On the other hand, there is the monarchic, inclusive monotheism of the more liberal, Palestinian Judaism. Here YHWH is imagined as standing at the top of a pantheon that is subordinate to him. According to Lang's model it is possible that monarchic monotheism gives way to old poly-theistic constellations; the juxtaposition of two divine figures, normally called duotheism, would, in this model, also exist within a monotheistic context. It is such a duotheism in a mono-theistic context that Lang sees in Proverbs 1–9.

It is not very plausible, however, to call a duotheistic constella-tion monotheistic. A constellation including two deities is not monotheism any more. It also has to be taken into account that the existence of the Wisdom Figure does not contradict YHWH-monolatry because the Wisdom Figure is not an object of wor-ship that would compete with YHWH-worship. One can honour or worship her by walking in her ways, and this way of life is, in most aspects, identical with an indirect form of worshipping

---

102. B. Lang, 'Der monarchische Monotheismus und die Konstellation zweier Götter im Frühjudentum: Ein neuer Versuch über Menschensohn, Sophia und Christologie', in W. Dietrich and M.A. Klopfenstein (eds.), *Ein Gott allein? YHWH-Verehrung und biblischer Monotheismus im Kontext der israelitischen und altorientalischen Religionsgeschichte* (OBO, 139; Freiburg: Universitätsverlag; Göttingen: Vandenhoeck & Ruprecht, 1994), pp. 559-64, esp. pp. 559-60, 562; and 'Monotheismus', *NBL*, II, cols. 834-44, esp. cols. 838-40.

YHWH: Obeying his commandments. If there had been a 'cult' of the Wisdom Figure at all, it coincided with the YHWH-cult and did not contradict it. The Wisdom Figure can therefore be seen as a figure in a context of exclusive YHWH-worship. Her existence is compatible with a form of monotheism that may be called 'inclusive'. Lang describes such a form as monarchic monotheism, open to old duotheistic constellations.[103] The Wisdom Figure stands at YHWH's side and vouches for the goodness of the order of the world. There is no rivalry between them. The Wisdom Figure does not compete with YHWH in Israelite religion. She stands beside YHWH as one part of the image of God.[104] What her exact relationship with YHWH is, however, is left open in the texts. It could be a constellation that ranges between duotheism—with the Wisdom Figure as a goddess at YHWH's side—and monarchic monotheism—with personified Wisdom as a figure subordinate to YHWH. How far Israelite theology diverged from the exclusive form of monotheism by the invention of the Wisdom Figure has to be decided by the readers and interpreters of Proverbs 1–9. It is clear, though, that it does leave exclusive monotheism behind.

A Feminist Review of the Results

As feminist scholars like Camp, Cady, Ronan, Taussig and Schroer pointed out,[105] the personified Wisdom Figure as a female side of the Old Testament imagery of God is a welcome phenomenon in feminist theology. She makes it possible to approach and worship God in a female, and yet biblical, image.

---

103. So far, Old Testament research has not come up with a convincing description of the changes the Israelite faith underwent at the time the Wisdom Figure was invented.

104. Camp, 'Woman Wisdom', pp. 45-76 (47) goes from this point in a different direction. In her interpretation of personified Wisdom she follows Clifford Geertz's works about religious symbols. Schroer, 'Die göttliche Weisheit', p. 167, also interprets the postexilic constellation differently; she calls the Wisdom Figure Israel's God in the imagery of a woman. In my opinion, Schroer does not sufficiently consider that YHWH also plays an important role in Prov. 1–9 and that personified Wisdom therefore is not the only divine figure in these texts.

105. See above, nn. 2-4.

There are some other aspects of the Wisdom Figure, however, which, from a feminist perspective, cannot be accepted as universally helpful and positive. Personified Wisdom is a complex figure with some ambiguous features, and therefore she should be looked at from a critical feminist viewpoint.

In the perspective of religious history, personified Wisdom appears as an indeterminate figure. Wisdom in Proverbs 1–9 is a figure close to men and women, approaching them in an almost intimate way. She explains the good world order of YHWH, who is perceived to be more distant than the Wisdom Figure. This role played by the Wisdom Figure resembles one of the roles of today's women in western countries: that of the mother who lovingly cares for her children (cf. Prov. 8.17), who nourishes (Prov. 9.4-5) and educates them (the teaching mother as a parallel to teaching Wisdom). She embodies the authority and will of the father while he is absent.[106] In the context of patriarchal structures in family and society, this role has no direct influence on relevant political decisions. Seen in this environment, the Wisdom Figure certainly does not appear as a role model for women who are politically active. On the contrary, when transferred into our context, this facet of the Wisdom Figure actually embodies a female role model of the past.

The relationship between YHWH and the Wisdom Figure is in itself ambiguous because of the wide range of possible interpretations, reaching from a goddess-like figure to a being completely subordinate to YHWH. This ambiguity can be related to the indirect influence of Israel's female counselors, which Camp and Schroer have shown.[107] The counselors and wise women do not hold a political office or position so they do not bring their influence to bear in an institutional way. Similarly, the Wisdom Figure does not have a recognized place in an Israelite pantheon or a constellation of gods. Her position as related to YHWH is not firmly established; therefore, no conflict is seen with radical monotheistic concepts. Otherwise, she is not as relevant as a real goddess standing at YHWH's side would be. Her ambiguous

106. For the maternal role of the Wisdom Figure also see Brenner in Brenner and van Dijk-Hemmes, *Gendering Texts*, pp. 126-27.

107. Camp, *Wisdom*, pp. 86-90, 120-23; and Schroer, 'Weise Frauen', pp. 53-54.

rank in relation to YHWH protects her from being suspected of transforming Israelite religion into polytheism; on the other hand, she is in constant danger of losing her relevance within the context of postexilic Israelite theology.

Another aspect of the Wisdom Figure is less problematic. Because she integrates both human and divine wisdom, the Wisdom Figure gives human experience a higher theological value than it had enjoyed before. This is especially significant in the context of the Protestant tradition of Dialectic Theology, a tradition that, simply put, denies the theological relevance of human experience. The Wisdom Figure's positive estimation of human experience, the fact that she establishes it 'in heaven' (i.e. in the divine sphere) may serve to strengthen contextual theologies and their estimation of human experience. In the view of sapiential theology it is relevant for the faith of men and women how they perceive life and its conditions. Even if the Wisdom Figure transfers an older theologoumenon into her time and therefore does not exactly correspond to the experiences of post-exilic men and women, through this act of contradicting human experience, the experience of crisis becomes the starting point of theology. In addition to this, put in terms of systematic theology, the Wisdom Figure establishes a synthesis of dogmatics and ethics. The dogmatic fundamentals of theology and their application are combined in the Wisdom Figure because she is a witness to the good world order and at the same time sets up rules of social behaviour. This can be of value especially for feminist theology, which also tries to bring together experience with theology and doctrine with action. The Wisdom Figure, however, is a synthesis of these motifs only on a very formal and abstract level. Therefore, she might be useful for feminist efforts by supplying some biblical fundaments for them, but this effort has to be flanked by theological criteria and concrete applications. These have to be developed in today's contexts.

The historical and theological difference between the Wisdom Figure of Proverbs 1–9 and today's feminist efforts becomes clearer when Wisdom's counterpart in Proverbs 1–9 is taken into account. The 'Strange Woman' in Prov. 2.16-19, 5; 6.24-36 and 7.5-27 is the negative image of a social outcast. Female behaviour deviating from rigid social norms, as represented by the Strange

Woman, is branded and denounced.[108] Such a split of the image of women into a 'good', transcendent figure like the Wisdom Figure and a 'bad' type like the Strange Woman raises the question whether the Wisdom Figure really depicts a turn for the better in the lives of Israelite women, as Camp believes.[109] It is more likely to assume that sapiential circles in postexilic Israel were open to a positive formulation of a female figure in the divine sphere. Those who shaped Proverbs 1–9 in its present form[110] also had an interest in creating a female 'type' to denounce deviating social behaviour. Maybe the polarization or even dualism in the imagery of women is an early stage of a pattern of thought which can still be found today and which divides women into 'whores' and 'saints'.[111] From a feminist perspective, this development cannot be approved of even if the Wisdom Figure herself can be seen as progress in the field of the imagery of God.

Therefore, I propose a more differentiated feminist approach to the Wisdom Figure. Her existence as transcendent female being should neither be isolated from the existence of the Strange Woman, nor should far-reaching conclusions for the lives of women in postexilic Israel be drawn from the formulation of the Wisdom Figure. The Wisdom Figure in Proverbs 1–9 includes different facets. She is a product of a wide range of different interests of sapiential circles in postexilic Israel. The female imagery of God is only one of several levels touched by the Wisdom Figure. She is a product of postexilic Israel that cannot easily be adapted to the legitimate needs and wishes of

108. Maier, *Die 'fremde Frau' in Proverbien 1-9*, pp. 252-59; also Maier, 'Conflicting Attractions'.

109. Camp, *Wisdom*, p. 290.

110. I have tried to show that the speeches of the Wisdom Figure and the teacher in Prov. 1–9 are not necessarily products of identical authors and do not belong to the same redactional stratum; see G. Baumann, '"Zukunft feministischer Spiritualität" oder "Werbefigur des Patriarchats"? Die Bedeutung der Weisheitsgestalt in Prov. 1–9 für die feministisch-theologische Diskussion', in L. Schottroff and M.-Th. Wacker (eds.), *Von der Wurzel getragen: Christlich-feministische Exegese in Auseinandersetzung mit Antijudaismus* (BIS, 17; Leiden: E.J. Brill, 1996), pp. 135-52.

111. As a contemporary example for such a dualism, cf. the film *Fatal Attraction*; see Newsom, 'Discourse', p. 157.

today's women. She should not be integrated into feminist theology without critical examination. If she is to play an important role as an image of God, she has to be examined with the help of feminist criteria—and, through this process, be partially transformed.

THE GENDER AND MOTIVES OF THE
WISDOM TEACHER IN PROVERBS 7

Alice Ogden Bellis

One of the givens of much contemporary biblical scholarship is that there is no such thing as an objective reading of a text. This conviction is akin to the often dogmatically held view that truth is never absolute. Both of these precepts are propounded as if they were objective, absolute truths. If this were true, however, the dogmas themselves would be proven false. If it is not true, then the validity of these views is also undercut.

Feminist biblical scholars, including myself, are often quick to point out the subtle and sometimes not so subtle androcentric, even sexist biases of our male colleagues. These biases sometimes hinder the commentator's attempts to hear the text unencumbered by twentieth-century perspectives and issues.

In a similar way, the subtle and sometimes not so subtle gynocentric, even sexist biases of feminist interpreters sometimes adversely affect interpretive work. In addition, contemporary western values shared by both male and female scholars color the way we read, eroding our ability to understand texts in their own historical, cultural and sociological contexts, and ultimately to consider their implications for today. These problems are illustrated in recent work on the gender and motives of the wisdom teacher in Proverbs 7.

In spite of the fact that it is Lemuel's mother who warns him against women and wine in Prov. 31.1-9,[1] biblical commentators

---

1. It is interesting to note that one ancient Sumerian text, 'The Instructions of Suruppak', refers to instructions to a son from both parents. See James L. Crenshaw, 'A Mother's Instructions to her Son (Proverbs 31.1-9)' in J.L. Crenshaw, *Urgent Advice and Probing Questions: Collected Writings on Old Testament Wisdom* (Macon, GA: Mercer University Press, 1995), p. 384.

have generally assumed that the implied voice of the wisdom
teacher who instructs son(s) to avoid the *'iššâ zārâ*, the 'strange'
woman,[2] in Proverbs 7 is male.[3] Feminist interpreters have for
the most part agreed with this consensus, though often with
negative assessments of the wisdom teacher's motivations.[4]
Athalya Brenner and Fokkelien van Dijk-Hemmes have raised
the possibility that the wisdom teacher is implicitly an F or
female voice. They cite the ancient Near Eastern tradition of the
female rebuker[5] and the fact that the speaker looks through a
window at a scene below, an action that is much more frequently
associated with women than men.[6] They, like their feminist

2.   The translation used here is simply for convenience. The term is mul-
tivalent, though in the various contexts in which it is used in Proverbs it is
clear that the 'strange' woman is one who is involved in illicit sexual relations. See Claudia V. Camp, 'What's So Strange about the Strange
Woman?', in David Jobling, Peggy L. Day and Gerald T. Sheppard (eds.),
*The Bible and the Politics of Exegesis: Essays in Honor of Norman K. Gottwald on
his Sixty-Fifth Birthday* (Cleveland: Pilgrim Press, 1991), pp. 17-31; and the literature cited there.

3.   See James L. Crenshaw, *Old Testament Wisdom: An Introduction*
(Atlanta: John Knox Press, 1981) p. 87; William McKane, *Proverbs: A New
Approach* (London: SCM Press, 1970), pp. 332-41; R.B.Y. Scott, *Proverbs and
Ecclesiastes* (AB; Garden City, NY: Doubleday, 1965), p. 15; R.N. Whybray,
Wisdom in Proverbs (Studies in Biblical Theology; London: SCM Press, 1965),
p. 33, and *The Composition of the Book of Proverbs* (JSOTSup, 168; Sheffield:
Sheffield Academic Press, 1994), p. 56.

4.   See, e.g., Camp, 'What's So Strange About the Strange Woman', in
which she views the male teacher as expressing male fears of female sexuality. See also Carol Newsom, 'Woman and the Discourse of Patriarchal
Wisdom: A Study of Proverbs 1-9', in Peggy L. Day (ed.), *Gender and Difference in Ancient Israel* (Minneapolis: Fortress Press, 1989), pp. 142-60; Carole
R. Fontaine, 'Proverbs', in C.A. Newsom and S.H. Ringe (eds.), *The Women's
Bible Commentary* (Louisville, KY: Westminster/John Knox Press, 1993),
pp. 146-48; Kathleen O'Connor, *The Wisdom Literature* (The Message of Biblical Spirituality, 5; Wilmington, DE: Michael Glazier, 1988), pp. 61-63; Gale
A. Yee, '"I Have Perfumed my Bed With Myrrh": The Foreign Woman (*'iššâ
zārâ*) in Proverbs 1-9', *JSOT* 43 (1989), pp. 53-68.

5.   See S.D. Goitein, 'Women as Creators of Biblical Genres', *Prooftexts* 8
(1988), pp. 1-33.

6.   Athalya Brenner and Fokkelien van Dijk-Hemmes, *On Gendering
Texts: Female and Male Voices in the Hebrew Bible* (BIS, 1; Leiden: E.J. Brill,
1993), pp. 57-62, 113-26; and Athalya Brenner, 'Some Observations on the

sisters who criticize the supposed male teacher's psychology, also negatively assess the supposed female teacher's ideology.

Both see the female wisdom teacher as having internalized androcentric values. Van Dijk-Hemmes writes:

> The voices of admonishing and rebuking women which can be heard in Proverbs, are not in disagreement with…androcentric discourse. They are the voices of women who have internalized this discourse.[7]

Brenner writes:

> I am aware that even when my reading is deemed viable it can nevertheless be argued that the textual voice is an M [male] voice, presented as typically guarding paternity and its ensuing morality. Could it not, however, be the reflected dominant voice of a culture as it is introjected by F [female] participants of that same culture…? The price, here as in other passages in Proverbs, is the subscription of an identifiable F voice to misogyny and self-inflicted gender depreciation and gender disparagement.[8]

How the wisdom teacher's injunction against the 'strange' woman guards paternity is not entirely clear. Indeed, androcentric Israelite society seemed to tolerate a certain amount of promiscuity on the part of its men as long as the sexual partner was not a married woman—the infamous double standard. This standard assured men that their wives' children were their own, while giving them the freedom to enjoy other women sexually,

Figurations of Woman in Wisdom Literature', in Heather A. McKay and David J.A. Clines (eds.), *Of Prophets' Visions and the Wisdom of Sages: Essays in Honour of R. Norman Whybray on his Seventieth Birthday* (JSOTSup, 162; Sheffield: JSOT Press, 1993), pp. 192-208.

The one exception to the generalization that women look out of windows is Gen. 26.8, where Abimelech looks through his window and sees Isaac fondling Rebekah. The biblical examples of women looking out of windows are Michal (2 Sam. 6.16), Jezebel (2 Kgs 9.30) and Sisera's mother (Judg. 5.28). Brenner (*Gendering Texts*) points out that the literary figure of the woman at the window is substantiated by archaeological finds, in particular the Samaria ivories (p. 120).

7. F. Van Dijk-Hemmes, 'Traces of Women's Texts in the Hebrew Bible', in Brenner and van Dijk-Hemmes (eds.), *Gendering Texts*, pp. 17-109 (62).

8. A. Brenner, 'Proverbs 1–9: An F Voice?', in Brenner and van Dijk-Hemmes, *Gendering Texts*, pp. 125-26.

typically prostitutes who operated on the margins of society.[9]

Thus, the voice that teaches son(s) to avoid the 'strange' woman is not necessarily any more an internalized androcentric one than the voices of twentieth-century feminists who challenge the remnants of the same double standard today. Rather, such a voice can be understood to provide an alternative to norms that were oppressive of women.

There is a difference, however, between modern feminists' strategies and the ancient Hebrew wisdom teacher's approach to undercutting the double standard. Generally, modern feminists wish to increase sexual freedom for women. The wisdom teacher in Proverbs 7 is trying to decrease male sexual freedom.[10] Either strategy, if effective, could lead to a more egalitarian ethic. However, the ancient Hebrew teacher's approach is clearly a more restrictive one than that of many modern feminists. Brenner's discomfort with this restrictiveness may be reflected in her statement that,

> Within the literary F voice, F self interest is silent through identification with M interest; control over female sexuality is recommended at least implicitly; maternal possessiveness merges with the internalized M voice for the purpose of preserving an existing world order and worldview.[11]

What Brenner calls 'F self-interest' is unstated, but would seem to be sexual freedom. This is suggested by her concern about what she terms 'control over female sexuality', a particularly odd designation since what the teacher is advocating is really male sexual self-control. It is true that such self-control would result in less female sexual activity, but to call this result 'control over female sexuality' obscures the fact that the speaker is trying to control the sexual behavior of males, not females. A man's choice not to engage in sexual relations with a woman can hardly be considered controlling female sexuality, any more than a

9. See Phyllis A. Bird, 'To Play the Harlot: An Inquiry into an Old Testament Metaphor', in Peggy L. Day (ed.), *Gender and Difference in Ancient Israel* (Minneapolis: Augsburg–Fortress, 1989), pp. 77-79.

10. It is also possible that the strange woman comes to represent foreign gods as well as illicit sexuality, as many have suggested, but the sexual meaning is the most obvious and probably the original meaning.

11. Brenner, 'Proverbs 1–9: an F Voice?', pp. 125-26.

woman's choice not to engage in sexual relations with a man should be called controlling male sexuality. Brenner's shifting the emphasis in the passage only makes sense if her underlying concern is sexual freedom in general, and female sexual freedom in particular.

Sexual freedom for both men and women, 'combined with competent birth control may' make sense in a modern western setting—where children are not economic necessities for individuals or couples, but rather may be viewed as expensive luxuries. This view is prevalent today. Nevertheless, the reality of sexually transmitted diseases mitigates against it. The risk especially of AIDS makes sexual freedom a dangerous game, even when so-called safe sex is practised.

Finally, although children are not the economic necessity to the individual or family in post-industrial society that they are in more agriculturally based economies, modern western society's failure to put a high priority on children 'to the point that one in five children in the United States is growing up in poverty' is creating social problems which affect everyone. Without a 'supply' of healthy, well-educated future adults, the future looks bleak.

My rejection of the common view is no doubt colored by my personal situation. I am a married woman with two daughters. My husband and I both devote many hours to our children, who are bright and multi-talented. Although we are privileged economically, educationally and socially, we must still stretch ourselves to what seem like our financial, emotional and energetic limits to provide what we consider the optimum environment for their development. Parenting, although not easy, is important not only to the lives of individual children, but also to the society in which they live. In a largely agrarian economy such as ancient Israel's, where children were highly valued commodities and where birth control was perhaps not highly developed for that very reason,[12] what made sense in terms of sexual behavior was perhaps a little different from prevalent attitudes in the West today.

The book of Proverbs probably came into its final form in the

---

12. For a different view see Athalya Brenner, *The Intercourse of Knowledge: On Gendering Desire and 'Sexuality' in the Hebrew Bible* (BIS, 26; Leiden: E.J. Brill, 1997), pp. 69-89.

postexilic period, although much of the material in it may go
back to earlier periods. Although particular verses may reflect
later dates, the concerns that run through Proverbs 1–9 in general
and are found specifically in Proverbs 7 regarding illicit sexuality could make sense at almost any period of Israel's agrarian
history.

Hebrew society was agriculturally based, even in the postexilic
period.[13] In agrarian economies many children are needed in
order to work the land and provide for family members who are
too old to work any longer. Because infant mortality was high,
many children had to be born to ensure that a few would live to
adulthood. The burden of producing children fell to women who
not only gave birth, but also nursed the children in their early
years.

Although women may have done much manual labor in addition to their child-nurturing responsibilities,[14] they could not
survive alone. They needed a partner, a helper, with whom to
share the load. A womanizing man would in one way or another
divert a portion of his material resources and energy in another
direction, thus diminishing the life of the family, including the
woman. It may be difficult for modern westerners who are
accustomed to a more individualistic approach to life to appreciate the communal, cooperative organization that apparently prevailed in ancient Israel,[15] though even moderns realize that a

13. We know very little about urban families during the monarchic
period. The typical nuclear family was agrarian, and consisted of two
parents and between two and four children. See Joseph Blenkinsopp, 'The
Family in First Temple Israel', in Leo G. Perdue, Joseph Blenkinsopp, John J.
Collins, and Carol Meyers, *Families in Ancient Israel* (Louisville, KY: West-
minster/John Knox Press, 1997), pp. 51-57. These nuclear families included
up to four generations and lived in compounds with several other similar
families. See Leo G. Perdue, 'The Israelite and Early Jewish Family', in
Families in Ancient Israel, p. 175. Although there were changes and developments in Israelite society from the settlement of Canaan in 1200 BCE to
the beginning of the common era, the family 'continued in largely the same
form and with some of the same character for twelve centuries' (Perdue,
'The Israelite and Early Jewish Family', p. 165).

14. Carol Meyers, *Discovering Eve: Ancient Israelite Women in Context*
(Oxford: Oxford University Press, 1988), pp. 168-73.

15. Meyers, *Discovering Eve*, pp. 123-24. See also Perdue, 'The Israelite

two-parent household is generally better for the children and makes for easier parenting than single-parent arrangements.

Thus it can be argued that it was in ancient Hebrew women's self-interest for men to be monogamous. Although there is much in the Hebrew Bible that is androcentric and misogynistic, Proverbs 7 may be read as a voice subversive of 'patriarchy', understood here in terms of one of its aspects, the double standard. Ironically, this conclusion strengthens the arguments of Brenner and van Dijk-Hemmes that the voice of the wisdom teacher in Proverbs 7 is an F voice. It is less likely that an Israelite man, the primary beneficiary of the double standard, would have argued against it.[16] It is more likely that those who opposed it were women. Mothers would have had an additional motivation. Grown sons might be their means of support in old age. We may ask to what kind of men the wisdom teacher speaks: single men, married men, or perhaps any man who was vulnerable to the seductions of a 'strange' woman. Since life expectancy was short, the need to produce offspring high, and the educational years for the average male brief, we may assume that men usually married young. Thus, most young men probably were not sexually mature for very long before they were married. It is likely, therefore, that premarital sex was less a problem than sexual activity outside of marriage and that the primary audience of the wisdom teacher in Proverbs 7 was married men. Not only were they the most numerous. They were also the most critical to the maintenance of families and thus to the health of the community. This conclusion does not preclude the possibility

and Early Jewish Family', p. 167, and *idem*, 'Household, Theology, and Contemporary Hermeneutics', pp. 237-39 in Perdue, *et al.*, *Families in Ancient Israel*.

16. The only suggestion I have found as to what might motivate a male writer to advise son(s) against relationships with 'strange' women is offered by Leo G. Perdue (*Wisdom and Cult: A Critical Analysis of the Views of Cult in the Wisdom Literature of Israel's Ancient Near East* [SBLDS, 30; Missoula, MT: Scholars Press, 1977]), who suggests that the motivation might be the sapiential disdain of any activity in which passions were given free rein. Thus, for example, ecstatic religious behavior would characterize the 'heated man', but not the true sage, the 'silent man' (p. 155). This is an interesting suggestion, but without textual support: it sounds more like a modern concern for control than a truly ancient motivation.

that the teacher spoke to all men, married and single. By indoctrinating young unmarried men against sexual liaisons with 'strange' women, the wisdom teacher would have engendered a habit that would hopefully follow the men into their marriages.

My suggestion that it was more likely that a woman would have counseled against men consorting with women other than their wives than a man assumes that the self-interest of either gender was a more significant motivating factor than the interests of the group. Much modern western analysis makes this kind of unexamined assumption, which in effect reads twentieth-century individualistic values and gender battles into ancient Israel. Given the communitarian orientation of the Hebrews, one could easily argue that the motivation behind the wisdom teacher's advice in Proverbs 7 is not narrowly construed female self-interest, but rather the preservation and health of the community, which in turn would benefit all of its individual members.

One could argue, then, that the gender of the wisdom teacher in Proverbs 7 is either impossible to determine or irrelevant. Certainly, it is impossible to be certain of the gender of the speaker in Proverbs 7, though we may nevertheless still find clues concerning the implied speaker. Here Brenner and van Dijk-Hemmes's arguments are helpful. The question of relevance is of another sort. If the clues suggest that the speaker is an F voice, that is of interest to modern readers for whom gender concerns are often burning issues.

A number of questions must still be addressed if the hypothesis of an F voice in Proverbs 7 is to be accepted. It might seem odd that a female wisdom teacher whose aim was in part to end the double standard would address son(s) rather than daughters. Would she not have been more successful counseling young women to shun liaisons with young men? The reality was probably otherwise. To the extent that the 'strange' women that the teacher had in mind were prostitutes,[17] counseling them to

17. In 'Who Would Blame Her? The "Strange" Woman of Proverbs 7', in Fokkelien van Dijk-Hemmes and Athalya Brenner (eds.), *Reflections on Theology and Gender* (Kampen: Kok, 1994), pp. 21-32, Mieke Heijerman describes the 'strange' woman as a needy woman, a woman with unspecified problems, who hopes religious vows may help her (Prov. 7.14), but needs

change professions would have been about as effective as advising the unemployed to get a job.

Prostitutes, then and now, are usually persons marginalized by society.[18] They are often products of families that cannot or do not provide for their needs and of societies that have weak safety nets. In ancient Israel perhaps they were young widows who had no familial home to which they could return after the death of their husbands nor grown sons to support them. Although the prophets admonished the people to care for the widows, orphans, and sojourners, it is fair to assume that such preachments were honored in the breach. In most cases prostitution is a career to which one turns in desperation. It is rarely a profession of choice. Married women and single women living in their father's houses were already heavily socialized against promiscuity. Advising them was in most cases like preaching to the converted. Those whose attitudes needed to be changed were probably men, not women.

Still, some may feel that there is something of self-hatred in advice given by a woman teacher to son(s) to avoid the seductions of 'strange' women. However, self-esteem does not require one to pretend that every member of one's group is worthy of praise. I am a citizen of the United States. I am proud of my

money in order to fulfill her vows. Her husband, literally 'the man', may be wealthy, but has taken his money bag with him (Prov. 7.19-20). Heijerman suggests that the woman resorts to prostitution in order to raise the needed money. She cites Karel van der Toorn ('Female Prostitution in Payment of Vows in Ancient Israel', *JBL* 108 [1989], pp. 193-205), who indicates childlessness as one of the reasons women made religious vows. Since childlessness could result in a woman being sent away, the stakes were high. If women learned that religious vows, or the ensuing adultery entered into to pay the vows (husbands could be infertile) led to pregnancy, then desperate women may easily have made such a choice. As plausible as this reconstruction is, it remains hypothetical. Scott (*Proverbs and Ecclesiastes*, p. 65) suggests that the vows in Prov. 7 may refer to the proceeds of sacred prostitution associated with pagan cults, vowed to a goddess of fertility. Such views, for which the evidence is scant, are generally repudiated today. See, e.g., M.I. Gruber, 'The Hebrew *qĕdēšāh* and her Canaanite and Akkadian Cognates', in M.I. Gruber, *The Motherhood of God and Other Studies* (Atlanta: Scholars Press, 1992), pp. 17-47.

18. See Phyllis A. Bird, 'The Harlot as Heroine: Narrative Art and Social Presupposition in Three Old Testament Texts', *Semeia* 46 (1989), pp. 119-39.

heritage. However, I do not believe that all the behavior of all my fellow citizens is above reproach. If I argued that all United States citizens are wonderful, it would imply that I am very insecure about my national identity. Only when our egos are strong can we tolerate self-criticism.

It may seem contradictory that I argued above that prostitutes did not choose their professions, and thus may be seen as victims rather than immoral characters; and now I argue that it is not contrary to one's self-esteem to be critical of certain members of one's group, that is, prostitutes. Society may force women into prostitution. That does not mean that their behavior is praise-worthy or that one should do business with them.

Another objection may be raised to the premise that there is nothing strange about a woman counseling men against liaisons with strange women. The admonition to young men to avoid 'strange' women may itself be viewed as strange, given the fact that there are more stories in the Hebrew Bible of men raping women than of women (prostitutes or otherwise) seducing men,[19] and the historical reality was probably even more skewed in that direction. Interestingly, except for the story of Tamar's seduction of Judah which is a special case, there is only one story of a Hebrew man consorting with a prostitute, that is, Samson with the prostitute from Gaza (Judg. 16.1-3). Hosea and Gomer might appear to be another such story, but she is not called a *zônâ*[20] and may be understood as a promiscuous woman rather than a prostitute. The Hebrew spies who stay at Rahab's house

19. Tamar is raped by her half-brother Amnon and the Levite's woman is brutally gang-raped and murdered. Lot's daughters are offered to the Sodomites to be raped, though the offer is refused. According to many interpretations Dinah is raped by Shechem, but for another view of this story see Lyn Bechtel, 'What If Dinah Is Not Raped', *JSOT* 62 (1994), pp. 19-36. Joseph is unsuccessfully seduced by Potiphar's wife. Tamar, Judah's daughter-in-law, pretends to be a prostitute in order to be impregnated by Judah when he fails to enforce the law of levirate on her behalf.

20. The verb *znh* has the broad meaning of 'fornicate' and the more narrow meaning of 'be a prostitute'. Phyllis Bird explains that the feminine participle is used of a woman who is 'a professional or habitual fornicator, a promiscuous or unchaste woman, whose role and profession are defined by her sexual activity with men to whom she is not married' (Bird, 'To Play the Harlot', p. 78).

may have been mixing business with pleasure, but the text does not say so directly. In spite of the lack of stories dealing with prostitution in the Hebrew Bible, it is clear that prostitution existed, was tolerated, and was probably more widespread than rape. Rape was a crime with harsh penalties.[21] Prostitution was less offensive, but probably impacted negatively more women than did rape. Since prostitutes in most cases had no other means of support, the only way to stop prostitution was to induce men to stop seeking the services of prostitutes.

If the wisdom teacher was successful, we must ask what would have become of the prostitutes. Clearly, in the short term their lives would have been made more difficult. It is unlikely, however, given human nature, that the supply of customers for prostitutes will ever be eliminated. If that were to happen, perhaps the same change of heart would provide a better social order in which women would not be driven to such work in the first place.

We may surmise that the wisdom teacher's strategy in addressing men in the particular way (s)he does involves a bit of psychology. (S)he counsels men to be strong enough not to allow themselves to be seduced, rather than nagging them to avoid the pleasures of the 'strange' woman.

Perhaps in a different world, where men were not more powerful physically, economically and politically than women, such a psychologically savvy approach would not be essential to success. In the world of the Hebrew Bible, the (female) wisdom teacher's strategy can be understood as carefully calculated to change men's sexual behavior in a way consistent with high female self-esteem. Such a change would not only enhance the lives of many women, but strengthen the entire community. Whether in fact the strategy worked is hard to gauge. The

21. The biblical definition of rape is different from the modern one. Today consent is the key to whether rape has occurred. In biblical law consent was not the issue. With or without consent, sex with an unbetrothed woman was a crime against the father, a minor offense. Sex with a married or betrothed woman was a crime against the husband or prospective husband, a capital offense, regardless of whether the women consented. See Carolyn Pressler, *The View of Women Found in the Deuteronomic Family Laws* (BZAW, 216; Berlin: W. de Gruyter, 1993), p. 37 n. 46.

teaching made it into the canon. That much is clear. Perhaps it contributed to the destruction of the ancient double standard. Perhaps it also contributed to the survival and health of ancient Israel.

Whether it can touch a postmodern western culture that is largely indifferent to the Bible is harder to assess. Our worlds are vastly different, yet some commonalities bind us together. These commonalities entice at least some of us who care about what the Bible says to continue reading the words of ancient wisdom teachers found therein. Many biblical scholars and persons of faith (not necessarily mutually exclusive categories) read these ancient teachers' words not only to debate them intellectually. We look at the texts not simply to confirm our own values as if the text were only a mirror and never a window into another world. We read the texts not simply to critique them, although critical reading is important. Rather, we listen to the ancient authors to glean from them something of value for today. In the process we see ourselves more clearly and are challenged to reconsider the common 'wisdom' of our day.

APPENDIX: A LETTER TO MY DAUGHTERS

Alice Ogden Bellis

Much of the book of Proverbs is advice from a parent, often a father, to a son to seek wisdom, personified as a woman, as his metaphorical mate in life. On a more practical level, he is being advised to marry a wise wife, literally 'a woman of strength' (Prov. 31.10). The choice of mate is one of the most important choices a person makes. Proverbs would not be nearly so effective if it were written only on an abstract level. By making it concrete as well, it delivers an emotional charge. However, if the reader is female, the imagery does not work, unless one is lesbian. The following letter was written in response to a challenge to rewrite Proverbs with reversed gender imagery. Since I have two daughters, aged 17 and 14, I have written it for them.

Dear Margaret and Elizabeth,
You know that I love you more than anything else in the world. I want you to be happy, but as you know, life is tough, life is real. It takes more than being an excellent student, world-class athlete or prizewinning dancer or

musician to lead a happy life. These things are important and you are on your way to achieving some of these goals, but it takes more to be happy.

And so I ask you to try to discover what is true and just and wise. These words are tired and overworked, but that does not mean they are devoid of meaning. Do not accept anyone else's word for the truth, but listen to what the great sages of the past have said and decide for yourselves what is right. Seek the truth in the midst of contemporary thought and accept nothing else. Make truth your lover, justice your muse. Truth will stand by you if you lose your friends or your job because you refused to do something unethical. Justice will encircle you with warmth more real than a fire, when people shun you for standing up for the dignity and worth of every person, regardless of their personal characteristics, or when you blow the whistle on wrongdoing.

Each new generation must understand the truth all over again. The issues are always slightly different; the contexts changed. Seek out truth diligently. Look for him not in the broad streets where most men hang out. Look for him not in the dim lights of bars and dance clubs. Look for him not in the illusions of power that fill the halls of Congress. Look for him not among the heroes on television or in the movie theaters. Look for him not on the athletic fields. You will not find truth in any of these places. Ego and vanity you will find there.

You may not even find him in the churches, as they are often too busy being lonely hearts clubs and too absorbed in being self-righteous to be very concerned about serious matters of truth and justice. You may not find him in the universities either, as many there seek only a meal ticket for the future. Others are just passing time, playing games.

Truth and justice are elusive. They present themselves to those who seek them persistently and seriously. They hide from everyone else. Do not be misled by handsome faces, by beautiful bodies, by the right clothes, or the correct manners. Especially do not be deluded by flatterers who tell you that you are beautiful (of course you are!) and then ask you to give them your body or your soul. The pretty boys and jocks will beckon to you. They will ask you to go out. Soon, they will ask you to bed. It's a dangerous world. Their ways lead to death, not just moral death, but physical death as well. Drugs and alcohol and cigarettes are some of the ways of those who want to show off, but inside are little boys. They want easy sex with no responsibility. Do not cavort with folly. Do not consort with the frivolous. Rather spend your time with men of substance and worth. A good man is hard to find, but he is more precious than jewels.

Love always,

Mom

CONFLICTING ATTRACTIONS: PARENTAL WISDOM AND THE 'STRANGE WOMAN' IN PROVERBS 1–9

Christl Maier

The figure of the 'strange' (אשה זרה) or 'foreign' (נכריה) woman in Proverbs 1–9 long stood in the shadow of its famous counterpart Lady Wisdom. Only in recent years has this female character become a topic of scholarly study[1] and, now, many valuable insights into the figure can be asserted. I would like to present my own position as viewed among this chorus of interpretive voices. As Gale A. Yee pointed out in the first volume of *A Feminist Companion to Wisdom Literature*, the interpretation of the 'strange' female figure is a twofold task.[2] First, the historical and social circumstances surrounding the literary production of the texts and their social encoding of gender ideology needs examining.[3] Second, one should analyze 'the text's rhetoric', that is, 'its artful ability to persuade its audience to accept a particular ideology'.[4] I followed this double reasoning in my PhD dissertation[5] and will pursue it in this article. In this way, I want to show the multifaceted portrait of this female character. I am going to analyze the text's rhetoric and to have a look at its authors and socio-historical setting. Finally, I will focus on the

1.   Five out of 12 articles of the first volume of A. Brenner (ed.), *A Feminist Companion to Wisdom Literature* (FCB, 9; Sheffield: Sheffield Academic Press, 1995), pick out this fascinating figure as a central theme.

2.   Cf. G.A. Yee, 'The Socio-Literary Production of the "Foreign Woman" in Proverbs', in A. Brenner (ed.), *A Feminist Companion to Wisdom Literature* (FCB, 9; Sheffield: Sheffield Academic Press, 1995), pp. 127-30.

3.   Yee, 'Production', p. 129.

4.   Yee, 'Production', p. 130.

5.   Cf. C. Maier, *Die 'fremde Frau' in Proverbien 1–9: Eine exegetische und sozialgeschichtliche Studie* (OBO, 144; Freiburg: Universitätsverlag; Göttingen: Vandenhoeck & Ruprecht, 1995).

role women played in formulating this characterization; and on modern feminist interpretations which respond to such forms of rhetoric.

The Portrait of the 'Strange Woman' in the Light of Hebrew Bible Traditions

The 'strange' woman is presented in four admonishing speeches within Proverbs 1–9. The genre of father-to-son instruction, known from Egyptian Wisdom tradition, is used in order to warn a single male against a female figure. The often-cited aim 'to save you from the "strange" woman' (2.16; 6.24; 7.5) is pursued by unmasking the woman's supposed negative intentions and by unfolding the disastrous consequences of being ensnared by her. Let us first look at the view of the speaker who describes her nature and deeds.

Considering the semantics of זר/זרה (strange) and נכרי/נכריה (foreign) one must conclude that both terms have negative overtones, while the literary context has a heavy bearing on the meaning. The adjective זר denotes 'otherness', referring to what is outside a delimited field.[6] In a cult context זר characterizes a person not allowed to serve as a priest (Lev. 22.12; Num. 17.5; 18.7) or an illicit cultic practice (Exod. 30.9; Lev. 10.1). As a social designation זר refers chiefly to a person outside a kinship group, be it family (Deut. 25.5; Prov. 6,1; 11,15) or nation (Isa. 1.7; 25.2; Jer. 51.2; Ezek. 28.7, 31.12). Typically נכרי denotes national or ethnic foreignness (Judg. 19.12; 2 Sam. 15.19; 1 Kgs 8.41). In Deuteronomy the נכרי, an economically independent foreigner, is separated from the so-called גר (stranger) who settles without land property among Israelites (Deut. 14.21, 15.3). But there are also occurrences where נכרי marks strangeness within a kinship group (Ps. 69.9; Job 19.15; Gen. 31.15). The female adjective נכריה is prominent in Ezra 9–10 and Neh. 13.26-27, where it denotes women outside the *gôlâ* (exilic) group, marriage to whom is forbidden. In Proverbs 1–9 the term זרה 'strange/other woman' is once mentioned on its own (5.3), whereas the term נכריה 'foreign

---

6. L.A. Snijders's detailed study, 'The Meaning of זר in the Old Testament: An Exegetical Study', *OTS* 10 (1954), pp. 1-154; and its summary, 'זר/זור', *ThWAT*, II (1977), pp. 556-64.

woman/outsider' always occurs as the second component of a parallel pair (2.16, 5.20, 6.24, 7.5). From this stylistic feature we may conclude that the meaning 'other/outsider' is prevalent.[7]

Although the 'strange' woman is variably characterized in Prov. 2.1-22, 5.1-23, 6.20-35 and 7.1-27, the different texts show common features. In every instruction her words are judged as 'slippery, seductive, false' (2.16, 5.3, 6.24, 7.5; cf. 9.17), and her ways as 'leading to death' (2.18, 5.5, 6.26, 7.26-27; cf. 9.18). When read from ch. 2 through to ch. 9, this figure is exposed more and more as ultimately destructive.

In Prov. 2.15-17 the 'strange' woman is first introduced as unfaithful to her human partner and to her God, whose covenant she has forgotten. These statements allude to the metaphor of God's unfaithful wife in Jer. 3.4 and 13.21, and to Deut. 4.23. The female figure is characterized as unreliable in any relationship. A similar danger is represented by so-called wicked men (2.12-15; cf. 1.10-19). They talk subversively, plan evil things and try to persuade people to join their crooked paths. In the speaker's view only those who are faithful to wisdom, who know righteousness and justice, will be able to resist that woman and those men (2.6-10). They will 'dwell in the land' (שכן ארץ) and will not be uprooted from it (2.21-22). The motif of land tenure takes up deuteronomistic tradition[8] and strongly refers to Psalm 37.

In Prov. 5.3-14 the male addressee is warned of the 'strange' woman's lips that drip honey and of her smooth tongue. If he does not keep away from her door, he will have to face 'social death': he will have to give his property to strangers, lose his dignity in the eyes of others and be shamed in the public assembly. In his last speech, the worthy Job draws a similar picture of the consequences of adultery (Job 31.7-12). In Proverbs 5 the issue is adultery too, although it is only implicitly mentioned: the male is advised to take his own wife as a source of sexual satisfaction and not to embrace the 'foreign' woman's bosom (5.15-20).

Prov. 6.20-24 asks the young man to wear the father's

7. See also A. Brenner in 'Proverbs 1-9: An F Voice?', A. Brenner and F. van Dijk-Hemmes (eds.), *On Gendering Texts: Female and Male Voices in the Hebrew Bible* (BIS, 1; Leiden: E.J. Brill, 1993), pp. 113-130, esp. 122-23.

8. Cf., e.g., Deut. 2.12, 3.12, 20; 5.31; 33.28.

commands on his heart and to bind the mother's teaching (אם
תורת) to his neck. Their words are supposed to guide the man's
way, to guard him in his sleep and to advise him in the morning.
This passage strongly alludes to Deut. 6.6-9 and 11.18-20.[9]
According to this tradition parents should recite the commandments of the divine Torah, given by Moses, to their offspring
several times a day. This relationship to God's Torah gives great
authority to parental instruction in Proverbs. The parents' words
are, like the Torah given by Moses, a Torah to live with, a
teaching for daily life. The intention in Proverbs 6 is again to
warn the young man of the 'strange' woman. She has, according
to 6.25-35, the power to light a fire of passion in a male. There are
many allusions here to the Decalogue, especially to the
prohibition of stealing (גנב), coveting a neighbour's wife (רעהו
חמד אשת) and committing adultery (נאף). Starting with an ardent
glance of the woman (6.25), a glance that provokes fire in the
male bosom (6.27), the offense is as damaging to the agent as
walking on hot coals (6.28). As with a thief who steals because of
hunger (6.30), a man who satisfies his sexual appetite must be
charged. Here, the death penalty for adultery (cf. Lev. 20.10;
Deut. 22.22) is not applied, but the outcome is again 'social
death': the community will despise such a man, publicly
denouncing him (6.33). The jealous husband will not show
mercy on the 'day of vengeance' (יום נקם), that is, of court proceedings. He will not accept a gift or a bribe (6.34-35) instead of a
trial. This allusion to commandments of the Decalogue and to
Deut. 6.6-9 and 11.18-20 belongs to a process of interpretation
that adapts a received authoritative text to a new context.

Prov. 7 draws the most detailed picture of the 'strange'
woman, describing a 'typical scene' of her life: The master of the
house being absent (7.19), the woman wanders in the streets of
the town under the shelter of darkness, waiting for her victim
(7.9, 12). She persuades a spineless young man with words of
seduction and trickery:

9. See my article, '"Begehre nicht ihre Schönheit in deinem Herzen"
(Prov. 6.25): Eine Aktualisierung des Ehebruchsverbots aus persischer Zeit',
BibInt 5 (1997), pp. 46-63.

I had to provide a sacrificial meal, today I have fulfilled my vows.
Therefore, I have come out to meet you,
to look for you and I have found you.
I have spread my couch with covers, with coloured linen from Egypt.
I have sprinkled my bed with myrrh, aloes and cinnamon.
Come, let us take our fill of caresses till morning,
let us delight each other in love.
For the man is not at home,
he has gone on a distant journey.
The bag of money he has taken with him,
when the moon is full he will come back to his house (7.14-20).

Thus she boldly embraces the male and lures him into her house and the bed covered with luxurious and perfumed cloth. The scene may be an allusion to the advances of Potiphar's wife towards Joseph (Gen. 39.7-12). Several words of the 'strange' woman's speech belong to the poetry of love and can be compared to S o S 3.1-5. But there is a warning overtone in Proverbs 7 which is reinforced by the drastic metaphors characterizing the woman's house as an anteroom to the underworld (7.26-27). The male addressee is compared to a weak-willed ox taken to the slaughterhouse (7.22), the 'strange' woman is presented as a victorious warrior slaying innumerable men (7.26). Although this image reminds us of Ishtar, the ancient Near Eastern goddess of love and war, the 'strange' woman of Proverbs 7 is neither a goddess[10] nor a goddess devotee. She has no divine qualities but, on the contrary, has to pick up her victims in the streets. She dresses like a prostitute (7.10) although she lives in a richly furnished house. Her wealth is shown by imported cloth and perfumes, the luxury goods *par excellence*. Her mentioning of sacrifices and vows refers neither to a divine banquet nor to a case of sacred prostitution. On the one hand, the existence of sacred prostitution in Israel is now strongly doubted.[11] On the other hand, the particular sacrifice of Prov. 7.14 (זבחי שלמים, 'shared offering') is thoroughly understandable within priestly

10. For a refutation of G. Boström's influential hypotheses cf. Maier, *Die 'freme Frau' in Proverbien 1–9* , pp. 198-206.

11. H.C. Washington, 'The "Strange" Woman (אשה זרה/נכריה) of Proverbs 1–9 and Post-Exilic Judaean Society', in A. Brenner (ed.), *A Feminist Companion to Wisdom Literature* (FCB 9; Sheffield: Sheffield Academic Press, 1995), pp. 157-184 esp. 164-65.

law and does not point to worship of a foreign god or goddess. According to Leviticus 3 it consists of burning the fat covering the entrails and kidneys of the sacrificial animal. The rest of the beast should be eaten on the same and following day in a state of purity (Lev. 7.15-20). It is strongly prohibited to leave the meat to the third day or to eat it under impure conditions. On the textual level of Proverbs 7, invoking the sacrifice by its precise term calls for urgent action and provides a pretext for the woman's sudden assault on the man. In the speaker's view the woman unmasks herself as unbearable, because she mixes a cult offering with sexual acts—a real abomination in Israel (cf. Lev. 15.16-18). As the entire instruction is a monologue delivered by a speaker, intended to show the woman's false character, her speech in 7.14-20 turns out to be a fiction, not an actual quote of her words.[12]

Finally, the 'strange' woman is directly confronted with personified wisdom in the poem of Prov. 9.1-6, 13-18. Here the woman is named 'Lady Folly' (אשת כסילות), but has the same features and produces the same outcome for the male as the 'strange' woman of the other texts. Both Lady Wisdom and Lady Folly invite the same audience to their houses by using almost the same words: 'Whoever is simple, let him turn in here!' (9.4, 16). Lady Wisdom owns a house. She is a wealthy member of high society who prepares a fine banquet. She invites fools to a meal but, in fact, offers teaching, so that the foolish may reach the 'path of understanding' (דרך בינה). By contrast, Lady Folly plays the harlot sitting lazily in front of her house, which is situated in the high places of the town. Her words, 'stolen water is sweet and bread eaten in secret is pleasant' (9.17), are a parody of Wisdom's invitation. The metaphor points to Prov. 5.15, where the man is asked to drink from his own cistern, that is, embrace his own wife. In the view of the poem's narrator, the harlot-like and foolish woman feeds sexual needs only; and her

12. Therefore, I do not agree with K. van der Toorn, 'Female Prostitution in Payment of Vows in Ancient Israel', *JBL* 108 (1989), pp. 193-205. He interprets Prov. 7 as a case of occasional prostitution, and understands the woman's words as referring to a 'real' problem, but overlooks their function as rhetorical device for conveying her false speech and abnormal behaviour.

male victim does not know that her followers are like shadows of Sheol, the underworld (9.18). In Proverbs 9 Wisdom and the 'strange' woman represent two different directions of the way of life. They challenge their male audience to choose between wisdom and folly. The choice is difficult, as its outcome—good life or becoming a social outcast—is not revealed from the beginning. Thus Proverbs 7 points back to the instruction: Whoever follows the advice of the speaker and one's parents will reach the path of wisdom, and that means a good life.

Compared to the material in Proverbs 10–29, which consists of mostly unconnected proverbs, the portraits of the 'strange' woman and Lady Wisdom prove to be extensions of existing tradition. Prov. 9.1-6, 13-16 can be read as a lively elaboration of Prov. 14.1: 'The wisdom of women builds up their house, foolishness breaks it down with her own hands.'[13] Furthermore, the motif of the 'strange' woman is already known to sapiential instructions of ancient Egypt and Mesopotamia.[14] In these earlier traditions the 'strange' woman appears as a prostitute. Her social status is, according to Phyllis Bird, 'that of an outcast, though not an outlaw, a tolerated, but dishonored member of society'.[15] Two sentences from older proverb collections also belong to this tradition:

> The speech of 'strange' women (זרות) is a deep pit.
> The curse of YHWH is on him who falls into it (Prov. 22.14).

> A prostitute[16] is a deep pit
> and a foreign woman (נכריה) a narrow well.
> For she lies in wait like a robber
> and increases the among unfaithful men (Prov. 23.27-28).

Compared with this tradition, the 'strange' woman of Proverbs 1–9 has more facets, is presented in a more lively way.

---

13. Cf. the opposition between wisdom (חכמה) and harlots (זונות) in Prov. 29.3.

14. See M. Lichtheim, *Ancient Egyptian Literature*. II. *The New Kingdom* (3 vols.; Berkeley: University of California Press, 1976), p. 137; W.G. Lambert, *Babylonian Wisdom Literature* (Oxford: Clarendon Press, 1960), pp. 102-103.

15. P. Bird, 'The Harlot as Heroine: Narrative Art and Social Presupposition in Three Old Testament Texts', *Semeia* 46 (1989), pp. 119-39 (120).

16. So the MT. The LXX speaks of the house of another man. This rendering is dependent on the pair זרה/נכריה in 'strange/foreign' Prov. 1–9.

So far I have followed the reasoning of the texts themselves, which build up the perspective of the admonishing speaker or the poem's narrator. In this view the 'strange' woman is fascinating, but destructive; enticing, but disreputable. Let us have a look behind that rhetoric in order to uncover the social setting of the instruction.

The Rhetoric of Otherness—
Its Authors and Socio-historical Background

Scholars have long tried to identify the 'strange' woman, debating the question of whether she is an actual[17] or allegorical figure. Most scholars favour a symbolic interpretation, as the polyvalent traits of this figure cannot be fused into a single character. Analyzing the rhetorical strategy for persuading the instruction's audience, the title 'strange woman' signifies a female figure as an 'outsider' and 'other' with regard to the audience. Her words and deeds are depicted as opposed to those of the textual speaker who, in the end, has the last word.

In my view, the figure represents several aspects of 'strangeness' and various social settings of women. First, it may represent 'foreign', that is, ethnically different women, as the term נכריה suggests. But the often-mentioned offense of 'adultery' strengthens the view that every woman outside the addressee's family is called 'strange'. So, even women belonging to the same ethnic group may become 'strange' if they do not adhere to social conventions. The 'strange' woman is accused of transgressing Torah commandments, such as the boundary between cult and sexuality (Prov. 7; cf. Lev. 7.19-21, 15.16-18). She is depicted as an adulteress who seeks various lovers. Herein the authors' androcentric stance becomes apparent. In their opinion a woman belongs to one man only, first to a father and then husband, and this is a matter not only of personal relationships but also of economics. Every sexual contact with another male destroys a woman's status as daughter or wife and, according to the instruction's rhetoric, turns her into a 'strange' woman. But the instruction argues further that a man who has

17. Cf. G. Boström, *Proverbiastudien: Die Weisheit und das fremde Weib in Spr. 1–9* (Lund: C.W.K. Gleerup, 1935), pp. 42-52, 134-45.

intercourse with a woman other than his wife will destroy his own social position. On the whole the texts offer an upper-class perspective whereby honor and personal integrity are essential values: to lose one's status in the public assembly (Prov. 5.14) and fall into disgrace (6.33) comes close to losing one's life.

Claudia V. Camp convincingly argued that Proverbs 1–9 forms an introduction or, together with Proverbs 31, framework for the selected older material of Proverbs.[18] Thus, the majority of scholars date these texts to the postexilic period of Persian rule. Concerning the socio-historical background of Proverbs 1–9, my research agrees with that of Harold C. Washington on several points, but differs in dating the material. Washington argues for an early postexilic setting when land tenure was a critical issue, as people returning from exile laid claim to their ancestors' landholdings meanwhile tilled by other Judaeans (cf. Jer. 39.10; 2 Kgs 25.12). In my opinion, this problem of continued land-holding is already solved in Proverbs 2. The speaker wants the addressee to keep the property he has already inherited as a prerequisite for upholding high social status, since being uprooted is the fate of the wicked (2.21-22) and penalty for the addressee's disobedience. The authors' interest in proper relations with other families and, especially, other women, comes close to the perspective of the genealogies in Ezra 2 and Nehemiah 7. Although these genealogical items may be 'fictive expressions of political and social solidarity rather than blood lineage',[19] they function as the postexilic community's membership lists. The so-called 'house of the fathers' (בית אבות) forms the fundamental social unit within this community.[20]

Several scholars link the topic of the 'strange' woman to the conflict about exogamous marriage in Ezra 9–10 and Nehemiah 13. Joseph Blenkinsopp connects the negative female imagery of Proverbs 1–9 to denunciations of alien cults in prophetic texts

18. Cf. Camp, *Wisdom and the Feminine in the Book of Proverbs* (Bible and Literature, 11; Sheffield: Almond Press, 1985), pp. 207-208.

19. Washington, ' "Strange" Woman', p. 175.

20. Cf. the collected studies of J.P. Weinberg, *The Citizen-Temple-Community* (trans. D.L. Smith-Christopher; JSOTSup, 151; Sheffield: Sheffield Academic Press, 1992).

(Isa. 57.3-13, 65.1-7, 66.3-4, 17; Mal. 2.10-16)[21] and in Nehemiah 13, and compares it to the religious and social objections to exogamous marriage. Washington emphasizes the problem of maintaining landholdings, which are the economic base of the community and may be inherited or disposed of by foreign women.[22] Kenneth G. Hoglund suggests that the Persians enforced a protected ethnic identity in the Judaean province in order to facilitate identification of the ruling group and regularity in administration and taxation.[23] Most scholars take it for granted that the Ezra narrative testifies to the prohibition of exogamous marriages in the Judaean community. But the Hebrew text fails to mention the dissolution of the offending marriages[24] and, also, names opponents of the divorce proposal (Ezra 10.15). According to Ezra 10.16 the *gôlâ*-group especially supported Ezra's demand. Nehemiah's banishment of a priestly son (Neh. 13.28) is not motivated by such a prohibition but is based on political grounds, as this man married a daughter of Nehemiah's personal enemy Sanballat. In fact, during the Persian rule many ethnic groups were living on the territory of the former Judaean Kingdom—descendants of refugees from the Northern Kingdom; Judaeans; members of the *gôlâ* Persian administrators; and former neighbours such as Edomites, Moabites and Ammonites who had enlarged their area of settlement after Jerusalem's fall in the sixth century.[25] Within that context, scholars differ in their

21. Cf. J. Blenkinsopp, 'The Social Context of the "Outsider Woman" in Proverbs 1–9', *Bib* 42 (1991), pp. 457-73, esp. 465, 71.

22. Women inheriting land are a topic of late addition to priestly law (Num. 27.1-11, 36.1-9; cf. Job 42.15). This is substantiated in Elephantine (cf. T.C. Eskenazi, 'Out from the Shadows: Biblical Women in the Postexilic Era', *JSOT* 54 [1992], pp. 25-43). See also Maier and Schroer's essay in this volume.

23. Cf. K.G. Hoglund, *Achaemenid Imperial Administration in Syria-Palestine and the Missions of Ezra and Nehemiah* (Atlanta: Scholars Press, 1992), pp. 437-42, and Blenkinsopp, 'Context', p. 472.

24. Ezra 10.44 is 'cured' by a conjecture from 3 Ezra 9.36, which reports an actual dissolution. Cf. T.C. Eskenazi and E.P. Judd, 'Marriage to a Stranger in Ezra 9–10', in T.C. Eskenazi and K.H. Richards (eds.), *Second Temple Studies*, II (JSOTSup, 175, Sheffield: JSOT Press 1994), pp. 266-85, esp. 271.

25. Cf. R. Albertz, *Religionsgeschichte Israels in alttestamentlicher Zeit, II*

viewpoints about the size and social status of the so-called
Citizen-Temple-Community: a modest number of people makes
endogamous marriage difficult because the number of potential
marriage partners may quickly decrease, and promotes the
control of such a measure. If only a leading group favours
endogamous marriage, what status are other residents granted?
The perspective of the Ezra-Nehemiah texts—the *golah*-group as
numerous and single-minded— sounds highly idealistic.

Although the polemics against exogamous marriages in Ezra-
Nehemiah and against the 'strange' woman in Proverbs 1–9
seem to be similar phenomena, the sapiential instruction of
Proverbs focuses on a different problem. The main issue here is
not marriage but adultery or sexual intercourse with unfamiliar
women, which are challenges to family integrity. Adultery in
this context threatens social status and property because the
injured husband may go to court (6.34-35) or seek financial compensation (5.9-10). Therefore, the instruction's authors aim at
controlling their and their sons' family ties and sexual relations,
and try to persuade by teaching. The authors adhere to social
values of in-group solidarity, such as righteousness and justice,
which are grounded in the faith of YHWH (2.6-10, 5.21-23, 6.30-
32).

This leads us to a third issue of postexilic Judah—the codification of Torah, that is, the formation of the Pentateuch. While
compelling evidence for the theory that the Persians initiated
and forced a codification of law[26] is lacking,[27] many scholars
assume that the basic stock of social and priestly law was
brought together during the fifth or fourth centuries BCE.[28] In

(Göttingen: Vandenhoeck & Ruprecht, 1992), pp. 504-506; Eskenazi and
Judd, 'Marriage', pp. 269-70.

26. German scholars speak of 'Reichsautorisation'. See P. Frei,
'Zentralgewalt und Lokalautonomie im Achämenidenreich', in P. Frei and
K. Koch, *Reichsidee und Reichsorganisation im Perserreich* (OBO, 55; Freiburg:
Universitätsverlag; Göttingen: Vandenhoeck & Ruprecht, 1984), pp. 7-43;
Hoglund, *Administration*, pp. 234-36.

27. Cf. Maier, *Die 'fremde Frau' in Proverbien 1–9*, pp. 54-55, 64.

28. Cf. Albertz, *Religionsgeschichte*, II, pp. 469-73; F. Crüsemann, *Die Tora:
Theologie und Sozialgeschichte des alttestamentlichen Gesetzes* (Munich: Chr.
Kaiser Verlag 1992), pp. 387-93; J. Blenkinsopp, *Ezra-Nehemiah: A Commen-
tary* (OTL; Philadelphia: Westminster Press, 1988), pp. 152-57.

Nehemiah 8–10 this process is linked to Ezra, the scribe presented as responsible for the community's self-commitment to the Torah. Several postexilic biblical texts overtly allude to legal materials of the Pentateuch, making it relevant to new circumstances and later theological viewpoints.[29] Thus the adaptation of the texts referred to shows them to be of a highly esteemed tradition. In the light of other references to the Torah and the formation of the Pentateuch, the allusions to the Decalogue and the teaching of children (Deut. 6.6-9, 11.18-21) in Prov. 6.20-34 point to a later dating, probably to the first half of the fourth century BCE.

Another reason for this later dating may be the depiction of a banquet scene in Prov. 9.1-6. During the fourth century the influence of Greek culture was increasing due to trade relations and Greek imports into the Eastern Mediterranean coast. From literary sources[30] we know that banquets, where upper-class men and women met, were an often-celebrated custom among Greeks[31] and Persians. Perhaps the authors of Proverbs 1–9 are to some extent challenged by this custom which favours social contact with unfamiliar women.

By and large, the sapiential instruction clearly reveals an upper-class perspective. Property and high social position are at stake. Because of the texts' language and artful style a high level of education can be assumed for its authors. To sum up, the authors of Proverbs 1–9 belong to urban upper-class groups of the Judaean community, with traditional religious values that highly influence social mores. The intention of their warnings is to advise their sons and give them guidelines for daily life. Obedience to the textual speaker becomes a matter of identity and in-

29. Cf. the regulations for the Sabbath in Jer. 17.19-27; Neh. 13.15-22; the remission of debts in Neh. 5; the liberation of slaves in Jer. 34.8-22. For Neh. 10 cf. D.J.A. Clines, 'Nehemiah 10 as an Example of Early Jewish Biblical Exegesis', *JSOT* 21 (1981), pp. 111-17.

30. Cf. Est. 1.1-20; Dan. 5; Xenophon, *Cyropaedia* 8.4.1-27; Josephus, *Ant.* 11.3.2-9.

31. The banquet-scene with male and female participants is often attested on Greek ceramic vessels and Cypriot metal bowls. Cf. Maier, *Die 'fremde Frau' in Proverbien 1–9*, pp. 234-46; J.-M. Dentzer, *Le motif du banquet couché dans le Proche-Orient et le monde grec du VIIe au IVe siècle avant J.-C.* (BEFAR, 246; Rome: Ecole française, 1982).

group position. In this context, the image of 'wicked men' (Prov.
1.10-19, 2.11-15) possibly reflects upper-class males who gain
their riches not through inherited wealth but by taking part in
international trade and usury. They probably oppose the authority of elder family heads and use new means for obtaining
wealth. Their negative characterization also has traits from the
paradigm of the 'wicked, impious man' (רשע; Ps. 10, 64, 73; and
Job 24.13-17) who opposes the pious and, in the end, God. Here
too the rhetoric of otherness tries to brand people who do not
adhere to a traditional lifestyle by characterizing them as God's
opponents.

Women's Contribution to the Rhetoric of Otherness

The admonishing speeches in Proverbs 1–9 name every person
not adhering to their definite values as an 'outsider' and a
danger to the social group. They show a gender-specific concept
of the 'enemy'. While the male 'outsider' transgresses conven-
tional behaviour in economic matters, the female 'outsider'
transgresses the sexual mores that are an important criterion for
boundaries and social organizations. The warnings against the
'strange' woman are examples of transposing any sign of independent female behaviour, that is, behaviour uncontrolled by
father or husband, under the label of 'harlotry', to the realm of
the undesired.[32]

If we consider the authors' gender, or at least the gender of the
group responsible for and using such instruction, I suppose that
male and female positions may emerge. On the textual level, the
mother is mentioned twice giving advice like the father (Prov.
1.8; 6.20). Although the sapiential pattern of father–son instruction is applied in Proverbs 1–9, the only passage specifically
referring to a father's instruction is 4.1-4. Contrary to the often
suggested father–son or teacher–pupil relationship of the
instructional genre, the speaker may also represent a mother
rebuking her son such as the mother of Lemuel, King of Massa,

32. I agree with Brenner on the marginalizing function of the term זנה 'to
whore' and its cognates. See A. Brenner, *The Intercourse of Knowledge: On
Gendering Desire and 'Sexuality' in the Hebrew Bible* (BIS, 26; Leiden: E.J. Brill,
1997), pp. 147-51.

in Prov. 31.1-9. The figure looking through the window in Proverbs 7 resembles Michal (2 Sam. 6.16), Jezebel (2 Kgs 9.30) and, above all, Sisera's mother (Judg. 5.28). Thus it follows a traditional motif. Fokkelien van Dijk-Hemmes has shown that this rebuking female 'knows how to reproduce the dominant discourse perfectly—first by calling on the voice of another woman who is qualified as "strange", then by "muting" it'.[33] Besides, in Prov. 7.4 another woman figure is called upon to save the addressee from the adulteress: it is Wisdom in the role of 'sister' or 'female familiar friend'.[34]

Looking at the assumed socio-historical background, women seem to be highly involved in the community. They are mentioned as members of the authoritative assembly (קהל)[35] and contribute to important decisions within the community, such as the building of the Jerusalem wall (Neh. 3.12), the call for debt remittance (Neh. 5.1) and the proclamation of the Torah (Neh. 8.2-3; cf. 10.29-30). Thus the admonishing speeches of Proverbs 1–9 can be understood as texts spoken, written and used by fathers *and* mothers, men *and* women.

Responding Readers

Finally, the parental wisdom outlined here also faces a gendered audience. Although the speeches directly address 'sons', they implicitly unfold a definite message for 'daughters', too. Daughters should not look for sexual contact with men apart from one lifelong husband but should behave like an industrious, loving wife who teaches her children the traditional way of life according to the Torah. In this line of arguing the speaking mother and Lady Wisdom function as shining examples of correct female behaviour, whereas the 'strange' woman represents the wrong behaviour. At this point the question

33. Van Dijk-Hemmes, 'Wisdom and Warning Discourse', in Brenner and van Dijk-Hemmes, *Gendering Texts*, p. 48-62 (62).

34. The terms אחות (sister) and מודע (close friend) do not belong to bridal imagery as in the S o S, where אחות (sister) is paralleled by כלה (bride), but denote kinship. Cf. G. Baumann, *Die Weisheitsgestalt in Proverbien 1–9:.Traditionsgeschichtliche und theologische Studien* (FAT, 16; Tübingen: J.C.B. Mohr, 1996), pp. 245-47.

35. Cf. Eskenazi, 'Out from the Shadows', pp. 41-42; and Ezra 10.1.

arises: How should modern male and female readers cope with such varied characterizations of women, and with women who take part in a rhetoric of otherness?

Carol Newsom analyzes the stabilizing function of the 'strange' woman and Lady Wisdom insofar as both figures define and secure the boundaries of the symbolic order of patriarchal wisdom.[36] She points to a similar symbolism in the film *Fatal Attraction*: a naive young husband is seduced by an attractive, but in the end violent and mad, woman who would have destroyed his life if his loving wife had not rescued him. While the film attempts to naturalize its discourse and to conceal the storyteller's viewpoint, Proverbs 1–9 makes known several competing voices and, as Newsom concludes, the speaker's position can be questioned.

So, I do not assume simply that a female reader of Proverbs 1–9 'is required to identify against herself',[37] as Gale Yee does. Reading is not just a matter of identification with literary figures, but also allows the adoption of a certain discourse. As a male reader may overcome identification with the simple male addressee by joining the father's discourse, so a female reader is not forced to identify with the 'strange' woman but may adopt the perspective of the rebuking mother or that of Lady Wisdom. However, in both cases the dominant discourse furthers an androcentric perspective and male interests or, as Brenner says, 'within the literary F voice, F self interest is silenced through identification with M interest…for the purpose of preserving an existing world order and worldview'.[38] According to the world view of Proverbs 1–9 women who do not adhere to traditional social conventions will be named 'strange' and are thus condemned as outsiders. Merging the 'strange' woman's deeds with her character, the description has a destructive effect on the image of women in general. The positioning of the admonishing speeches as an introduction to sapiential tradition emphatically supports such a generalization. The 'strange' woman figure

36. C. Newsom, 'Woman and the Discourse of Patriarchal Wisdom: A Study of Proverbs 1–9', in P.L. Day (ed.), *Gender and Difference in Ancient Israel* (Minneapolis: Fortress Press, 1989), pp. 142-60, esp. 157-59.

37. Yee, 'Foreign Woman', p. 126, in a citation from Fetterly.

38. Brenner, *Gendering Texts*, pp. 125-26.

mirrors the long-lasting patriarchal cliché of women being sexually deviant and uncontrolled.

Although I appreciate the instruction's intention to maintain identity and to make Torah commandments relevant in a time of political and social crisis, I cannot accept that the female figure is made responsible for illicit intercourse. In this regard the very positive role of Lady Wisdom does not neutralize the androcentric perspective, as the two female figures are opposed to one another in Proverbs 9 and maintain a distinction similar to that of the madonna and the whore. However, I would like to emphasize that women are not only victims of such anti-woman propaganda but also co-agents of its existence, thus helping to maintain androcentrism and, in the end, patriarchy[39]—in past and present times. Modern male and female readers should not perpetuate such a biased rhetoric but deconstruct it. Mieke Heijerman, for example, variably portrays the 'strange' woman of Proverbs 7 as a mother's rival, a man's scapegoat or a needy woman, thus resisting the one-sided negative view of the text's speaker.[40] Camp offers another deconstructive reading of the female imagery when she interprets it in light of trickster mythology known from tribal folklore. She argues for a paradoxical unity of Lady Wisdom and the 'strange' woman, and for a positive valuation of women's power as 'anti-structural, regenerative because of its liminality'.[41] I would like to add that the speaker's misogynous image of the outsider woman also offers a quite miserable image of a common young man portrayed as weak-willed, naive and even stupid, a man who can easily be

39. The German expression for this is 'Mittäterschaft', which means 'acting together with/at the side of the (male) agent'. The term was introduced by the German sociologist Christina Thürmer-Rohr in an article, 'Aus der Täuschung in die Ent-Täuschung: Zur Mittäterschaft von Frauen,' in C. Thürmer-Rohr, *Vagabundinnen: Feministische Essays* (Berlin: Orlanda Frauenverlag, 1987), pp. 38-56.

40. M. Heijerman, 'Who Would Blame Her? The "Strange" Woman of Proverbs 7', in A. Brenner (ed.), *A Feminist Companion to Wisdom Literature* (FCB, 9, Sheffield: Sheffield Academic Press, 1995) pp. 100-109.

41. C.V. Camp, 'Wise and Strange: An Interpretation of the Female Imagery in Proverbs in Light of Trickster Mythology', in A. Brenner (ed.), *A Feminist Companion to Wisdom Literature* (FCB, 9; Sheffield: Sheffield Academic Press, 1995), pp. 131-56, esp. 155.

inflamed by a single wink of the eye or an encouraging word from any woman.

While accepting that group identity is formed by defining insiders and outsiders, I oppose the power structure of the texts. A male or female speaker here offers a monologue that not only fails to present other voices, but also exerts a negative judgment from the very beginning. However, the characterization of the attractive female who seduces unsuspecting males blurs the actual power structure in patriarchally organized communities. Authority is not only claimed by referring to the Torah tradition, but also by threatening the addressee with a shameful end and by creating a negative image of female sexuality. In the end the parental wisdom of Proverbs 1–9 turns out to be as attractive and, at the same time, as dangerous as its depiction of the 'strange' woman.

QOHELETH THE 'OLD BOY' AND QOHELETH THE 'NEW MAN': MISOGYNISM, THE WOMB AND A PARADOX IN ECCLESIASTES*

Eric S. Christianson

The perception of Qoheleth's attitude to women has had a long and chequered history. He has vacillated between a woman-hater and a freethinker whose thoughts fit comfortably in a modern age. Typical, then, is the question posed by N. Lohfink's article: Was Qoheleth a woman-hater? ('War Kohelet ein Frauen-feind?'[1]). Roland Murphy has recently captured well the elusive-ness of the answer: 'Obviously the final word on this text [Eccl. 7.25-29 and Qoheleth's attitude as a whole] has not yet been written. Thus far, it refuses to yield its secret.'[2] But this essay is only partly concerned with that question. I am asking other questions, both explicit and implicit from my approach: What kind of evidence is there for the answers proposed to Lohfink's question? Are the answers, at least in part, determined by whom we would like Qoheleth to be? And what does the more indirect approach (i.e. apart from reviewing the usual texts: 2.8, 7.25-29, 9.9) of reviewing Qoheleth's attitude to the womb offer?

As will become apparent, there is something potentially

*   I would like to thank Athalya Brenner for inviting me to write some-thing I have found challenging, and Rosemarie Kossov for her fine help with translations.

1.   N. Lohfink, 'War Kohelet ein Frauenfeind? Ein Versuch, die Logik und den Gegenstand von Koh. 7:23–8:1a herauszufinden', in M. Gilbert (ed.), *La sagesse de l'Ancien Testament* (BETL, 51: Leuven: Leuven University Press, 1979), pp. 259-87.

2.   R.E. Murphy, *Ecclesiastes* (WBC, 23a; Dallas, TX: Word Books, 1992), p. 78. Compare his similar remarks elsewhere: 'feminist study of the Bible has not remarked a recent change in the verdict concerning Qoheleth's misogynism' ('Recent Research on Proverbs and Qoheleth', *CR:BS* 1 [1993], pp. 119-40 [135]).

explosive about Qoheleth's attitude to women, and reviewing how people have understood it will be the most interesting entry into other considerations. So, the procedure of this essay will be first to map out the ways in which scholars have attempted to come to terms with Qoheleth's attitude to women (I) and then to supplement that with Qoheleth's treatment of the womb (II). Finally, I will discuss the interpretive paradox(es) that the overall enquiry highlights (III). To begin to map the terrain, then, it makes most sense to start with the largest and most charted area of dispute.

I

Ecclesiastes 7.25-29 is Qoheleth's most conspicuous discussion about woman[3] (women are mentioned, in passing, in only two other places: 2.8; 9.9). For good reason, then, the passage has loomed large in discussions about Qoheleth's attitude to women as a whole. In fact, without this text it is doubtful that any serious discussion would have ever arisen.

> (25) I turned, with all my being, to understand, to search out and to seek wisdom and the sum of things; and to understand evil, folly and the folly of madness. (26) And I found more bitter than death the woman who is traps, her heart nets, her hands chains. He with whom God is pleased will be delivered from her, but he who sins will be taken by her. (27) See, this I have found, said Qoheleth ([adding] one to one to find the sum, (28) which my soul has sought continually but I have not found): one man among a thousand I have found, but a woman among all of these I have not found. (29) See, this alone I have found: that God made humanity upright, but they have sought many devices.

However clear the text may seem to be in its sentiments, many have found need to dispute its clarity.

First, there are some problems with v. 26 that affect the whole passage. Is Qoheleth really saying, in his own words, that

---

3.   Many perceive the markers of this passage differently, particularly its end, which may be 8.1 (see Murphy, *Ecclesiastes*, p. 75, for the discussion). The verses of contention concerning Qoheleth's attitude to women, however, are generally limited to 7.25-29 (with the exception of a few, notably T. Krüger, who refer to 7.23-24 as well; more on which, see below).

women, or at least one type of woman, are inherently a trap? Is a woman really more bitter than death? There are translation problems. The Hebrew of v. 26b reads אשׁר־היא מצודים וחרמים לבה אסורים ידיה (lit. 'who / that-she [is] traps, nets her heart, chains her hands…'). If we translate, as is most common, 'a woman *who is* traps', then the woman whom Qoheleth finds to be more bitter than death is a type of woman: the type who traps men.[4] If, however, we translate 'a woman, she is traps…', Qoheleth may be referring to a bitter personal experience of a particular woman. Or, following R. Gordis and, less committedly, R.N. Whybray, he may be referring to women in general.[5]

There are ways of excusing Qoheleth from any of the above sentiments, such as, for example, suggesting that he is quoting someone else. O. Loretz would have us think that Qoheleth 'rejects the negative evaluation of woman and [this] is thus an attempt to correct his predecessor'.[6] Even more adamant are Lohfink and K. Baltzer. Lohfink thinks first that מר ממות in 7.26a means that woman is *stronger* than death, an idea remote to the Hebrew Bible[7] and, as Fox points out, rather absurd in itself.[8] Lohfink further takes the אשׁר of 7.26b not to be the usual humble

---

4.   אשׁה with ה (the definite article) in the wisdom literature occurs only here at Eccl. 7.26, which gives weight to the idea that a particular type of woman is under consideration; i.e. '*the* [kind of] woman who is traps…' Given the wholly uncommon use of the article, then, this particular application of the noun is likely at least, if not an assertion about womankind in general.

5.   R.N. Whybray, *Ecclesiastes* (NCB; Grand Rapids: Eerdmans; London: Marshall, Morgan & Scott, 1989), p. 125; R. Gordis, *Koheleth—The Man and his World* (repr; New York: Bloch Publishing, 1962 [1955]), p. 272. The argument is strengthened by the use of אשׁר, which, according to Whybray, as elsewhere in Ecclesiastes, could mean 'because, for'.

6.   O. Loretz, 'Poetry and Prose in the Book of Qohelet (1:1–3:22; 7:23–8:1)', in J. de Moor and W. Watson (eds.), *Verse in Ancient Near Eastern Prose* (Neukirchen–Vluyn: Neukirchener Verlag, 1993), pp. 155-89 (183).

7.   Indeed, the only direct connection of 'woman' to death in another passage that I can find suggests the opposite idea: 'From a woman sin had its beginning, and because of her we all die' (Sir. 25.24 NRSV; cf. 26.22). Given Qoheleth's fascination with Genesis (more on which, see below), this is more like the sentiment he had in mind.

8.   M.V. Fox, *Qohelet and his Contradictions* (JSOTSup, 71; Sheffield: Almond Press, 1989), p. 238.

relative pronoun, but to somehow be a marker of indirect speech: hence, '[I keep coming up against the view that] woman is stronger than death...' T. Krüger excuses Qoheleth by suggesting that אשר is demonstrative, specifying 'that one woman who is...', which Qoheleth goes on to elaborate. The comment is therefore not 'a misogynistic remark, but a declaration in agreement with the traditional wisdom topic of warning against a strange woman'.[9] Baltzer follows Lohfink and further suggests that the אשר at 7.28 must refer to the חשבון just mentioned at 7.27, yet at 7.29 אשר conveniently introduces another quote![10] (It has even been suggested, quite unnecessarily, that we amend the אשר of v. 28a to אשה, 'woman', and hence have, 'a woman I continually sought'.[11]) In a manner seemingly as strained, Murphy suggests that Qoheleth is refuting the 'one in a thousand' saying of 7.28 by understanding the verse as follows: 'what my soul has always sought without finding [is this]: one man among a thousand...' Ergo Qoheleth is citing someone else. Yet the only (and insufficient) reason Murphy can suggest for the insertion of 'is this' is that it simplifies a complicated style.[12]

The strain of such readings is easy to see and it is very tempting to regard such efforts as attempts to modernize Qoheleth instead of seeing him more logically as 'a child of his time' (a notion Murphy explicitly rejects).[13] The real weakness of the quotation theory lies in its argument from silence. Who is to say, for example, that if Qoheleth is in fact quoting that he is not doing so approvingly? And if we cannot know (what criteria

9. 'Dann läge hier keine generell frauenfeindliche Äusserung vor, sondern eine Aussage, die dem traditionell-weisheitlichen Topos der Warnung vor der "fremden Frau" entspricht' (T. Krüger, ' "Frau Weisheit" in Koh 7,26?', *Bib* 73 [1993], pp. 394-403 [395]).

10. K. Baltzer, 'Women and War in Qohelet 7:23–8:1a', *HTR* 80.1 (1987), pp. 127-32 (131).

11. So Fox, following Ehrlich, in M.V. Fox and B. Porten, 'Unsought Discoveries: Qohelet 7:23–8:1a', *HS* 19 (1978), pp. 26-38 (31).

12. Murphy, *Ecclesiastes*, pp. 75, 77.

13. Interestingly, Lohfink criticizes, without a hint of self-irony, ways in which the LXX translators, and eventually church fathers, attempted to explain away, through a process of allegorization, a generally misogynistic reading ('War Kohelet ein Frauenfeind?', p. 265).

could we possibly have?), what difference does it make? It would be better to pay attention to the only markers that do exist, that is, the narrative speech markers that serve to highlight certain points of Qoheleth's story.[14]

Another problem concerns the use of חטא, sinner, and טוב לפני אלהים, one who is pleasing/good to God, in 7.26b. The one who is pleasing to God (note the passive sense) escapes the woman, while the one who sins is ensnared (lit. captured) by her (note the lack of responsibility implied in וחטא ילכד בה—even the one who sins is not responsible for his actions). The statement is part of Qoheleth's overall strategy of searching. Because wisdom has proven inadequate in all of his questing for understanding, here too wisdom will not help that man escape that woman; the outcome is solely in the hands of God. One can only *be* one who pleases God and, like wisdom itself, God's reasons for making that so are hidden.[15] As Murphy helpfully points out, in 7.26 the 'good' and the sinner are not moral classifications, but are 'designations of human beings in terms of the inscrutable divine will. Some will fall victim to this type of woman, but some will not, as God pleases.'[16] Wisdom failed Qoheleth and it will fail the man who attempts to flee this woman, for it does not matter if he is wise or a fool. In the end the fate of the sinner and the one who is 'good' before God are ultimately the same—death (9.1; cf. 2.16)—and God's decisive control over the matter remains intact.

One of the most seemingly offensive (while at the same time 'key') aspects of this passage is the 'one in a thousand' saying of 7.28. As others have observed before, the real issue is the value that Qoheleth attributes to finding as opposed to not finding. 'See, this I have found...' (7.27), he says, 'One man among a thousand I have found, but a woman among all of these I have not found' (7.28). This has been read several ways. Krüger, following D. Michel, contrasts the one in a thousand saying to Sir. 6.6: 'Let those who are friendly with you be many, but let your

14. See my *A Time to Tell: Narrative Strategies in Ecclesiastes* (JSOTSup, 280; Sheffield: Sheffield Academic Press, forthcoming), 'Introduction: Reading Ecclesiastes as Narrative'. As the markers relate to this passage see Chapter 3.2 of the same.

15. Similarly, see Whybray, *Ecclesiastes*, p. 125.

16. Murphy, *Ecclesiastes*, p. 76.

advisers be one in a thousand' (NRSV). The one man to be found is, like a treasure, a true friend (*wahren Freund*). This should make the fact that a woman cannot be found even worse. But like so many commentators, Krüger takes Qoheleth's slight harshness to men to soften his opinion about women: the conclusion now is that 'men are upright one thousandth "better" than women!', and this cannot be taken to be 'evidence' (*Beweis*) that Qoheleth devalues women.[17] Furthermore, a crucial point is overlooked here. Little can mollify Qoheleth's sentiment that, according to Krüger, a woman not only cannot be found but cannot even be a good friend.

Jacques Ellul offers a rather extraordinary and solitary reading of 7.28:

> When Qohelet claims he has not found a woman among all of them, he cannot have in mind 'the' woman, according to his description of her [at 7.26]. Consequently, 'woman' is not a snare, etc., in herself, otherwise, obviously, he would have found her… [Qoheleth has never found a] true woman…a woman as God created her, fulfilling her true woman's essence.[18]

And from this he eventually draws a disturbing conclusion:

> [because the] woman's vocation was infinitely more complex [than the man's]…it may be possible to find, at length, a man after God's own heart. But a woman never manages to achieve the fulness of her kind.[19]

What makes this reading alarming is the feeling that Ellul perceives himself thus to be giving women everywhere a sort of backhanded compliment: he assumes that there is an ideal—an 'angelic' opposite to the woman 'who is a snare'—to which the woman (reader) is to aspire.

Although I have already discussed some weak points in Baltzer's position, he is strikingly original in his delineation of the military language that permeates the whole passage: אסורים (nets), מצודים (siege-works) and אלף (brigade) in particular.

---

17. 'Männer sind gerade ein Promille "besser" als Frauen!' (Krüger, '"Frau Weisheit"', p. 396).

18. J. Ellul, *Reason for Being: A Meditation on Ecclesiastes* (trans. J.M. Hanks; Grand Rapids: Eerdmans, 1990), p. 201.

19. Ellul, *Reason for Being*, p. 203.

Hence, instead of one man among a thousand, we have one man among the brigade(s) I found, but not a woman, because, simply, war 'is a male affair'.[20] One problem with reading the passage this way, however, is that Qoheleth's extremes are suspiciously eased. The potential challenge to the reader (is Qoheleth's finding good, bad or neither?) is clinically dispensed with.[21] In a similar vein, Lohfink dispenses with the severity by suggesting that the numbers אחד and אלף 'direct your thoughts to statistical rather than moral qualifications. One should take the saying as literally as possible. Then it simply implies that the people subject to Kohelet's observations after a certain time were no longer to be found.'[22]

In general, as many have noted, the passage is about discovering. As Fox and Porten have shown, the verbs בקש (seek) and מצא (find) play off of one another, the occurrence of one generating occurrences of the other, and the wordplay is often rich or ironic (as in Qoheleth's *discovery* [מצא] that there is too much *seeking* [בקש], 7.29).[23] The presence of such intense searching raises the question of value, a point crystallized by Athalya Brenner's revealing reading:

> whereas a 'real' man is one in a thousand, 'a woman' (presumably one who is reliable/worthy) is not to be found among those few choice individuals… While it is not clear what the reference is to[24]…a reading of less (unspecified) than 1:1000 ratio for female

20. Baltzer, 'Women and War', pp. 130-31.

21. There are other problems with Baltzer's overall approach. For example, Baltzer argues that while the second and third 'military' terms applied to the woman in v. 26 have counterparts (her 'heart' and 'hands'), the first does not and one must be offered (he suggests 'breasts'). But this is unnecessary as it is likely that a counterpart is already present in the pronoun היא ('Women and War', pp. 128-29).

22. Lohfink, 'War Kohelet ein Frauenfeind?', pp. 280-81.

23. Fox and Porten, 'Unsought Discoveries', pp. 37-38.

24. Whybray helpfully points out that the text '*does not state what it is* that the speaker has sought, and which he has, or has not, found in his extensive research', and further that we do not know precisely what is meant by the hyperbolic 'one man among a thousand' (*Ecclesiastes*, p. 127; his italics).

human integrity, perhaps even no human integrity rating for
women, makes sense.[25]

To take offense she must assume that, at least to Qoheleth, the
man in question is worthy and that *the act of finding* confirms
human integrity. The fact that he found a man among a thousand (even though we cannot know exactly what is meant by
this), but among the same amount of people he found no
woman, is presented by Qoheleth as a kind of evidence that
humanity was first upright, but they now have sought many
devices ('reasonings')[26] which led them astray. A thoroughly
negative tone is conveyed in that the failure to discover,
regardless of the object, is Qoheleth's vexation in life. Also, the
image of searching in this passage serves to illustrate his struggle
on the whole. The point is that he is unable to find the sum of
what should be *like* the answer to a (seemingly) simple
mathematical problem: $1 + 1$.[27] As with the rest of his searching,
the answer eludes him.

Several scholars have pointed out Qoheleth's underlying
homage to Genesis 2–3 in this passage.[28] D. Garrett points out
parallels such as the curse of toil and the inaccessibility of knowledge.[29] According to Fox, Adam is 'trapped' by the woman as is
Qoheleth, hence Qoheleth's point is that woman is predatory.[30]
For Ellul Qoheleth had in mind the ideal of Eve by depicting the
'bad' woman of the passage as her opposite: 'She *should* be the
marvel that dazzled Adam.'[31] Ecclesiastes 7.29, according to

25. A. Brenner, 'Some Observations on the Figurations of Woman in
Wisdom Literature', *idem* (ed.), *A Feminist Companion to Wisdom Literature*
(FCB, 9; Sheffield: Sheffield Academic Press, 1995), pp. 50-66 (59 and 59 n.
4).

26. חשבנות, 'sums'; LXX λογισμούς. Cf. Wis. 1.3: 'crooked reasonings
[λογισμοί] separate one from God' (and see Wis. 3.10).

27. Further on this mathematical aspect of the passage, see my *A Time to
Tell*, chapter. 8.3.

28. For a recent analysis of Genesis in Qoheleth's text as a whole, see
William H.U. Anderson, 'The Curse of work in Qoheleth: An exposé of
Genesis 3:17-19 in Ecclesiastes', *EvQ* 70.2 (1998), pp. 99-113

29. D.A. Garrett, 'Ecclesiastes 7:25-29 and the Feminist Hermeneutic',
CTR 2.2 (1988), pp. 309-21 (313-15).

30. Fox in Fox and Porten, 'Unsought Discoveries', p. 33.

31. *Reason for Being*, p. 201 (italics mine); further, when this 'earthly

Krüger, echoes Gen. 6.5 in its condemnation of humanity.[32] Qoheleth most certainly had, according to the commentaries, at least the primeval history of Genesis before him as he wrote. In scrutinizing the 'Fall' passage proper (Gen. 2.15–3.24), then, several parallels become apparent. At 2.20, for example, Adam gives names to all the cattle, birds and every beast (לכל חית), but for Adam, no helper could be *found* (לא־מצא עזר). As a result of this, God goes on to form a woman from Adam. Hence, as a result of Adam's not finding, the woman is created—out of the man's failure. Similarly, in Ecclesiastes, the failure to find, to discover, is in itself a curse. Knowledge and death are paralleled as well. The result of the fruit-eating is that Adam and Eve know, like God, good and evil (Gen. 3.5 [twice], 7, 22). Qoheleth wants to know wisdom, folly and the folly of madness (Eccl. 7.25 [twice]). When they eat, God says that they will surely die (Gen. 2.17; 3.3-4). Like Qoheleth, they desired knowledge, but God *made* it unattainable. (Of course we will never know whether Qoheleth was in fact paying homage to a suppressive relationship or whether he saw the resulting curse of the Genesis story as something with which he was simply resolved to cope.)

We can now turn to the question of the passage's overall gist. Commentators have differed starkly on whether Qoheleth's psyche is misogynistic or simply misunderstood. Some see quite plainly that the misogynistic overtones dictate a clear message: Qoheleth was irredeemably a misogynist. The most striking, and for me unexpected, example of this comes from Christian D. Ginsburg, who stated in 1861 in regard to this passage that men making women the embodiment of wickedness 'in all ages' has been 'to the detriment of themselves, the female sex, and society at large'.[33] Others have followed this assessment, although not always as forcefully. Gordis, refreshingly, makes no attempt to excuse Qoheleth, except perhaps to point out (very typically among commentators, as it happens) that Qoheleth is *nearly* as

representation of divine love turns into degradation and indecency…the best goes bad… This is why Qohelet becomes so violent when he speaks of women.'

32. Krüger, ' "Frau Weisheit" ', p. 399.

33. C.D. Ginsburg, *Coheleth (Commonly Called the Book of Ecclesiastes)* (repr.; New York: Ktav, 1970 [1861]), p. 387.

harsh on men as he is on women, as if that somehow pacifies his misogynism.[34] But he goes further: 'This famous passage in which Koheleth expresses his distrust of women testifies to the attraction they hold over him... Their physical charms ("her hands", v. 26) and their emotional appeal ("her heart", v. 26) are alike dangerous to man, because honor, rare among men, is non–existent among women.'[35] Baltzer is, on the whole, close to Gordis in his assessment: in the ch. 7 passage, 'Qoheleth is saying "perfect men are rare, perfect women are non-existent"... [thereby] more than reflecting the Oriental view...' Like others he comes to the view that 'Qoheleth was something of a misogynist.'[36] Like Gordis and Baltzer, Fox refuses to pay heed to the idea that Qoheleth has somehow avoided the charge of misogyny, stating that Qoheleth happily participates in a tradition in which 'escaping from a woman...is fortunate, a sign of God's favor'.[37] Fox further sees Qoheleth's rather mundane observation as a let down: 'There is bathos in these words: the result of his search in the lofty realms of intellect is just this: a woman is dangerous.'[38]

From this middle ground we may move to the opposite side of the field. A recent and staunch defender of Qoheleth's reputation is D. Garrett. His purpose in his article, 'Ecclesiastes 7:25-29 and the Feminist Hermeneutic', is clear enough: 'to uphold the Bible's authority'; that is, not to understand better this difficult passage, but to 'save the Bible from the accusation of misogyny'.[39] The outcome is predetermined. Any notion that Qoheleth

---

34. Gordis, *Koheleth*, pp. 273, 275. Compare G. Ogden's suggestion: 'that one man in a thousand escaped the wily woman is in no sense a commendation of the male at the expense of the female. To posit, as is usual, that Qoheleth took a negative attitude to women, is absolutely unjustified' (*Qoheleth* [Readings; Sheffield: JSOT Press, 1987], p. 123). One wonders if Ogden would be comfortable to say the reverse had Qoheleth said the reverse.

35. Gordis, *Koheleth*, p. 272. Here it is difficult to tell whether Gordis is merely attempting to summarize Qoheleth or is extrapolating in agreement with him.

36. Baltzer, 'Women and War', p. 147.

37. Fox, in Fox and Porten, 'Unsought Discoveries', p. 31.

38. Fox, *Qohelet and his Contradictions*, p. 241.

39. Garrett, 'Ecclesiastes 7.25-29', pp. 310, 311.

participates in a tradition that vilifies women (a tradition that Garrett amazingly believes does not even exist) is dismissed and any possible severity in Qoheleth's views is quashed. Ellul follows Garrett closely (although not, so far as I can tell, knowingly) in this camp. As we have already seen he arrives to some startling conclusions. Ellul's procedure is to assume that there is by necessity a flipside to this 'awful text against women' (he finds it in the praises of companionship in 4.9-12).[40]

Less ideologically invested are the approaches of N. Lohfink, K. Baltzer, G. Ogden, D. Rudman and T. Krüger to this passage. As we have seen, Lohfink seems to be the one who got the modern ball rolling to explain the passage in a more favourable light, and I have discussed how Baltzer took it further. Ogden sees the woman of v. 26 as a metaphor or 'figure for premature death', making the whole mean that an untimely death is more bitter than death itself, which might fit well with other passages on death such as 9.11-12 (cf. 7.17). This lends support, he claims, to the idea that the charge of misogynism is unfair.[41] But Ogden's reading is tenuous. The meaning that metaphors or figures create cannot be isolated so easily from the language used to convey them, as Ogden would have it, and the extent to which Qoheleth elaborates the wicked figure *as a woman* makes this view less likely. Elsewhere Qoheleth chose less offensive ways of saying that death may come unexpectedly.

Dominic Rudman has made a recent and interesting attempt at understanding woman in Ecclesiastes in yet a new light.[42] Rudman makes it clear from the start that he will interpret the passage in the context of Qoheleth's notion of divine determinism, which he argues pervades the whole book. Ecclesiastes 7.23-29 therefore presents woman as an agent of God's judgment which will entrap a man, but not Qoheleth who seems to have escaped her. Rudman aligns himself with Fox, explicitly against Baltzer and Lohfink, in not wishing to mitigate Qoheleth's misogynism.[43] This said, we are quickly and implicitly requested

40. Ellul, *Reason for Being*, p. 196.
41. Ogden, *Qoheleth*, pp. 120-21.
42. Dominic Rudman, 'Woman as Divine Agent in Ecclesiastes', *JBL* 116 (1997), pp. 411-27.
43. Rudman, 'Woman as Divine Agent', p. 414.

to ignore it. At the heart of his argument is the notion that מצוד
(net), חרם (dragnet) and אסור (bond), used to describe the woman
in 7.26, all have some connection to Yahweh's divine judgment.
There are some convincing examples, particularly from the
prophetic literature, but there are exceptions, as he admits. The
most serious problem, however, arises from the use of these
words elsewhere in Ecclesiastes, where of the other two uses of
מצוד one is a literal human trap used in war (9.14; an example
Rudman ignores) and the other (9.12) is not so clearly a divine
net as Rudman suggests.[44] The other two terms do not even
appear in Ecclesiastes, and אסור, as Rudman remarks, is generally a 'neutral' term at any rate. Even if one grants that the
woman in ch. 7 is God's agent of wrath, her ultimate purpose
remains a negative one, for she exists to thwart human knowledge and to entrap men.[45] Although Rudman tries to avoid the
parallel, woman's purpose becomes not unlike that of the wicked
woman of Proverbs: in both the woman lies in wait—like a
trap—for men, and is nothing but bad news.

Krüger has made perhaps the most credible attempt at avoiding the ascription of misogynism to Qoheleth. His thesis is that
the whole passage (7.23-29), including the reference to woman, is
to do with the inaccessibility of wisdom, particularly wisdom
personified.[46] Ecclesiastes 7.24 sets the tone by determining
wisdom as a distant quality (Fern-Sein).[47] Qoheleth thereby

44. 9.12: 'Indeed, humanity does not know their time. Like fish that are
caught in an evil net (מצודה רעה), and birds being caught in the snare; so
will human beings be snared by an evil time, when it falls upon them suddenly.' Even if the evil time is linked to God's providence (as in ch. 3), it is a
result of the way God has structured the world that people do not know
when evil will happen. That is very different to saying that God himself is
casting the net, thereby creating the evil that happens to them. Evil has
human sources as well as divine in Ecclesiastes (e.g. 1.12; 4.1-3). There is no
Divine Hunter here, but rather the image of the net is a metaphor for the
experience of life as beyond human control.

45. Therefore, 'Qoheleth supposes such pleasures [described in ch. 2] as
the woman embodies as antithetical to wisdom' (Rudman, 'Woman as
Divine Agent', p. 420).

46. Contra Lohfink, 'War Kohelet ein Frauenfeind?', pp. 261-62.

47. Krüger, ' "Frau Weisheit" ', p. 398. In support of Krüger, Alphonse
Maillot similarly remarked that 7.26-29 echoes the idea of the 'impossibility

critiques traditional ideas of wisdom being the road to ethical perfection. Making reference to Sir. 6.24-31, in which wisdom personified is 'fetters' that will teach discipline and eventually give joy, Krüger suggests that Qoheleth's wicked woman is a seductive version of Dame Wisdom. Therefore, 'The process of the acquisition of knowledge becomes "erotic".'[48] In 7.26, then, Qoheleth becomes even more disillusioned about wisdom than in vv. 23-24: Dame Wisdom herself turns out to be more bitter than death. Wisdom personified, in her own way, is as seductive as the 'strange woman' of traditional wisdom. Krüger does not claim that Qoheleth was *not* a misogynist, but endeavours to show that the passage has nothing to do with women per se. This is why he can conclude his article by not excusing Qoheleth's overall attitude: '[according to Qoheleth] one encounters only men on the search for wisdom, and no woman (v. 27f.), not even "Dame Wisdom" (v. 26a)—fortunately (v. 26b), here we are dealing with a questionable product of male fantasy'.[49]

Other texts are relevant to Qoheleth's 'explicit' attitude towards women and contribute, as we shall see, to an overall tone of objectification.[50] First, Qoheleth lists women among a list of vanities by which he attempted to define himself and failed (2.7-11):

of finding wisdom' expressed in 7.23-24 (*La Contestation: Commentaire de l'Ecclésiaste* [Lyon: Cahiers de réveil, 1971], p. 131; as cited in Ellul, *Reason for Being*, p. 199). Maillot makes some further extraordinary remarks: 'Wisdom is inaccessible, and as versatile as a woman… But wisdom is not found with women… Women compel wise men to err…they make them…lose their heads… This is a delightful confession for Qohelet to make: "I have always been taken in"… Furthermore, this entire passage is a direct tribute to love and its power… Qoheleth puts Don Juan on trial here rather than women… This passage amounts to indirect and unconscious… praise of exclusive, monogamous love' (pp. 131, 133, 135). Ellul remarks that he finds 'Maillot's meditation quite remarkable' (p. 199).

48. Krüger, ' "Frau Weisheit" ', p. 402.

49. Krüger, ' "Frau Weisheit" ', p. 403.

50. As Brenner points out, objectification is one of the more subtle tones of the whole book ('Some Observations', pp. 59-60). Similarly, for C. Fontaine, in Qoheleth's world Qoheleth is the 'only true subject', since he never speaks of entering a relationship ('Ecclesiastes', in C.A. Newsom and S.H. Ringe [eds.], *The Women's Bible Commentary* [London: SPCK; Louisville, KY: Westminster/John Knox Press, 1992], pp. 153-55 [154]).

> (7) I acquired menservants and maidservants, and the sons of the
> house were [born] to me; along with heads of cattle and sheep. A
> great deal was mine, more than all who were before me in
> Jerusalem. (8) I also gathered for myself silver and gold, and the
> wealth of kings and the provinces. I got myself male and female
> singers, and the delights of the sons of humanity: concubines and
> concubines![51] (9) And I became great and surpassed all who were
> before me in Jerusalem. Furthermore, my wisdom remained with
> me. (10) All that my eyes sought I did not keep from them. I did
> not withhold my heart from any kind of mirth; for my heart was
> merry from all my toil, and this was my portion from all my toil.
>
> (11) And I considered all the deeds my hands had done and the
> toil in which I had toiled to do it. And behold, everything was
> absurd and a pursuit of wind, and there was no profit under the
> heavens.

While it is perhaps not unusual to list women among a list of
other objects (among the possessions of 'your neighbour', Exod.
20.17 [cf. Deut. 5.21]; or the 'spoil', Judg. 5.30), the rhetorical effect
is clear: women are to be gathered (like sheep and cattle) for the
purpose of appearance and pleasure (2.7-8). Qoheleth's ensuing
experience is, not surprisingly, unsatisfactory in every sense, as
the following verses (10-11) suggest. In other words, women
formed part of the material plunder—among 'all that his eyes
desired' (v. 10)—which in turn formed the basis of his experi-
ment of pleasure announced in 2.1. Qoheleth judged the whole
enterprise a failure, but on the activity of objectification involved
in arriving at his conclusion, he withheld judgment—a 'justifi-
able' means to an end.

Other parts of Qoheleth's text, as Brenner has shown, may
more subtly betray misogyny, even violence. In her close reading
of 3.1-9 she undertakes to discern the gender of the voice
of/behind the text as well as that of the intended audience. Like
the conjectured, fictive author, the voice of the poem is male.
Brenner convincingly draws out threatening overtures, particularly in the central v. 5: 'A time to cast stones and a time to gather

---

51. This difficult and much commented upon *hapax*, שדה ושדות, has, as
Murphy puts it, 'never been satisfactorily explained' (*Ecclesiastes*, p. 17). See
esp. G.A. Barton, *The Book of Ecclesiastes* (repr; ICC; Edinburgh: T. & T.
Clark, 1959 [1908]), pp. 91-92, for a host of options (he eventually settles on
'mistress' or 'concubine').

stones, a time to embrace and a time to refrain from embracing.'
Through the 'rough' handling of such polyvalent BH and MH
symbols as stones (suggesting stoning, grinding [and, by
extension, violent sex], millstone around the neck etc.), women
are 'metaphorized' in a subjective and violent relationship to the
male voice.[52] Although there are perceptibly weak points in her
argument (as she admits),[53] her reading is provocative and
shows how Qoheleth's language is laden with the latent tokens
of a predominantly male culture.[54]

In the much discussed sentiment at 9.9, Qoheleth repeats in
part his attitude of the ch. 2 passage discussed above:

> Enjoy life with a woman whom you love,
>   all the days of your absurd life that he has given you under the sun
>   —all your absurd days.
> For this is your portion in life, and in the toil at which you toil.

Some commentators bring out clearly the element of objectification here. Ogden, for example, says of the woman in 9.9 that
Qoheleth's imperative to his students is that they 'appreciate her
as a divine gift'.[55] Ogden's remark, perhaps unintentionally,
highlights the fact that to Qoheleth the woman is functional and
nothing else (an aspect augmented by the use of עם, 'with'). She
is an allotment, a portion in life (חלקך בחיים), that is measured to
men along with toil, riches and good food (cf. 2.10; 3.22; 5.18,
19).[56] With the notable exception of Lohfink,[57] Qoheleth's

52. A. Brenner, 'M Text Authority in Biblical Love Lyrics: The Case of
Qoheleth 3.1-9 and its Textual Relatives', in A. Brenner and F. van Dijk-
Hemmes, *On Gendering Texts: Female and Male Voices in the Hebrew Bible* (BIS,
1; repr., Leiden: E.J. Brill, 1996 [1993]), pp. 133-63 (143-45).

53. Other points in the poem become far more difficult to establish in
terms of their oppressive quality, and, apart from vv. 2a-b and 5, other
verses 'are not strongly associative' (Brenner, 'M Text Authority', p. 149).

54. Brenner, however, states it more strongly than I would: the poem 'is
chiefly motivated by sex rather than by any other vertex' ('M Text Authority', p. 150).

55. Ogden, *Qoheleth*, p. 153.

56. The negative aspect of this 'portion' I am highlighting is contrary to
Rudman, who thinks that the portion of woman for a man is 'potentially a
positive thing' (Rudman, 'Woman as Divine Agent', p. 421). Strictly from a
male perspective I am sure Qoheleth would have agreed.

57. In Eccl. 9.9, 'Woman is placed in a list along with good food, sweet

'objective' remark goes widely unnoticed.

One problem of the passage is how to translate its first six words: ראה חיים עם־אשה אשר־אהבת, lit. 'see life with a woman whom you love'. 'See' is easy enough to understand as 'enjoy' due to Qoheleth's consistently similar use of the word elsewhere (e.g. 2.1, 24; 3.13; 5.18; 6.6). Some think it easy to understand 'a woman whom you love' as a wife. The problem is that the definite article before 'woman' in the Hebrew is missing here, and in classical Hebrew we would expect the article to indicate that 'wife' is meant. But the wisdom literature *has* no instances of אשה with the article except, as noted above, in Eccl. 7.26. As elsewhere in the wisdom literature, whether this is a woman or a wife depends on the context. Likewise, how readers perceive Qoheleth, as a family man or as a bachelor, for example, is often clearly a motive in the preference of translation. Some do little to hide that motive. Loretz, for example, translates עם־אשה 'with thy wife', following Luther. His motives are made clear when he refutes two other scholars' translation, 'woman' (R. Bartelmus: the kind of love referred to is like marriage anyway; and Lohfink: '"who she is" is not at issue and there is insufficient evidence to solve it anyway'), by stating that the 'Jewish wisdom teachers, who warn against the "alien woman", would have been highly amused at these interpretations of progressive authors'.[58]

Other translations assume that Qoheleth was of a certain disposition towards marriage. Ginsburg held that אשה in 9.9 must mean 'any woman' since it was clear from the context that 'sensual gratification, and not "the enjoyments of the matrimonial state", is here urged'.[59] He goes on to qualify this reading by stating that in ch. 7 Qoheleth 'enjoined moderation' and was basically of sounder mind than in ch. 9, where he has 'reached that point from which he could see no moral government at all...nothing left for man but momentary enjoyment and the gratification of every desire'.[60] In other words, Qoheleth must be

wine, clean clothes and sweet smelling hair oil. She is one of many ways of getting pleasure' (Lohfink, 'War Kohelet ein Frauenfeind?', p. 260; Krüger follows in his assessment, ' "Frau Weisheit" ', pp. 394-95).

58. Loretz, 'Poetry and Prose', p. 188.
59. Ginsburg, *Coheleth*, p. 417.
60. Ginsburg, *Coheleth*, p. 416.

vulgarized into moral bankruptcy for Ginsburg's reading to work. Barton proceeds similarly: the passage 'urges enjoyment with a woman, not the placing of trust in her'.[61] And he goes further: 9.9 constitutes 'a command to embrace whatever woman pleased one, and so gain the "delights of the sons of men" alluded to in $2^{8'}$.[62] Others assume that Qoheleth is more favourably disposed to marriage. For instance, despite the complexity of the context and the possibility of readings, M. Eaton states without argument in relation to 9.9 that 'Marriage is a further help in the midst of the frustrations of life.'[63]

Remembering the suspicion that is easily raised by the use of the quotation theory at the end of ch. 7, it becomes even more dubious when applying the approach to 9.9. The effect of the theory in ch. 7 is invariably to help us to see Qoheleth in a kinder light. Without it Qoheleth would be permitted to remain an uncomplicated 'child of his time', rallying against the 'wicked woman'. But in 9.9, if *Qoheleth* were understood to be saying that a woman is to be enjoyed (a woman who is *not* your wife), the opposite becomes true. He is no longer a traditionalist. A strange interpretive paradigm thereby arises. For example, Loretz uses the quotation theory at ch. 7 to suggest that Qoheleth rejects the negative evaluation of women endorsed by traditional wisdom. But when at 9.9 'thy wife' is insisted upon in order that Qoheleth agree with the 'Jewish wisdom teachers', Qoheleth's perceived conservatism is played off against his misogynism at the expense of logical consistency. Two instances that on the surface convey Qoheleth's shirking of intimacy and responsibility (7.25-29; 9.9), and which could portray Qoheleth as a bigot and a libertine respectively, are transformed into portrayals of liberal minded-ness and conservatism respectively! Eaton similarly illustrates the paradigm by using 9.9 to justify the idea that Qoheleth could not be a misogynist in ch. 7: 'Any accusation of misogyny misses the Preacher's point, as we see from the contrasting picture of married life in 9:9.'[64]

61. Barton, *Ecclesiastes*, p. 148.

62. Barton, *Ecclesiastes*, p. 163.

63. M. Eaton, *Ecclesiastes* (TOTC; Downer's Grove, IL: InterVarsity Press, 1983), p. 128.

64. Eaton, *Ecclesiastes*, p. 116.

I have dwelt on these questions because they are, obviously, pertinent to Qoheleth's attitude to women, at which the purpose of this article is aimed, but they are tired old questions. Therefore, having sketched out ways in which the 'traditional' texts have been used to construct Qoheleth's attitude to women, I would like now to supplement the picture.

II

As to why the womb merits discussion, it is interesting to note that in Ecclesiastes the womb and its cognates (birth etc.) are more frequently touched on than the topic of women proper. So, the question can easily be returned: why has the topic *not* been reviewed? But before continuing, some qualifying remarks are in order.

It is difficult to say whether a certain type of speech or even content of speech is 'genderable'. It is therefore important to avoid the use of such emotive words as 'feminine' to describe an aspect of Qoheleth's language. As Brenner has pointed out, the narrating voice of Ecclesiastes is exclusively male. It is a male outlook and Qoheleth, although his name is a feminine verb form, is a man. Ecclesiastes is what Brenner calls an M text; not a male author, but a text whose transmitting voice is distinctly male.[65] But while the voice is male, some of the content is distinctly female; for talk of the womb is female in that it involves 'the value of practices, processes and modes of being that have been biologically or historically associated with women'.[66] This minimal distinction brings into focus the importance of investigating, along with the more traditional 'explicit' texts, the more peripheral and implicit 'female' language—'modes of being'—with which Qoheleth expressed himself.

In the history of Western literature the 'womb' and its synonyms (e.g. Heb. 'a full belly'), it has been argued, have signified a rich host of ideas from mystery to profanity. Even today

65. The distinction is necessary since some texts written by men have a female voice and vice versa; see Brenner, in Brenner and van Dijk-Hemmes, *Gendering Texts*, esp. pp. 6-7.

66. M. Raphael, *Thealogy and Embodiment: The Post-Patriarchal Reconstruction of Female Sacrality* (Sheffield: Sheffield Academic Press, 1996), p. 16.

'womb' can call to mind anything from a hospital to a sense of religious awe. Men have brought their own unique, if often negative, perspective to the 'womb'. M. Raphael, referring to Simone de Beauvoir, suggests that men in 'high' civilizations, for example, have tended to see themselves as gods who have fallen 'from the brightness of an infinite heaven into the mud of the female earth. The womb then signifies a prison, cave or abyss from which a man's birth marks the beginning of his death.'[67] Rosemary Ruether suggested that the womb may even be linked to the history of the subordination of women in that men have felt alienated from 'the great mysteries of gestation and birth', and hence have subordinated women in an attempt to compensate.[68] For Raphael, the womb is 'metaphorically and actually the central locus of female sacral power'.[69] But that power, when we get to the Hebrew Bible, has gone from sacred originator to 'unclean place...subject to taboos and purificatory rites'. And in Old Testament stories, 'God's will is carved in the seed or sperm; the matriarch's wombs are simply vehicles.'[70] Similarly, at least in Job, that a man comes from the womb means that he cannot achieve purity, while more ironically it means that while there is hope for him, there is none for the true possessor of the womb.[71]

There are three texts I will consider in relation to the womb. The first is 5.13-17:

> (13) There is a grievous ill I observed under the sun: riches were stored up by their owner to his own harm. (14) But those riches were destroyed in a bad venture. And he had a son, and there was nothing for his hand. (15) Just as [that man] came from his mother's womb, naked he shall return, going as he came, and he will not take anything from his toil that he carries in his hand. This too is a grievous ill: (16) precisely as he came, so shall he go; and what profit has he from toiling for the wind? (17) Indeed, he

67. Raphael, *Thealogy and Embodiment*, p. 57.
68. Cited in Raphael, *Thealogy and Embodiment*, p. 65.
69. Raphael, *Thealogy and Embodiment*, p. 133.
70. Raphael, *Thealogy and Embodiment*, pp. 65, 272.
71. So Lillian R. Klein, 'Job and the Womb: Text about Men, Subtext about Women', in Brenner (ed.), *A Feminist Companion to Wisdom Literature* , pp. 186-200 (199). Interestingly, Job claims to 'own' the womb when it suits him (p. 198; see Job 19.7).

> consumes all his days in darkness and great vexation, and sick-
> ness and resentment.

The person Qoheleth 'observes' here was in a business deal gone
horribly wrong. He has a son, the most eminent blessing
for which he could hope, but with nothing to pass on that
blessing becomes a curse. The state in which he enters the world
illustrates, for Qoheleth, the depravity of human striving: naked
and materially bankrupt. The observation is saved from mind-
numbing ordinariness by the connection to the man's departure.
This is 'you can't take it with you' with a vengeance. Even what
little he carries in his hand is made meaningless by death, for it
will die with him since there is no son to carry it farther.
Remembering the connections to Genesis that have been made, it
is worth noting that the state of nakedness (*having* nothing) is
absurd to Qoheleth. It is the stark opposite of one of his few
instances of joy (9.8; linked to woman in 9.9). It is not what he
expects in that one works under the curse of toil seemingly to
'gather' and 'collect' (cf. Eccl. 2.8, 26; 3.5) and expects to have
something of intrinsic worth, that is, something that cannot be
taken away. As the author of Wisdom recognized as well, neither the status, such as Qoheleth's, of king, nor any other status,
enables escape from this 'tainted' way in and out of the world:
'For no king has had a different beginning of existence; there is
for all one entrance into life, and one way out' (Wis. 7.5-6).[72]

The commentaries point us to Job 1.21 for a ready parallel.
After Job has suffered an *absurd* loss (an undeserved loss), he
tears his robes and says, 'Naked I came from my mother's womb
and naked I will return. The Lord gave and the Lord has taken
away.' Job's is a statement of belief while Qoheleth's is a statement of plain fact. For Job it is even an act of worship (1.21b-22),
whereas for Qoheleth it comes after a section in which God is
both distant and to be unhealthily feared (5.1-6). The womb has
become, for Qoheleth, a harbinger of death. That which has
given life will take it. Qoheleth was *born* into absurdity and, like
the quality of wisdom (inaccessible), he has not asked for it
to be so. On the contrary, even here he is made ill from his

72. Other notable occurrences of the image of going forth from the
womb (יצא מבטן אמו) occur in Job 1.21, 3.11, 38.29 and Isa. 46.3.

confrontation with that absurdity. And although compared to Job's formulation Qoheleth's comments may strike us as shallow or materialistic,[73] the depth comes from the womb being somehow implicated in his lament, for he clearly sees it to be bound up with the structure of an unjust and painfully bewildering world. Unlike Job's references to mother earth and the more cosmic notions of the womb found elsewhere (cf. 2 Esd. 4.38-42; 16.38), Qoheleth's 'problem' with the womb is earthly and bound to human experience. The womb is the matrix through which is delivered a sorrowful inheritance (cf. Eccl. 1.12).

The second text, 6.3-5, is thematically connected to the first:

> (3) If a man begets one hundred children, and lives many years, though many be the days of his years, and his soul is not satisfied by [these] good [things]—and indeed, there is no burial for him—I said, 'The stillborn child is better off than he.' (4) For in absurdity it came and in darkness it shall go, and in darkness its name is covered. (5) [And] although it has not seen the sun, or understood it, it finds rest rather than he.

Here is a man whose loins have been prolific, has lived to a good age and yet has no *real* satisfaction in life (cf. 4.8; 5.10). The notion that it was better not to have been born than to have lived at all was expressed frequently in antiquity.[74] Even Qoheleth has expressed it elsewhere in the book (4.2-3; cf. 7.1). But what does it mean that the stillborn actually finds rest, an idea that Gordis described as 'obvious to the point of banality'?[75] And, as

73. So G. Vall: Qoheleth at 5.15, in contradistinction to Job 1.21, 'does not encourage the reader to further "contemplate the likeness" of womb and tomb or of birth and death' ('The Enigma of Job 1,21a', *Bib* 76 [1995], pp. 325-42 [340]); cf. the parallel idea in Ps. 49.17: 'For when they die they [the rich] will carry nothing away; their wealth will not go down after them' (compare 1 Tim. 6.7). This is again contrary to Job who in 1.21, according to Vall, 'is either vowing to remain in a state of mourning…or he is anticipating the decay of his own skin and flesh in the tomb—or both' (pp. 334-35).

74. For examples, see D.J.A. Clines, *Job 1–20* (WBC, 17; Dallas, TX: Word Books, 1989), pp. 89-90; and cf. Job 3.11, 16-18; 10.18-19; 2 Esd. 5.35. Interestingly, such an untimely birth (נֶפֶל), who will never see the sun, is in Ps. 58.8 (9) likened to a curse, an idea reversed here in Qoheleth.

75. Gordis, *Koheleth*, p. 249. He argues that rest (נחת) here simply means

Whybray points out, *how* could a foetus experience anything anyway,[76] for, its name (its memory) is covered in darkness? Qoheleth now affirms that the failure not to come out of the womb (birth; cf. Job 3.11; 31.18) means rest. There is a progression, then, from the first text. The coming and going from and to the womb is now more directly clothed in absurdity and darkness. The 'rest' of the stillborn is not an experience but consists of a peaceful *lack* of experience; for it is precisely the overload of experience that has oppressed Qoheleth elsewhere. In other words, there is something redemptive about *staying* in the place of origin, having never to return to it empty handed.

The third and perhaps most important of our texts is 11.5:

> Just as you do not understand the way of the life-breath in the formation of bones in the womb[77] (בבטן המלאה), so too you do not understand the activity of God who does everything.

The place of the womb, and the acknowledgment of its mystery, is chosen to convey one of Qoheleth's most fundamental tenets: the inscrutability of the divine will. If elsewhere in the Hebrew Bible antagonism towards women is rooted in the fact that men cannot accept that they do not participate in the mystery of the creative act of gestation and birth (in which God's will is present; cf. Ps. 139), then Qoheleth could perhaps be a chief perpetrator of that antagonism. Here is a plausible root, then, to Qoheleth's anger—he is devastated throughout by the fact of this inscrutability, and that fact is inextricably linked to women.

Perhaps there is *something* redemptive in Qoheleth's use of the womb in that he represents a break with tradition. His advice is to accept mystery, and that is the point of 11.5: just as you cannot know the mystery of the womb, so you cannot know (as Qoheleth discovered through failure) the mystery of God. In

satisfaction: the stillborn had greater satisfaction because it had 'no knowledge or exposure'. Similarly, see Barton, *Ecclesiastes*, p. 130.

76. Whybray, *Ecclesiastes*, p. 106.

77. The MT has 'as you do not understand the way of the life-breath, so [you do not understand] the formation of bones in the womb, so too you do not understand the activity of God...' The extra comparison is unnecessary if we read, following most commentators and translations, כעצמים (*as the* [formation of] bones) as בעצמים (*in the* [formation of] bones). See esp. Gordis, *Koheleth*, p. 322.

other words, do not even attempt to understand it; that may lead to the kind of frustration that is taken out on women, and is witnessed in ch. 7. And so he may be dealing with the root of female profanization. Furthermore, if the stillborn is better off remaining in the place of its origin, it has escaped the curse of death and toil and it has in this way been redeemed (cf. 1 Tim. 2.15). But even this smacks of excuse-making by assuming a sophisticated strategy of redemption that readers subsequently must fashion for themselves.

Some have remarked upon Qoheleth's obsessions with female anatomy and, by extension, sexual gratification (cf. Gordis's comment above, pp. 117-18). On the surface only 2.8 and 9.9 seem to offer any case for that. But when we consider the womb texts as well, it may be that Qoheleth, as Klein says of Job, exhibits a 'preoccupation with female reproductive powers', and his 'suppressed interest in woman's sexual functions discloses a significant fissure in the overt male concerns about righteousness'.[78] Furthermore, in Job, 'Woman is so identified with childbearing [and nothing else] that she may vanish in the image: the womb frequently becomes a synecdoche for woman, with woman "disappearing" in the anatomical part'.[79] For Qoheleth the case is the same, if more subtle, in that on the surface (at *least* on the surface) of the texts reviewed in the first section he denigrates woman plainly, while elsewhere she is silenced except for her anatomy. She is at once the recipient of lingual abuse and the cipher of the absurd.

III

Theories abound as to *why* Qoheleth said what he said. Qoheleth was speaking in the guise of King Solomon when he described his search for a (pleasing?) woman among a thousand concubines.[80] Or, 'Qoheleth was almost surely a bachelor, and was

78. Klein, 'Job and the Womb', p. 200.
79. Klein, 'Job and the Womb', p. 197.
80. Ellul (*Reason for Being*, p. 202), F. Zimmermann (*The Inner World of Qohelet* [New York: Ktav, 1973], p. 86) and Barton (*Ecclesiastes*, p. 147) all suggest a general Solomonic context. I offer a 'Solomonic approach' to the passage in *A Time to Tell*, chapter 6.1. Interestingly, Elizabeth Cady Stanton,

certainly no apologist for the marriage institution.'[81] On the other hand, Zimmermann argues that Qoheleth *was* married, for the image of a 'full womb' (11.5) occurred to him and he denounced women bitterly, a practice that could only come from 'one who has experienced marriage with that kind of wife'![82] Similarly, Garret suggests that the ch. 7 passage, *'from a man's perspective,* describes the miseries of the domestic relationship' (italics his).[83] Barton thought that a 'bitter personal experience' underlies the passage in ch. 7.[84] Lohfink elaborates his theory on Qoheleth's personal life with admirable detail:

> [Qoheleth's comments in ch. 7 come] from the vocabulary of a closed male culture. This is the way men talk among themselves, when, for instance, they are told one of their number is going to get married. In those circumstances someone quotes a similar saying and everyone laughs about it. Psychologists might be interested in the significance of that sort of thing.[85]

Lohfink works with a very clear psychological portrait of the speaker. Whybray offers a different, perhaps more balanced view:

> It has…been alleged, on very flimsy evidence, that Qoheleth was that very rare phenomenon among the Jews of the Old Testament period, a bachelor, and even a misogynist. This notion is based mainly on a single very obscure passage, 7.23-29, which is certainly capable of being interpreted as expressing contempt or hatred of women in general, but is also capable of other interpretations. Against it has to be set the passage (9.7-10) in which Qoheleth includes the companionship of a beloved woman or

writing at a time when Solomonic authorship was still widely accepted, remarked of 7.26-29 that 'Solomon must have had a sad experience in his relations with women. Such an opinion is a group reflection on his own mother, who was so devoted to his success in the world. But for her ambition he would never have been crowned King of Israel' (*The Woman's Bible* [2 vols.; Edinburgh: Polygon Books, 1985 (1898)], II, pp. 99-100).

   81. Gordis, *Koheleth*, p. 296. Cf. Ginsburg's comments above, p. 124.
   82. Zimmermann, *Inner World*, pp. 2-3.
   83. Garrett, 'Ecclesiastes 7.25-29', p. 318.
   84. Barton, *Ecclesiastes*, p. 148.
   85. Lohfink, 'War Kohelet ein Frauenfeind?', p. 279; Baltzer follows, 'Women and War', p. 128.

wife among the pleasures of life. All these theories about the nature of the man Qoheleth are attempts to discover what we are in fact not told.[86]

Whybray's implicit warning should be heeded.

Along with psychological portraits, it helps readers little that in confronting Qoheleth's attitude commentators offer explanation after explanation of how, for example: Qoheleth quoted; Qoheleth was referring to warplay (if he was he could have done so more clearly!); Qoheleth was rather harsh on men too, so it's excusable; Qoheleth was a lad, give 'em a break. In other words, Qoheleth must *be seen to be* what we think he should be.

For some the case is clear (so Fox: 'Qohelet remains a misogynist').[87] But even when the case is clearly *for* misogynism, there are qualifications. Most are along the lines of, 'the wisdom teachers were certainly aware that not every woman was a blessing'.[88] In 1898 Elizabeth Cady Stanton stated well why women feel unable to accept such soothing mollifications warmly:

> The commentators vouchsafe the opinion [for example] that there are more good women than men. It is very kind…of the commentators to give us a word of praise now and then; but from the general tone of the learned fabulists, one would think that the Jezebels and the Jaels predominated. In fact, Solomon says that he has not found one wise woman in a thousand.[89]

And here is where Qoheleth's text runs aground as well: the 'general tone'. Qoheleth remains unclear in his motives, and the simple fact that he said what he said is all that remains. And it is difficult to assume the best. We cannot really fathom, for example, that someone would speak positively of an object of which not one in a thousand could be found, especially when we say such things as 'you're one in a million' or 'you're a star' in positive contexts! At least in our common vernacular that failure to discover a woman will succeed in offending a feminist sensibility. When one speaks of the Bible's affect on the reader one does not (can not!) really mean a close reading of the Hebrew that

86. R.N. Whybray, *Ecclesiastes* (OTG; Sheffield: JSOT Press, 1989), p. 22.

87. *Qohelet and his Contradictions*, p. 238; similarly Barton, *Ecclesiastes*, pp. 147-48.

88. Fox and Porten, 'Unsought Discoveries', p. 32.

89. Cady Stanton, *The Woman's Bible*, II, p. 100.

unearths a reference to war, or a veiled reference to woman wisdom. Instead, one must mean the tone. The simple fact of 'woman is more bitter than death' stares us in the face. Even if we could stretch that to mean 'woman is stronger than death', millions of Bibles in hundreds of translations say otherwise. In other words, when it comes to tone and the naked power of language, what readings are feasible is what matters.

Despite the plain offensiveness of Qoheleth's text, at least two feminists have found in Qoheleth's thought a model for feminist action. Esther Reed, in her article, 'Whither Postmodernism and Feminist Theology?',[90] has suggested that Qoheleth's is an 'irregular discourse' to which feminist theology can look to help to form its agenda. Feminists can turn to Qoheleth because 'the only kind of feminist theology which can survive in the post-modern era speaks from the margins', and, like Ecclesiastes, is a type of wisdom that is 'eccentric' (p. 18). The condition for reading Qoheleth 'in the postmodern context of feminism is its thematic statement of vanity' (p. 19). Qoheleth informs feminist theology by propagating what Reed calls a 'performative function of memory' from which feminist theologians can learn (p. 23). Furthermore, Qoheleth's views on time are creatively applied to the need for feminist theology to 'discern the moment' of its crisis and to act accordingly for the future—in the proper time (pp. 25-28). Like Reed, Carole Fontaine, in her contribution to *The Women's Bible Commentary*, picks up on the same positive potential to sanction a movement dedicated to overturning orthodox male hierarchies.[91] This paradoxical shift of power (oppressive text to liberation text) highlights again the power of Qoheleth's language and overall strategy of subversion. Qoheleth's 'feminist' potential is cast against/over his likely misogynistic sentiments. Perhaps the scenario is best described as ironic, the kind of irony that brings a knowing smile to the corners of the mouth. However, for those whom I have reviewed above who suggest that Qoheleth could not possibly be a misogynist, the irony is lost. This is the kind of irony created when

90. Esther D. Reed, 'Whither Postmodernism and Feminist Theology?', *Feminist Theology* 6 (1994), pp. 15-29.

91. I note here that Carole Fontaine has recently indicated to me in personal correspondence that she would no longer hold to this view.

Qoheleth's story is taken at least at face value: 'I found woman more bitter than death.'

Finally, then, the title of this essay comes into context. Psychological portraits, explanations and the readerly dilemma created by Qoheleth's language I have just suggested, all point to an anxious paradox in Ecclesiastes. Qoheleth has been made an 'old boy'—'married' to the old stock of wisdom's trade—by those who read his text plainly (e.g. Barton, Fontaine, Fox, Ginsburg, myself[?]); and made a 'new man' by those who insist that Qoheleth somehow managed to avoid participation in the oppression of his age (e.g. Eaton, Ellul, Garrett, Lohfink, Loretz). The 'old boy' school is far less susceptible to being accused of fitting Qoheleth into a mould for their own reading strategies. But perhaps that can be put down to a lack of boldness, for the readings of the 'new man' school provide valuable confrontations that, in the helpful words of John M.G. Barclay (although concerning another matter altogether), 'force us to re-examine the consensus and test whether it rests on a secure basis'.[92]

Qoheleth's remarks in ch. 7 were used in the fifteenth-century Inquisitor's witch-hunting manual, *Malleus Maleficarum*, 'to sanction torture of women accused of witchcraft'.[93] While such an abuse of the text is hardly evidence in itself of inherent misogyny, it does lay bare the power of Qoheleth's emotive language—one which seemingly lies in wait to be 'exploited' for suppression (*Malleus*) or liberation (Reed, Fontaine); 'old boy' or

92. John M.G. Barclay, describing radical theories—which he regards to be dubious but valuable—that attempt to rethink the slavery situation in Philemon, in *Colossians and Philemon* (NTG; Sheffield: Sheffield Academic Press, 1997), p. 99.

93. So Fontaine, 'Ecclesiastes', p. 154. I have been unable to acquire the text but found the following interesting remark at the Malaspina University-College website: 'According to York University Social Science researcher Peter Paolucci, the misogyny in the Malleus is arguably the most blunt and extensive attack against women in western civilization. The Malleus "observed" that Midwives offered newborns to the devil at birth. Women's "venereal delectation...is of a weaker sort". Citing Ecclesiastes, the Malleus notes that, "...a woman knows no moderation in goodness or vice". "Devils do these things through the medium of women"' (Russell McNeil, 'Vindication of the Rights of Women: Mary Wollstonecraft, 1792' [www.mala.bc.ca/~mcneil/vinda.txt, 26 September, 1996]).

'new man'. The author of *Malleus* had the easy task of adapting a ready-made language for its purpose. Reed and Fontaine, on the other hand, somehow divorce the image of Qoheleth the misogynist from the image of Qoheleth the freethinker in order to make use of the Qoheleth they need most. That 'divorce' is perhaps made easy by the fact that, as regards those issues that he discussed the most (particularly the acquisition of knowledge), Qoheleth broke away radically from so much of what we have constructed to be the 'old boy' school (i.e. the world-view epitomized by Proverbs). In other words, the explanation that Qoheleth was simply 'a child of his time' does not satisfy the desire to make our radical picture of Qoheleth complete. We expect more from the Bible's great sceptic.

'MANY DEVICES'(QOHELETH 7.23–8.1): QOHELETH, MISOGYNY
AND THE *MALLEUS MALEFICARUM*

Carole R. Fontaine

As I was conducting a training session on the topic of 'Women in the Biblical Wisdom Traditions' for lay Sunday school teachers, male and female, of the United Church of Christ, the following interchange, termed 'proverb performance'[1] in paroemiological studies, occurred. The subject was a 'hot' one: not only had biblical scholars been rediscovering the implications of the female personification of Woman/Lady Wisdom and her wicked twin, Woman Stranger/Lady Folly for the study of women's roles in 'ancient Israel', but significant leakage of such inquiries into the area of New Testament theology had begun to occur.[2] Not only was 'Sophia' Christology coming to the forefront as a feminist re-reading of the early traditions of the Jesus Movement, but that very fact had begun to spawn counter-groups within several

1.   The meaningful transmission of a 'proverbial' statement in a social interaction to provide an evaluation or reinterpretation of a situation, especially one involving conflict by persons or groups of different status. The 'proverb' acts as a traditional authority which shields its lower status user from the implications of the point of view just raised. For a discussion of this linguistic interaction in the Hebrew Bible, see Carole R. Fontaine, 'Proverb Performance in the Hebrew Bible', reprinted in David J.A. Clines (ed.), *The Poetical Books: A Sheffield Reader* (The Biblical Seminar, 41; Sheffield: Sheffield Academic Press, 1997), pp. 316-32.

2.   Susan Cady, Marian Ronan and Hal Taussig, *Wisdom's Feast: Sophia in Study and Celebration* (San Francisco: Harper & Row, 1989); Robert Wilckens (ed.), *Aspects of Wisdom in Judaism and Early Christianity* (Notre Dame: Notre Dame University, 1975); Claudia Camp, *Wisdom and the Feminine in the Book of Proverbs* (Bible and Literature, 11; Sheffield: Almond Press, 1985). For an extensive bibliography on Sophia and Christology see Cady, Ronan and Taussig, *Wisdom's Feast*, p. 215 n. 5.

Christian denominations, including the UCC, claiming that such Christologies constituted a modern heresy to be put down at all costs. Hence, into such a mixture, it seemed good to place some actual reflection on the foundational texts themselves before jumping to any ecclesial conclusions about their meaning for modern followers of the New Testament.

The Interaction Situation: Why Quote a Folk Saying?

After a general background on the multiple origins of the wisdom tradition—from concrete tribal problem solving to the elite, abstract productions of bureaucracies and schools of scribes—we began to delve into a close reading of Proverbs 1–9 and Proverbs 31, texts which contain both positive and negative stereotypical reflections on the subject of the female, cosmic and human. Moving from there to texts that had received less attention by the Sophia-Christology groups, we began looking at the distinctively *un*flattering passages to be found in Qoheleth and Ben Sira, where it seemed that the dignity and value of Cosmic Woman Wisdom was inversely proportional to that of *real, human* women. In general, we agreed with scholars like Camp and others that while negative evaluations of females in Proverbs were usually limited to *certain kinds of females* (the loose, garrulous, nagging, adulterous, idolatrous, foreign, seductive females who give content to the characterization of Woman Stranger), by the time of the later sages it appeared as though *all females* were being lumped into a single, negative category. This trend might be explained by reference to the strong influence of classical Hellenistic and Greco-Roman dualism, or to the changing social circumstances of Judah under Persian home rule, or later domination by harsh invading groups bent on imperialist expansion in first Hellenistic and finally Roman Judea.

Under such circumstances two impulses might be discerned in the literature produced. The first is an apologetic desire to respond to the challenges of Greek philosophy by recasting Hebrew wisdom into the categories and discourse of one's supposedly culturally 'advanced' conquerors. This could be done either by showing that Wisdom (equivalent to Torah in Ben Sira) was *superior* to that of one's conquerors (Ben Sira), or by suggesting that Hebrew Wisdom was sufficiently *similar* to classical philosophy, that it could naturally and suitably be reframed as a concurrent rather than competing tradition (Wisdom of Solomon). In the former case, it was a natural move to bring the 'category' of 'woman' into harmony with the surrounding philosophical traditions, which were largely negative in tone, although paradoxically, elite women were achieving more social prominence and power in the later periods (Hellenistic through Roman). These social gains may have spurred on the conservatism and misogyny of the classical and biblical writers of late antiquity.[3] Add to this the later effects of Roman misogyny propagated throughout its empire during the very time from which some of our texts come and the recipe for the symbolic and literal exclusion of women from consideration as full human beings is complete.[4]

The second impulse behind the learned misogyny of the sages under political domination grew up more as a survival strategy. While the ancestor stories of Genesis and 'early' Israel are notable for their positive evaluations of the crucial roles women might play in Salvation History, during the later time of foreign domination, our sages may have been anxious to differentiate the conduct of *their* women from those of the surrounding cultures, as yet another way to reinscribe 'difference' and social control.[5] When exercise of control in the political, 'public' domain

3.   Sarah B. Pomeroy, *Goddesses, Whores, Wives, and Slaves: Women in Classical Antiquity* (New York: Schocken Books, 1975), pp. 92-189; *idem, Women in Hellenistic Egypt From Alexander to Cleopatra* (New York: Schocken Books, 1984). As always, possibilities open to women in the 'public domain' varied by social class and status. For selections of classical and clerical misogynist texts, see Alcuin Blamires (ed.), *Woman Defamed and Woman Defended: An Anthology of Medieval Texts* (Oxford: Clarendon Press, 1992), pp. 17-98.

4.   Luise Schottroff, *Lydia's Impatient Sisters: A Feminist Social History of Early Christianity* (trans. Barbara and Martin Rumscheidt; Louisville, KY: Westminster/John Knox Press, 1991), p. 77.

5.   Warren Trenchard concludes that Ben Sira is 'personally negative' towards women, since he reworks positive traditional material from Proverbs in such a way as to render it negative in tone (*Ben Sira's View of Women: A Literary Analysis* [BJS, 38; Chico, CA: Scholars Press, 1982],

is denied the patriarchal male, a compensatory mechanism is required. In the case of the later wisdom period and the postexilic period in general, this took the form of close control of the household and its residents.[6] Growing concern in this area leads to a fixation on mixed marriages, dietary, ritual observance and inheritance laws, all of which provide an enhanced sense of control over one's life, at least at the private level. Clearly, since females are required in the process of getting a son for inheritance of land critical to family survival, in the preparation of foods, the performance of household religious observances, and were key players in interracial/'interfaith' marriages, the compulsive need to control their sexuality becomes part of the male response to a specific social predicament.[7] Male honor required no less than an obsessive preoccupation with the sources of female shame, that is, sexuality.[8] It was against this background

pp. 167-73); see also Claudia V. Camp, 'Understanding a Patriarchy: Women in Second Century Jerusalem Through the Eyes of Ben Sira', in A.-J. Levine (ed.), *'Women Like This': New Perspectives on Jewish Women in the Greco-Roman World* (SBL Early Judaism and its Literature, 1; Atlanta: Scholars Press, 1991), pp. 3-39; 'Honor and Shame in Ben Sira: Anthropological and Theological Reflections', paper read at the First International Conference on Ben Sira, Soesterberg, the Netherlands, July 28-31, 1996; and 'Honor, Shame and the Hermeneutics of Ben Sira's Ms C', in Michael Barré (ed.), ' "*Wisdom, You are My Sister!*": *Studies in Honor of Roland E. Murphy, O. Carm., on the Occasion of His 80th Birthday* (CBQMS, 29; Washington: Catholic Biblical Association, 1997), pp. 157-71.

6.   Tamara C. Eskenazi, 'Out from the Shadows: Biblical Women in the Post-Exilic Era', in Athalya Brenner (ed.), *A Feminist Companion to Samuel and Kings* (FCB, 5; Sheffield: Sheffield Academic Press, 1994), pp. 252-71.

7.   It may also have been the case that females were at special risk of sexual exploitation by the various overlords of Judah and Judea. For a grisly example, examine a coin minted in the region about three years before the fall of Masada (70 CE): a Roman soldier looms over a prone Jewess, while the legend reads 'Judea Capta'. Rape is often a 'symbol' for imperialist conquest, suggesting that the actual practice of rape under such circumstances was, if not customary, at least commonplace (Susan Brooks Thistlethwaite, ' "You May Enjoy the Spoil of Your Enemies": Rape as a Biblical Metaphor for War', *Semeia* 61(1993), pp. 59-78).

8.   For a general introduction to the categories of honor and shame in biblical literature, see Victor H. Matthews, Don C. Benjamin and Claudia

of shifting cultural paradigms for 'faithfulness' to one's tradition that the vicious evaluations of womankind were to be understood, I suggested. Always grateful for a 'way out' of having to disagree with or challenge the Bible's views, the readers/hearers responded positively…until we actually opened to Qoh. 7.23-8.1a:[9]

> 23 All this I have tested by wisdom; I said, 'I will be wise'; but it was far from me. 24 That which is, is far off, and deep, very deep; who can find it out? 25 I turned my mind to know and to search out and to seek wisdom and the sum of things, and to know the wickedness of folly and the foolishness which is madness. 26 And I found more bitter than death the woman whose heart is snares and nets, and whose hands are fetters; he who pleases God escapes her, but the sinner is taken by her. 27 Behold, this is what I found, says the Preacher, adding one thing to another to find the sum, 28 which my mind has sought repeatedly, but I have not found. One man among a thousand I found, but a woman among all these I have not found. 29 Behold, this alone I found, that God made man upright, but they have sought out many devices. 8.1 Who is like the wise man? And who knows the interpretation of a thing? (RSV)

Before she could be 'shushed' by her elders, a young woman in her twenties called out from the back of the room, 'Them's fightin' words!'

This was a classic occasion of proverb performance by the young woman.[10] Although she disagreed with *both* the text *and*

Camp (eds.), *Honor and Shame in the World of the Bible,* (Semeia, 68; Atlanta, GA; Scholars Press, 1994).

9.   We use the RSV translation here as that was the text to which our young reader responded. Some scholars begin this passage at v. 25; we choose to add in vv. 23-24, since the identity of the referent there is included in some modern readers' attempts to mitigate the misogyny of Qoheleth's great findings (Thomas Krüger, ' 'Frau Weisheit' in Koh 7, 26?', *Bib* 73 (1993), pp. 394-403.

10.   In an Interaction, X (female Sunday School teacher, low status) says to Y (female Bible 'expert', high status), 'Just as A equals B in this proverb ('them's', A = 'fightin' words', B), so C (Qoheleth 7:23-8:1) equals D ('fightin' words') in this context!' The user of the proverb is concealed behind its traditional authority; the correlation of terms A, C = B, D with a negative evaluation associated with Y (and *not* X!) is typical of twentieth–century proverb performance. In modern contexts, proverb users almost always

the validity of my scholarly attempts to nuance it, she herself did not have the specialized training or the social power needed to challenge the 'expert'. Further, though relations are often strained, it may be that she had no wish to discomfit the learned speaker out of bonds of common sisterhood—how often does a woman expert speak on the Bible in the world of the Church, after all? In such a multifaceted interaction, she chose to let 'tradition' speak and offer the challenge.[11] As it happened, I agreed wholeheartedly with her proverbial assessment of this piece of traditional wisdom, enshrined as 'authoritative' due to its inclusion in 'Holy Scripture'. Though I might offer many ways of understanding the background of these misogynist passages, I could not displace the 'plain sense' being conveyed by the anti-female sentiments expressed. Further, I began to wonder how the Christian community had heard such texts in the past, and the impact of those responses on the lives of actual women (e.g. had Qoheleth's words *always* been perceived as 'fightin' words'? Were they 'performed' by the community on *behalf of* women and their dignity, or used to denigrate the female sex? Were/are they perceived as generalities which may not apply in specific situations, or as universals which always hold true?). The following study is in many ways a response to that young woman, and takes her characterization seriously in choice of method: we will fight these passages with words…

apply positive proverbs to themselves or their own evaluations of a situation, whereas negatives are applied to their opponents in the interaction.

11. The verbal context which usually evokes this proverbial response might be characterized as gendered 'trash talk', often in the form of shaming remarks about one's female relatives. These ritualized exchanges are still frequent and customary in military and sporting contexts (e.g. between offensive and defensive linemen before the snap of a football in order to lure the opponent 'offsides'). Similar 'fightin' words' may also be used *by* men to shame other men into acting in accordance with male codes: see the statements by the Philistine army in 1 Sam. 4.9, before the battle of Shiloh, which they win after originally losing heart: 'Take courage, and be men, O Philistines, in order not to become slaves to the Hebrews as they have been to you; be men and fight!' Similar men-to-men proverbial usages in war are recorded in Hittite texts from LBA Anatolia (O.R. Gurney, *The Hittites*, [Harmondsworth: Penguin Books, rev. edn, 1981], pp. 180-81).

Establishing the 'Plain Sense' in Qoheleth 7.25–8.1a

The Context Investigated

The passage under discussion is in many ways typical of Qoheleth's preferred style of discourse (experiential 'tests'; citation and contradiction;[12] tallying up of examples and statement of conclusions) and is linked by keywords to many of the catch-phrases already encountered in the book (seek/find; wisdom/folly; straight, wicked, 'see', etc.). There is, however, no denying that the text bristles with grammatical difficulties and/or ambiguities which render the search for its 'plain sense' almost as difficult as Qoheleth's search for deep Wisdom.[13] The King James Version, with its technique of indicating ellipses by setting off interpolated words in italics, gives the reader in English a taste of the problems:

> 23 All this have I proved by wisdom: I said, I will be wise; but it *was* far from me. 24 That which is far off, and exceeding deep, who can find it out? 25 I applied mine heart to know, and to search, and to seek out wisdom, and the reason *of things,* and to know the wickedness of folly, even of foolishness *and* madness: 26 And I find more bitter than death the woman, whose heart *is* snares and nets, *and* her hands *as* bands: whoso pleaseth God shall escape from her; but the sinner shall be taken by her. 27 Behold, this have I found, saith the preacher, *counting* one by one, to find out the account: 28 Which yet my soul seeketh, but I find not: one man among a thousand have I found; but a woman among all those have I not found. 29 Lo, this only have I found, that God hath made man upright; but they have sought out many inventions. 8.1a Who *is* as the wise *man?* and who knoweth the interpretation of a thing?[14]

---

12. Even the acceptance of this penchant in interpretation still leaves the reader to puzzle out what is being cited and whether it is being affirmed or disputed.

13. As one commentator wryly notes, 'Our difficulties are many' (Graham Ogden, *Qoheleth* [Sheffield: JSOT Press, 1987], p. 120).

14. סבותי אני ולבי לדעת ולתור ובקש חכמה וחשבון ולדעת רשע כסל והסכלות

7.25: הוללות ומוצא אני מר־ממות את האשה אשר־היא מצודים וחרמים לבה אסורים

7.26: ידיה טוב לפני האלהים ימלט ממנה וחוטא ילכד בה

7.27 ראה זה מצאתי אמרה קהלת אחת לאחת למצא חשבון

7.28: אשר עודבקשה נפשי ולא מצאתי אדם אחד מאלף מצאתי ואשה בכל־אלה לא מצאתי

Referents and antecedents are not always clear (what *or who* exactly is 'far off and deep' in v. 24? To what does the *'this'* in v. 27 refer?), nor are the connections between some clauses and main verbs;[15] a piling up of double accusatives in v. 25b ('wickedness *of* folly' or 'wickedness *and* folly'; 'foolishness *and* madness' or 'foolishness *which is* madness'?) leads to a variety of difficulties and translation possibilities. Syntactic obscurity routinely leads modern scholars to redivide consonants,[16] reconstruct from Syriac and the LXX, and repoint the vowels as needed, as well as adopting other stratagems (positing Aramaisms in v. 29 or new Hebrew roots like מרר for 'strong' instead of 'bitter' in v. 26) to render meaning from the sage's musings.[17]

Even where syntax is not peculiar, it is often difficult to know just what the writer is referring to: what kind of wisdom did the sage achieve, if he also says it was beyond him? What, then, is supposed to be the great finding (Hebrew *ḥešbôn*, or the sum of one's calculations) of this sage who is not wise[18] (and if the latter is really the case, then why are we listening?)? That women are, at worst, dangerous; at best, ambivalent, from the point of view of men? *All* women or just a certain type? Or is this what he has *not* found? No wonder this sage begins and ends his essays on the meaning of life by characterizing all as 'vanity'—evanescent, insubstantial, an exhalation of hot air, gone in a moment![19]

לבד ראה־זה מצאתי אשר עשה האלהים את־האדם ישר והמה בקשו חשבנות רבים: 7.29
מי כהחכם ומי יודע פשר דבר 8.1a

15. Is the woman more bitter than death *because* she is snares and nets, or is it 'the woman *whose* heart is snares and nets…', that is, only women of that type? The *'ašer* clause may be interpreted either way (M.V. Fox, *Qoheleth and his Contradictions* [JSOTSup, 71; Sheffield: Almond Press, 1989]), p. 241).

16. Based on supposed *content*?

17. For a summary of linguistic and grammatical considerations, see Fox, *Qoheleth and his Contradictions*, pp. 236-44; R.E. Murphy, *Ecclesiastes* (WBC, 23A; Dallas, TX: Word Books, 1992), pp. 74-75.

18. Michael V. Fox and Bezalel Porten, 'Unsought Discoveries: Qoheleth 7:23-8:1a', *HS* 19 (1978), pp. 32, 34.

19. Unfortunately, the standard effect of Qoheleth's words, whatever the reason for them, have had a longer impact than the male vanity which might be responsible for them, as will be seen in the discussion below.

Grammatical difficulties and their limits to our understanding of the 'plain sense' of the text may not be the only ambiguity a responding reader is up against, as is suggested by the many devices employed in translations by critical commentators. In fact, what we may have in Qoheleth's digressions, uneasy juxtapositions, dangling clauses, and hanging rhetorical questions is not simply or even primarily a disorganized text or compilation of competing traditional teachings, but a *deliberate* use of the 'dialogue' genre to convey content *and* method.[20] Commentators have long posited at least two voices in Qoheleth: that of the sage himself (pretending to be a king in his use of 'royal fiction'), and a pious editor who introduces and ends the book on a note of orthodoxy (12.8-14); others have seen as many as nine different hands adding glosses to resolve contradictions.[21] Beyond that, it has been the fashion to understand that in many sites of contradiction in the text, Qoheleth is deliberately citing a proverb or saying encapsulating traditional wisdom, with which he then argues.[22]

In one of the more ingenious solutions to the problem of contradictions in Qoheleth, T.A. Perry proposes that the sage here allows two sides, 'voices' if you will, of a dialogue on the meaning of life to emerge by letting each position 'have its say'. Thus we hear the words of *K*, a voice in Koheleth which Perry identifies as a 'seeker of experiential knowledge', a greedy Collector of people, things and experiences (Qoheleth 2.4-10), King, Pedagogue and Pessimist. The counterpoint to this voice, 'differentiated by tone and style', intentionally adopted to provide a 'second opinion' before judging life totally worthless, is that of the 'Presenter', 'Antagonist' or 'Arguer'. Perry writes of this

20. See T.A. Perry, *Dialogues with Koheleth: The Book of Ecclesiastes* (University Park, PA: Pennsylvania State University Press, 1993), pp. 3-50, for a compelling solution to the problem of 'voices', contradictions and pessimistic content in Qoheleth. Perry's contribution to the standard 'quotation and argument' interpretive tradition is his view that this is not just a matter of style or content, but a method of pedagogy for the sage who uses it.

21. R.N. Whybray, *Ecclesiastes* (OTG; Sheffield: JSOT Press, 1989), pp. 23-24.

22. The so-called 'zwar-aber Aussage'. See Murphy, *Ecclesiastes*, pp. xxxii-xli, for a full discussion of critical theories regarding integrity and authorship of the book.

literary *pas de deux* in 1.4-7 (where *K*'s words are presented in italics and 4b, 5b-6a; 6c; 7b belong to the Presenter):

> *A generation goes forth, only to die!*
> But the earth endures forever.
> *The sun rises, only to set!*
> Yet it pants to return to its starting point, where it rises again.
> Moreover, it goes southward but returns northward.
> *The wind goes forth around and around!*
> Yet it can reverse its direction.
> *All rivers flow to the sea!*
> But the sea is not filled. And the rivers must return to their source, since they continue to flow to their destination.
>
> …K the Pessimist tends to poetic assertion, uses the enchantments of rhythm and generalizations to support an otherwise weak argument, namely everything in nature dies and therefore humans have no hope. By contrast, the Presenter's reply is cool, deliberately prosaic, unwilling to skip to hasty conclusions, and perhaps joyously contradictory. To configure this scene as a dialogue not only makes perfect sense but is consistent with the dialogic nature of both the wisdom genre and the essay…[23]

The very contradictions which caused the book's canonicity to be questioned in antiquity[24] have now become the interpretive key to the text's meaning for modern readers whose experience of history may have spawned something of the same pessimistic world-view and paralysis that afflicts the *K* voice. In Perry's translation of our 'fightin' words' of 7.23-29 we then read:

> *All of these things I tested for the sake of wisdom. I said:*
> *'I shall grow wise, even though it is far from me.'*
> *What has always been is far and deep indeed.*
> And what is deep who can find!
> *(I and my heart turned repetitively to know and explore and seek wisdom and strategies, and to know the wickedness of folly.*
> But foolishness is insane!)
> *For example, I personally find woman more bitter than death, for her heart is full of traps and snares and her hands are chains.*
> He who is good in God's eyes will escape from her, but the wicked will be entrapped.
> Said Koheleth:

23. Perry, *Dialogues*, p. 10.

24. See discussion in Murphy's 'History of Interpretation' section, *Ecclesiastes*, pp. xlviii-lvi.

Look, I have found this, as I set out step by step to discover a strategy,
and anything beyond this I did not find: I found one good man in a
thousand, but not even one good woman in the same number.
Except that I have found this, and note it well: At the outset God
made all human beings righteous.
But they have invented many strategems.[25]

The Arguer continues to present the basic tenet of the 'goodness
of creation'—a basic wisdom theme—which Perry feels that *K*
only questions indirectly. The 'they' of 7.29 refers to humanity as
a whole, and the 'strategems' refer back with irony to their cognates in 7.25, where the 'devices', 'calculations', 'plans' of great
wisdom thinkers lead to so few results in the end. The Snarehearted Woman is a symbol for all of the worldly pleasures
which the king found so worthless. The 'thousand' is also understood through the vehicle of the royal fiction: in all of Solomon's
extraordinary harem, not one good woman was to be found.[26]

For Perry, the recognition that *K* is in fact *not* referencing the
wisdom tradition's full, typical stance on women is heightened
by the assumption and indentification of a counter-voice that
brings the grandiose claims of the sage *K* back to the bar of
experience. Still, this pedagogical literary device is sufficiently
obscure that readers through the ages largely have been unaware
of it, and have heard the content of this text quite differently (see
below).

Typically, Qoheleth contradicts himself later (cf. 9.9, 'Enjoy life
with the wife whom you love, all the days of your vain life
which he has given you under the sun, because that is your
portion in life and in your toil at which you toil under the sun').
Elsewhere, in Proverbs, 'traditionally' ascribed to the same
'King' who speaks in 7.23-8.1, we read a broader range of men's
experiences of women finding their way into proverbial forms:

Let your fountain be blessed, and rejoice in the wife of your
youth...(Prov. 5.18 RSV)

A gracious woman gets honor, and violent men get riches. (Prov.
11.16 RSV)

25. Perry, *Dialogues*, pp. 125-26.
26. Perry, *Dialogues*, p. 131-32. Perhaps the one who got away (the
Queen of Sheba in 1 Kgs 11) was the virtuous one and had good reason to
flee (cf. the Ethiopic version of this legend in the *Kebra Nagast*).

> A good wife is the crown of her husband, but she who brings shame is like rottenness in his bones. (Prov. 12.4 RSV)
>
> He who finds a wife finds a good thing, and obtains favor from the LORD. (Prov. 18.22 RSV)
>
> House and wealth are inherited from fathers, but a prudent wife is from the LORD. (Prov. 19.14 RSV)
>
> A good wife who can find? She is far more precious than jewels...(Prov. 31.10 RSV)

Further, the acrostic poem begun in Prov. 31.10 continues in a paean of praise to the dutiful, industrious, wise, gracious, compassionate female who is the one who, in the words of the modern saying, 'makes a house a home'.[27] Exemplary wife, eager mother, thoughtful household manager, business woman, speaker of Torah, Proverbs gives us a biblical portrait of a veritable 'SuperMom', a picture of efficiency and approved domestic values[28] to which few real human women are able to live up—at least, not without her staff of servants or willingness to stay until all hours to get everything done.[29] As 'off the scale' as this figure might be, she provides a necessary counterweight to all the nagging, jealous, adulterous females that also frequent the pages of wisdom literature. Indeed, this may, in fact, be the reason why she is there in the 'last' place: to answer former charges of frivolity lodged against most or all of womankind.

27. The full citation in folkspeech is, 'It takes a heap o' livin'/ to make a house a home'; the literary version is, 'It takes a heap o' livin' in a house t' make it home/A heap o' sun an' shadder, an' ye sometimes have t' roam/ Afore ye really 'preciate the things ye lef' behind,/ An' hunger fer 'em somehow, with 'em allus on yer mind' (Edgar Guest, 'Home', in John Bartlett, *Bartlett's Familiar Quotations* [rev. by Emily Beck; Boston: Little, Brown and Company, 14th edn, 1968], p. 963).

28. Barbara H. Geller Nathanson, 'Reflections on the Silent Woman of Ancient Judaism and her Pagan Roman Counterpart', in Kenneth Hoglund *et al.* (eds.), *The Listening Heart: Essays in Wisdom and the Psalms in Honor of Roland E. Murphy, O. Carm.* (JSOTSup 58; Sheffield, England: Sheffield Academic Press, 1987), pp. 259-80.

29. Is this a virtue or a symptom of dysfunction? Does she, like the Hebrew God (Ps. 121.4), suffer from sleep deprivation? Is her sleeplessness a sign of something to which we should be paying more attention?

For the lips of a loose woman drip honey, and her speech is smoother than oil...(Prov. 5.3 RSV)

And lo, a woman meets him, dressed as a harlot, wily of heart. She is loud and wayward, her feet do not stay at home... Her house is the way to Sheol, going down to the chambers of death. (Prov. 7.10-11, 27 RSV)

Like a gold ring in a swine's snout is a beautiful woman without discretion. (Prov. 11.22 RSV)

It is better to live in a corner of the housetop than in a house shared with a contentious woman. (Prov. 21.9 RSV)

It is better to live in a desert land than with a contentious and fretful woman. (Prov. 21.19 RSV)[30]

The mouth of a loose woman is a deep pit; he with whom the LORD is angry will fall into it. (Prov. 22.14 RSV)

For a harlot is a deep pit; an adventuress is a narrow well. She lies in wait like a robber and increases the faithless among men. (Prov. 23.27-28 RSV)

It is better to live in a corner of the housetop than in a house shared with a contentious woman. (Prov. 25.24 RSV)

A continual dripping on a rainy day and a contentious woman are alike; to restrain her is to restrain the wind or to grasp oil in his right hand. (Prov. 27.15-16 RSV)

This is the way of an adulteress: she eats, and wipes her mouth, and says, 'I have done no wrong.' (Prov. 30.20 RSV)

Under three things the earth trembles; under four it cannot bear up: a slave when he becomes king, and a fool when he is filled with food; an unloved woman when she gets a husband, and a maid when she succeeds her mistress. (Prov. 30.21-23 RSV)

Seen from the perspective of the earlier voices of tradition, Qoheleth's reflections in ch. 7 are not so out of line with what is said elsewhere; what is new is that the K voice may be translated in such a way that it fails to note that not *all* women fall into the

---

30. We might add to this list Prov. 22.10, 'Drive out a scoffer, and strife will go out, and quarreling and abuse will cease', which rabbinic Judaism interprets as referring to a contentious wife who should be divorced, although the term 'scoffer' (לץ, *lēṣ*) is masculine singular as it appears in Proverbs.

category of 'snare'. That young male students should be warned
of the 'wiles' of females for whom the only hope of status and
fulfillment offered them by patriarchal culture is in the capture,
acquisition and annexation of the unwary male who cannot
escape their machinations: this is surely the stock in trade of
patriarchal pedagogy.[31] It recognizes the trap into which *women*
are forced by the limitations placed upon them, though of
course, it condemns them for acting in accordance with the messages their culture has sent. Even the Queen Mother of King
Lemuel says as much in her instruction to her son ('What, my
son? What, son of my womb? What, son of my vows? Give not
your strength to women, your ways to those who destroy kings',
Prov. 31.2-3). The Egyptian *Instruction of Ptahhotep* gives even
clearer warnings to young men entering court service:

> If you want friendship to endure
> In a house you enter
> As master, brother or friend,
> In whatever place you enter,
> Beware of approaching the women!
> Unhappy is the place where it is done,
> Unwelcome is he who intrudes on them.
> A thousand men are turned away from their good.
> A short moment like a dream,
> Then death comes for having known them.[32]

That wisdom tradents should reflect on the tricky matter of
dealings with 'work-related' females, or finding a woman
worthy of becoming the wife of a man on 'the way up' should
occasion no surprise, and we find here that once more, men by
the thousands are endangered by their interest in women who
are 'off-limits'.[33] This is simply another area in which scribal
goddess Wisdom seeks to equip her male followers with the

31. Carol A. Newsom, 'Woman and the Discourse of Patriarchal
Wisdom: A Study of Proverbs 1–9', in Peggy Day (ed.), *Gender and Difference
in Ancient Israel* (Minneapolis: Fortress Press, 1989), pp. 142-60.

32. Miriam Lichtheim, *Ancient Egyptian Literature: A Book of Readings.*
I.*The Old and Middle Kingdoms* (3 vols.; Berkeley: University of California
Press, 1975), p. 68.

33. These characterizations are certainly not flattering to males: they
seem more like lemmings in the grip of ineluctable instinct than rational
humanoids.

survival skills needed for success in an ambiguous world. Since the phrase 'to find a woman' (*māṣā' 'iššâ*) also means 'to take a wife', it may be that Qoheleth, who is not known for his celebration of family life,[34] is simply announcing in v. 7.28b that he never found a female who could meet his high standards for the mate of a sage.

There are, of course, other possibilities: his statement may be meant literally. Following the 'royal fiction' that makes our speaker into Solomon, the author of Proverbs and Song of Songs, we might conclude that his harem relations were singularly unsatisfying. Perhaps *K* may even be telling us *not* to take what he says too rigidly! He does *not* comment specifically on the nature of the one man who escapes from the Snarehearted Woman,[35] and one can hardly conclude that his opinion of males is much higher than his estimation of women. But there is more: the adjective 'bitter' (*mar*) used to describe the Snarehearted Woman is masculine, and *K*'s verb in 7.27's 'said Qoheleth' is feminine in gender![36] Does he mean that *he* too is no more reliable than the woman/wife he could not find?

Beyond the intertextual links to proverbial thoughts about woman and her place, our text displays other connections which help us understand the sage in his test of wisdom and folly. Genesis 1–11, with its depiction of the original human couple's exit from Eden and humanity's descent into sinful nations, may have influenced the thoughts expressed in 7.29: Qoheleth's plaintive questions about 'what is good' (for a person) is a cynical

34. More Egyptian advice makes clear the link between a woman at home and founding a family: 'When you prosper, found your household, take a hearty wife, a son will be born you. It is for the son you build a house, when you make a place for yourself'('The Instruction of Prince Hardjedef', Lichtheim, *Ancient Egyptian Literature*, I, p. 58). Since Qoheleth has no use for his successors, he has little incentive to acquire a woman/wife.

35. So with Murphy, *Ecclesiastes*, pp. 75-76; Fox, *Qoheleth and his Contradictions*, p. 241; Ogden, *Qoheleth*, p. 123. If we take 'adam' as generic in this verse, we might even say that women could be counted among those who please God and escape the snare.

36. Elsewhere, the word *Qoheleth* presumably a title or job description, takes a masculine verb (1.12; 12.8, 10). Most commentators redivide the consonants to create 'says (masc.) *the* Qoheleth'.

reversal of the Creator's pronouncements of goodness on creation.[37] As in the Eden story, both human quests for knowledge end in frustration, and women are implicated in men's stymied desires to grasp and know. For some commentators, this explains the unusual use of '*ādām*, the generic term for human, in v. 28 in opposition to 'woman/wife', '*iššâ* ' (the more usual choice would be '*îš* , 'adult male human').[38]

Some critics have argued that this passage should also be heard against the intertextual backdrop of the SoS— yet another play on the Solomonic royal fiction. In SoS 3.1-5 the same word-pair, 'seek/find',[39] from our 7.27-28, is used to describe one of the sequences in which the beloved searches for her lover in order to bring him to a secure, private trysting place. More fortunate than Qoheleth, our pursuing 'bride' finds what she seeks, but not without an initial setback. This theme is reduplicated in the dream sequence of SoS 5.2-8, with a further venture into the territory of honor and shame: this time when the watchmen find the beloved, they mistake her for a less savory person on a similar errand (a prostitute?) and commit violence against her for her boldness. Here, her quest is defeated as she transgresses the boundaries of female honor, is shamed by the watchmen, and forced to enlist the help of the daughters of Jerusalem in her pilgrimage to love.[40] If we take the beloved's case as a paradigm for Qoheleth's search for a wife/woman, a dialogue between the two voices of these texts suggests that Qoheleth might have succeeded had he tried harder (left his usual habitat to search in all sorts of places, however unlikely), looked more eagerly and insistently, showed a willingness to be shamed as a test of the worthiness of his quest, or enlisted aid in his investigation. Even

37. So with Midrash and Targum (Whybray, *Ecclesiastes*, pp. 60-61; Fox and Porten, 'Unsought Discoveries', p. 33).

38. Fox and Porten, 'Unsought Discoveries', pp. 27, 33. In v. 29, the meaning of '*ādām* reverts to its more typical meaning, 'human being'.

39. Fox and Porten, 'Unsought Discoveries', pp. 34-37. See also Gen. 27 and 1 Sam. 9 for other examples of intensive use of this word-pair to build plot.

40. Contra Dianne Bergant, ''My Beloved is Mine and I Am His' (Song 2:16): The Song of Songs and Honor and Shame', *Semeia* 68 (1994), pp. 23-40, who reads the beloved as displacing the honor/shame paradigms of the brothers and watchmen by means of her own unmediated speech.

though our text suggests that his search was repetitive, exhaustive, and relentless ('adding one to one to find an answer'; 'repeatedly'), and is discussed with terms used to denote physical 'motion', it is clear from the outcome that Qoheleth—and his personified 'heart' which accompanies him[41]—have not gone very far.

Qoheleth among the Commentators: A Selective Sampling

It is beyond the scope of this essay to present an exhaustive treatment of this passage as it occurs in the history of the Synagogue's and Church's exegesis; bibliography for such studies is readily available, but many Christian sources are known only through later references to them in other works, or are unpublished, or survive only in fragmentary form.[42] We will, however, dip our feminist ladle into the waters of interpretation as they flowed from the world of the Jewish Diaspora into late medieval and modern Europe. Nowhere does it become more clear that 'time and chance' (9.11) affect the interpretations given a passage, even though the text translated has not changed its original words. Clearly, the 'plain sense' of our passage from Qoheleth, K, the Arguer, King Solomon or a later masquerader is to be found in the eye of its beholder![43]

The Babylonian Talmud, Targum of Qoheleth and Qoheleth Rabbah

In most of the places where this passage is quoted in the *Babylonian Talmud* it is routinely paired with Prov. 18.22, 'He who finds a wife finds a good thing, and obtains favor from the LORD', whose Hebrew, טוב מצא אשה מצא (*māṣā' 'iššâ māṣā' ṭôb*), forms a wordplay on Qoheleth's אני ומוצא (*ûmôṣē' 'ănî*) 'and I found'.[44]

---

41. This may represent Egyptian influence; at any rate, it is a peculiarity of Qoheleth's speech. It should be remembered that the heart in Hebrew *and* Egyptian is the perceiving, rather than the feeling, organ. Fox, *Qoheleth and his Contradictions*, pp. 86-88, 241.

42. See Murphy, *Ecclesiastes*, pp. xlviii-lv for extensive references on patristic, medieval and Jewish exegesis of the book; cf. also Beryl Smalley, *Medieval Exegesis of Wisdom Literature* (Atlanta: Scholars Press, 1986).

43. The eye is not satisfied with seeing (1.9).

44. *Yeb.* 63a; 63b; *Ber.* 8a.

The word 'woman' is clearly taken to mean 'wife' instead of all women, or as a metaphor for something else. The rabbinic authors sublate the negative implications of Qoheleth's statement by contrasting it to an earlier saying of 'Solomon's giving a view which is exactly opposite of Qoheleth's in 7.23-8.1: the blessing of a (good) wife is *indeed* a Good Thing, and comes directly from the Hebrew God. Apparently, in the matter of seeking and finding a mate, for these rabbis, things can go either way; it is in the hand of the LORD. Thus, by finding a contrast to the text's (purported) view, it casts into doubt the universal validity of the *K*'s statement.[45] In this interpretive move we clearly see a *zwar-aber* ('to be sure', 'however') construction composed by juxtaposing two contrary statements attributed to the same author: a mode of discourse worthy of Qoheleth himself. This paradigmatic contrast between the state of a man who finds a good wife and the one who finds a woman more bitter than death becomes enshrined in 'folk-speech': newly married men are asked 'מצא או מוצא?', '*Happy or not?*'[46]

It is worth noting that when our passage appears in the *Babylonian Talmud* without its sublating partner from Proverbs, the interpretation and context do not go well for women. In *Soṭah* 8b, v. 27, 'adding one to one to find the sum' is quoted to heap punishment on the wife suspected of adultery: just as she schemed by her acts, one upon one, to do that which would bring her to her lover's bed, so the judges should place like punishments upon her, one by one.[47] In *Giṭṭin* 45a, the citation of 'no woman in a thousand' of v. 28 is used to render sense out of the experiences of the righteous daughters of R. Naḥman. These females were so pious that they could stir a boiling cauldron with their bare hands and not be burned. When they are later taken captive and placed into forced marriages with their captors, they are overheard talking in the privy. They reject the option of escaping to return to their former Jewish husbands, in order to remain with their captors. The Jew who overheard them

---

45. *Well done!* The process of sublating patriarchal texts through the juxtaposition of contrary authoritative statements is a useful tool for feminist interpretation which seeks to stay in dialogue with traditional texts.

46. *B. Yeb. 63b.*

47. *B. Soṭ. 8b*

returns to tell the tale, much to the chagrin of the community. The passage concludes with the view that they must have been protected by witchcraft rather than righteousness in their former culinary feats. If even such righteous women as these could fall so far from the ideal, is it any wonder that the sage says he could not find even *one* woman who was better than she should be![48]

The *Targum of Qoheleth*, of Palestinian provenance and provisionally dated to a time after the *Babylonian Talmud* (based on *Targ. Q*'s use of that text) but before the Islamic conquest of the region, and the *Midrash Qoheleth Rabbah* (similarly difficult to date), struggle to understand the 'plain sense' of our ambiguous text.[49] Both follow the rabbinic interpretive scheme which posits Qoheleth as King Solomon, and both make use of interpolations based on Genesis 1–11. But King Solomon for rabbinic readers is now more than simply the king of Israel's 'glory days': he is the wonder-full king with knowledge of demons, magic and the deep things of the world.[50] He has gone from King to Beggar to King once again, as part of his dealings with the demon Ashmodai (Ashmodeus of Tobit) whom he took captive.[51] Magician, lover and sinner with many foreign women (one thousand in all!), folklore hero punished by God for his arrogance and sent into exile, who would know better than this man about what is more bitter than death?[52] For the Targum, Qoheleth the king has

48. *B. Giṭ.* 45a.

49. Peter S. Knobel, *The Targum of Qohelet, Tr. with a Critical Introduction, Apparatus and Notes* (The Aramaic Bible, 15; Collegeville, MN: Liturgical Press, 1991), pp. 12-15; for a discussion of the history of texts and interpretations see Murphy, *Ecclesiastes*, pp. xxiv-xxvi; xlviii-lvi.

50. Solomon's mastery of demons and magic is based on the Babylonian Jewish interpretation of שדה ושדות in 2.8 to mean 'male and female demons' rather than 'carriages' (*Talmud Yerushalami*), 'concubines' (preferred by modern translators) or 'cupbearers' (preferred by ancient versions), *b. Giṭ.* 68a.

51. At one point Ashmodeus masquerades as Solomon, whom he has exiled, and rules in his place. Is the passage in question a typical demonic trick played on humanity?

52. *B. Giṭ.* 68a; contra Murphy, *Ecclesiastes*, p. liv, Ashmodai does *not* 'depose Solomon'; this is rather a consequence of his seeking to be free of enslavement. It should be noted that Solomon is restored to his throne after three years of exile through the offices of a good woman. In one version the

become a sage of the 'rabbinic' sort,[53] for whom Wisdom is best known as Torah (interpolations in italics):

> All that, *I said,* I have tested with wisdom. I said *to myself,* 'I will be wise *also in all the wisdom of the Torah,* but it eluded me. *Behold, already* it eluded *man to know everything* which was *from the days of old and the secret of the day of death and the secret of the day when King Messiah will come.* Who will find it out *by his wisdom?* I turned *to reckon* in my mind and to know how to examine and to seek wisdom *and* the reckoning *of the reward of the deeds of the righteous and to know the punishment of* the sin of the fool and folly and the intrigues *of government.* I found a thing *which is more bitter to man* than *the bitterness of the day of* death (that is), the woman *who causes her husband many sorrows and in whose* heart is nets and snares. Her hands are tied *so that she cannot work with them.* Upright before the Lord *is the man who divorces her with a bill of divorcement* and escapes from her, *but guilty before the Lord is the man who marries her and* is caught in her *harlotry.* See, this *is the matter I found,* said Qoheleth who *is called Solomon the king of Israel. I determined the relationship of the planets* one to the other to find the reckoning *of men what will be at their end.* There is *another thing which* my soul still sought but I have not found; (namely) *a perfect and innocent* man *without blemish from the days of Adam until Abraham the Righteous was born, who was found faithful and innocent* among the one thousand *kings who were assembled to make the Tower of Babel* but I did not find a *worthy* woman among all *the wives of those kings.* Only see this, I have found *that* the Lord made *the first* man upright *and pure before him, but the serpent and Eve seduced him to eat from the fruit of the tree whose fruit enables those who eat it to know the difference between good and evil, and they caused the day of death to be imposed upon him and upon all the inhabitants of the world and* they tried to find many calculations *in order to bring a plague upon the inhabitants of the earth.*[54]

beggar Solomon is taken in by a kindly old lady who shows him a fish she bought, which turns out to contain his very own signet ring (formerly thrown in the sea [or: swallowed] by Ashmodai). When he puts it on, he is transformed and returned to the throne; in a different version, it is his wife, Naamah, daughter of the King of Ammon, who guts the fish, finds the ring and brings about the beggar's return to kingship (Angelo S. Rappoport, *Myth and Legend of Ancient Israel* [New York: Ktav, 1966]), III, pp. 131-39. These legends, perhaps of Indic or Iranian origin (as is Ashmodai) find their way to medieval Europe, probably via Byzantine transmission.

53. Murphy, *Ecclesiastes*, p. liv.
54. Knobel, *Targum*, pp. 40-41.

We see here not only the glossing of the 'hidden' things of vv. 23-24, 28 with the coming of the Messiah and the day of death (things sought out by the 'prophet' Solomon looking ahead at Israel's future), but the addition of other elements to explicate the ellipses of the original Hebrew text. The 'one thousand' which will become important in modern attempts to save Qoheleth from the charge of misogyny (see below) now refers to the builders of the Tower of Babel and their unworthy wives. The woman more bitter than death is the noxious and lazy wife who ought, by Talmudic law, to be divorced speedily (*b. Yeb.* 63b) and shunned for purposes of remarriage. This is something of an improvement since it acquits *all* women of being guilty as charged. This slight gain is balanced, however, by the imputation of guilt to womankind through Eve's conspiracy with the Serpent: now v. 29 is read to mean that 'Man' (the male creature, not humanity in its generic form) was created upright. He—and they do mean 'he'!—was then corrupted by Eve & Company, the referents of the cryptic 'they' who seek devices, bringing many plagues upon the earth (and not just the plague of a bad wife, as in Prov. 22.10). In the same place, Qoheleth Rabbah reads:

> He (Adam) was upright, as it is said: 'That God made Adam upright' (7.29) and it is written, 'Behold Adam was one of us' (Gen. 3.22) one of the ministering angels. When however he became two then 'They sought out many inventions' (7.29).[55]

From a feminist perspective, the Midrash is somewhat better than the Targum—but only somewhat—in its general implications: in the latter, Eve and the Serpent were the seekers of many devices against the noble Adam (and presumably, his god); in the midrash, however, *both* humans bear the responsibility for those machinations. The impetus which causes the move from being upright, however, is clearly to be found in the creation of the female gender as a 'free-standing' entity. The alternative traditions of Gen. 1.27 where *both* humans, male and female, are created simultaneously and *both* in the divine image, offer no apparent challenge to the male interpreters of womankind in these reworkings of the Hebrew text.

55. Quoted in Knobel, *Targum*, p. 41.

Qoheleth among the Christians: Literary Proverb Performance in the Malleus Maleficarum

Long before Talmud, Targum or Midrash sought to inscribe a patriarchal ethic of female guilt in Qoheleth's puzzling words, the New Testament entered the lists in favor of a Fall to be attributed primarily to women. Ironically, without the falling women of the world, men would have had no need for a savior; Woman's deception by the Serpent (now attributed to all women throughout all history) is a critical element that brings about the drama of Salvation History. However, She receives no particular reward for this key role in helping God fulfill *His* plans for humanity. Instead, we hear in 1 Tim. 2.12-14, 'I permit no woman to teach or to have authority over men; she is to keep silent. For Adam was formed first, then Eve; and Adam was not deceived, but the woman was deceived and became a transgressor'.[56] The text continues by telling us that women may be saved by the bearing of children, with 'modesty' as their watchword in all things. Despite some arguments that try to make the early Jesus Movement into a sort of 'women's liberation' event, at present two things are clear: (1) we do *not know* what attracted Jewish and pagan women to the Jesus Movement in the early days, or if they were attracted *as women* to the movement; and (2) whatever egalitarian impulses toward women and slaves may have existed in the Jesus Movement at its inception, by the time of the formulation of the 'doctrines' of the Church Fathers and Councils, women had been put firmly in their place as inferior, misbegotten males defined by Aristotle, less-than-fully-human creatures whose duty was to be submissive to the men who rule over them.[57]

---

56. See Schottroff, *Lydia's*, pp. 69-78. Cf. Sir. 25.24; for discussion of the 'sexual' nature of Eve's seduction by the Serpent see John A. Phillips, *Eve: The History of an Idea* (San Francisco: Harper & Row, 1984), pp. 38-51. Speculation about the origins and nature of evil remained fairly fluid in the early centuries before and during the rise of Christianity; it is by no means clear that this passage attributed to Paul can be 'blamed' on any sort of normative position of the Judaisms of the time.

57. A.-J. Levine, 'Second Temple Judaism, Jesus, and Women: *Yeast of Eden*', in Athalya Brenner (ed.), A *Feminist Companion to the Hebrew Bible in the New Testament* (FCB, 10; Sheffield: Sheffield Academic Press, 1996),

Within this philosophical and social matrix of female inferiority Qoheleth's words on Woman, read with the customary negative slant, were scarcely perceived to be out of place among the teachings of the learned doctors of the Church.[58] This is not to say that Churchmen did not have *other* problems with Qoheleth (such as the pessimistic statements suggesting that all activity is more or less futile, unacceptable to a world redeemed by Christ), but his purported views on women were not among them. Commentator James Crenshaw notes, 'Qoheleth added his voice to the choir that sang about the weaknesses of women, but he viewed men as only slightly better...'[59] Qoheleth's surly estimation of his own sex, however, never similarly contributed to a doctrinal stance which had direct and dire impact on the lives of those so evaluated. And how could Qoheleth's words be disbelieved, when it was the wise and experienced 'King Solomon' who uttered them? If some women were driven to look to a different, heavenly King, a kind of 'knight in shining armor'[60] who defended prostitutes and healed women in their bloody 'impurity', we will not dispute with them here the emotional validity of that interpretative move, given their time and place. We will only note that, unfortunately, such allegiances did nothing to protect observant Christian women when they fell into the hands of the Church's all-male inquisitors.[61]

pp. 306-08, 326-28; see also Schottroff, *Lydia's*, pp. 3-42; Elizabeth A. Clark, *Women in the Early Church* (Message of the Fathers of the Church, 13; Wilmington, DE: Michael Glazier, 1983); Karen Jo Torjesen, *When Women Were Priests: Women's Leadership in the Early Church and the Scandal of Their Subordination in the Rise of Christianity* (San Francisco: Harper & Row, 1993), esp. pp. 118-20; 136-49; 203-41. All of these writers attempt to trace the legacy and impact of classical misogyny on Jewish and Christian traditions, as well as delve into the social circumstances of the increasing restrictions placed upon women during the rise of Christianity.

58. In fact, Qoheleth's words in this passage are 'obsessively quoted in the Middle Ages' (Blamires, *Woman*, p. 34 n. 56).

59. *Ecclesiastes: A Commentary* (OTL; Philadelphia: Westminster Press, 1987), p. 147.

60. Schottroff, *Lydia's*, pp. 14-15.

61. Trial transcripts from torture sessions indicate that Christian women routinely called to God the Father, Jesus Christ, Mary, Our Lady of Guadeloupe to bear witness to their innocence and stop the torture. They received

Many factors came together in early modern Europe to create the several centuries' long reign of terror for Christian[62] and pagan women. These governmental and social shifts include but are not limited to the rise of the modern state and its use of coercive power against its citizens, the ceding of witchcraft prosecutions to secular courts as the capital crime of 'treason' rather than ecclesiastical courts who had previously treated such charges as 'heresy', changes in jurisprudence,[63] the Roman Church's attempts to curb the nascent Protestant Reformation which ensued in almost continuous 'wars of religion'. At the same time the First World saw continent-wide inflation caused by the influx of gold from the exploited 'New World', modernization of economies which moved peasant workers out of the agrarian feudal system into cities, resulting in record numbers of unemployed causing the average age of marrying couples to soar and the size of families to decrease. Added to this was the collapse of medieval medical paradigms which had failed miserably to respond to the Black Plague, the transmission of syphilis from the New World to the First World through soldier 'carriers' infecting prostitutes,[64] and the rise of the university-trained,

no recorded reply (Claudia Lewis, 'Requiem for a Jew', *Tikkun* 11 [1996], pp. 77-79). Although this particular case concerns a converso, many others could be cited.

62. Both Protestant and Catholic women were at risk. The outbreaks of the witchcraze were worst in Scotland, Germany and France. England, which refused to sanction the use of torture to obtain confessions, had a rather different experience because of this fact. See Anne Llewellyn Barstow, *Witchcraze: A New History of the European Witch Hunts* (San Francisco: Pandora/Harper Row, 1994); and Erik H.C. Midelfort, 'Witchcraft and Religion in Sixteenth-Century Germany: The Formation and Consequences of an Orthodoxy', *Archiv für Reformationsgeschichte* 62 (1971), pp. 266-78.

63. The first occurrence ever of large numbers of women in the penal system; the admission of 'spectral' evidence in trials and other changes in the understanding of what constituted 'proof' of the crime; the accused having no right to counsel nor to confront their accusers; the use of torture to obtain confessions, with no cessation of the torture even after confession (Barstow, *Witchcraze*, pp. 15-55).

64. Advanced symptoms of syphilis created many of the dreaded effects of the 'witches' disease': impairment of fertility, changes in male genitalia,

male-exclusive medical profession now in direct competition with village folk healers (wise women). A large group of unmarried or widowed older women was created by the confluence of these factors. These were women past the age of bearing children, without means of self-support and, hence, of no use to the patriarchal state but deserving of 'alms' by traditional Church teachings.

Theologies of demonic 'conspiracy theories', each with an appropriate ideological 'twist' as required by Protestants or Catholics, held sway as the Church's general explanation for disruptive social change, especially once most heretical groups, lepers, homosexuals and Jews had been either wiped out or expelled. These theories were quickly made available across the continents, along with lurid descriptions of the proceedings of witchcraft trials, by the invention of Gutenberg's printing press. Indeed, the *Malleus Maleficarum*, or 'Hammer of Witches' was an immediate best-seller in the fifteenth century, second only to the Bible. As is often typical, women of the underclasses were some of the first casualties of technological advances. It is no wonder that modern students of medicine, law, government, colonialism, psychopathology, anthropology, sociology of the modern era, heresy and feminist theology all turn a fascinated—if horrified—gaze upon this period as they try to discern the mechanisms that caused the people of Europe to go stark, raving mad, almost in unison. This period left the modern world with a legacy of intolerance and public cruelty that it has yet to successfully renounce.[65]

While the *Malleus Maleficarum* was not the first nor the last treatise on witchcraft, its origins, abilities and remedies for it, it is arguably the most important (with Jean Bodin's *Demonomanie* perhaps taking second place) in its impact.[66] Certainly, it was

---

dementia, and 'cold spots' with no sensation on the body (Brian P. Levack [ed.], *Articles on Witchcraft, Magic and Demonology: A Twelve Volume Anthology of Scholarly Articles. X. Witchcraft, Women and Society* [New York: Garland Publishing, 1992], pp. 273-306).

65. Barstow, *Witchcraze*; Levack (ed.), *Witchcraft, Women and Society*.

66. Sydney Anglo, 'Evident Authority and Authoritative Evidence: The *Malleus Maleficarum*', in S. Anglo (ed.), *The Damned Art: Essays in the Literature of Witchcraft* (London: Routledge & Kegan Paul, 1977), p. 14.

accorded a status which its opponents never obtained with their fierce denunciations or carefully argued legal or medical insights. The *Malleus Maleficarum* remained 'the' text which any detractor of the witchcraze must confute. Penned by two Dominicans, Henrich 'Institoris' Kramer and Jacob Sprenger, with the blessing of the conspiracy-minded Pope Innocent VIII in his Bull, *Summis desiderantes affectibus* (9 December 1484) directed specifically toward his beloved Inquisitors.[67] Composed shortly after this, the work was approved—though not without some hostility—by the Doctors of the Theological Faculty at the University of Cologne in 1487.[68]

Truly a 'child of its time', this treatise is marked by the full use of the rhetorical devices of its age: citation of 'classical' references piled up in circular fashion, analogical reasoning,[69] arguments from silence, all deployed with an entirely cavalier attitude toward what might constitute 'proof' of such activities as alleged by its authors. Modern readers—though not all![70]— might take particular note of the 'enthusiastic sadism'[71] of the Inquisitors as they give directions for the dehumanization and torture of their unfortunate captives. I can imagine no scenario short of direct, divine intervention with a host of 'special effects' that could have convinced these talented theological torturers of the innocence of their prisoners. As one later medical detractor,

67. Heinrich Kramer and James Sprenger, *The Malleus Maleficarum* (trans. with an introduction, bibliography and notes by Montague Summers; New York: Dover, 1971), p. xxv.

68. Kramer and Sprenger, *Malleus*, p. xxxvii.

69. E.g. the evidence of naturally caused sickness is used to 'prove' the occurrence of demonically induced illness.

70. The modern translator Montague Summers turns his attention to the usefulness of the purported misogyny of the text: 'Possibly what will seem even more amazing to modern readers is the misogynic trend of various passages... However ... I am not altogether certain that they will not prove a *wholesome and needful antidote* (italics mine) in this feministic age when the sexes seem confounded, and it appears to be the chief object of many females to ape the man, an indecorum by which they not only divest themselves of such charm as they might boast, but lay themselves open to the sternest reprobation in the name of *sanity and common-sense*' (Kramer and Sprenger, *Malleus*, p. xxxix).

71. Anglo, 'Authority', p. 27.

Johann Weyer, commented sourly in his own refutation of the *Malleus Maleficarum*, the only evidence of demonic possessions and pacts with the Devil were to be found in the behavior of the Inquisitors and civil authorities.[72]

Naturally, for men of the cloth the Bible must be seen to both prove their claims and sustain their arguments for speedy legal redress of the heinous crimes of old women. The Bible was not entirely on their side, however: for every 'Witch of En-dor', one could put forward a universalistic statement about the ultimate power of God and the triumph of good over evil. The problem of God's participation in the witches' evil deeds, by allowing them to occur, was readily solved by deferring to doctrines of 'free will'. Certainly, the Satan's behavior in the book of Job might suggest to some that no evil is done to a good man unless the Lord wills it, but such considerations do not trouble our authors. Nor do they look to the preaching of the prophets, as did other writers arguing for and against the existence of witchcraft, which identified cosmic, natural and personal misfortunes *not* as a deed done by an enemy, but as the natural and just retribution for one's sins at the hands of the Lord.[73] Our text on Qoheleth 7 commences in answer to Question 6 of Part One, *'Why it is that Women are chiefly addicted to Evil Superstitions'*:

> It is this which is lamented in Ecclesiastes vii, and which the Church even now laments on account of the great multitude of witches. And I have found a woman more bitter than death, who is the hunter's snare, and her heart is a net, and her hands are bands. He that pleaseth God shall escape from her; but he that is a sinner shall be caught by her. More bitter than death, that is, than the devil: Apocalypse vi, 8, His name was Death. For though the devil tempted Eve to sin, yet Eve seduced Adam. And as the sin of Eve would not have brought death to our soul and body unless the sin had afterwards passed on to Adam, to which he was tempted by Eve, not by the devil, therefore she is more

72. Gregory Zilboorg, *The Medical Man and the Witch During the Renaissance* (The Hideyo Noguchi Lectures; Publications of the Institute of the History of Medicine, 3.2; The Johns Hopkins University Press, 1935; New York: Cooper Square Publishers, 1969), pp. 111, 131-32, 141.

73. Weyer writes caustically 'It is fortunate that [Job and Nebuchadnezzar] are not among us today, for if they were hereabouts some old woman would have to shoulder the responsibility for their distress, and the brains of these old women are so inflamed that under torture they would confess to having caused all these terrors' (Zilboorg, *Medical Man*, p. 152).

bitter than death. More bitter than death, again, because that is natural and destroys only the body; but the sin which arose from woman destroys the soul by depriving it of grace, and delivers the body up to the punishment for sin.

More bitter than death, again, because bodily death is an open and terrible enemy, but woman is a wheedling and secret enemy.

And that she is more perilous than a snare does not speak of the snare of hunters, but of devils. For men are caught not only through their carnal desires, when they see and hear women: for S. Bernard says: Their face is a burning wind and their voice the hissing of serpents: but they also cast wicked spells on countless men and animals. And when it is said that her heart is a net, it speaks of the inscrutable malice which reigns in their hearts. And her hands are as bands for binding; for when they place their hands on a creature to bewitch it, then with the help of the devil they perform their design.

To conclude. All witchcraft comes from carnal lust, which is in women insatiable. See Proverbs xxx: There are three things that are never satisfied, yea, a fourth thing which says not, It is enough; that is, the mouth of the womb. Wherefore for the sake of fulfilling their lusts they consort even with devils. More such reasons could be brought forward, but to the understanding it is sufficiently clear that it is no matter for wonder that there are more women than men found infected with the heresy of witchcraft. And in consequence of this, it is better called the heresy of witches than of wizards, since the name is taken from the more powerful party. And blessed be the Highest Who has so far preserved the male sex from so great a crime: for since He was willing to be born and to suffer for us, therefore He has granted to men this privilege.[74]

The theological methods of these exemplars of the privileged, preserved male sex are clear enough: the eternally valid biblical text which at all times must be true and applicable is freely used to give meanings to the passage which, while certainly inherent in previous interpretations, were held in check to some degree by the contrary contours of Qoheleth's own text. Now, the Preacher's words delineate a collective character for women which, were it true, should leave men frightened indeed.[75] Along with classical authors, Augustine and Thomas Aquinas are trotted out in force to bolster the claims made concerning woman

---

74. Kramer and Sprenger, *Malleus*, p. 47.

75. We might note here that the witches' malevolent control of both male and female fertility, as well as her preoccupation with damage to the male genitals, are salaciously narrated by our theologians. Cf. *Malleus*, Part 1, Question x; Part 2, Question i, chs. vi-vii, xiii, *et passim*.

(see Noonan). Even Proverbs 31.10-31, with its praise of the Woman of Worth and continued affirmation that a good wife is a gift from the great God, is turned to the witchmonger's needs by piecemeal readings interpreted with extreme prejudice.

Several elements are of particular interest in the inquisitors' use of the passage from Qoheleth. First, it is rather interesting that Qoheleth's dictum about not even 'one in a million' does *not* appear here, though it was much quoted by male authors during the period. Is it perhaps the case that such inclusion might cast some doubt upon the theologically and morally privileged status of males as a gender? Further, Solomon, the all-knowing king and great enemy of demons who supposedly authored our text, is not invoked, though it would have been natural, given the context, to do so.

Most telling of all, beyond generalizations and late medieval/early modern isogesis, is the uncanny transfer of the traits of the witch-hunters which they project onto their victims. Their torture was more bitter than death or devil, for the accused were suffering at the hands of their own duly authorized 'saviors'; similarly, the trauma of captives went far beyond the torment of the body, leaving captives destroyed in soul and betrayed by a faith that had no deliverance for them. The 'wheedling' of the 'secret enemy' more aptly describes the procedures of the inquisitors than the behavior of the women they sought to destroy. The 'bands' and 'nets' of the Churchmen's 'inscrutable malice' found their manifestation in the shackles that manacled the wrists of the accused, supposedly the 'more powerful party' against whom any extreme measures of cruelty were warranted. It would appear that Weyer and others were correct after all: the crimes against humanity committed during this age must be attributed largely to those in power.[76] We disagree with the good friars: the male sex has been preserved from nothing in this matter; any devils in evidence during these centuries wore the guise of Adam. Following the reasoning of Sprenger and Kramer, we must name this movement for the more powerful party and proclaim it a heresy of male hierarchy.

---

76. Such opinions caused Weyer's work refuting the *Malleus* to be dubbed 'Weyer's Poison' by the Church (Zilboorg, *Medical Man*, p. 201).

Many Devices of the Modern Commentators

We have seen in the discussion above that critical commentators are of many minds about how to translate, resolve or make palatable the sentiments expressed in one of Qoheleth's most famous passages—and one of his few mentions of women.[77] The trend by modern critics, as noted by Christianson, is to find a way to excuse Qoheleth for the views on women he expresses, either by deferring to the 'quotation' model which has him citing, then rejecting, the attitudes that most moderns find repellent, or using grammatical ambiguities to nuance the passage, or both.[78] We will take up two interpretations which return us to our original metaphor: the 'plain sense' of this passage to many hearers and interpreters alike is one which invites conflict, rather than settling it (more typical of the way of Wisdom, even when it means supporting the *status quo* sometimes challenged by other more prophetic elements in the culture).

Fightin' Words, One More Time.

One approach to sanitizing Qoheleth 7 is taken by critics who note that the Tanak, from time to time, cites women as exemplars of strength.[79] In the wisdom tradition this is also true of the rhetoric used to warn young men against the foreign, strange or adulterous woman.[80] But it is not only wicked women, or their mother Eve who brought death to all men, who are associated with the moral, physical and emotional strength that is the hallmark of the 'coping' female: the 'Woman of Worth' of Prov. 31 is designated by the term *ḥayil*, used of men to designate their champion-like natures as (primarily) warriors. Further, such

77. For further discussion see Eric S. Christianson, 'Qoheleth the "Old Boy" and Qoheleth the "New Man": Misogyny, the Womb and a Paradox in Ecclesiastes' in this volume.

78. So Murphy, *Ecclesiastes*, pp. 75-77; T. Krüger, ' "Frau Weisheit" ', pp. 394-95; K. Baltzer, 'Women and War in Qoheleth 7:23-8:1a', *HTR* 80.1 (1987), pp. 127-32; see Christianson's discussion, 'Old Boy'.

79. Claudia Camp and Carole R. Fontaine, 'The Riddles of the Wise and their Riddles', in Susan Niditch (ed.), *Text and Tradition: The Hebrew Bible and Folklore* (Semeia Studies; Atlanta, GA: Scholars Press, 1990), pp. 127-52.

80. Krüger, ' "Frau Weisheit" ', p. 395.

critics read in the SoS that 'love'—surely the province of women and their mates—is 'stronger than the grave' (8.6). Could it be that Qoheleth is *really* lauding women, experts in the realm of emotions and relationships, perhaps claiming they are 'as strong as' death, rather than more bitter than death?! Baltzer makes a case for this reading by pointing out that the 'thousand', 'nets' and 'devices' (e.g. 'siege-works') are typical of military vocabulary. The point would be then that when Qoheleth examined the brigades composed of a thousand soldiers, replete with their technologies of death, he found no woman among them, for this is *not* the way of women. That is, women may be 'death machines' through their 'original' sins and their come-hither biological differences from men, but at least they have no part in the official killing machines of the Persian or Hellenistic state.[81] The critic has *indeed* located words about fighting in our passage, but his device is to relocate their referents in order to deflect their impact on the biblical theory of womankind evinced here. It is interesting to note that the postbiblical Jewish and Christian male readers of Qoheleth, who must surely have been more familiar with the *'true'* military meaning of these words, should have never before put forward this interpretation—until they started reading in the company of learned women. Previously, the only war intuited from this text prior to our century was the 'gender war' which women, by nature (through means of their carnal lust, weakness of intellect and propensity toward witchcraft),[82] wage against helpless males. The views of Sprenger and Kramer stand as the rule, and *not* the exception.

One final modern interpretation is of interest for its different tack on freeing Qoheleth from the charge of misogyny: Krüger suggests that, given the passage's emphasis on seeking and (not) finding, perhaps the one woman in a thousand Qoheleth could not find was Woman Wisdom herself![83] Certainly, one might support this from Qoheleth's own musings: he says that he made

81. Baltzer, 'Women and War', p. 131.
82. Note, too, the use of such language of extremes during the witch-craze: Judge Boquet of Burgundy writes to Henry IV that 'the Sorcerers reach everywhere by the thousands; they multiply on this earth like the caterpillars in our gardens' (Zilboorg, *Medical Man*, pp. 73-74).
83. Krüger, ' "Frau Weisheit" ', p. 398.

a test of wisdom, but it ended in the puzzle of the grave ('How can the sage die like the fool?!' Qoh. 2.16). Later he claims that Wisdom remained far off and very deep, despite all his struggles to know her and grasp her (7.23-24). That this is true we cannot deny: the content of his words on women reveals how little he found out about the nature of women's ways, or relationships in general. Perhaps he shakes his fist angrily at an indifferent cosmos which gave him no reason to think differently, hoping to provoke a better answer than any he could devise by himself. The many devices of those who interpret him cannot disguise the man's ambivalence about human-to-human contact, and his 'more bitter than death' disappointment with women in particular. Though we may explicate all the various meanings of his grammatical ambiguities and put forth gentler readings, interpreters should not and cannot ignore the very real, negative effects on the lives of actual women that the 'plain sense' of this text, read over the centuries, created. Here are words from tradition which *must* be fought: to do otherwise would be only more vanity, and a striving after wind.[84]

84. I would like to thank my research assistants, Brian Noonan, Margaret Tabor, Mary Jane Jenson and Nancy Citro, for their help in the preparation of this manuscript.

WISDOM LITERATURE AMONG THE WITCHMONGERS

Brian B. Noonan

Patriarchal societies by definition discriminate against women, relegating them to roles lacking the power men take for granted, and to generally low repute. Also, European-style societies— among others—tend to justify their institutions by appealing to Scripture and/or to God (Himself) for authority. Taking these two premises together, Professor Carole Fontaine and this writer, working on a project of assessing the impact of Wisdom literature on attitudes towards women, assumed that apologists for misogyny in medieval Europe would seek to justify their beliefs by citing pertinent exerts from the Bible. To test this assumption by quantitation we looked closely at one particularly egregious example of this genre, the *Malleus Maleficarum*[1] ('The Hammer of Evil-doers', or 'Smashing Witches').

Source	Number of Authors	Number of Citations	% of 509
Tanak	19	89	17
New Testament	20	59	12
Apocrypha	6	18	4
Christian	54	294	58
Other	13	49	10
Total	112	509	100

Table 1. Distribution of author/source citations among five categories in the *Malleus Maleficarum* (due to rounding, percentages do not add up to exactly 100)

Published with the encouragement of Innocent VIII soon after his bull commissioning the Inquisition in Germany (1484), the

---

1. H. Kramer and J. Sprenger, *The Malleus Maleficarum* (trans. M. Summers; New York: Dover Publications, 1971).

Hammer was an early literary manifestation of a 'demon mania' that seemed to sweep over Western Europe in the fifteenth and sixteenth centuries. In fact it became an important handbook for those in pursuit of witches and other heretics. This book not only provided a theological basis for the existence (and danger) of witchcraft, it instructed readers on how to identify occasions of witchcraft, and counselled them on juridical stratagems for prosecution. It is replete with the worst kind of anti-woman sentiments and prejudices, against which even the modern translator attempts to forewarn the reader. However, we discovered that the Rev. Summers was a rather sympathetic translator, reinforcing our suspicion that in this book we had a superb example of Bible-based misogyny (see Fontaine above).

Joshua	1
Judges	2
1 Samuel	1
2 Samuel	2
1 Kings	6
2 Kings	1
Isaiah	8
Jeremiah	1
Ezekiel	2
	24

Table 2. Distribution of author/source citations among the
Former Prophets in the *Malleus Maleficarum*

As a test of our hypothesis that the Bible, and its wisdom literature in particular, was a major resource for the authors, we proceeded to count the numerous citations in the original text, deciding that frequency of appearance would correlate positively with degree of authority and influence upon the author's thinking. Our inventory involved a seemingly simple process of scanning the text and recording each occurrence of any author or work. Indeed, in the 1971 edition such citations are italicized, making it relatively easy to pick them out. In addition, the editor supplies brief biographies, and footnotes identifying some incomplete references. But the task was still not simple.[2] For

2. Never again will this scholar begrudge a professor a full citation worthy of Turabian herself! Throughout, book titles have several different

instance, on p. 62 the text reads '...*But against this*, S. Augustine says (*de Civitate Dei*, XVIII) that the transmutation of men into brute animals...' Later on that page we read '...but S. Augustine says that he creates shapes...' The former contains a nugget of 'library fact', the latter merely an assertion. To references like the former, which contained the author's name, the title of the work and a chapter number, I applied the term 'hard'. Mere anecdotal *innuendoes* or passing glosses I termed 'soft' even if a modern footnote furnishes more precise information. As a matter of fact, given the wide variety of types of citations, if the text mentions two out of three possible identifying data (name of author, title of work, chapter number), I called it a hard reference. Some references were so vague I had to omit them completely; for example, 'as mentioned before'.

Overwhelmed by this profusion at first, I had to resort to the use of a Claris *FileMaker Pro* database to keep track of all the citations in all their various forms. Once organized, I exported the data to a Microsoft *Excel* spreadsheet to massage the figures (all on a Macintosh platform).

As mentioned above, in this project we were only examining the quantity of citations, not the quality. We fully expected to prove that the Bible had a strong influence on the social and theological values of Kramer and Sprenger. Accordingly, I sorted my list under five categories: Tanak, New Testament, Apocrypha, Christian and Other. 'Christian' included both patristic and medieval authors; 'Other' contained classical pagans, Arabs, medieval Jews and a few unidentifiable people. We also assumed that this would be the order of decreasing frequency/influence. For the purposes of this study, we assumed that each book in the Bible had but one author each. Table 1 shows the distribution among our five major categories. We are particularly curious about the relative importance of wisdom literature on Kramer and Sprenger, especially *Qoheleth* with its

---

names or spellings, authors are quoted with no indication of location, sections are mentioned as if the reader could then infer the source. One may tolerate this lack of precision in scriptural allusions because familiarity (and concordances, etc.) allows even a novice to locate exact verses; but it is harder to relate to a culture wherein so many classical books and authors were as familiar to the typical scholar as the Bible is to us.

possible contributing world-view. Carole Fontaine places its composition 'sometime between 250 BCE and the Maccabean revolt of 167 BCE'.[3]

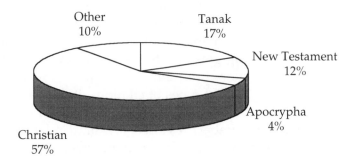

Figure 1. Distribution of citations in the *Malleus Maleficarum*

We finally tallied approximately 509 different citations, among 113 authors/sources. As can be seen in Figure 1, the Bible was far less important than patristic and medieval material in the formation of Kramer and Sprenger's ideas. As a matter of fact, we found only one citation from *Qoheleth*! After a litany of terrible comments about woman worthy of Tertullian (their voice, gait, posture etc.) they say:

> It is this which is lamented in Ecclesiastes vii, and which the Church even now laments on account of the great multitude of witches. And I have found a woman more bitter than death, who is the hunter's snare, and her heart is a net, and her hands are bands. He that pleaseth God shall escape from her; but he that is a sinner shall be caught by her.[4]

Similarly, they cited 1 Samuel 28 only once, the 'Witch of Endor' episode in which Saul visits a necromancer. Among the books of the Tanak, Job was the most heavily cited, 15 times. In the New

---

3.   C.R. Fontaine, 'Ecclesiastes', in C.A. Newsom and S.H. Ringe (eds.), *The Women's Bible Commentary* (Louisville, KY: Westminster/John Knox Press, 1992), p. 153.

4.   For a fuller quotation and discussion see Fontaine, ' "Many Devices" ', esp. 160-61.

Testament, Matthew was most popular, with 7 occurrences. Tobit (6 times) was almost as popular among the Apocryphal books. Among Christian authors Augustine of Hippo took

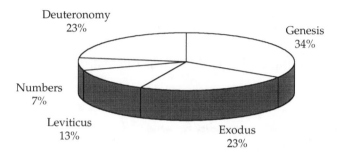

Figure 2. Distribution of Torah citations in the *Malleus Maleficarum*

second place, being referred to 62 times (10 per cent). The Grand Prize among all authors went to took second place Thomas Aquinas, whom they cite 71 times, a full 12 per cent of all the citations of 112 different authors! Finally, Aristotle had 26 citations, making him the most influential non-Christian, non-biblically 'inspired' or sanctioned author. Table 1 contains the more general data. Figures 2, 3 and 4 show the distribution of citations within larger categories.

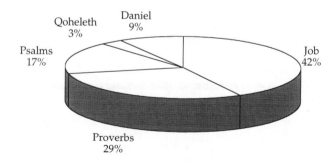

Figure 3. Distribution of Wisdom citations in the *Malleus Maleficarum*

We found that our thesis, that Wisdom literature and other intertestamental materials influenced by Hellenistic dualism and misogyny played the deciding role in Kramer and Sprenger's thinking, was not supported by our inventory. At most, citations by such scriptural authorities constituted only a minor voice in the libretto of classical and Christian authors informing the ancient legacy of woman-hating. Popular post-Christian feminism which locates the Hebrew Bible as a primary source authorizing the Early Modern war against woman needs to reframe its charges in the light of statistical evidence drawn from close scrutiny of foundation texts such as the *Malleus Maleficarum*.

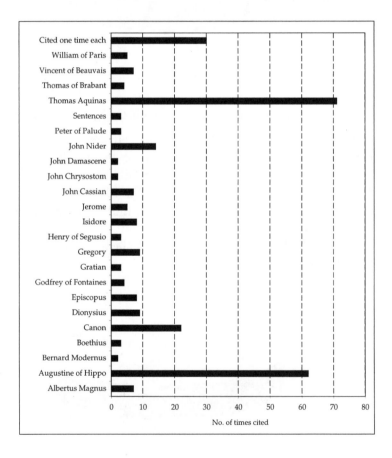

Figure 4. Distribution of 54 Christian (non-biblical) authors in the *Malleus Maleficarum*. Twenty-four are listed alphabetically by name and quantity, while 30 others who were cited only once each, were included under Other.

WHAT ABOUT JOB? QUESTIONING THE BOOK OF 'THE RIGHTEOUS SUFFERER'

Christl Maier and Silvia Schroer[1]

Fundamental Questions about the Book

The book of Job is the only biblical book which has been recognized as world literature. Its history of interpretation is considerable, and up to this day the name of Job is associated with at least a vague knowledge of a man who experienced great disaster and whose patience is proverbial. The patience of female readers is severely tested, too: men speak and act in the 42 chapters of the book, rich and educated men at that, as well as a male God. Against those long male speeches there are a few verses in which women are at least mentioned, and one single verse in which a woman speaks (Job 2.9). Most of these short remarks can be found in the frame story of the book (chs. 1–2; 42.7-17): in the actual dialogue there are only marginal references to women, the life of women or femininity. Can a book which is so clearly and explicitly written from an androcentric point of view claim to deal with questions that are relevant for both men *and* women?[2] Are we women touched by Job's suffering, his protest and his righteousness? Surely some skepticism is in order here. Suffering has its own female face—this is true today as, probably, in ancient Israel. How do we, in view of this knowledge, read this book about the righteous sufferer? Are we convinced by Job?

---

1. A shorter German version of this article is L. Schottroff and M.-Th. Wacker (eds.), *Kompendium Feministische Bibelauslegung* (Gütersloh: Gütersloher Verlag, 1998) pp. 192-207.
2. See also D.J.A. Clines, *Interested Parties: The Ideology of Writers and Readers of the Hebrew Bible* (JSOTSup, 205; Sheffield: Sheffield Academic Press, 1995), p. 124. He characterizes the implied audience as male, highly literate, intellectual and leisured.

Are his problems our problems? Or are we faced with a book in which, in the usual fashion, problems made by men are discussed by men, with no conclusion? Do the images of God in this book offer us approaches? Are the well-known speeches of YHWH plausible answers to the questions of Job or to our questions?

It is difficult to find feminist readings of the book of Job. This is one reason why we are trying to approach the book with various methods and questions that, nevertheless, are based on historical-critical methods. We are trying to reconstruct the social and religious context of this book and its authors, and to illuminate its history of interpretation. We are linking our exegesis to a feminist option: we are not setting out to justify this biblical book, but want to show how far it conceals or mentions women, their experiences or their world, and to what extent it represents suppression or liberation for women today (in accordance with the hermeneutics of Elisabeth Schüssler Fiorenza).

The Frame of Reference for a Feminist Exegesis of Job

In the context of this essay we are not able to discuss or even touch on all topics necessary for a thorough understanding of the book. We are not concerned with feminist aspects of the text; rather, we wish to define the framework of reference within which our feminist exegesis of Job will move.[3] A summary of a few conclusions that we reached in the course of our research is given below.

The Tradition of the Righteous Sufferer in Ancient Near Eastern Wisdom Literature

The book of Job belongs to the wisdom literature of Israel that, to a great extent, was molded by the literature and tradition of the surrounding great cultures and sought 'international' contact with those cultures. Viewed from a literary-historical perspective, neither the figure of Job nor the theme of 'unjust suffering' are new ideas. After the collapse of the Old Kingdom in Egypt, at the end of the third millennium BCE, appear the first writings

---

3.   J. Ebach's article ('Hiob/Hiobbuch', *TRE* 15 [1986], pp. 360-90) offers a thorough overview of the current research and has a good bibliography.

which describe the disintegration of all order[4] in the form of a lament or in a fictitious dialogue about injustice and chaos.[5] In the *Admonitions of Ipuwer*[6] the speaker accuses God in no uncertain terms of not being a good shepherd, of hiding himself away and not at all feeling the people's misery. In Mesopotamia the question of the 'righteous sufferer' seems to have been discussed over centuries. In the Akkadian writing *ludlul bel nemeqi* a desperate, sick man bewails his misery and testifies to his righteousness until he is saved and healed by the god Marduk.[7] In the so-called *Babylonian Theodicy* a righteous sufferer pours out his misfortune to his friend, protesting his innocence in several cycles of speeches; his friend, however, does not share his view that the world is unjust.[8] When we read the book of Job we must therefore remember that behind it stands an old literary and theological tradition that influenced it. The discussion of suffering through the device of a fictitious male character to whom male friends are attached; the carrying out of theological discourse in the form of disputations; the presentation in the discussion of a certain repertoire of solutions to the problem; and, finally, the fact that a solution can come about through the deity's direct intervention—all these features belong to the Ancient Near Eastern traditions.

Job as the Person Affected and Having a Problem

The reading of Job is usually strongly influenced by the frame narrative. In this frame story Job is above all a man affected by concrete misfortune; thus, the book can be read as the

4. Cf. 'Complaints of Khakheperre-Sonb', in M. Lichtheim, *Ancient Egyptian Literature: A Book of Readings* (3 vols.; Berkeley: University of California, 1973–80 [cited as *AEL*]), I, pp. 145-49. 'The Eloquent Peasant', in *AEL*, I, pp. 169-84 and J.B. Pritchard, *Ancient Near Eastern Texts Relating to the Old Testament* (Princeton: Princeton University Press, 2nd edn, 1955 [cited as *ANET*]), pp. 407-10.

5. Cf. 'Dispute between a Man and his *Ba*', also called 'Dispute over Suicide', in Pritchard, *ANET*, pp. 405-407.

6. 2000 or 1580-1200 BCE, in Lichtheim, *AEL*, I, pp. 149-63 and Pritchard, *ANET*, pp. 441-44.

7. Twelfth century BCE; cf. W.G. Lambert, *Babylonian Wisdom Literature* (Oxford: Clarendon Press, 1960 [cited as *BWL*]), pp. 32-62.

8. 800-750 BCE; in Lambert, *BWL*, pp. 70-91.

examination by an individual of his situation as a suffering person. This dimension is important and indisputable, but also too narrow. The biblical character of Job also carries a problem, that is, this fictitious character becomes the literary vehicle for fundamental ideological and theological questions of certain social groups.[9] Job not only laments his misfortune but, above all, also reproaches his friends, circumstances, the world order and the God behind all this. The dialogue is a wisdom discourse in which various ideological positions come under fire, including the divine speeches which—eventually—bring in a new acceptable position.

The 'Tun-Ergehen-Zusammenhang' (the 'actions have built-in consequences' concept)

What, then, is the underlying problem of Job (and precursory Ancient Near Eastern literature)? The experience of suffering was accepted in Israel, much more than today, as a basic constituent of the frail human existence (cf. Job 14.1-4; Ps. 103.15-16). The problem as such is due to the fact that, according to common oriental thought, there is a connection between a person's actions and his or her well-being. This connection is firmly anchored in the world order established and guaranteed by the deities, a world order which comprises all aspects of life and in which the individual is bound to his or her family and the succession of generations. Therefore the just and god-fearing will experience happiness and blessing in their lives, while the godless will fail. Klaus Koch showed more than 40 years ago that this way of thinking is not couched in terms of reward and punishment categories.[10] Already early on, the 'Babylonian Theodicy' points to the reverse (l. 70-71; cf. Job 21.7-26 and elsewhere):

9. Cf. O. Keel, *Jahwes Entgegnung an Ijob: Eine Deutung von Ijob 38–41 vor dem Hintergrund der zeitgenössischen Bildkunst* (Göttingen: Vandenhoeck & Ruprecht, 1978).

10. K. Koch, 'Is there a Doctrine of Retribution in the Old Testament?', in J.L. Crenshaw (ed.), *Theodicy in the Old Testament* (Issues in Religion and Theology, 4; Philadelphia: Fortress Press, 1983), pp. 57-87; cf. further details of this in B. Janowski, 'Die Tat kehrt zum Täter zurück: Offene Fragen im Umkreis des "Tun-Ergehen-Zusammenhangs" ', *ZTK* 91 (1994), pp. 247-71.

Those who neglect the god go the way of prosperity,
while those who pray to the goddess are impoverished
and dispossessed.[11]

Misfortune is considered the greatest injustice because it not only
makes the affected person lose the 'deserved' reward for his
righteousness, but also defames him on top of everything as an
evil-doer who secretly or at least unknowingly did something
wrong in the deity's eyes. Contrary to all experience, Israelites
too clung to this postulated axiom, as many psalms show (Ps.
1;14; 26; 37.1-2, 9-12; 75; 112). This is true both for individuals and
for groups. For example, in Deuteronomy 28 the curses which
are to descend upon the guilty people are painted in drastic
colors, recalling the great misfortune afflicting Job as an individual. Israel's prophets of the exile initiated a clear shift, with built-
in consequences, in the theology of action. Since the catastrophe
of the Southern and Northern kingdoms' fall was considered a
generations-long punishment for the fathers' sins,[12] the basis for
individual ethical behavior became fragile and fatalism took
over. Thus Ezekiel and Jeremiah's pupils pleaded for the aboli-
tion of the idea that the whole people (or group) should be
punished for individual wrongdoings according to the *Tun-
Ergehen-Zusammenhang* principle—stating that from now on each
individual should be responsible for his or her sins and nobody
else's (Jer. 31.29-30; Ezek. 18.3-20). The book of Job presupposes
those developments (21.19 onwards). It revolves around the
dramatically intensified question about the significance of Job's
misfortune if, as he claims, he really is a righteous man and
around what God has to say about this insoluble contradiction.
In the prologue, the problem of the *Tun-Ergehen-Zusammenhang*
is formulated slightly differently from the (assumed) perspective
of God. The question in 1.9, asked by the satan and the cause of
all Job's misery, is: Does Job fear God חנם—that is, for nothing,
without reason, without compensation? Is Job's prosperity,
therefore, the result of his piety? Or is it the other way round?[13]

11. Lambert, *BWL*, p. 75.
12. Cf. 'the saying of the sour grapes' in Ezek. 18.2; Jer. 31.29.
13. See J. Ebach, *Hiobs Post: Gesammelte Aufsätze zum Hiobbuch, zu Themen
biblischer Theologie und zur Methodik der Exegese* (Neukirchen–Vluyn:
Neukirchener Verlag, 1995), pp. 15-31.

In the dialogue section of the book, Job complains to and against this God who inflicts wounds on him 'for no reason' (9.17; cf. 2.3). But in his laments and disputes, does he hold onto God תֻּם?

The Relationship between the Dialogue and the Frame Narrative
Scholars do not agree on which of the two parts—the larger dialogue section (3.1–42.6) or the frame story (chs. 1–2; the end of ch. 42)—is older. Both parts are put together strikingly loosely. In 3.1–42.6 the story of the prologue and epilogue is never actually referred to: there is only the presumption that Job has been afflicted by great misfortune. Mentioning the three friends in 2.11-13 and 42.7-10 has the purpose of linking the narrative and the dialogue. We assume that the whole book, in its final form, dates from the postexilic period, although older oral and also literary traditions may have been preserved in the speeches.[14] The dialogue uses Ancient Near Eastern wisdom literature. This is one reason why it can be considered older than the frame story. In view of Ezek. 14.14 it is, however, assumed that the frame story is old. But from the exilic text of Ezek. 14.13-23 we only learn Job's name and that he was a very righteous man. Indeed, it is possible that there existed an old narrative about a man called Job who suffered misfortune, endured it and was restored. Yet, in our opinion, both the prologue and the epilogue are literary creations with the aim of framing the dialogue and giving the listeners or readers a relevant interpretative context for reading it. This is why, even today, it is difficult to read the dialogue and at the same time pretend that the frame story does not exist. The prose section is, in our opinion, a secondary addition framing the poetic corpus. In the dialogue, up to God's speeches, an existing and complex concept of God and the world is developed dramatically, with no simple solutions. The frame story, on the other hand, tries to dissolve the tensions by comparatively simple theological means. Thus evil is excluded from the concept of God and wrapped up in the figure of the satan. In contrast to

14. On the final form of the book cf. A. Brenner, 'Job the Pious? The Characterization of Job in the Narrative Framework of the Book', *JSOT* 43 (1989), pp. 37-52; and C. Fontaine, 'Folktale Structure in the Book of Job: A Formalist Reading', in E.R. Follis (ed.), *Directions in Biblical Hebrew Poetry* (JSOTSup, 40; Sheffield: Sheffield Academic Press, 1987), pp. 205-32.

the sparkling, rebellious figure of Job as presented in the dialogue, the frame story only shows the pious sufferer who is completely vindicated at the end, so that hardly any trace of his suffering is left. Also, the epilogue concludes the *Tun-Ergehen-Zusammenhang* dispute with a simple solution, namely with the reward of Job's unsupported piety. A further reason for our assumption that the frame story is a later addition is the observation that, in other biblical writings, the beginning and the end were frequently added later on. This is certainly true in the cases of Proverbs 1–9 and 31.10-31; Deuteronomy 1–3; 32–34; and the Psalms; it is also possible that the first two chapters of Samuel, or Esther, indicate a kind of later 'retellings' of the writings concerned. A third reason for our thesis is the mention, in the epilogue, of daughters who are entitled to inherit. This should be linked to the texts about Zelophehad's daughters in Numbers 27 and 36 which presuppose postexilic circumstances.[15]

An Attempt to Place the Book Socially, Historically and Religiously
The book of Job is part of the literature of the educated higher classes of Israel, as indicated by its elaborate and difficult language.[16] The Job of the dialogue is depicted as an influential and affluent village potentate (ch. 29); the Job of the prologue and the epilogue as a very wealthy owner of herds and farmer at the edge of the desert, somewhere in a fictitious North West Arabia.[17] It is characteristic of the wisdom books to support the claim of the universal validity of their teachings by avoiding precise references to their own place or time. Nevertheless, it is possible to find indications for contextualizing the book.[18] It will

15. More on this see below.
16. Cf. Clines, *Interested Parties*, p. 124.
17. E.A. Knauf, 'Ijobs Heimat', *WO* 19 (1988), pp. 65-83.
18. See above all F. Crüsemann, 'Hiob und Kohelet: Ein Beitrag zum Verständnis des Hiobbuches', in R. Albertz *et al.* (eds.), *Werden und Wirken des Alten Testaments* (Festschrift C. Westermann; Göttingen: Vandenhoeck & Ruprecht; Neukirchen–Vluyn: Neukirchener Verlag, 1980), pp. 372-93; R. Albertz, 'Der sozialgeschichtliche Hintergrund des Hiobbuches und der 'Babylonischen Theodizee', in J. Jeremias and L. Perlitt (eds.), *Die Botschaft und die Boten* (Festschrift H.W. Wolff; Neukirchen–Vluyn: Neukirchener Verlag, 1981), pp. 349-72; W. Schottroff, 'Zur Sozialgeschichte Israels in der Perserzeit', *Verkündigung und Forschung* 27 (1982), pp. 46-68.

probably have been written in the postexilic period by and for Judah's (formerly) affluent circles. It is exactly those circles which in the fifth and fourth centuries BCE were afflicted by social, economic and religious troubles. The book of Job is 'crisis literature', just as its Ancient Near Eastern precursors were. Under Persian rule, the population of Judah had to pay taxes in natural produce and make monetary payments. Years of drought and maladministration appear to have worsened the already precarious economic situation (cf. Hag. 1.11, 2.17; Mal. 3.11). Personal righteousness is no longer a guarantee for one's welfare, the *Tun-Ergehen-Zusammenhang* is invalidated, and more and more people fall into poverty and debt. Well-off Judaeans are especially afflicted by showing their solidarity with the poorer men and women and giving them loans, legal advice and alms. Other Judaeans, however, take part in the exploitation of their fellow countrymen, since the blame for the desolate situation of the poorest—described in Job 24.2-14 and 30.2-8 (cf. also Isa. 58)—is placed with the doings of the godless (probably not members of the Persian administration but rather Judaean compatriots).[19] The accounts of the sinful rich and the suppressed poor in Job 22.6-9; 24.1-17; 31 are a literary reference to the social legislation of Deuteronomy, especially Deuteronomy 19–25 and the Decalogue but also certain curses in Deuteronomy 28.[20] Job 24 bewails the inhuman effects of the pledge law, and formulates provisions for the poor which go much further than those prescribed by the law. In Job 31 Job curses himself if he may have broken the commandments of the Decalogue, and, in so doing, demonstrates clearly his comprehensive concern for servants, maids and other fringe groups. The postexilic interpretation of the deuteronomic Torah demonstrates how relevant God's demand to express solidarity with the poor was, especially in times of economic difficulty. By showing himself to be a member of society's upper strata, in solidarity with the poor, Job heightens his reproach to God, who obviously brings disaster

19. Cf. the similar background in Neh. 5.
20. Cf. G. Braulik, 'Das Deuteronomium und die Bücher Ijob, Sprichwörter, Rut: Zur Frage früher Kanonizität des Deuteronomiums', in E. Zenger (ed.), *Die Tora als Kanon für Juden und Christen* (Freiburg: Herder, 1996), pp. 61-138.

especially to those who live according to his law.

Several religious or theological developments presupposed by the book of Job imply that the book belongs in the postexilic period. As already mentioned, the collective extension of the *Tun-Ergehen-Zusammenhang* is no longer an issue, which suggests that the book was written after Ezekiel. Also, the author expects from its audience a YHWH-monotheism that is no longer questioned. On the one hand, the names for God in the dialogue (אלהים, אל) and the poetic forms אלוה, 'deity' as well as שדי, 'the almighty' are quite ambiguous. The proper name YHWH occurs in the heavenly council scenes in the prologue, in the introductions to the speeches by YHWH and Job's replies, and in the epilogue (cf. 12.9). This means that the book's deity, where seen in relation to another character, is quite without any doubt the God of Israel. Although Job and his friends are not Israelites, they confront YHWH, who presents himself as Lord over the whole world. Although the moon cult of Harran is possibly hinted at in 31.26-28 (cf. Deut. 4.19, 17.3), we know that this book's readers tended to relate all areas of creation and human existence to the one God—with the exception of the netherworld, the abode of the dead. At the same time it becomes clear that a huge religious effort to see this monotheism through is required. In his long laments Job wishes, in passing, for a witness in heaven (16.18-21) or a redeemer (גאל) who will release him (19.25-27). If both passages can be interpreted as inquiries from the one God,[21] then only in Elihu's speech in 33.23 a messenger, a heavenly mediator, suddenly appears who presents himself as the savior in mortal anguish. Now the only One has company. With the same outcome, the prologue explains the cause of suffering and evil by introducing a quasi-divine figure. Like in Chronicles (1 Chron. 21.1; cf. Zech. 3), this figure is called 'accuser'[22] (השטן) yet is subordinated to the only One. This kind

21. R. Kessler, "Ich weiß, daß mein Erlöser lebet": Sozialgeschichtlicher Hintergrund und theologische Bedeutung der Löser-Vorstellung in Hiob 19, 25', *ZTK* 89 (1992), pp. 139-58, esp. p. 153.

22. For a detailed discussion of this figure see P.L. Day, *An Adversary in Heaven: Satan in the Hebrew Bible* (HSM, 43; Atlanta: Scholars Press, 1988), esp. pp. 69-106. For her, the positioning of this divine intermediary in the council scenes creates irony, as the audience knows his function whereas

of phenomenon can quite definitely be placed in the postexilic period.[23] Even before the exile the whole symbolic, religious system had gone through a process of strong 'uranization' and 'astralization', that is, removal of the divine powers to the sky and the attribution of increasing significance to the nocturnal stars. The late effects of these developments are still tangible in Job. The God of Israel is remote, he seems unapproachable and uninvolved. Job rebels against this concept of God, he fights for a 'closer' God. The disciples of Isaiah (the so-called Trito-Isaiah), who were contemporaries of the authors of Job's dialogue, did the same in their own way, since they proclaimed that YHWH sits enthroned high up but, at the same time, is among the lowly and contrite (Isa. 57.15).

Feminist Criticism of and Approaches to the Book of Job

This essay cannot provide a critical analysis of the whole book. For this reason we have selected topics which seemed productive for a feminist reading. According to the premises presented above, we will start from the dialogue, move on to the frame story (prologue and epilogue) and, finally, to the book's history of interpretation in both Judaism and Christianity.

The Dialogue: A World without Women?
With a clap of thunder, ch. 3 starts off the long sequence of speeches and replies which constitute the main part of the book. Job curses the day of his birth, he wants to wish the whole of creation back to chaos and his only hope is the peace of the netherworld. His lament is however not just a complaint, but a targeted accusation against a God who has created a world in

---

the characters in the dialogue do not. In her view Job's heavenly witness, whom he strongly seeks, is the satan himself (cf. p. 149). In our view, her interpretation shows the impact of the prologue on the reading of the dialogue section.

23. For an opposite view see H. Spieckermann, 'Die Satanisierung Gottes: Zur inneren Konkordanz von Novelle, Dialog und Gottesreden im Hiobbuch', in I. Kottsieper *et al.* (eds.), '*Wer ist wie du, HERR, unter den Göttern?*': *Studien zur Theologie und Religionsgeschichte Israels für O. Kaiser zum 70. Geburtstag* (Göttingen: Vandenhoeck & Ruprecht, 1994), pp. 431-44.

which people, though trapped in misery, have to go on living
(3.20). It is God who hedges them in (3.23), with no route of
escape. Thus Job not only speaks of his personal misery but also
makes a general statement, and directs his reproaches against
God from this general, universal position. Generalizations of this
kind can be found again and again in the dialogue section. A
characteristic of this is the use of the Hebrew words for man or
mankind, אדם, and its equivalent אנוש which is only used in
poetry. Both terms describe the human, but from a semantic
point of view they are closely associated with the male (cf. 4.17,
10.5). Being male is seen as exemplary for being human. Whenever אדם and אנוש are used women are at best implied, but do not
appear as such. It is here that the fundamental criticism of the
book's androcentrism has to start. In the patriarchal perspective
women, their world and their experience are mentioned only in
passing and only in specific roles. Typically the mother's womb
(בטן, רחם), from which Job or the human steps into the world, *is*
mentioned (1.21; 3.10-11; 10.18-19; 19.17; 24.20; 31.15,18). Lillian
Klein even assumes that 19.17 talks of Job's wife as the womb
which belongs to him. For him, being a woman is reduced to the
function of giving birth.[24] Also, the idea that man is born of
woman is associated with the fundamentally sinful condition of
human life several times.

> What is man, that he could be pure,
> or one born of woman, that he could be righteous?
> (15.14; cf. 14.4; 25.4)

Where else are women mentioned, apart from woman as the one
who gives birth? In 19.15 Job's maidservants are referred to as no
longer recognizing their master; even worse, 19.17 talks about
the fact that Job's breath is offensive to his own wife. In the dialogue Job's wife plays no part as a person in her own right. She is
mentioned only one more time when, in 31.10, Job connects a
kind of negative confession of his sins with a self-curse: if he
really had committed the offenses mentioned, then his wife 'may

---

24. L.R. Klein, 'Job and the Womb: Text about Men, Subtext about
Women', in A. Brenner (ed.), *A Feminist Companion to Wisdom Literature*
(Sheffield: Sheffield Academic Press, 1995), pp. 186-200, esp. 198-99; we
consider her interpretation too narrow.

grind another man's grain', that is, serve him (possibly also in a sexual sense) and be handed over to strangers. Thus Job puts at stake the integrity of his wife, whom he considers his personal possession. Real relationships between Job and women in the personal sphere are not perceptible here: the women remain shadows, be it Job's neighbor's young wife whom he–theoretically—could look at lustfully (31.1-9), the maidservant whose justice he respects (31.13), and the widow who represents a challenge for him to fulfill the law by helping her (31.16-17).[25] The description of misery in the difficult ch. 24 mentions widows whose infants are used as pawns because their mothers are in debt, as well as infertile childless women. In the wider context Job's options seem clear: as a respectable patriarch it is his duty to help the poorest and, in Israel, this means (as it does today, all over the world), women amongst others.

In the dialogue section no woman speaks. It is Job, his three friends Eliphaz, Bildad and Zophar, and later on a younger man called Elihu as well as the God of Israel (presented as a male God), who talk. These are talks among men, motivated initially by Job's great misery and the friends' desire to give comfort through explanations and deliberations. Then, in the divine speeches, it is a male God's decision to reply to Job's lamentations and accusations in order to correct the friends' words. The speeches are exhaustingly long and repetitious; the friends often talk at cross purposes or around Job (and vice versa). In effect, what frequently remains is incomprehension, hurt and outrage on all sides. A development of real communication, of changes in the speakers' positions can hardly be detected. Points of view are clarified, but positions harden.

Although, on closer inspection, the book of Job contains several concepts of God, most of them do not contain any components that can be specifically allocated to women or to 'the female'. Divine care demonstrates itself in the careful handling of the human child by the Creator in 10.8-10 and in the womb (31.15; cf. Ps. 139.13b, 15). More frequently, however, the text speaks of God as a sovereign God or a God who treats Job with hostility, attacks and even persecutes him (6.4; 16.7-17; 19.6-12).

---

25. The protection of widows, orphans and strangers (גר) is one of the basic laws concerning fringe groups, cf. Exod. 22.20-21, 23.9; Deut. 24.17.

In the divine speeches there are 'male' characteristics of God, such as his being 'master of animals' and 'fighter against Behemoth and Leviathan'. In 5.8-16 God is presented as a God of subversion, in the old tradition of the weather gods,[26] a God who lifts up the humble and brings down the mighty. Yet this concept of God is no consolation for Job since, for him, it is bound up with the experience of arbitrariness.

Male Suffering and Female Suffering in Israel and in the Book of Job
What does Job suffer from? What did women suffer from at that time? Can this book claim to express the problems of women, too?

Job loses his herds and his children, then his health and physical integrity. On this last point Job is affected worse than his wife. In his speeches he rebels against God because he is sure that he has lead an upright life, and cannot understand why so much misery has come upon him. He suffers because he is excluded from the community of the living, has lost his status and his standing through his impoverishment and disease, and has become a stranger to those closest to him. He suffers because of the inflexibility of his friends, who do not believe in his uprightness.

Let us attempt a kind of corrective counter-reading of the book, with the help of other biblical texts in which women's suffering is described specifically. Women suffer at this time because of extremely dangerous, frequent pregnancies (noted as early as Gen. 3.16). Many women lose their lives in childbirth (e.g. Rachel in Gen. 35). Many infants and children will also have died in front of their very eyes without their mothers being able to help them. Women suffer because of their childlessness, since the only really acceptable social standing they can have is due to being a mother (cf. Michal's fate in 2 Sam. 6.23). Women suffer due to sexual violence (e.g. Gen. 19 and 34; Judg. 19), and in the case of rape they do not only have to bear a man's violence but also be prepared for the social ostracism which rape entails (1 Sam. 13). Women suffer due to the machinations of male politics, as, for example, Rizpah who loses several sons because they

26. Cf. 12.13-25; 26; 34.20; 36.26–37.6; Ps. 113.4-9; Hannah's Prayer in 1 Sam. 2.

were killed in a political act of revenge (2 Sam. 21.8-14). Women suffer due to wars with all the attendant hunger, thirst and expulsion (Lam. 2.11-12). Women have to live in fear of being raped by foreign soldiers or abducted as prisoners of war (cf. Judg. 5.30; Lam. 5.11). Women suffer particularly when the population becomes impoverished. If they are widows, they fall very quickly through the social net and are exposed to the corruption of more influential people without any protection. Somebody might move the boundary stone of their small field (cf. Prov. 23.10), and the next harvest will not be enough to feed their children; a rich man may take their children as pawns because they are in debt (cf. Job 24.2-3).

There are just as many references to specific women's suffering in Israel, great suffering which would have deserved to become the topic of a great book and the subject of a battle with the god-head—just as Job's material losses and disease did. However, the women who are mentioned only briefly in those texts, only rarely turn to the God of Israel in their suffering. One fears that women's suffering was not important enough for the authors of Job to deserve being written about, either. If women participated in writing this book—which we doubt—then they were not able to include their personal experiences of suffering, or made a conscious decision to support the upper social strata perspective of their male co-authors.

The Divine Speeches as Answer to Job's Lament and Accusation
The two divine speeches (38.1–42.6) are also primarily introduced as disputations. God challenges Job to brace himself like a man and battle with God. Job has repeatedly asked in this debate for a direct meeting with God. God accepts the challenge, and now God and the man who has been wronged face each other. The imagery of war and battle seems offensive. But, for Israelites, faith was always associated with the firm conviction that the godhead is great enough for people to shake and struggle with. On the Jabbok, Jacob wrestles with a demon who turns out to be YHWH (Gen. 32). The sisters Leah and Rachel struggle with God over their fertility and their children, struggles which can be recognized in the names of their children (Gen. 29-30). In the Psalms God is asked quite directly to be partial and to intervene.

Such a concept of God seems to us remarkable despite the battle imagery.

The content of the divine speeches has to provide an answer to Job's lament and accusations. To claim that what God says is not that important, and that the very fact that God answers at all is proof enough of the all-powerful God's mercy, leads to a theology which is in danger of becoming cynical. Yet it is not easy to recognize immediately the plausibility of the speeches when reading them for the first time, since they are imbued with images and ideas of the Israelite world picture which, in turn, is part of the Ancient Near Eastern background. Othmar Keel[27] presented a thorough exegesis of the divine speeches against this background which, in our opinion, is a workable basis for more detailed feminist research.

According to Keel the first divine speech is a reply to Job's accusations which are condensed in ch. 3, namely, that the world order is bad. Job has darkened the counsel, indeed blackened it (38.2). In ch. 38 God replies with extensive references to his cosmic creation, which in Ancient Near Eastern thought establishes orders and upholds them daily, and within which human life is in fact possible. In the second part of the divine speech (38.39-39.30) God presents himself as the shepherd of an initially mysterious flock of ten animals grouped in pairs. Keel has shown that the selection of the animals is determined by a motif that is very common in Ancient Near Eastern and Israelite art, namely the so-called 'master of animals'. This divine figure grasps on each side an animal or a mythical creature, each allotted to the steppe or the desert, areas that are inaccessible or even dangerous for humans. In the iconography of seals the 'master of animals' is frequently depicted next to a symbol of the ordered world, the stylized tree above which the sky arches. The divine power which dominates the animals, and at the same time protects and defends them, is therefore probably responsible for the dynamic upholding of the world order. In his answer to Job the God of Israel presents himself expressly as the caring custodian of this animal world which, for humans, represents chaos, a threatening world. He allocates specific regions to these animals

27. Cf. Keel, *Jahwes Entgegnung an Ijob*.

and defends their right to exist as well, an existence which does not serve man and can even be dangerous for him. The role of a shepherd in the Ancient Near East included both keeping and protecting as well as mastering and controlling.[28] The horse is an exception in these ranks of animals; for Israelites it was associated mainly with war, which in turn allowed chaos to break into the well-ordained order and to spread terror.

The second divine speech deals in more detail with the accusations made in ch. 9, esp. 9.22-24. There Job had made the outrageous claim that God is completely indifferent to human fate, that he kills the good and the wicked indiscriminately. Earth is, Job concludes, in the hands of a sadistic criminal. Answering this rebuke in chs. 40–41, God presents himself as the successful fighter against Behemoth (hippopotamus) and Leviathan (crocodile). They represent, also in well-documented (Egyptian, in this case) iconography, the chaos and evil which are overcome in Egypt by the king or the god Horus. Thus the God of Israel is engaged in the battle against injustice and the powers of evil. Although he allows chaos—as it were—its own space, niches in the cosmos, he controls those powers and lays down limits for them. This reply would be disappointing only if Job expected God to be the absolute controller of all this order. Obviously, such a concept of God would not be in accordance with a feminist theology.[29] Job accepts God's speeches as a genuine answer to his inquiries and accusations. Already in his initial reaction (40.3-5) he promises to be silent from now on. He acknowledges the greatness of creation, compared with which he himself feels slight and insignificant: 'I put my hand over my mouth'. His final statement (42.1-6) makes it even clearer that Job

28. Against M. Oeming, ' "Kannst du der Löwin ihren Raub zu jagen geben?" (Hi 38,39): Das Motiv des "Herrn der Tiere" und seine Bedeutung für die Theologie der Gottesreden Hi 38–42', in M. Augustin and K.-D. Schunck (eds.), *Dort ziehen Schiffe dahin… Collected Communications to the XIVth Congress of the International Organization for the Study of the Old Testament, Paris 1992* (BEATAJ, 28; Bern: Peter Lang, 1996), pp. 147-63. He only sees the mastering aspect (cf. pp. 152-58).

29. See also L.M. Bechtel, 'A Feminist Approach to the Book of Job', in A. Brenner (ed.), *A Feminist Companion to Wisdom Literature* (FCB, 9; Sheffield: Sheffield Academic Press, 1995), pp. 222-52, esp. 223-24.

was not simply overcome or persuaded, but actually convinced:

> My ears had heard of you but now my eyes have seen you.
> Therefore I change my mind and comfort myself on dust and ashes.
> (42.5-6)

The vision of God makes knowledge of the divine possible, and only a few are granted this knowledge. For Job this moment means a change, it is a moment of conversion. But this is a conversion without an attitude of repentance—although the old translations and the majority of exegetes disagree on this count.[30] Job is no longer interested in what he has said before because he has been convinced and consoled (but not put off!). While still sitting in dust and ashes, Job becomes a different person.[31] Is it possible for us to understand this development? Is God's answer an answer to questions about the purpose of the world order—an answer for Job as a 'problem bearer'? Is it an answer in a situation of real suffering, to a Job as somebody afflicted by actual suffering? We would answer these questions in the affirmative. For, within the various biblical models of creation, the divine speeches offer, together with Psalm 104, a concept which is not anthropocentric. Creation is not calculated for humans, as presented in different forms in Genesis 1 and 2. In the world-view of wisdom literature creation is a structure in which humans take the place which has been allocated to them, next to animals and many other created beings and things. The creation of man and woman is not mentioned in ch. 38—and this is no coincidence! Thus Job who was brought into dire straits by suffering is taken into the expanse of creation, an expanse which makes his relative importance clear, but which also unburdens him. Job is not in the center of creation, something which he learns in a long, painful process of disillusionment and also allows new beginnings. This concept of humanity should offer an opening for feminist exegesis, theology and ethics, since it offers solutions to problems which our western culture and its

30. As can still be found in Bechtel, 'A Feminist Approach to the Book of Job', p. 250.

31. In accordance with J. Ebach, *Streiten mit Gott. Hiob. Teil 2: Hiob 21–42* (Neukirchen–Vluyn: Neukirchener Verlag, 1996), pp. 158-160; and E. van Wolde, 'The Development of Job: Mrs Job as Catalyst', in A. Brenner (ed.), *A Feminist Companion to Wisdom Literature*, pp. 201-21, esp. 219-20.

attendant androcentrism has not overcome to this day. On the basis of the divine speeches, a new relationship between human and creator can be called for. In those speeches there is no criticism whatsoever of 'man as the measure of all things', that is, the distancing from anthropocentrism is not coupled with a criticism of patriarchal orders. Even a world-view which presupposes a single divine power, but which nevertheless allows the existence of 'niches for chaos', is in our opinion worth discussing in terms of a feminist theology, since the separation of evil onto a semi-divine figure is out of the question.

Where Can Wisdom Be Found?
Just before Job starts his final plea, his speeches and those of his three friends are interrupted in ch. 28 by a self-contained poem on wisdom. The verse, 'But where can wisdom be found?', is repeated like a refrain. 'Where does understanding dwell?' (vv. 12, 20). Wisdom poems in which personified wisdom appears or is picked out as a central theme can also be found in Proverbs 1–9, Sirach 1 and 24 as well as in Wisdom of Solomon 6–10, in each case with a specific emphasis. In the book of Job wisdom is a hidden, incomprehensible quantity only God has access to.

> When he established the force of the wind and measured out the waters,
> when he made a decree for the rain and a path for the thunderstorm,
> then he looked at wisdom and appraised it; he confirmed it and tested it
> (28.25-27).

For humans wisdom is untraceable. It hardly ever appears in human shape: in the final verses it looks like a secret plan which runs through everything. The personification is in keeping with the theme of the whole book: for Job the human, it seems impossible to find ultimate wisdom and knowledge; the paths leading to it are closed. Such feelings of deepest skepticism can already be found in the older wisdom literature of Egypt and Mesopotamia. Job 28 is an important chapter for a feminist reading of the book, as in it thoughts critical of patriarchy are expressed implicitly. Such thoughts could become a starting point for the reading of the whole book.

Job 28.1-11 uses numerous images from mining. It describes the things *homo faber* is able to do in his resourcefulness, and how he manages to get access to the most inaccessible entrails of the earth. This technical approach has something almost offensive about it, as in all those actions people do things which are actually reserved for God, such as raging like fire, overturning mountains and splitting rocks.[32] In spite of crossing the frontier in this area, man (28.13) does not find wisdom and his skills fail. Verses 15-19 contain, in accordance with the traditional *topos* of wisdom theology, the praise of the preciousness of wisdom, the possession of which exceeds all wealth and riches known to man at that time. This thought too contains a crux of argument: wisdom cannot be bought, it is hidden from all, rich or poor. Only God, who has established it in creation, knows the way to it (28.23-27). In this sense ch. 28 prepares the need for the divine speeches. Absent wisdom and knowledge can only be found in the encounter with God.

Chapter 28 gets to the heart of the powerlessness of Job's friends, who consider themselves wise and are so sure of themselves that they accuse their friend, despite his protestations to the contrary, of being a sinner since he has suffered so much. In terms of content and structure, the chapter is so closely bound up with its context that we do not consider it to be a later extension of the book.[33] The last verse (28.28) may very well be a gloss, but it is a meaningful continuation of the preceding thought: wisdom is the fear of the Lord, a piety which has ethical consequences such as avoiding evil. Wisdom does not consist of philosophizing about God and the world, but proves itself in just actions.[34]

Job's Wife and Daughters in the Frame Narrative

According to the prologue Job, the rich man, has seven sons and three daughters. None of the children whom he loses all at once

32. For a detailed discussion see R. Zimmermann, 'Homo Sapiens Ignorans: Hiob 28 als Bestandteil der ursprünglichen Hiobdichtung', *BN* 74 (1994), pp. 80-100, esp. 88-91.

33. Cf. Zimmermann, 'Homo Sapiens Ignorans', pp. 97-98. From a different perspective, Fontaine draws the same conclusion. Analyzing the book of Job as a folktale, in accordance with the studies of the Russian structuralist Vladimir Propp, she sees Job 28 as a necessary thematic bridge to the 'provision or receipt of a magical agent' and Job's reaffirmation of his own position (Fontaine, 'Folktale Structure in the Book of Job', pp. 218-19).

34. Cf. the very concise summary at the end of Ecclesiastes, in 12.13-14.

is mentioned by name. Job's relationship with them is raised only in so far as his offering sacrifices for potential sins they may have committed, and his mourning of their deaths. Neither does Job's wife have a name in the prologue. Job does not lose his wife through his misfortune; and in the epilogue she is not even mentioned again, since she is not one of the gifts Job receives anew. And yet, she bears him ten other children. In the prologue she does not appear until ch. 2, when her critically ill husband is already sitting in ashes. Job's wife speaks only one verse, and Job replies with one verse:

> His wife said to him: Are you still holding on to your integrity (תמה)?
> Bless/Curse (ברך) God and die!
> He replied: You speak as one of the foolish women speak (אחת הנבלות).
> Shall we accept good from God and not trouble? (2.9-10)

Traditionally the wife's statement or question (which in Hebrew is open) is interpreted either as an expression of incomprehension, or of mocking. Her suggestion that Job should bless/curse (ברך) God and die has been related to the satan's announcement (2.5) that Job would ברך God to his face. This is why Augustine called the wife a *diaboli adiutrix*, Satan's helper who was to tempt Job. This interpretation, however, has to be countered on several counts.[35] Initially, at least, the wife speaks with God's words (cf. 2.3). She states or asks if Job will hold on to his integrity. The term ברך is used in the book of Job consistently in its ambivalent meaning of blessing and cursing. The common interpretation of ברך only as a euphemism for 'cursing' would be too narrow, both in this passage as in others. The text deliberately leaves the meaning undecided: as a curse in the sense of a fending off of disaster, or a blessing in the sense of praise of the admirable.[36] It is possible that the wife suggests that Job bless God once more as long as he holds on—or is able to hold on—to his integrity, then die at peace with God after this farewell.[37] It is also possible that she points out to Job the absurdity of his holding on to God and

35. Cf. also Ebach, *Hiobs Post*, pp. 68-70.
36. Cf. T. Linafelt, 'The Undecidability of ברך in the Prologue of Job and Beyond', *BibInt* 4 (1996), pp. 154-72.
37. See also the midrash on Job 2.9, in S.A. Wertheimer (ed.), *Battei Midrashot II* (Jerusalem: Mossad Ha-Rav Quq, 2nd edn, 1968), p. 165.

suggests that he curse and turn away from this God, a God who has abandoned him, and then die, since blasphemy always carried the death penalty (Lev. 24.16).[38] Both cases could involve compassion or, at any rate, common sense instead of mockery or sarcasm. Job's wife wants a way out of this hopelessness, even if this means death. Job does not accept this and rejects her as 'one of the foolish women', אחת הנבלות. The counterpart Hebrew masculine term represents, above all, socially inferior people (cf. 30.8) but also the godless (cf. Ps. 14.1). Job does not want to escape through death but, instead, to bear his suffering. Together with his wife—as is suggested by the use of the plural—he wants to accept evil from God as much as good. This is the only passage in the Hebrew Bible where a husband does not listen to the wife advising him, as was expected of Israelite and Jewish wives.[39] An important observation was made by Ellen van Wolde: due to his wife Job becomes a questioning person, and it is only through her that he, who in 1.20-22 is still highly loyal to his God and simply mourns his loss, reaches a point where he even considers the possibility of *not* accepting evil from God.[40] This brief confrontation between Job and his wife is not unambiguous, thus leaving readers dissatisfied. It is not surprising, then, that the Greek text tradition has preserved a much longer version of this passage which is, however, dated even later than the Septuagint, as it represents an expanding interpretation:

> After much time had passed his wife said to him,
> 'How long will you endure, saying,
> "Behold, I shall wait a little longer, expecting the hope of my salvation."
> Behold, your memory is already blotted out from the earth,
> the sons and daughters, the travail and pangs of my womb,
> whom I reared with toil in vain.

38. Cf. J. Ebach, *Streiten mit Gott. Hiob. Teil 1: Hiob 1–20* (Neukirchen–Vluyn: Neukirchener Verlag, 1996), p. 37.

39. As can be found already in the midrash on Gen. 3.12: *Gen. R.* 19.

40. Van Wolde, 'The Development of Job', p. 205. Fontaine ('Folktale Structure in the Book of Job', p. 215) characterizes Job's wife as a 'princess tester' in the plot structure, and her question as a critical theological reflection on the matter at hand. From the perspective of the tale, the wife's answer must be suppressed for further tests by the friends.

> And you sit in decay caused by worms, spending the nights outside,
> and I am a wanderer and a servant,
> going from place to place and from house to house,
> looking for the sun to set, in order that I might rest from my toils and pains which now oppress me.
> But say some word against the Lord and die.'[41]

In this expansion the wife also remains nameless. But the suggestion that Job should speak against God and then die is now put into a wider context. The wife refers to herself as one involved in Job's suffering. It is her children who were snatched from her, her toil was in vain. Without rest she roams about in search of a source of support, fleeing from pain.

Job's wife has a sister in Tobit's wife, who works equally hard for the support of her husband (Tob. 2.11-14). In this case, however, the wife's provocative question about the reward for Tobit's piety stems from an argument about a small billy goat. Tobit does not believe that it was given to his wife as a present.

The *Testament of Job*, written in the first century before or after the birth of Christ, is probably based in its description of Job's wife on the verses quoted above. There at last she is given a name: Sitis, reminiscent of *Ausitis*, the Greek translation of Uz, the home of Job; or Sitidos, an allusion to Greek σιτίζειν, 'to give bread'. Sitidos who, full of compassion, takes care of her husband and feeds him, eventually dies and, in the end, Job has Dinah for a second wife.

For a feminist reading of the book of Job the wife is a challenge in various respects. Through her, the patriarchal character of the book becomes dramatically apparent. Although she is afflicted by the same disasters as Job, apart from the disease, her suffering is not recognized; in fact, she herself is hardly mentioned. Contrary to all biblical role-conventions her advice is not accepted by Job: she is called foolish and dishonorable, and is removed from the story that follows. At the same time, however, the later narrative traditions show that this important gap had a stimulating effect on readers' imagination and called for more details. It is no coincidence that the *Testament of Job* devotes so

41. J.E. Hartley, *The Book of Job* (NICOT, 18; Grand Rapids: Eerdmans, 1988), p. 83.

much attention to this wife and to Job's daughters. A Job as devoid of relationships as the one in the Hebrew tradition was not acceptable. And it was seemingly also unbearable that the suffering and co-suffering of this woman was not mentioned at all.

Job's three daughters also provide a starting point for a feminist reading of the book. The first three daughters die without their names being given, whereas the three later daughters are mentioned by name: Jemimah (turtle dove), Keziah (cassia)[42] and Keren-Happuch (horn of antimony).[43]. It is worth noting that neither the first set nor the second set of seven sons are mentioned by name, although the daughters are. The names come from the area of aesthetics and cosmetics and, to us, sound cute. The daughters' beauty is emphasized and brings glory to Job everywhere in the country. Despite this renewed androcentrism, which forces the women into a specific role, it is worth noting that by naming the women their status is enhanced quite significantly as compared with the sons. This revaluation becomes obvious in the fact that the sisters are given a share in the father's inheritance together with their brothers, quite an improper way of organizing one's will by Israelite standards. We have to relate this short comment to Numbers 27 and 36, texts which were also written in the postexilic era when many of the properties in Judah had to be reorganized. Those passages speak of the daughters of Zelophehad, who are also mentioned by name. [44] These daughters come and speak to Moses, because they consider it unjust that their father's inheritance (נחלה) should be lost only because he had no sons. Their appeal is granted: in such cases daughters shall be entitled to inherit from now on. The amendment of this law, restricted again in Numbers 36, is in order to prevent the tribe from losing the inheritance in the event of the daughters' marrying out of it. Henceforth those women

42. An aromatic plant used in perfumes and for incense; see, e.g., Exod. 30.24; Ps. 45.9.

43. A black metallic powder used as mascara; see, e.g., 2 Kgs 9.30; Jer. 4.30.

44. Cf. A. Sterring, 'The Will of the Daughters', in A. Brenner (ed.), *A Feminist Companion to Exodus to Deuteronomy* (FCB, 6; Sheffield: Sheffield Academic Press, 1994), pp. 88-99.

are only allowed to marry within their tribe. Job's settlement exceeds these legal guidelines. His daughters are entitled to be heirs, just as their brothers are. What caused the change in Job's relationships? Could it be that, through his suffering and the content of the divine speeches, he has come to realize that his name is to continue in his daughters, and that these women are also entitled to a self-sufficient and financially secure life, independent of men? If this were the case, then the detached Job of the prologue would have, at least, found a new role as a father through the dialogue.

The three daughters' subject status is also strongly emphasized in the *Testament of Job*. The whole of the third part of the book is dedicated to them.[45] However, their share in their father's inheritance is no longer material but spiritual. Whether this is an advantage remains to be seen. It is interesting to note that the three women are regarded as entitled to inherit as far as piety and revelations are concerned. They are full religious subjects. The brief verses about Job's wife and daughters in the book of Job call, as it were, for a reinterpretation, possibly by female authors.

A Glance at the History of Interpretation
A feminist exegesis cannot skip the history of interpretation, since sometimes interpretation may imply patriarchal constraints while, at other times, it offers a key to a diverse reading of the biblical text. The book of Job has influenced an immense amount of works of literature, art and music.[46] Thus we are going to limit ourselves to the theological reception of the book.

In the Jewish history of interpretation the book of Job is not used for reading in the synagogue, but passages of it are quoted

45. For a detailed discussion see R. Lesses, 'The Daughters of Job', in E. Schüssler Fiorenza (ed.), *Searching the Scriptures* (2 vols.; New York: Crossroad Publishing, 1994), II, pp. 139-49; and L. Sutter Rehmann, 'Das Testament Hiobs', in L. Schottroff and M.-Th. Wacker (eds.), *Kompendium Feministische Bibelauslegung* (Gütersloh: Gütersloher Verlag, 1998), pp. 465-73.

46. Cf. Ebach 'Hiob/Hiobbuch', pp. 370-73; G. Langenhorst, *Hiob unser Zeitgenosse: Die literarische Hiob-Rezeption im 20.Jahrhundert als theologische Herausforderung* (Mainz: Grünewald Verlag, 2nd edn, 1995).

or referred to in sermon-like and ethical texts.[47] Interpretation centers on the frame narrative and the character of Job. For example, the book's significance becomes obvious in the fact that according to the Babylonian Talmud (*b. B. Bat.* 14b.) Moses is its author and Job is compared to Abraham (*b. B. Bat.* 15b; cf. *M. Soṭ.* 5.5; *Gen. R.* 49.9). The rabbis see Job as a historical character, but place him in completely different epochs. The Babylonian Talmud reports the contrary opinion of an unnamed individual according to whom Job never existed and who says that the story of Job was a fairy tale (*b. B. Bat.* 15a). The rabbinical interest centers on Job's piety: more precisely, on the discussion of the sentence in Job 13.15 which was read completely differently in the Hebrew version. Sometimes it was seen as the result of Job giving up, as in the translation of the consonantal text and in Martin Luther's translation: 'even if he kills me I will not (i.e. לֹא) place my hope (in him)'. Sometimes it is understood as indicating a revolt of Job's, as read by the Masoretes who vocalized the text and in the New International Version: 'though he slay me, yet I will hope in him (i.e. לוֹ)'. The rabbis represent the latter opinion, referring to Job 27.5 and thus interpreting Job as a man who feared God throughout and until the end (*M. Soṭ.* 5.5; *b. Soṭ.* 27b). The identification of Job's wife with Dinah, Jacob's daughter who is already mentioned in the *Testament of Job*, is also widespread in the Jewish history of interpretation. In the midrash on Genesis (*Gen. R.* 57 for Gen. 22.21) it is based on a compilation of the name for Job's wife as one of the foolish women (נבלות) and the verse in Gen. 34.7 which talks about the scandalous deed (נבלה) which Shechem committed with Dinah (cf. also *b. B. Bat* 15b; *Gen. R.*19; Josephus, *Ant.* 8.8; *y. Soṭ.* 5.8). The midrash on Gen. 3.12 (*Gen. R.* 19) even draws a parallel between her and Eve, and Job becomes the counterpart of Adam[48] because he does not accept his wife's advice. On the whole Job's wife is presented in a more positive light than in the Christian tradition: her reaction is interpreted as an expression of

47. S. Schreiner, 'Der gottesfürchtige Rebell oder Wie die Rabbinen die Frömmigkeit Hiobs deuteten', *ZTK* 89 (1992), pp. 159-71.

48. A similar interpretation is given by S. Meier, 'Job I–II: A Reflection of Genesis I–III', *VT* 39 (1989), pp. 183-93.

love and loyalty towards Job.[49]

The Qur'ān too knows Job as the patient, good servant of God and names him, together with other well-known men such as David and Solomon, the patriarchs, Moses and Aaron (surah 4.163; 6.84; 21.83-84; 38.41-44). As in the Christian interpretation with regard to Job's wife, the Qur'ān commentaries are more misogynous than the original text itself. In surah 38.44, for instance, Job is issued with the hard-to-understand challenge to keep a formerly given oath through lashes with a sheaf (of twigs). In the commentaries this is explained thus: Job had sworn to give his wife 100 cane strokes and this oath was to be kept in the mildest manner, with a light cane.[50]

Christian interpretation continues the tradition of the good sufferer Job. However, it is worth noting that the New Testament, on the one hand, does refer to Job's endurance (Jas 5.11); but, on the other hand, it does not reduce him to the image of the good sufferer but takes up phrases and statements about divine knowledge from the book of Job.[51] The above-mentioned pejorative view of Job's wife by Augustine is continued by calling her 'Xanthippe' and, thereby, comparing her with the pugnacious wife of Socrates.[52]

The History of Art contains interesting views of Job interpretation.[53] Byzantine book miniatures demonstrate a notable

---

49. R. Gordis, *The Book of God and Man: A Study of Job* (Chicago: Chicago University Press, 1965), p. 11; cf. Wertheimer, *Battei Midrashot II*, p. 165.

50. R. Paret, *Der Koran: Kommentar und Konkordanz* (Stuttgart: W. Kohlhammer, 2nd edn, 1980), p. 422.

51. Similarly T. Hainthaler, '*Von der Ausdauer Ijobs habt ihr gehört' (Jak 5,11): Zur Bedeutung des Buches Ijob im Neuen Testament* (Bern: Peter Lang, 1988).

52. As noted by Ebach, *Hiobs Post*, pp. 68-69; and also J. Ebach, *Feministische Aspekte des Hiobbuches*, unpublished manuscript, n.d. A similar type of 'female rebuker figure' or female scold can already be found in the women characters of Prov. 1–9 and 31. Cf. A. Brenner and F. van Dijk-Hemmes, *On Gendering Texts: Female and Male Voices in the Hebrew Bible* (BIS, 1; Leiden: E.J. Brill, 1993), pp. 56-62, 113-17.

53. See, e.g., the work of William Blake on this topic, in M. Perry-Lehmann (ed.), *There Was a Man in the Land of Uz: William Blake's Illustrations to the Book of Job* (Jerusalem: The Israel Museum, 1992); and Fontaine's Preface to this volume.

interest in the family of the rich man Job,[54] in the figure of the satan and in all those details in the (Greek!) text which inspire the imagination such as certain animals, Leviathan and Behemoth, or personifications such as the earth or the demons of sickness. In these pictures Job's wife is sometimes presented as compassionately helpful or preaching, more often as gripped by revulsion. Quite frequent in such illuminations, as in the rest of Christian art, is a typological connection between Job and Christ.

Until now we have not discussed one form of Job interpretation which we consider particularly worthy of note. In the Jewish tradition, especially since Auschwitz, and in liberation theology, there are collective interpretations of Job which significantly differ in their approach from the possibilities discussed up to now.[55] One example for a Jewish collective interpretation is the 1946 book by Margarete Susman.[56] For the philosopher and essayist, writing under the shock of the *Shoah*, the fate of the beaten Jewish people is mirrored in Job; it is a people that looks back to a brilliant past, a people that laments its boundless suffering, a people that cannot comprehend its repudiation and shame and, yet, wants to understand the will of God for whose sake it suffers. Just as Job, the Jewish people does not atone for an individual sin, but for the offense of the human race[57] and, like Job, in this question about the 'Why' and in its struggle with God, encounters its God and itself anew. Thus the character of Job helps the author to understand the incomprehensible, namely the cruel fate of her people, and to understand the One whom this people in deep piety experienced as its God.[58]

54. P. Huber, *Hiob—Dulder oder Rebell? Byzantinische Miniaturen zum Buch Hiob in Patmos, Rom, Venedig, Sinai, Jerusalem und Athos* (Düsseldorf: Patmos Verlag, 1986).

55. See S. Schroer, 'Entstehungsgeschichtliche und gegenwärtige Situierungen des Hiob-Buches', in Ökumenischer Arbeitskreis für Bibelarbeit (ed.), *Hiob (Bibelarbeit in der Gemeinde)* (Basel: Reinhardt Verlag; Zürich: Benziger Verlag, 1989), pp. 35-62, esp. 57-62.

56. M. Susman, *Das Buch Hiob und das Schicksal des jüdischen Volkes* (Freiburg: Herder, 1968 [1946]).

57. M. Susman, *Das Buch Hiob und das Schicksal des jüdischen Volkes*, pp. 72-73, 77.

58. Other Jewish writers such as Hans Jonas and Richard L. Rubinstein criticize or even refuse to take Job as a figure for interpreting the Shoah. See

In the 1980s Latin-American liberation theologians presented collective interpretations of Job.[59] Enrique Dussel sees the people of El Salvador as a collective Job, and his interpretation of the book is based on the background of this people's suffering. This people—like Job—knows about its suffering and, at the same time, its innocence. Job's lament is made topical with the witness of martyrdom of Christians in that country. Dussel interprets the whole of the Job dialogue in the context of the frame narrative: God has given way to the satan, thus Job's friends too are the satan's agents who wish to convince Job that he is suffering because he has sinned. The system of rule, 'Satan' and his 'Wise Men', are only interested in the oppressed people's belief that they are to blame for their own suffering.[60] Although the biblical Job is not a representative of the poor, he is at most a representative of society's impoverished upper strata. Although there are no grounds for the description of the friends as agents of the satan in the text, it is surely legitimate to consider Job the representative of the affected and wise people that are no longer deceived by *status quo* theology which aims at sanctioning unjust conditions by placing the burden of injustice on the individual. After all, the biblical Job is not an individual but a symbolic figure whose theme is the problem of many people, both in an exemplary and certainly also an extreme fashion.

Conclusion: Feminist Keys to the Book

For a feminist reading, a look at the widely differing interpretations of Job is very encouraging. In the past, interpretations have been presented which made Job topical and were triggered by specific groups and concrete situations. History is really only waiting for a feminist continuation of this practice. The feminist Job project can start from the gaps in the text, for example, with

Langenhorst, *Hiob unser Zeitgenosse*, pp. 209-13.

59. E. Dussel, *Herrschaft und Befreiung: Ansatz, Stationen und Themen einer lateinamerikanischen Theologie der Befreiung* (Fribourg: Edition Exodus, 1985); cf. also G. Gutiérrez, *Hablar de Dios desde el sufrimiento del inocente: Una reflexión sobre el libro de Job* (Salamanca: Ed. Sigueme, 1986). A discussion of Gutiérrez's work is given in Langenhorst, *Hiob unser Zeitgenosse*, pp. 365-75.

60. Cf. Dussel, *Herrschaft und Befreiung*, pp. 184-85.

Job's wife;[61] with Job's daughters as his heiresses, not only beautiful but also equal to their brothers; or with the collective experience of the female people of God, with the unjust suffering of women. The latter approach is brought up in Käthe Kollwitz's images of women and children 'in misery', since the art-historical tradition knows both 'Job in misery' and 'Christ in misery'. A key for an inclusive reading of the book could be a righteous female sufferer, for example, the poor widow in 24.3, 21 and 31.60 as a representative of marginalized people, above all women. Their existence can be compared with that of the desert animals (24.4), seen as chaotic by other people and who, according to the first divine speech, are nevertheless under God's loving care. Job's wife too is a righteous (female) sufferer, deprived of her status as a religious subject and banned from the book. The search for her voice, the suppressed voices of women in the book, can be compared with the approach by Athalya Brenner and Fokkelien van Dijk-Hemmes that they call 'gendering texts'. It means looking for textual voices that reflect female or male gender, in this case the experience of female suffering or the female struggle with God. Job's wife—not a subject but a nameless womb which is associated with finiteness and impurity, the violated Dinah, the Sitidos who demeans herself for bread, the woman who has been handed over to strangers (31.10)—passages such as Job 3.20-22, 7.2-8, 10.8-14 and 16.7-19—can be read as the laments of such female figures. The 'hymns of subversion', such as 5.8-16 and 12.3-25, can be read as their songs of hope for a change in their circumstances; this is an interpretation which is already part of the biblical tradition, as in Hannah's Prayer (1 Sam. 2) and Mary's Song (Lk. 1). In this context the interpretations of the deuteronomic Torah in Job. 24 and 31 have to be seen as an ethical admonition—stronger than usual—to alleviate the suffering of women. The righteous female sufferer can become a subject once more. This is, however, a per-spective which in the book itself appears only on the horizon; it becomes a reality in the case of the righteous woman's daughters

61. Cf. G. Deninger-Polzer, 'Hiobs Frau: Leidtragende, nicht Randfigur', in K. Walter (ed.), *Zwischen Ohnmacht und Befreiung: Biblische Frauengestalten* (Freiburg: Herder, 1988), pp. 109-21; and the narrative exegesis by A. Chedid, *La femme de Job* (Paris: Editions Calmann-Lévy, 1993).

with their names and inheritance.

A further key for the feminist reading could be the divine speeches in chs. 38–41, together with wisdom's description in ch. 28. From a theological point of view, ch. 28 implies several areas which can be filled with feminist criticism: the criticism of a male world and an almost scientific understanding of wisdom which subjects all areas of the world, does not leave any secrets and yet does not manage to find the life-giving wisdom mysteriously given at the creation. It is a criticism of a wisdom which is open only to the rich and does not go hand in hand with a fear of God. Within the framework of this criticism of androcentrism, the non-anthropocentric concept of God and the world in chs. 38–41 open up a perspective that may liberate women. The divine speeches not only lead Job out of the confinement of his suffering, but also give readers a view of the wider context of creation. God shows himself as a power of life which is not focused on the male individual but gives scope to everyone, man and woman alike. At the same time, a world-view becomes obvious in which suffering and chaos have their place but are limited. After his change of heart Job, who until then was isolated, can build his relationships with his friends, his relatives and the daughters whom he now treats differently from the expectations of a patriarchal order. He can only continue to live once his point of view has changed. Read from this perspective, the book of Job stands for a theology which is based on experience, a theology which is not androcentric, which gives its readers ethical standards not only in relation to their fellow human beings but also in relation to the world about them.

What we have shown is that feminist interpretations of Job start at its fringes or gaps. We think that this should be reflected on and continued. For example, a comparative reading of the Masoretic and Septuagint texts does not exist as yet. It was important to us to put aside the interpretative context of the prologue and the epilogue and to fathom the depths of a least some of the texts in their contrariness and diversity.

LADY WISDOM AND DAME FOLLY AT QUMRAN

Sidnie White Crawford[1]

The female figures of Lady Wisdom and Dame Folly, found in the postexilic wisdom literature, have always attracted much debate and speculation. The questions of who they are and what they stand for, particularly in the case of Lady Wisdom, have been hotly debated. Is she merely a literary creation, driven by the fact that the nouns for 'wisdom' in Hebrew and Greek, *ḥokmâ* and *sophia*, are feminine in gender? Or is she an actual divine figure, a female hypostasis of Yahweh, the god of Israel, indicating a female divine presence in Israelite religion? These debates have yet to be resolved. Now that the large corpus of sapiential texts from Qumran is beginning to be studied, new light may be shed on the figures of Lady Wisdom and Dame Folly. This paper investigates these two figures in three Qumran texts, 4Q184, 'The Wiles of the Wicked Woman'; 4Q185, 'A Sapiential Work'; and 4Q525, 'Beatitudes,' to see if the presentation of these figures in three otherwise unknown texts can shed any light on their function in Second Temple Jewish thought. First, I will begin with a brief overview of the wisdom texts containing these two figures, starting with the biblical evidence.

Hebrew Bible

Lady Wisdom, or Wisdom personified as a female figure, appears in one canonical wisdom text, the book of Proverbs. Wisdom also appears in the book of Job, but less as a personified figure and more as an abstract concept. Both books are generally considered to be postexilic, and both are found at Qumran. The

1. This article originally appeared in a volume of *Dead Sea Discoveries* honoring Eugene C. Ulrich of the University of Notre Dame.

parade text for the figure of Lady Wisdom is Proverbs 1–9, where she appears in three major pericopes, 1.20-33, 8.1-36 and 9.1-6, 10-12. In these pericopes Wisdom speaks for herself, on her own authority. Her primary relationship is with God, since she is the first thing created by God, and she is with God during the entire act of creation. However, her chief delight and focus is men, to whom she constantly calls. It is through her that men are able to attain knowledge of God and the good life (3.13-18).[2] In Wisdom's main speech in ch. 8, she claims that she was created by God before the cosmos, dwells with God, and participated with, or at least observed, God in the creation of the world. All these attributes make her status as a divine being, at least in Proverbs 1–9, seem unquestionable.[3]

Her opposite number, Dame Folly (Heb. אשתכסילות is, however, clearly human. She is identified with the 'strange woman' (Heb. אשה זרה), the adulteress whose purpose is to lead the young man astray (the androcentric nature of the text here should not require comment). She is also the 'foreign' woman (נכריה), who, like many foreign women in the Israelite tradition, leads men from the right (Israelite) path.[4] The most interesting

2. I am using the term 'men' advisedly here. As Carol Newsom has convincingly demonstrated, Prov. 1–9 is written in a male voice to a male audience; women, whether as wisdom or folly, function only as the other against which men measure themselves. Carol A. Newsom, 'Woman and the Discourse of Patriarchal Wisdom: A Study of Proverbs 1–9,' in Peggy L. Day (ed.), *Gender and Difference in Ancient Israel* (Minneapolis: Augsburg– Fortress 1989), pp. 142-60.

3. Wisdom's attributes and actions can be related to Ancient Near Eastern tutelary gods such as the Sumerians' Nisaba and Inanna and the Egyptians' Ma'at and Isis, thus reinforcing her divine status. See Carole R. Fontaine, 'Proverbs', in Carol A. Newsom and Sharon H. Ringe (eds.), *The Women's Bible Commentary* (Louisville, KY: Westminster/John Knox Press, 1993), pp. 145-52.

4. Cf. the condemnation of Solomon in 1 Kgs 11.1-8 for being led astray by his foreign wives. Solomon is, of course, traditionally credited as author of the Book of Proverbs (1.1). For further discussion of the אשה זרה in Proverbs, see Gale A. Yee, ' "I Have Perfumed my Bed with Myrrh": The Foreign Woman ('iššâ zārâ) in Proverbs 1–9'; and Harold C. Washington, 'The Strange Woman (אשה זרה/נכריה) of Proverbs 1–9 and Post-Exilic Judaean Society', both in Athalya Brenner (ed.), *A Feminist Companion to*

thing to note about the portrayal of Folly is that, while Wisdom's gifts cover all aspects of life (e.g. riches, insight, a life of ease), Folly's snares are almost entirely sexual (a telling comment on male fears of female temptation). This is in spite of the fact that other parts of Proverbs 1–9 mention other types of wicked or foolish behavior (e.g. theft, lying, murder, haughtiness; cf. 1.11-19, 4.24, 6.12-19). So while Wisdom, the positive female figure, embraces all aspects of human life, Folly the negative female encompasses only sexual sin. In her two main speeches, 7.10-20 and 9.13-18, her allure is sexual, although the consequences of heeding her are cosmic, leading to 'the depths of Sheol', pointing to a dark, chthonic side of Folly.[5] This is a theme that will recur.

The wisdom poem in Job 28.12-28 is thought by many to be a separate wisdom piece incorporated by the author of Job into his book. In it, wisdom is clearly associated with God, and is said to be created by God at the time of creation. However, wisdom is not a personified figure here, and no particular emphasis is given to its feminine characteristics. Interestingly, it is God who shows the way to wisdom, rather than vice versa. A variation on this theme appears in later apocryphal and pseudepigraphical literature.[6]

Apocrypha and Pseudepigrapha

There are several passages in the apocryphal and pseudepi-graphical literature in which the figure of Wisdom appears, in which two distinct strands of the understanding of that figure begin to emerge. These passages draw heavily on Proverbs 1–9, although other influences also appear. The Wisdom of Jesus Ben Sira, or Ecclesiasticus, opens with the praise of Wisdom, a female

Wisdom Literature (Sheffield: Sheffield Academic Press, 1995), pp. 110-26, 157-85.

5. I would like to thank Carole Fontaine for drawing my attention to this aspect of Folly. See Fontaine, 'Proverbs', and also Claudia Camp, 'What's So Strange about the Strange Woman?' in D. Jobling, P.L. Day and G.T. Sheppard (eds.), *The Bible and the Politics of Exegesis: Essays in Honor of Norman K. Gottwald on his Sixty-Fifth Birthday* (Cleveland: Pilgrim Press, 1991), p. 31.

6. For commentary on Job, see, e.g., Norman Habel, *The Book of Job: A Commentary* (OTL; Philadelphia: Westminster Press, 1985).

figure, created by God before all other things, and poured out on
all flesh (1.1-20). Her manifestation in human beings is the 'fear
of the Lord', which is the beginning, the fullness, the crown, and
the root of Wisdom. In ch. 24, Wisdom describes herself as a
divine being, whose home is in the heavens, seeking a dwelling
place on earth, among humans. Here the relationship to Wisdom's speech in Proverbs 8 is clear.[7] Finally, God commands her
to dwell with Israel, and this leads Ben Sira to his great declaration, that Wisdom is the Torah, the special possession of Israel:
'All this is the book of the covenant of the Most High God, the
law that Moses commanded us as an inheritance for the congre-
gations of Jacob' (24.23; see also 15.1). This important theme will
recur in other literature. Finally, Ben Sira 51.13-20 is a poem
detailing the author's search for wisdom as a youth; the description of wisdom has erotic overtones (51.15), but Wisdom's overall characterization is as an abstract concept rather than a
personified being. Ben Sira does not mention Folly as a
personification of wickedness; however, his book is rife with
warnings concerning the dangers of women's sexuality, which
he considers ready to burst out and wreak havoc at a moment's
notice (e.g. 22.3-6; 25.16-26; 26.7-12).[8] Ben Sira is found in fragmentary form at Qumran (where it was found in Cave 2, but not
in Cave 4) and Masada, although ch. 24 has not been found
either at Qumran or Masada. Chapter 51 surfaces at Qumran in
an unexpected place, in 11QPsalms[a] as a free-standing psalm,
indicating that before its location in Ben Sira it was a 'free-float-
ing' composition.[9]

The Wisdom of Solomon, which is not found at Qumran, also
declares that Wisdom is a divine being, present at creation
(7.22b-8.1), but the book moves in a completely different direction, heavily influenced by Hellenistic thought.[10] In the Wisdom

---

7.   Eileen M. Schuller, 'The Apocrypha', in C.A. Newsom and S.H.
Ringe (eds.), *The Women's Bible Commentary* (Louisville, KY; Westmin-
ster/John Knox Press, 1992), p. 237. Wisdom's speech is also similar to the
self-laudatory Isis hymns from the Hellenistic period.

8.   For further discussion, see Schuller, 'Apocrypha', p. 237.

9.   James C. VanderKam, *The Dead Sea Scrolls Today* (Grand Rapids:
Eerdmans, 1994), pp. 35-36.

10. David Winston, *The Wisdom of Solomon* (AB, 43; Garden City:

of Solomon, Wisdom is an eternal emanation of the deity, both immanent and transcendent, that permeates all creation and makes those who seek her the friends of God. There are also erotic elements in the portrayal of Wisdom, when Solomon seeks to make her his bride and desires 'intercourse' (συναναστροφή) with her (8.2-16). Nowhere, however, does the Wisdom of Solomon equate Wisdom with the Torah.[11] This portrayal of Wisdom, with its clear Greek overtones, is unique in the Apocrypha and the Pseudepigrapha.

Two other short passages from the Apocrypha and Pseudepigrapha are worth mentioning. The Book of Baruch, 3.9-4.4, which is not found at Qumran, seems to draw on Job 28 and Ben Sira for its portrayal of Wisdom. In Baruch, Wisdom is created by God, sought by humans, and, as in Ben Sira, equated with the Torah of Israel: 'She [Wisdom] is the book of the commandments of God, the law that endures forever. All who hold her fast will live, and those who forsake her will die' (4.1). A different interpretation of Wisdom is found in *1 Enoch* 42, part of the 'Similitudes of Enoch' (the only section of *1 Enoch* not found at Qumran), which utilizes the theme of Wisdom seeking a dwelling among humans and not finding one. However, unlike Ben Sira, Enoch does not go on to say that Wisdom finds its particular dwelling among the people of Israel, and there is no equation of the divine figure of Wisdom with the Torah.[12]

Doubleday, 1979), pp. 172-90. Winston also points out the parallels in the portrayal of Wisdom to the Isis aretologies of the Hellenistic period, continuing the pattern of analogy to ancient Near Eastern goddesses.

11. However, Jack T. Sanders points out that while the Wisdom of Solomon does not equate Wisdom and Torah, it does use the Torah narrative to illustrate its points about Wisdom's capacity to save and protect the one who seeks her (cf. chs. 10–11). I would like to thank Professor Sanders for providing me with a copy of his paper 'When Sacred Canopies Collide: The Reception of the Torah of Moses in the Wisdom Literature of the Second-Temple Period', presented at the Annual Meeting of the Society of Biblical Literature in 1996.

12. George Nickelsburg suggests that *1 En.* 42 is a parody of the claim by Ben Sira 24 and Bar. 4.1 that Wisdom is gained by the study of the Torah; for Enoch, Wisdom is only accessible through divine revelation (*Jewish Literature Between the Bible and the Mishnah* ([Philadelphia: Fortress Press, 1981], p. 216).

Rather, the figure Iniquity, or Folly, which appears to be here a divine or semi-divine figure, goes out among humans and finds a dwelling place among them. No more is said about either figure in the Similitudes.

Several themes, therefore, are present in the apocryphal and pseudepigraphical literature which were also noted in the biblical literature: Wisdom as a divine creation, female in gender, with a particular role in creation and a particular relationship with humanity (or, more probably, men). In a separate development, Wisdom also begins to be equated with the Torah as the special possession of Israel. Folly, on the other hand, is still associated almost exclusively with sins having to do with women's sexuality (with the exception of *1 Enoch* 42, where she is a more general figure). These themes continue at Qumran.

Qumran Evidence

The main sources for the figures of Folly and Wisdom at Qumran are the manuscripts 4Q184 and 4Q185, both published by John Allegro in *Discoveries in the Judaean Desert* V, and extensively commented on by John Strugnell.[13] 4Q184 is perhaps the better-known text, for Allegro gave it an intriguing title, 'The Wiles of the Wicked Woman', while 4Q185 was merely called 'A Sapiential Work'. 4Q184 discusses a female figure who can be clearly associated with Dame Folly, while 4Q185 features a female figure who is probably to be equated with Lady Wisdom. Both texts draw heavily on Proverbs 1–9, but they do not appear to utilize the apocryphal and pseudepigraphical texts discussed above. They both exist in single prototypes, and both manuscripts date paleographically, according to Strugnell, to the first century BCE. Since 4Q184's subject, Dame Folly, is beyond doubt, I will begin with that text.[14] The text begins by introducing a female figure whose every action is sinful:

13. J.M. Allegro, 'Qumran Cave 4 I (4Q158–4Q186)', in *Discoveries in the Judaean Desert of Jordan,* V (Oxford: Clarendon Press, 1968); J. Strugnell, 'Notes en marge du volume V des "Discoveries in the Judaean Desert of Jordan"', *RevQ* 7 (1970), pp. 163-276.

14. All translations, unless otherwise noted, are taken from F. García Martínez, *The Dead Sea Scrolls Translated* (trans. Wilfred G.E. Watson; Leiden: E.J. Brill, 1994).

She […] utters futility and in […]
She is always looking for depravities,
and whets the words of her mouth, and implies insult,
and is busy leading the community astray with nonsense.
Her heart weaves traps, her kidneys [nets.]
[her eyes] have been defiled with evil
her hands go down to the pit
her feet sink to act wickedly and to walk towards crimes. (lines 1-5)

4Q184 is almost a pastiche of allusions to Proverbs 1–9, where Dame Folly's sins are sexual, and only sexual, in nature. Here in 4Q184, too, her wicked actions lead to the corruption of men through illicit sexuality: 'Her eyes scan hither and yon, and she raises her eyebrows impudently, to spot the just man and overtake him…' (lines 13-14). The idea of the wanton woman speaking with 'smooth words' (line 17) and leading the simple astray with her sexuality occurs in Prov. 2.16, 5.3, 6.24, 7.5, 7.21 and 9.13-18. Her paths as 'paths of death' and 'tracks to sin' and her gates as the 'gates of death' and 'entrance to Sheol' (lines 8-11) echo Prov. 2.13-15, 25.18-19, 5.5-6, 7.25-27 and 9.18. The idea that she sits in the city gates, where she entraps men into fornication ('In the city squares she veils herself, and stations herself in the gates of the village, and there is no-one who interrupts her in [her] incessant [fornicating.]'), is taken directly from Prov. 7.10-12 and 9.13-18; and the notion that she does this to pervert a righteous man is a reversal of the role of Lady Wisdom, who cries out in the city gate in order to set the simple on the path of righteousness (cf. Prov. 1.21-22, 3.23-26, 8.1-5, 9.3-6). The sin contemplated here is clearly fornication, as in Proverbs 1–9, and will lead to ruination.

However, the female figure here appears to be more cosmic in scope than the simple 'loose woman' of Proverbs 1–9. Her clothing is not merely flashy, as in Prov. 7.10 ('decked out like a prostitute'), but are 'shadows of twilight' and 'diseases of corruption'. Her attire has bat-like 'wings' (line 4). Her dwelling is in the 'heart of night', the 'foundation of gloom', the 'tents of silence', and 'the eternal fire'. One is reminded of the various divine beings associated with death in the Ancient Near East: the Canaanite god Môt, whose residence is referred to as 'Muck' and 'Phlegm'; Ereshkigal, queen of the Mesopotamian underworld, where the goddess Inanna is turned into a rotting piece of meat hung on a hook; and perhaps most especially, the winged night demon Lilith who appears, for example, in Isa 34.14 as an inhabitant of a destroyed Edom, a 'land of burning pitch'. Lilith goes on to a spectacular career in Hebrew folklore, and in most tales her sin is sexual; she refuses, in one way or another, to be a proper wife to Adam, and so is driven out of Paradise; she now preys on innocent men and on women in childbirth.[15] All of these figures are associated in mythology with cosmic disorder; their counterparts (Ba'al, Inanna, Eve) are associated with the proper divine order of the world. Thus the Wicked Woman in 4Q184 becomes the personification of chaos opposed to God's established order.[16] The chthonic qualities of Dame Folly, hinted at in Proverbs, become clear in 4Q184. In fact, as Baumgarten notes, 'most pronounced is the emphasis on her association with the netherworld'.[17] Dame Folly has ceased to be simply human and become demonic. This 'catastrophization' of Dame Folly may be similar to the cosmological struggle between good and evil that one finds in certain Qumran sectarian literature, particularly the doctrine of the Two Spirits in the Community Rule, cols. 3 and 4. The Spirit of Darkness, in that text, leads those who walk in its way (characterized as 'paths of darkness') into, among other things, 'impudent enthusiasm, appalling acts performed in a lustful passion, and filthy paths for indecent purposes'. Those who follow the Spirit of Darkness will end, like those enticed by the Wicked Woman, in the netherworld, 'with the humiliation of destruction by the fire of the dark regions'.[18] Thus sin, for the Qumran community, is not simply human frailty, but part of the cosmic struggle between God and Satan.

15. For a fuller discussion of this and other demonic figures and a complete bibliography, see Joseph M. Baumgarten, 'On the Nature of the Seductress in 4Q184', *RevQ* 15 (1991), pp. 133-43.

16. Rick D. Moore, 'Personification of the Seduction of Evil: "The Wiles of the Wicked Woman"', *RevQ* 10 (1979-81), p. 512.

17. Baumgarten, 'Seductress', p. 137

18. García Martínez, *Scrolls*, pp. 6-7. A major factor in the doctrine of the Two Spirits found in the Community Rule is the idea of individual predestination, a notion that does not occur in the texts so far investigated. Rather, each individual is free to choose his own path.

This may account for the 'more-than-human' quality of the Wicked Woman/Dame Folly in 4Q184.[19]

References to Lady Wisdom are less clear in the Qumran sapiential texts, given the fragmentary nature of that material. She seems to appear in a second text published by Allegro in *Discoveries in the Judaean Desert* V, 4Q185. 4Q185 is a somewhat longer work than 4Q184, with three columns of text preserved. The portion relevant to our concerns comes from col. 2, lines 8-15.

> Blessed is the man to whom she has been given, the son of man [...]
> The wicked person should not brag, saying:
> She has not been given to me and I [shall not look for her.]
> [God has given her] to Israel, and like a good gift, gives her.
> He has saved all his people, but has destroyed...
> Whoever glories in her will say:
> he shall take possession of her and find her (lines 8-12).

The figure in question appears to be a personified female figure, given by God, sought (or not sought) by men, whose possession gives the good life. Once again, the text is a pastiche of allusions to biblical texts. Compare, for example, Prov. 3.13-18:

> Happy are those who find wisdom, and those who get understanding, for her income is better than silver, and her revenue better than gold. She is more precious than jewels, and nothing you desire can compare with her. Long life is in her right hand; in her left hand are riches and honor. Her ways are ways of pleasantness, and all her paths are peace. She is a tree of life to those who lay hold of her; those who hold her fast are called happy.

with lines 11-14:

> Whoever glories in her will say:
> he shall take possession of her and find her, and get her as an inheritance.
> With her there are long days, and greasy bones, and a happy heart, riches and honor.
> Her youth [increases] favours and salvation.
> Blessed the man who does it [her], and does not [...

19. However, it should be noted that this 'demonization' is part of a larger pattern of the continuing denigration of human women in some of the wisdom literature of the postexilic period from Dame Folly in Prov. 1–9, through the human women who cause Ben Sira such misgivings, to Qohelet who, in spite of his best efforts, cannot find any woman who is wise (7.28)! Cf. Fontaine and Christianson's essays in this volume.

> and does not look for her with a fraudulent spirit,
> or grow fond of her with flattery.

Further, the idea that wisdom is something that is passed on
from parents to children is prevalent in wisdom literature (e.g.
Ben Sira 4.16: 'If they remain faithful, they will inherit her; their
descendants will also obtain her'), and appears in 4Q185, lines
14-15 as well:

> As it was given to their fathers so will he inherit her.
> [He will grow fond of her] with all force of his strength
> and with all his vigour without restraint.
> And he will give her in inheritance to his descendants.

However, unlike the active female figure found in Proverbs, this
figure is an object, not a subject; she is given by God, sought by
humans, and possession of her brings reward; but, at least in the
material we have, she does not act. In fact, she more closely
resembles the non-personified figure of Wisdom in Job 28, where
Wisdom is described as established by God but is not active; or
Bar. 3.9-4.4, where Wisdom is essentially passive and, impor-
tantly, is given by God to Israel ('He found the whole way to
knowledge, and gave her to his servant Jacob and to Israel,
whom he loved', 3.36).[20] The notion that Wisdom is a special gift
from God to Israel is also prominent in Ben Sira 24.8, 10-12:

> Then the Creator of all things gave me a command, and my Cre-
> ator chose the place for my tent. He said,'Make your dwelling in
> Jacob, and in Israel receive your inheritance. In the holy tent I
> ministered before him, and so I was established in Zion. Thus in
> the beloved city he gave me a resting place, and in Jerusalem was
> my domain. I took root in an honored people, in the portion of the
> Lord, his heritage.

Here, of course, Wisdom is a far more active figure; however, the
result is the same: Wisdom becomes the special possession of the
people of Israel. This raises the question of whether Wisdom is
being equated with the Torah in 4Q185, as in Ben Sira and
Baruch. A case can certainly be made for that contention.
Wisdom is given specifically to Israel; she is inherited from the
fathers and passed on to the descendants; possession of her

---

20. Sanders, 'Canopies', p. 5, again notes that 4Q185 also uses the Torah
to illustrate its concept of Wisdom.

brings blessing, and she is to be loved by the possessor; and, in line 13 we find the admonition, 'Blessed the man who does it [her], and does not [...].' 'Doing' wisdom can certainly be understood as following the Law, and this seems to be the best understanding of the female figure in this text. Thus, in 4Q185 we find the same movement toward equating wisdom with the Torah that we found in Ben Sira and Baruch.

One other text from Qumran also mentions a female Wisdom figure, although the referent is not as clearly personified as in 4Q185. 4Q525, 4QBeatitudes, which exists in only one copy (like 4Q184 and 185), is dated by its editor Emile Puech to c. 200 BCE.[21] The type of literature to which 4QBeatitudes belongs is Wisdom, since it contains, as de Roo notes, 'striking resemblence[s] between 4Q525 and traditional Jewish Wisdom books such as Proverbs and Ben Sira'.[22] However, as George Brooke has observed, 4QBeatitudes also contains eschatological language, which represents a change from Proverbs and Ben Sira, and places 4Q525 in relationship with 4Q184's cosmic description of the Wicked Woman.[23] The passages that mention the figure of Wisdom are, first, frag. 2, col. 2, lines 2-7:

> Blessed are those who rejoice in her,
> and do not explore insane paths.
> Blessed are those who search for her with pure hands,
> and do not importune her with a treacherous heart.
> Blessed is the man who attains Wisdom,
> and walks in the law of the Most High,
> and dedicates his heart to her ways,
> and is constrained by her discipline
> and always takes pleasure in her punishments;
> and does not forsake her in the hardship of [his] wrongs,

21. E. Puech, 'The Collection of Beatitudes in Hebrew and in Greek (4Q525 1-4 and MT 5, 3-12)' in F. Manns and E. Alliata (eds.), *Early Christianity in Context: Monuments and Documents* (Studium Biblicum Franciscanum; Collectio Maior, 38; Jerusalem: Franciscan Printing Press, 1993), p. 356.

22. Jacqueline C.R. de Roo, 'Is 4Q525 a Qumran Sectarian Document?', in Stanley E. Porter and Craig A. Evans (eds.), *The Scrolls and the Scriptures: Qumran Fifty Years After* (Sheffield: Sheffield Academic Press, 1997), p. 345.

23. G. Brooke, 'The Wisdom of Matthew's Beatitudes (4QBeat and Mt. 5.3-12)', *Scripture Bulletin* 19 (1988–89), p. 37.

and in the time of anguish does not discard her,
and does not forget her [in the days of] terror,
and in the distress of his soul does not loathe her.
For he always thinks of her,
and in his distress he meditates on [the law,]
[and throughout] his [whole] life [he thinks] of her,
[and places her] in front of his eyes
in order not to walk on paths [of evil…]

Frag. 2, col. 3:

She cannot be obtained with gold…
with any precious stone[…[24]

And frag. 4, lines 6-11:

do n]ot seek her with [wic]ked heart […
Do not] se[ek her] with arrogant heart […
Do not] abandon [your inh]eritance to the na[tions,]
or your lot to the sons of foreigners.
For, the wise [man…
they instruct with tenderness.
Those who fear God keep her paths and walk in her laws,
and do not reject her reproaches.
Those who understand will acquire […
Those who walk in perfection keep away from evil
and do not reject her admonishments […

In these passages Wisdom, which is sought for by men, is unquestionably equated with the Torah, most clearly in frag. 2, col. 2, lines three and four, where the parallelism demands the equation: 'Blessed is the man who attains Wisdom, and walks in the law of the Most High.'[25] Wisdom / Torah, according to frag. 2, should be followed and meditated on in order to obtain blessing (lines 12-13). Wisdom / Torah is the special inheritance of Israel, the 'special path' for those who love and fear God. Thus, Wisdom has lost the special status we observed in Proverbs 1–9, Job 28, 1 *Enoch* 42 and the Wisdom of Solomon, and become subsumed under the Torah, as in Ben Sira 15.1, 24.23 and Bar. 4.1. This equation of Wisdom and Torah in 4Q525 and, probably, 4Q185, might have been expected in the literature of a group that

24. Cf. with Prov. 3.15.
25. Brooke, 'Wisdom', p. 36. See also Emile Puech, 'Un Hymne Essénien et les Béatitudes', *RevQ* 13 (1988), pp. 57-88.

places such emphasis on the study of and obedience to the Law as do the inhabitants of Qumran.

What can finally be said about the figures of Lady Wisdom and Dame Folly in the Qumran literature? The development of these figures in 4Q184, 185 and 525 takes place along lines already discernible in non-Qumran literature. This is particularly important in the case of Wisdom, whose separate identity is lost in the growing emphasis on Torah. If she ever was a separate female divine figure, as can be argued from Proverbs 1–9, *1 Enoch* 42 and the Wisdom of Solomon, she is no longer so in Ben Sira, Baruch, and 4Q525. Equally important, this is not a 'Qumranian' phenomenon only, but occurs broadly in Second Temple literature. This would lead to the conclusion that these texts are not 'sectarian,' but are part of the general theological trends of Second Temple Judaism, within which we continually find the elevation of Torah.[26] This trend continues to develop until it becomes 'normative' in Judaism, as it remains until the present day. As for Dame Folly, she undergoes a major change, from human figure (Prov. 1–9), to semi-divine being (*1 En.* 42), to chthonic night demon (4Q184), but in all cases her portrayal continues an unfortunate emphasis on women's sexuality as sinful. This latter development takes exceptionally strong root in Christianity, with consequences felt until the present day. Thus we again see texts from Qumran not as isolated or unique, but as part of the general mix that we call Judaism in the Hellenistic and Roman periods.

26. Thomas Tobin had already reached the conclusion, on other grounds, that 4Q185 was not a sectarian text. See T. Tobin, '4Q185 and Jewish Wisdom Literature', in H. Attridge, J. Collins and T. Tobin (eds), *Of Scribes and Scrolls* (College Theology Society Resources in Religion, 5; Maryland: University Press of America, 1990), pp. 145-52. Puech likewise argues that 4Q525 is not a Qumran composition ('Collection', p. 384); however, de Roo makes a case that 4Q525 was composed at Qumran. While the parallels she finds between 4Q525 and the so-called sectarian literature are interesting (see especially the parallel she draws between frag. 4, line 12, 'the skillful dig her paths', and CD 6.25), it could be argued that 4Q525 affected the texts that she cites rather than vice versa (if Puech's date is accepted, this must be the case). The question of what makes a composition 'sectarian' and how to determine what, if anything, was actually composed at Qumran, is not yet resolved.

ASENETH AS WISDOM

Ross S. Kraemer[1]

Introduction

Despite its potential oddity, the union of the biblical Joseph to the daughter of an Egyptian priest receives only passing notice in the book of Genesis. But sometime during the Greco-Roman period, a tale was composed in Greek purporting to set forth precisely what happened when Aseneth (Heb: Asnath) met Joseph. In this tale, conventionally titled *Joseph and Aseneth* after the manner of ancient Greek romances but which I now prefer to call *Aseneth*, Joseph's future bride was a beautiful 18-year-old virgin. Devoted to her native gods, she lived in chaste seclusion with her father, Pentephres (Heb. Potiphera) and her unnamed mother in the Egyptian city of the sun (Heliopolis). When Pentephres learns that Joseph, Pharaoh's second-in-command, is about to visit their home on his grain-collecting rounds, he proposes to his daughter a match with the eminent and eligible Joseph. Although she initially dismisses the idea, when Joseph enters the family courtyard Aseneth is thunderstruck with his heavenly appearance. But when, at her father's command, she finally meets this vision of a man, he keeps her at arm's length and prays for her transformation.

Fleeing to her upper chamber, Aseneth experiences precisely this. While Joseph travels the countryside, Aseneth renounces her idolatry, fasts, weeps and mourns for seven days and nights, only to see at the conclusion of her repentance a human-like

1. This essay is extracted from portions of my book, *When Aseneth Met Joseph: A Late Antique Tale of the Biblical Patriarch and his Egyptian Wife, Revisited* (New York: Oxford University Press, 1998), esp. Chapters 2 and 7, revised and abridged as necessary.

figure descend from heaven and enter her bedroom. Astonishingly, this divine being looks precisely like Joseph. He proceeds to tell Aseneth that her repentance has been accepted and that henceforth she will marry Joseph. Before he departs, he shows her a mystery involving bees and a honeycomb and feeds her a small portion of the honey itself, declaring that 'this honey the bees of the paradise of delight have made, and all who eat of it shall not die for eternity'. Shortly thereafter, this heavenly figure ascends into heaven. When Aseneth meets Joseph a second time, he takes her in his arms and embraces her as his spouse. With the blessings of Pharaoh and of her parents, Aseneth and Joseph get married, consummate the wedding and produce their sons Manasseh and Ephraim. They live, more or less, happily ever after.

'Rediscovered' by a French scholar in the late nineteenth century, the tale of Aseneth and Joseph was briefly taken for an early Byzantine Christian composition.[2] The vast majority of scholars who studied it came to the conclusion that the story was composed by a Jewish author prior to the early second century CE, despite the fact that the earliest manuscripts of any version of the story are seventh-century CE, no ancient source cites the tale, and there is no evidence for Jewish knowledge of the story prior

---

2. P. Batiffol, 'Le Livre de la Prière d'Aseneth', *Studia patristica: Etudes d'ancienne littérature chrétienne*, I-II (Paris: Leroux, 1889–90), pp. 1-115. Subsequently, Marc Philonenko published a Greek text and French translation of a so-called shorter version *Joseph et Aséneth: Introduction, texte critique, traduction et notes* (Studia Post-biblica; Leiden: E.J. Brill, 1968). An English translation based on this text may be found in H.F.D. Sparks, *The Apocryphal Old Testament* (Oxford: Clarendon Press, 1984), pp. 465-503. I translated Chs. 1–21 in *Maenads, Martyrs, Matrons, Monastics: A Sourcebook of Women's Religions in the Greco-Roman World* (Philadelphia: Fortress Press, 1988), pp. 263-79. A preliminary Greek text of the so-called longer version was disseminated by Christoph Burchard: it is most conveniently available in Albert-Marie Denis, *Concordance grecque des pseudépigraphes d'Ancient testament: Concordance, corpus des textes, indices* (Avec la collaboration d'Yvonne Janssens et le concours du CETEDOC; Louvain-la-Neuve: Université Catholique de Louvain, 1987). Burchard also published an English translation with extensive notes and commentary: 'Joseph and Aseneth: A New Translation and Introduction', *OTP*, II, pp. 177-247. For additional references and discussion, see *When Aseneth Met Joseph*.

to the modern period (it is transmitted, instead, in Christian manuscripts). Having thus located the work, most scholars proceeded to consider it evidence for Hellenistic Jewish ideas about conversion from paganism to Judaism, if not a fictionalized narrative of actual conversion rites.[3] Until very recently, no scholar gave serious thought to the significance of Aseneth's gender.[4]

It is my current conviction, as set forth in *When Aseneth Met Joseph*, that contrary to the position many scholars have taken, Aseneth is more likely to have been composed in the third or even the fourth century CE by one or more persons whose cultural identity and religious self-understanding we cannot determine with any degree of certainty. While that person or persons may have been Jewish, there is good reason to consider the likelihood of Christian authorship, and there are even several other possibilities. Still contrary to a prevailing scholarly consensus, I think that the earliest form of *Aseneth* is almost certainly the so-called shorter version, while the so-called longer version appears to represent intentional revision. While the process by which the tale(s) was composed is quite complex, it is clear that ideas about gender are central to its construction. The shorter and longer versions display intriguing tensions around the representation of gender difference, but both versions of the story are essentially in accord with pervasive late antique understandings of gender and gendered hierarchy.

In these extracts, I consider the role that Wisdom traditions play in the construction of the figure of Aseneth, in both the shorter and longer reconstructions. In general, the quotations and text references in this essay are taken from the shorter reconstruction. However, to facilitate analysis of the relationship between the shorter and longer reconstructions, I occasionally employ a combined citation whose format is designed to allow the reader to see where the texts are essentially in agreement and

3. For a fine summary of this consensus, see Randall Chesnutt, *From Death to Life: Conversion in Joseph and Aseneth* (JSPSup, 16; Sheffield: Sheffield Academic Press, 1995). Chesnutt's work is also itself a good representative of these positions.

4. One important recent exception, though, is Angela Standhartinger, *Das Frauenbild im Judentum der hellenistischen Zeit: Ein Beitrag anhand von Joseph und Aseneth* (AGJU; Leiden: E.J. Brill, 1995).

where they differ. In these combined citations, text printed in common typeface is essentially identical in both texts. Text in bold face is found only in the longer text.[5] Versification in common typeface (e.g. 8.3-4) is either common to both texts, or that of Philonenko. Versification in bold face (e.g. **8.4-5**) is that of Burchard's text, following his system of notation in his English translation. Translation of the shorter text is my own; translation of the longer is based on Burchard's, with occasional modifications.

Wisdom Traditions in the Construction of the Figure of Aseneth

The tradition of Wisdom personified as female and her antithesis, the Strange or Foreign Woman, looms large beneath the tale of *Aseneth*, which is in some ways a tale of the transformation of the latter into the former.[6] The opening verses of the story reflect a tension between these two representations. The daughter of an Egyptian priest, Aseneth is by definition foreign in relation to Joseph, yet the narrator claims that she was in no way like (the daughters of) the Egyptians (1.7).[7] Further, Aseneth's dress and

5.   In addition, text in parentheses in common typeface is found only in the shorter text. Square brackets contain editorial and explanatory material as necessary, regardless of typeface. Boldface text in parentheses denotes Burchard's additions, usually to improve the sense in English.

6.   Interestingly, though other scholars are quite well aware of the predominance of Wisdom motifs in the texts, they may have tended to focus on Joseph as Wisdom, or at least on Joseph as sage (see, e.g., Karl-Gustav Sandelin, 'A Wisdom Meal in the Romance Joseph and Aseneth', in *Wisdom as Nourisher: A Study of the Old Testament Theme, its Development Within Early Judaism and its impact on Early Christianity* (Abo: Abo Akademi, 1986), pp. 151-57.

7.   The textual traditions here are quite complicated. Philonenko's reconstruction of v. 7 ('And she was in no way like the daughters of the Egyptians but was in all ways like the daughters of the Hebrews') is actually a pastiche of readings from the shorter and longer manuscripts. The reading common to all appears to be 'and she was in no way like the Egyptians'. The words 'daughters of' are found in one of the shorter manuscripts (B) but not in D; the phrase 'but was in all ways like the daughters of the Hebrews' is taken from one of the longer manuscripts, A (the basis of the text printed by Batiffol's); a variant occurs in another long manuscript, H.

demeanor will momentarily contradict this claim, for what good Israelite daughter venerates foreign gods (2.5) and clothes herself in their images (3.10)?

Not only Aseneth's initial garments but also her possessions, as described in the opening chapters (her gold and silver, her jewelry and linens), conform to this dual association. Her storerooms filled with costly goods are just such riches as Prov. 24.3 assigns to Woman Wisdom: 'By Wisdom a house is built: by knowledge the rooms are filled with all precious and pleasant riches.' But if her rooms allude to Wisdom's house, they initially contain the representations of Aseneth's Egyptian gods and, like Aseneth herself, require transformation. While the presence of such idols is consistent with Aseneth's identity as the daughter of an Egyptian priest and fulfills an important need for the narrative, it also accords with the presentation of the Foreign or Strange Woman, particularly in Proverbs, who is the antithesis of Woman Wisdom. As the Strange Woman's house is filled with the dead (Prov. 9.18), so Aseneth's gods are also ultimately shown to be dead, and deaf and dumb as well (8.5; 12.6).

As with her rooms, Aseneth's garments encode this dual association of the Strange Woman and Woman Wisdom. The garments which Aseneth wears, both at the beginning and the end of the story, accord well with traditions about Woman Wisdom. At the outset of the dramatic action, learning that her parents have returned from their ancestral estate, Aseneth adorns herself in clothing and jewelry that has multiple referents (3.7-3.11). She wears a linen robe the color of hyacinth, woven with gold, and trousers of gold cloth: over these she wears a gold girdle. Her bracelets and necklace are made of precious stones. A tiara rests on her head; a diadem around her temples; a veil on her head completes the arrangement. In this respect, her clothing resembles that of the virtuous woman in Proverbs 31, who wears fine linen and purple (*byssus* and *porphyra*), the same terms which occur in *Aseneth*. In Sirach Wisdom wears an ornament of gold, and her bonds are a purple (*hyakinthos*) cord. The wise man 'will wear her like a robe of glory and put her on like a crown of gladness' (Sir. 6.30-31).[8] But in one crucial detail Aseneth's initial

See Philonenko's textual note to 1.7, *Joseph et Aséneth*, p. 130.

8.   LXX: Hebrew is slightly different.

ensemble points to her foreignness, for her bracelets and necklace are made of precious stones that bear engraved on them the images and names of the gods of Egypt.

After her initial encounter with Joseph, Aseneth strips off all this fine, idolatrous clothing and dons, instead, the black robe of mourning she had worn at the death of her brother. This act thus symbolizes the 'death' of the Foreign Woman, and the beginning of Aseneth's transformation into Wisdom. In 18.3, after her repentance and transformation, Aseneth again adorns herself in clothing and jewelry that are described almost identically to her initial garments, except that, unsurprisingly, they contain no images or names of Egyptian gods.

Aseneth's representation as the Strange Woman is heightened in the initial scene with her parents (4.1-16). Greeting her father and mother in clothing that also signifies her identity as a bride, a motif to which we will return, it is not surprising that Aseneth immediately finds herself in a discussion with her father on the subject of marriage.

Pentephres proposes to marry Aseneth to Joseph, whom he describes as 'a man who reveres God' (*theosebēs anēr*) and who is temperate and virgin like Aseneth herself. Aseneth responds with horrified anger. Recounting a version of the story found in Genesis 39, in which, contrary to the biblical text, Joseph did indeed sleep with Potiphar's wife, she accuses her father of wishing to enslave her to a foreigner, and counters that rather than marry Joseph she will instead marry the firstborn son of Pharaoh.[9] The narrator's voice informs us that Pentephres was ashamed to speak any further with his brazen daughter. By her response, the as yet untransformed Aseneth is here an exemplar of the Foreign/Strange Woman and of the person devoid of Wisom. As in Prov. 9.13, the Strange Woman is foolish (*aphrōn*), arrogant (*thraseia*) and without proper understanding;

9. For the most part, rabbinic (and other) traditions concur that Joseph was blameless and did not have sex with Potiphar's wife, as explored by James Kugel, *In Potiphar's House: The Interpretive Life of Biblical Texts* (San Francisco: HarperCollins, 1990; repr. Cambridge, MA: Harvard University Press, 1994). However, Kugel also surveys a number of traditions in which Joseph is suspected of varying degrees of complicity (*In Potiphar's House*, pp. 94-98).

so Aseneth is ignorant (of the truth about Joseph as demonstrated by the false rumors which she accepts), foolish, arrogant and lacking in filial piety.

This portrait of Aseneth as the paradigm of the Strange Woman is further reinforced in subsequent scenes. On the heels of Aseneth's rejection of her father's suggestion that she marry Joseph, a courtier announces Joseph's imminent arrival, whereupon Aseneth flees back to her upper chambers. At the sight of the glorious Joseph, Aseneth realizes instantly the error of her prior judgments. The language she uses is identical to that of Prov. 8.5: *aphrōn kai thraseia*.[10]

As Aseneth has seen Joseph so, too, Joseph has seen Aseneth by her window. In lovely ironic reciprocity, Joseph initially makes the same erroneous assumptions about Aseneth that she previously made about him. Imagining Aseneth to be a foreign woman who, like other Egyptian women, desires to seduce him, Joseph asks Pentephres to send her away. The narrator informs us that many Egyptian women, including all the wives and daughters of Egyptian officials, were overcome by sexual desire for Joseph, so great was his beauty. Joseph, it turns out, was able to resist the advances of these women by remembering the commandments of his father Jacob to stay away from intercourse with foreign women, which is 'perdition and corruption' (7.6). Though absent in the biblical text, Jacob's 'commandments' are found in some rabbinic sources and in *Jub.* 39.6-8, where the commandment is, however, to stay away not from strange women but from the wives of other men.[11] The message here is clear: Joseph initially perceives Aseneth as a foreign woman, with whom intercourse (*koinōnia*) is death.

Aseneth's representation as Strange or Foreign Woman is most apparent in a scene which occurs shortly thereafter. In response to Joseph's characterization of his daughter, Pentephres responds that Aseneth is in fact not a foreigner, but his daughter and a virgin who detests men. He offers to have Joseph meet

10. 6.6. In 6.7 she repeats the designation ἄφρων. Elsewhere, though in different language (12.7 and 13.10), she confesses to insolence, arrogance and ignorance of Joseph's true identity.

11. This material is treated extensively in Kugel, *In Potiphar's House*, pp. 106-112.

Aseneth, whom he designates as Joseph's sister (7.8). Rejoicing that Aseneth is a virgin who detests men, Joseph agrees. After her mother brings Aseneth down to meet Joseph, Pentephres suggests that Aseneth kiss Joseph, whom he calls 'your brother.' But when Aseneth attempts to comply, Joseph balks. Putting out his right hand on Aseneth's chest, he utters a long speech, asserting that 'a man who reveres God' (*theosēbes anēr*), blesses God with his mouth, eats blessed bread, drinks a blessed cup and is anointed with blessed oil, cannot possibly 'kiss a foreign woman, who blesses dead and deaf idols with her mouth, eats the bread of strangling from their table and drinks the cup of ambush from their libations and is anointed with the ointment of perdition' (8.5). Pentephres' assertions aside, Aseneth remains a foreign woman, and Joseph will not have any physical contact with her that might be construed as *koinōnia*. (This prohibition, though, apparently does not prevent him from placing his hand against her chest!).

Still, within this same scene, Aseneth's identity as Strange Woman and as Wisdom are intermingled. First, there are the contradictory assessments in the mouths, respectively, of Pentephres and Joseph. Second, Aseneth has already demonstrated the beginnings of her transformation to Wisdom when, on first seeing Joseph, she correctly perceives both his true identity and the error of her earlier ignorance. Third, in her compliant obedience to her father and mother, she has resumed the role of dutiful daughter, consonant with the idea of filial piety as an aspect of wisdom.

In addition, a small element in these same scenes also points to Aseneth's beginning transformation into Wisdom. When Pentephres introduces the now dutiful Aseneth to Joseph, he remarks upon the affinity between the two: 'Greet your brother, for he is a virgin as you are today, and detests all foreign [strange] women as you detest all foreign men'(8.1). Only three verses earlier Aseneth was said only to detest men in general, but now her animosity is directed either specifically, or particularly, at foreign men. At least in the shorter version, which (unlike the longer) does not subsequently catalogue misandry as one of Aseneth's sins, this may mitigate her hatred of men, transforming it from misandry to a virtue and an analogue of the wise son's rejection of strange women.

In addition, the designation of Aseneth as Joseph's sister points to the underlying framework of the traditions in Proverbs.[12] Consider, for example, Prov. 7.4-5:

> My son, keep my words and store up my commandments with you;
> Keep my commandments and live...
> Say to Wisdom, you are my sister
> and call insight your intimate friend,
> that they may keep you from the strange woman
> from the adulteress with her smooth words.[13]

Of particular interest is the translation of the Old Greek (OG), which seems to speak only of one woman, the 'strange and wicked one', rather than two, the Strange Woman and the adulteress. In fact, the OG reading makes sense of *Asen.* 7.6, where Jacob taught his sons to guard themselves from foreign women, whereas *Jub.* 39.6, perhaps drawing on the Hebrew, has Joseph remember Jacob's teachings to guard himself from any woman who belongs to another man.[14]

Early sections of the story thus cast Aseneth primarily as the Strange Woman, with hints of her true or ultimate identity as Wisdom intermingled. Many of Aseneth's characteristics are equally those of Wisdom; from such general traits as her beauty to more idiosyncratic details such as her height.[15] In classic praises of Wisdom found in Wisdom of Solomon 6–11, for instance, or Sirach 24, Wisdom is beautiful, radiant, pure. Once Aseneth's transformation begins, the depiction of her as Wisdom intensifies.

For instance, immediately after Joseph refuses to let Aseneth kiss him, he prays for her transformation. In 8.11 he says, 'And may she drink the cup of your blessing, she whom you chose

---

12. It points also to imagery from Song that I consider elsewhere in *When Aseneth Met Joseph*.

13. Trans. NRSV from the Hebrew, adapted slightly.

14. Interestingly, though, Prov. 6.24 asserts that the teachings of parents (both father and mother, 6.20) protect the wise son from the woman who belongs to another man, and from the smooth words of the Strange Woman.

15. At 1.8, Aseneth is tall (μεγάλη) like Rebecca; in Sir. 24.13-14 Wisdom grows tall like various trees; though the Greek is here verbal: ἀνυψώθεν.

before she was conceived.' The notion that Aseneth was chosen by God before her birth clearly puts her into an elite class that includes only male figures, including Samuel, Jeremiah, Isaac and Samson, and may reflect biblical traditions of the pre-existence of Wisdom, as explicitly expressed in Prov. 8.22; Ps. 139.16;[16] Sir. 24.9; Wis. 9.9, etc.

Aseneth's relationship to her seven virgin companions also appears to draw from an association with Wisdom. That the companions specifically number seven accords with Prov. 9.1: 'Wisdom has built her house; she has hewn her seven pillars.' This association is at best implicit in the shorter text but is much clearer in the longer version, where in 17.6 the angelic figure blesses the seven virgins and explicitly calls them 'the seven pillars of the City of Refuge'. Not only the seven pillars, but also the city of refuge calls to mind the figure of Woman Wisdom in the book of Proverbs (e.g. 9.1, etc).[17]

The association of Wisdom with the word of God may undergird the strange scene in *Asen.* 16.6-7, where Aseneth speculates that the newly materialized honeycomb has come forth from the angel's mouth, and he appears to assent, saying: 'Blessed are you Aseneth, that the secrets of God have been revealed to you.' In Sirach, Wisdom is said to come forth from the mouth of the Most High. Similar imagery occurs in Prov. 2.6: 'For the Lord gives wisdom; from his mouth come knowledge and understanding.' Honey and honeycombs are also closely associated with Wisdom, as in Sir. 24.19, where Wisdom herself says: 'Come to me, you who desire me, and eat your fill of my fruits. For the memory of me is sweeter than honey, and the possession of me sweeter than the honeycomb.'[18] These passages suggest a complex relationship between Aseneth and Wisdom, one where not only is the honeycomb from the angelic figure's mouth Wisdom,

16. LXX/OG 138.

17. See also Philonenko, *Joseph et Aséneth*, p. 187.

18. In the Christian *Odes* 30.4-5, a similar description occurs for the water of the living spring of the Lord: 'Its waters are far pleasanter than honey, and the honeycomb of bees is not to be compared with it. Because it comes out from the lips of the Lord, and from the heart of the Lord is its name.' For extensive discussion of the significance of the *Odes* for *Aseneth*, see *When Aseneth Met Joseph*, chapter. 9.

but the consumption of that Wisdom transforms Aseneth not merely into a wise person but also into Wisdom herself.

Yet another detail of the text associating Aseneth with Wisdom may be seen in 10.12-13, where the repentant Aseneth throws her rich clothing and her gold and silver idols out the window to the poor. That she divests herself of these tangible signs of her former identity needs no particular explanation, but that she throws them to the poor is more intriguing. While such concern for the poor is associated with true repentance in Isaiah 58, it is also the case that concern for the poor characterizes the Virtuous Woman (the human version of Woman Wisdom) in Prov. 31.20.

The characteristics of Wisdom especially undergird the description of Aseneth's heavenly counterpart, Metanoia, whose identity is revealed to her by the angelic figure after her transformation.

> For Metanoia (Repentance) is a daughter of the Most High, and she appeals to the Most High on your behalf every hour, and on behalf of all those who repent, because he is the father of Metanoia and she is the mother of virgins, and at every hour she appeals to him for those who repent, for she has prepared a heavenly bridal chamber for those who love her, and she will serve them for eternal time. And Metanoia is a very beautiful virgin, pure and holy and gentle, and God the Most High loves her, and all the angels stand in awe of her (15.7-8).

As far as I know, this description of Metanoia, and indeed the entire personification of Metanoia, is unique to the texts of *Aseneth*. In both the shorter and longer versions, Metanoia's attributes are those of Woman Wisdom, particularly in her various virtues such as beauty, purity and holiness,[19] her intercessory functions, and God's love for her and those who love her. 'I [Wisdom] love those who love me, and those who seek me diligently find me' (Prov. 8.17); 'The Lord loves those who love her' (Sir. 4.14); 'The Lord of all loves [Wisdom]' (Wis. 8.3); 'Wisdom is radiant and unfading, and she is easily discerned by those who love her' (Wis. 6.12). Metanoia's hourly petitioning of God on behalf of the repentant resembles Wisdom's daily petitioning of God: 'I was daily his delight; rejoicing before him always'

19. Wis. 7.22 (Wisdom as ἅγιον); 7.24 Wisdom as most pure (καθαρότητα).

(Prov. 8.30). To the extent that Metanoia is Aseneth's divine double, Metanoia's traits are also those of Aseneth. These attributes are expanded and given more explicit expression in the longer text.

Particularly noteworthy is a general consonance between the experience of the speaker in Wis. 7–8 and the experience of Joseph in *Aseneth*, particularly in the longer version. The portrait of Wisdom in these chapters is consonant (though not identical) with Aseneth and with Metanoia. As Aseneth is portrayed as sunlight (18.7/**18.9**), so Wisdom is described in similar imagery, 'more beautiful than the sun, excelling the constellation of stars' (Wis. 7.29). She is initiate in the knowledge of God and, like Aseneth, of noble birth. Wisdom of Solomon 8 is also, at least generally, reflective of the narrative of Joseph, particularly vv. 10 and following, which describe the benefits of Wisdom to the man who loves and desires her. Such a one has glory among the multitudes and honor in the presence of elders, though he is young. He is keen in judgment, admired in the sight of rulers, governing peoples; with nations subject to him, and monarchs afraid; capable and courageous in war (this last is a little less like Joseph!). Similarly, life with Aseneth brings Joseph rest, gladness and joy, and immortality, at least in the form of their children, if not also in the immortality conferred in the scene with the angel.

Wisdom, Gender and Aseneth's Transformation: from Dangerous Foreign Woman to Theosebēs Gynē

Paramount among the aspects of Aseneth's transformation is her change from a foreign (Egyptian) idolater, wholly unsuitable as a wife for a man who reveres God (a *theosēbes anēr*), to the diametric opposite: a pious woman (*theosēbes gynē*) who herself worships only the same God, and renounces all her former idolatry. To phrase it slightly differently, the story of Aseneth recounts her transformation from the Other to the Self, viewed of course from the perspective of the author(s), who here clearly identifies with the household and community of Joseph.

Aseneth's otherness has many dimensions. She not only worships Egyptian gods, but embodies her otherness by wearing emblems of her idolatry on her clothing and jewelry, and eating

food unacceptable to 'Hebrews'. Nowhere in this text is this otherness more forcefully conveyed than in the scene where Joseph
prevents Aseneth from kissing him (in obedience to her father's
instructions), by holding her at arm's length. After reciting 8.5,
quoted earlier, Joseph continues:

> But a man who reveres God (*theosebēs anēr*) will kiss his mother;
> and his sister **by his mother and his sister** who is of his own tribe
> and family; and his wife, who shares his bed; those women who
> with their mouths bless the living God. Similarly, also it is not
> appropriate for a woman who reveres God (*theosebēs anēr*) to kiss
> a strange man, because such is an abomination before **the Lord**
> God (8.6-7).

In this passage, the Self and the Other are clearly differentiated
with respect to food, worship and physical contact, both sexual
and filial.

Aseneth's otherness has additional components. She is ignorant in her idolatry and her slandering of Joseph, insolent
toward her father and arrogant in her hatred of men. Her transformation from Other to Self incorporates all of these elements.
At the conclusion of the story, Aseneth worships the living God,
eats proper food and wears pristine, primordial garments devoid
of idolatrous images. She displays her newly acquired wisdom
in appropriate ways: in her humility before her father (and
mother); and in her subordination to her husband Joseph, whose
feet she washes and whose commands she obeys.

The significance of gender in the representation of Aseneth's
transformation should not be underestimated. In the first place,
it is the Other, the Egyptian, who is here represented by a
woman, while the Self, the one who reveres God, is represented
by a man.[20] Given the story's grounding in the tale we have now
in Genesis, this assignment may seem inevitable and unremark-
able. However, this begs the question of whether the foreigner
is a woman because Joseph is said to have married an Egyptian;
or whether the story of Joseph and Aseneth receives such extensive articulation precisely (though certainly not only) because it
offers the opportunity to elaborate upon the transformation of
a woman. The choice of a woman as the exemplar of one

20. The primary signifiers of identity in the text are *theosebēs* for Joseph,
his brothers and his community, and 'Egyptians'.

transformed (or even 'converted'), most familiar in the biblical story of Ruth, may reflect an idea of woman as a more natural exemplar of the Other and therefore as a better candidate for transformation. The ideal transformation narrative, then, may well be one that utilizes gender as a central component of difference.[21]

Both Joseph and Aseneth are described in language that is sometimes significantly gender-specific. Joseph is not only *dunatos* (powerful)—an attribute of God in 8.10—he is also *anēr dunatos en sophia kai epistēmē*: a man strong (or powerful) in wisdom and knowledge. He is called *sōphrōn*: wise, temperate, reasonable: one of the cardinal virtues of the Greek (male) philosopher. (*Sōphrosynē*: is also applied to women, but usually with different connotations, primarily of chastity.) This wisdom and temperance is manifest in, among other things, his ability to remain chaste despite the temptations of seductive Egyptian women, and to refuse Pentephres' offer of additional hospitality in order to continue with his task of collecting grain.

In contrast to Joseph's wisdom and self-control, Aseneth is miserable and foolish (*aphrōn kai thraseia*). Her initial failure to perceive the truth about Joseph and her acceptance of false Egyptian gossip about him exemplify her ignorance, a stereotypical trait of women in ancient sources. That is, not only is Joseph obviously male and Aseneth obviously female, but, in her initial state, Aseneth exemplifies the most negative aspects of ancient constructions of the feminine, while Joseph exemplifies virtuous masculinity. The only exception to this concerns Aseneth's sexuality: she, like Joseph, is chaste from beginning to end. But since the outcome of the story must be Aseneth's marriage to Joseph and the conception and birth of their sons, Manasseh and Ephraim, that is probably the one characteristic that the story cannot manipulate.

Aseneth's transformation utilizes gender in yet another, central way. In her preconversion state Aseneth is not only a woman but also, in several respects, the wrong sort of woman. Despite the (reconstructed) reading that Aseneth was in no way like the

21. It would be interesting to speculate on the connection between this, and the perception (itself problematic) that the majority of converts to Judaism in antiquity were women.

daughters of the Egyptians, but in all ways like the daughters of the Hebrews, Aseneth lacks the virtues of the Israelite matriarchs and is initially arrogant, unsubmissive and disdainful of men.

Even in small details, the text(s) may draw upon prevailing ancient gender constructions. When Joseph refuses to kiss Aseneth, as Pentephres has instructed, Aseneth breaks into tears and gazes intently at Joseph. Many ancient authors claim that the gaze of a woman was sexual and highly dangerous to men, and insist that proper women should never look directly at a man. Typical is Sir. 26.9: 'The licentiousness of a woman is made known by her raised gaze, and by her eyelids.'[22] Aseneth's action here may thus contribute to her pre-transformation portrait as an insolent foreign woman. It may also, however, be intended to intensify the portrait of Aseneth as a woman overcome with sexual desire, though less so in the shorter text, where such a portrait is as false an image of Aseneth as her initial slanders are of Joseph. And of course, the two readings are by no means mutually exclusive.

After her transformation, Aseneth is the epitome of the good woman: she is submissive, willing if necessary to be servile, appropriately affectionate toward men, the ideal wife and, soon, mother. This, by the way, may point not so much toward a conception of the Other as woman as to a characterization of the Other in which 'their' women are not properly submissive and do not conform to appropriate gender categories, whereas 'our' women are and do.

Such an analysis tempers other readings of the story, such as that by Doty in which Aseneth's transformation is viewed as the ultimate result of a personal quest for self-knowledge and redemption. Doty reads this tale as that of a female protagonist who gains the knowledge and insight that lead to personal transformation, comparable to quest narratives for male heroes.[23]

---

22. Translation mine. On ancient understandings of the gaze see Blake Leyerle, 'John Chrysostom On the Gaze', *Journal of Early Christian Studies* 12, 8 (1993), pp. 159-74.

23. Susan Elizabeth Hog Doty, 'From Ivory Tower to City of Refuge: The Role and Function of the Protagonist in "Joseph and Aseneth" and Related Narrative' (Ph D dissertation; The Iliff School of Theology and the Univer-

Her analysis is problematic not the least because the final outcome of Aseneth's story is the traditional ending for tales of
women—marriage to the hero. But even if *Aseneth* has elements
of ancient quest narratives, we must still acknowledge that the
catalyst of her transformation is a male authority figure, and that
Aseneth's initial response to her newly acquired wisdom is to
pray to be subservient to that male figure for the rest of eternity:

> Deliver me to [Joseph] as a servant **and slave**, (that) **and** I (may)
> **will make his bed** and wash his feet and wait on him **and be a**
> **slave to him** and serve him for all the rest of my life (13.12/**13.15**).

In a hierarchical system at which Joseph stood at the top,
Aseneth hopes only to assume a position at the very bottom, the
precise antithesis of the social position which she held only
instants earlier as the virgin daughter of an aristocratic family
who aspired to marry the (false) son of (the false) God.

I argue in several chapters of *When Aseneth Met Joseph* that
Aseneth's desire to assume the position of slave or servant may
be read as an integral part of narratives that depict the encounter
between humans and angelic or other divine beings, and formulas for such encounters. In virtually all of these examples, the
human assuming the status of slave or servant is male (perhaps
because *Aseneth* is one of the few non-biblical depictions of an
encounter between a woman and an angel). Certainly, for later
Christian readers of the story, the pious person who seeks to be a
slave to God was in the company of such exemplaries as the
apostle Paul himself. This may appear to suggest, then, that
Aseneth's desire to subordinate herself to Joseph has no particular significance with regard to gender. But on the contrary, I
wish to suggest that it is precisely the construction of feminine
gender as subordinate and submissive that is at work in this
imagery. Before the masculine God, or angel, or other powerful
divine emanation, petitioners are as women, and as slaves whose
status itself incorporates an element of gender differentiation.
For in their relation to their owners slaves, too, assumed the role
of women in relation to men. Nowhere is this perhaps more
apparent than in the matter of sexual behavior, where male slave

sity of Denver, 1989); an interpretation that is further challenged, I think, by
recent postmodern criticism of ancient novels.

owners easily availed themselves of the sexual services of both male and female slaves. For a woman, then, the acquisition of wisdom appears to include recognition and acceptance of her subordinate status.

The Uses of Gender in the Longer Version

Though both versions of *Aseneth* draw upon ancient construc-tions of the feminine, it is particularly noteworthy that the alterations of the longer text consistently address matters of gender, often introducing themes of gender that are only mini-mally present or absent altogether from the shorter text.[24] In *When Aseneth Met Joseph*, I consider numerous examples of this phenomenon. Here, I focus on those that draw on Wisdom motifs.

One instance occurs in the final lines of Joseph's initial prayer for Aseneth:

> And may she drink the cup of your blessing (she whom you chose before she was conceived), and **number her among your people, that you have chosen before all (things) came into being** and may she enter into your rest, which you have prepared for your chosen ones **and live in your eternal life for ever and ever** (8.10/**8.11**).

Earlier, I note some of the ramifications of the language of the shorter text, particularly its association of Aseneth with Wisdom, and with a plethora of male biblical figures chosen by God before their birth. The reading of the longer text eradicates these associations, particularly the classification of Aseneth with a list of chosen men.

---

24. For another consideration of these differences see Standhartinger, *Das Frauenbild*, who suggests (esp. pp. 189-204) that the shorter text presents Aseneth, Metanoia and Wisdom (all identified with one another) as unequivocally female, while the longer text undercuts these associations and attempts to masculinize Wisdom, for instance, in its arrogation of Aseneth's roles to Joseph. These differences reflect, in her view, debates in hellenistic Jewish circles over the gender of Wisdom/Logos, discernible particularly in Philo. Such debates reverberate also, she thinks, in early Christian circles, discernible beneath Paul's correspondence with the Corinthians. While her thesis is interesting, it is too dependent, in my view, on the unexamined assumptions that *Aseneth* is both early and Jewish.

The two silent soliloquys inserted prior to Aseneth's prayer in ch. 12 afford a more complex example. In my book, I argue that inserting these soliloquys addresses a number of redactive concerns. From a feminist perspective, it is quite tempting to see the longer narrative as reflective of ancient ideas about gender and speech. Many ancient sources evince a widely held belief that, in women, silence was ideal. 'A silent wife is a gift from the Lord' (Sir. 26.14). Even more interestingly, many ancient writers also connect women's speech and women's sexuality, drawing a clear analogy between the mouth and the vagina. The chaste woman had a closed mouth and a closed vagina (except, of course, to her licit husband): the unchaste woman opened her mouth to speech and her vagina to illicit intercourse.[25] So closely connected were these mouths seen to be that some writers offer up the public speech of a woman as *de facto* evidence of her unchastity.[26] Interestingly, the traditions in Proverbs make a somewhat more subtle distinction, by associating Woman Wisdom with speech which leads to righteousness, and the Foreign/Strange Woman with speech which leads to sexual immorality.[27]

We might then view the insertions of the longer text as the product of a redactor who is concerned with these issues, and who may even intend to connect Aseneth's virginity with her silence here, blurring the fine distinction in Proverbs, and stressing the blunter association of women's speech with women's unchastity. This Aseneth might be understood to utter her first two prayers silently to counter the possible implication that the seemingly chaste Aseneth was engaged in unchaste, inappropriate speech. Though these insertions clearly have multiple functions in the text, such a reading is consistent with the general pattern of revisions in the longer text.

25. These associations are present in rabbinic sources as well, e.g., *b. Ber.* 3a, where marital intercourse is described as a woman 'conversing' with her husband; also *b. Ned.* 20a-b (the marital intercourse of R. Eliezer and his wife, Imma Shalom).

26. See especially Kathleen E. Corley, *Private Women, Public Meals: Social Conflict in the Synoptic Tradition* (Peabody, MA: Hendricksen, 1993), pp. 24-79, and esp. 42-44.

27. E.g. Prov. 8.1-8; 31.26, on the speech of the Wise Woman; 2.16; 5.3; 6.24; 7.4; 7.21 for the Strange Woman, and the adulterous woman.

In *Aseneth* 13, Aseneth recapitulates in hymnic form the prior narrative of her abasement:

> But pardon me, Lord, because I sinned against you in ignorance **being a virgin and erred unwittingly and** spoke blasphemy against my lord Joseph (13.9).

The small but remarkable additional words 'being a virgin' appear to connect Aseneth's ignorance either with her virginity or with her gender. Since all versions of the text repeatedly emphasize Joseph's virginity as well, I am tempted to conclude that the redaction has in mind the latter—Aseneth's ignorance is associated with her gender.

The longer version's revisions of the description of Metanoia in ch. 15 may display similar tendencies, offering a diminished portrait of Metanoia more reliant on ancient constructions of the proper woman. This Metanoia is defined not only as the daughter of God but also as the sister of the angelic being, and she is loved by them not for her role in the salvation of the repentent but for her qualities of beauty, chastity, good disposition and meekness. Though these are frequently stereotypically feminine characteristics in ancient constructions of gender, in late antique fiction, they were extended to men as well. Further, since I show in the book that these changes are the result of the addition of traditional details, it is difficult to say whether the redactor's intention was to domesticate the image of Metanoia, or whether the effect is accidental. But nevertheless, it appears to be there and is consistent with other changes.

One of the most fascinating gender-related alterations in the longer text occurs in the scene with the honeycomb. In the shorter version the angel simply breaks off a piece of the comb and eats it, and puts some honey into Aseneth's mouth with his hand. In the longer version, before he gives her the honey, he instructs her, saying 'eat', and she does:

> And the figure stretched out his right hand and broke off (a piece) from the comb and ate, and **what was left he** put [(a piece of) the honey] into Aseneth's mouth with his hand **and said to her, 'Eat.' And she ate** (16.9 / **16.15-16x**).

This seemingly modest change nevertheless transforms the text into an inversion of Genesis 2–3. There a woman eats the fruit of mortality and shares it with her husband; here a husband figure eats the food of immortality and then gives some to the woman, explicitly telling her to eat it.

This passage is enormously suggestive and problematic. It appears that the divine couple of Joseph and Aseneth restore the damage done by Adam and Eve, affording human beings a means to return to their original angelic state and, indeed, acquiring precisely the immortality which God feared Adam and Eve might aquire had they remained in Eden (Gen. 3.22-24). What does this mean for Aseneth's identity as a woman? What, precisely, is Aseneth's role in the reversal of Eve's actions? Must Eve's deeds be compensated for by those of another woman? (as some Christian writers intepreted the perfect obedience of Mary as the reversal of Eve's disobedience).[28] And what precisely must that compensation be? Genesis 3.1-5 and following may be read (and indeed, has been so read) to imply that Eve learned of the forbidden fruit not from God directly but, rather, from Adam and, therefore, it is Eve's disobedience *to her husband* that leads to their shared mortality. By contrast, it is Aseneth's obedience to the angelic double of her husband, Joseph, which obtains immortality for her. And while the masculine figure also eats, thus formally reversing the actions of Adam and Eve, he is already an angelic being, and it is hardly necessary for him to eat angelic food in order to receive immortality.[29] It is significant that the actions of Aseneth and 'Joseph' undo death, but not sexuality, as opposed to other ancient interpretations (virtually all Christian) in which angelic identity, and/or restoration to the primordial state, undid both. But given the inescapable parameter of this story, that Aseneth must marry Joseph and give birth to both Manasseh and Ephraim, we could hardly expect otherwise!

It is fairly obvious that Aseneth here functions as a salvific figure, not only for her reversal of Eve's actions but also for the

28. E.g. Irenaeus, *Haer*. 3.22.4.

29. It is interesting that whether or not angels actually ate is a matter of concern to ancient writers. The angels who appear to Abraham in Gen. 18 are said, without nuance, to eat; while the angel who appears in Judg. 13 declines the proffered meal. The angel Raphael, who appears to Tobit and his son Tobias, says pointedly of his apparent consumption of food, 'I did not really eat or drink anything—but what you saw was a vision' (12.19).

role she will play as City of Refuge. Female saviors are fairly rare
in the religions of the Greco-Roman world, with the important
exception of Isis, so that this portrait of Aseneth may be quite
significant precisely for its presentation of a salvific female.[30]
And it is also obvious that Aseneth is depicted in all versions of
this story as the recipient of divine mysteries and wisdom. But if
my reading of this section of the longer text is correct, its sublim-
inal message is that Paradise is restored when women are properly obedient to their husbands. Then do they regain the immortality which Eve traded for knowledge. This, too, is consonant
with the identification of Aseneth with Wisdom, and of Wisdom
with the Virtuous Woman who is similarly obedient, industrious
and fruitful.

The longer text's revisions to Aseneth's prayer in the wake of
the angel's departure may intentionally reinforce the gendered
imagery of Aseneth's prior ignorance. In the shorter text Aseneth
utters only a brief prayer, asking forgiveness for having spoken
evil in ignorance. In the longer text she is far more self-deprecat-
ing. Calling herself audacious and lacking sense (an attribute, as
I have noted several times above, of the Strange Woman in Prov.
9.13), Aseneth berates herself for having said that an *anthrōpos*
came into her room from out of heaven, and not having realized
that it was [G]od. Her final comment here resembles that in the
shorter text, but with two subtle differences. First, she says it 'in
herself', recalling her earlier silent prayers. Second, where the
shorter text has her confess to having spoken evil in ignorance,
consonant with the earlier scenes in which Aseneth slanders
Joseph in ignorance, the longer text claims that she has spoken
all her words in ignorance, a broader and more devastating
claim.

Both versions of *Aseneth* utilize ancient stereotypical associations of gender. It is the female Aseneth who is foolish, ignorant
and lacking self-discipline: the male Joseph who is wise and self-
controlled. It is the woman who is Other, the male who is Self,
the woman who is human, the male who is divine. But none of
this is absolute. By drawing particularly on the dichotomy of the
Wise and Strange Women in numerous Wisdom traditions, the

---

30. Gail Paterson Corrington, *Her Image of Salvation: Female Saviors and
Formative Christianity* (Louisville, KY: Westminster Press, 1992).

authors are able to portray the transformation of Aseneth from foolish and ignorant to wise and discerning, from Other to Self, from mortal human to angelic immortal, from Egyptian idolater to one who reveres the true God. In this endeavor they may also be aided by the subtler, less dichotomous constructions of gender in late antique fiction.

It is not inconceivable that this subtlety intends at least a modest critique of certain ancient constructions of gender. This is even more likely if we imagine the alternatives to be the more overtly hostile writings such as The Wisdom of Jesus ben Sira (Sirach). Alternatively, we might argue that *Aseneth's* relative lack of hostility to women is nothing more than a by-product of the author's need to transform her into an acceptable wife for Joseph; and that in the desire to accomplish this, Aseneth's negative femaleness becomes subordinated to her positive *theosebeia*, her inclusion in the community of those who revere God.

Such an interpretation becomes less persuasive when we consider the differences between this account of the marriage between Aseneth and Joseph and rabbinic legends, legends that occur in sources whose dates are probably fourth century CE and later.[31] None of those legends is anything like our Aseneth story, and several claim that Aseneth was really the daughter of Joseph's niece, Dina (who had been raped by a Canaanite named Shechem according to Gen. 34) and only the adopted daughter of Pentephres. It is tempting to speculate that these different stories circulated in communities with somewhat different ideas about gender, and with somewhat differing social structures consonant with those ideas—although the key differences among the stories seem not to be gender constructs, but the identification of Aseneth as really an Israelite and not a Gentile after all. And, of course, if *Aseneth* is Christian, then rabbinic legends are almost beside the point, since each tradition would be oriented to fundamentally different interests in the Joseph narrative.

31. See the appendix to *When Aseneth Met Joseph*.

Part III

FEMINISTS READ THE PSALMS

'O GOD, HEAR MY PRAYER':
PSALM 55 AND VIOLENCE AGAINST WOMEN[*]

Ulrike Bail

'No-one Hears my Cry'

The psalms of lament allow individuals to articulate human experiences of violence, experiences which destroy social, psychological and physical integrity. The wall of silence which keeps the victim an isolated prisoner is broken down by such a naming of violence; the downtrodden can regain their strength and their identity through identification with the 'I' of the lament psalms: 'In this way the lament itself becomes a source of liberation.'[1] Scholars of the Psalms are agreed that the psalms of lament are open to human needs of all kinds and that their liberating potential is directed towards the end of all violence.[2] Despite this general assertion, no one has ever considered whether particular experiences of violence towards women can be located in the Psalms. This is the question with which this

---

[*] This article originally appeared in German: Ulrike Bail, 'Vernimm, Gott, mein Gebet'. Ps 55 und Gewalt gegen Frauen', in Hedwig Jahnow (ed.), *Feministische Hermeneutik und Erstes Testament* (Kohlhammer: Stuttgart, 1994), pp. 67-84. It is reprinted here with some corrections by the author. Translated from the German by Charlotte Methuen. Also on this theme see Ulrike Bail, *Gegen das Schweigen klagen: Eine intertextuelle Studie zu den Klagepsalmen Ps 6 und Ps 55 und der Erzählung von der Vergewaltigung Tamars* (Gütersloh: Gütersloher Verlagshaus, 1998).

1. Konrad Raiser, 'Klage als Befreiung', *Einwürfe* 5 (1988), p. 27.

2. Odil Hannes Steck, *Friedensvorstellungen im alten Israel. Psalmen. Jesaja. Deuterojesaja* (Zürich: Theologischer Verlag, 1972), p. 36 n. 84; Hans Seidel, *Das Erlebnis der Einsamkeit im Alten Testament: Eine Untersuchung zum Menschenbild des Alten Testaments* (Berlin: Evangelische Verlagsanstalt, 1969), p. 39; Hans-Jürgen Hermisson and Eduard Lohse, *Glauben* (Stuttgart: Kohlhammer, 1978), p. 39.

article will be concerned. The intention is not to offer a reconstruction of a historically identifiable distress or of a so-called real problem as the background to a specifically female experience of violence;[3] instead, the question is whether the structure of the language used in the Psalms can give space to the specific experience of violence suffered by women.

One of the most radical and painful forms of specifically female experiences of violence is rape.[4] Rape is primarily an act of violence, albeit an act of violence which takes a sexual form. According to Feldmann, the primary aim of the perpetrator is

> to subdue his victim, to control her, to break the woman's will, and to force her to obey his will, to use the victim as an object to release anger and resentment, to put her down, to humiliate her. Sexual satisfaction is secondary to the perpetrator (...). The perpetrator's sexuality is not central here; it is an instrument for the practice of violence and power in the form of sexualised

3. Seybold and Ruppert have demonstrated the questionable nature of such monolinear reconstructions. With the help of four viewpoints (language elements, imaginative forms, social implications and religious practices), Seybold attempts to identify psalms which refer to sickness and healing (Klaus Seybold, *Das Gebet des Kranken im Alten Testament: Untersuchungen zur Bestimmung und Zuordnung der Krankheits—und Heilungspsalmen* [Stuttgart: Kohlhammer, 1973]). Ruppert searches for prayers which reflect the situation of those who are accused (Lothar Ruppert, 'Klagelieder in Israel und Babylon: Verschiedene Deutungen der Gewalt', in Norbert Lohfink [ed.], *Gewalt und Gewaltlosigkeit im Alten Testament* [Freiburg: Herder, 1983], pp. 111-58). See also the summary of recent research in Joachim Becker, *Wege der Psalmenexegese* (SBS, 78; Stuttgart: Verlag Katholisches Bibelwerk, 1975), esp. pp. 24-33. The situations of distress implied in the Psalms are always 'a multi-factorial network of cause and effect', not a monocausal portrayal of distress, according to Frank Crüsemann, 'Im Netz: Zur Frage nach der "eigentlichen Not" in den Klagen der Einzelnen', in Rainer Albertz *et al.* (eds.), *Schöpfung und Befreiung: Festschrift für Claus Westermann* (Stuttgart: Calwer-Verlag, 1989), pp. 139-48.

4. On rape see Karin Flohtmann and Jochen Dilling, *Vergewaltigung. Erfahrungen danach* (Frankfurt: Fischer Verlag, 1987); Susan Brownmiller, *Gegen unseren Willen: Vergewaltigung und Männerherrschaft* (Frankfurt: Fischer Verlag, 1980); R. Emerson Dobash and Russell Dobash, *Violence Against Wives: A Case Against the Patriarchy* (New York: The Free Press, 1979); Beatrix Schiele, 'Die Gewalt gegen Frauen als Herausforderung einer feministischen Ethik', *Schlangenbrut* 25 (1991), pp. 6-12; Sylvana Tomaselli and Poy Porter (eds.), *Rape* (Oxford: Basil Blackwell, 1986).

aggression. On the other hand, a sexual attack on a woman is
particularly effective in attacking the core of her self-determina-
tion, her self-respect, her personal being.[5]

Women are degraded to objects and feel their identity to have
been destroyed.

Although acts of sexual violence against women are repeated
day after day, night after night, this theme remains taboo. 'No
one hears my cries' is the experience of many raped women.
Women's extreme experience of violence is scarcely noticed by
the church or considered in academic exegesis.

Taking Psalm 55 as an example, I will consider the extent to
which a conscious acknowledgment of violence against women
can influence and change the interpretation of lament psalms.
What possibilities of interpretation offer themselves if the psalms
of lament are open to women's experience of violence, and when
an awareness of this distress is attributed to the language of the
Psalms?

As the psalm stands, its first verse—added during the process
of its transmission and assimilation within the First Testament—
names David as the speaking subject of the prayer. In this way
Psalm 55 is not only drawn into the network of texts dealing
with David's biography but also, at the same time, becomes
restricted to this particularly 'male' context. This article will ask
whether it is also possible to draw other connections. Since I
assume that the speaking subject of Psalm 55 *could have been* a
woman, I shall speak of the speaker, the person praying this
psalm as a 'she' rather than 'he'. I assume that in Old Testament
times a woman's experience could have shaped a psalm. It is not
necessary, although it is certainly possible, to assume that the
woman who prayed this psalm also composed it. Its title could,
therefore, read: 'A Woman's Lament: Speaking against Silence.'

5.   Harald Feldmann, *Vergewaltigung und ihre psychischen Folgen* (Forum
der Psychiatrie, Neue Folge, 33; Stuttgart: Ferdinant Enke Verlag, 1992),
p. 27; and cf. Ruth Seifert, 'Krieg und Vergewaltigung: Ansätze zu einer
Analyse', in Friedel Schreyögg (ed.), *Nirgends erwähnt—doch überall
geschehen...Vergewaltigung im Krieg* (Munich: Gleichstellungsstelle für
Frauen, 1992), pp. 1-19.

The Text of Psalm 55

2.   O God, hear my prayer,
   and do not hide from my plea.

3.   Attend to me and answer me.
   I am restless in my despair,
   and am confused

4.   by the cries of the enemy
   by the onslaught of the wicked.
   They bring down trials upon me
   and with anger they persecute me.

5.   My heart quakes within me,
   and the terrors of death fall upon me.

6.   Fear and trembling come upon me,
   and terror overwhelms me.

7.   So I said,
   Had I the wings of a dove,
   I wanted to fly away and have rest.

8.   See,
   I wanted to flee far off,
   and settle in the wilderness,

9.   to hurry to my refuge,
   away from the blast of the wind, from the storm.

10.   Confuse, my Lord,
   split their tongues.
   Yes, I see violence and strife in the city.

11.   They surround it day and night on its walls,
   and trials and tribulations dwell at its heart.

12.   Ruin dwells at its heart,
   oppression and deceit do not retreat from its market.

13.   Yes, if an enemy had abused me,
   I would have borne it.
   If a foe had set himself over me,
   I would have hidden myself from him.

14.   But you: one of my own,
   my companion, my friend,

15.   with whom I enjoyed sweet fellowship,
   walked in the crowd in the house of our God.

16.   Let death fall upon them,
   let them go down alive to Sheol,
   for evil is in the heart of where they live.

17.   For I, I call to God,
   and GOD will rescue me.

18.   At evening, at morning, at midday I lament and moan,

and he will hear my voice.

19.   He will rescue my life for salvation
      from the quarrel against me,
      for they are too many about me.

20.   God will hear and will humble them,
      he, who has been enthroned from the beginning of time,
      for they do not keep their word,
      and neither do they fear God.

21.   He lays hands upon those who are at peace with him,
      he breaks his trust;

22.   His mouth flatters more smoothly than butter,
      but strife is in his heart;
      his words flow more gently than oil,
      but they are daggers [drawn swords].

23.   Cast your desire upon GOD,
      and he, he will sustain you,
      he will not allow the righteous to stumble forever.

24.   But you, God,
      you will bring them down into the deepest pit,
      the men of blood and deceit
      will not achieve even half of their days.
      But I, I trust in you.

From both text-critical and source-critical perspectives, the text of Psalm 55 is viewed in exegetical literature as extremely difficult.[6] Innumerable suggestions for 'repairs' have been and

6.   Comments to the translation, which change the Masoretic Text as little as possible.

v. 3: 'restless' comes from רוד; 'to be confused' is derived from הום (a form of המה).

v. 4: עקה is a hapax legemenon. Following Kraus (Hans-Joachim Kraus, *Psalmen* [*BKAT*, 15; Neukirchen–Vluyn: Neukirchener Verlag, 5th edn, 1978), p. 598, I translate 'onslaught'—but, against Kraus, in the singular.

v. 9: סעה is a hapax legemenon. However, in my opinion the fact that this word only appears here and that its meaning must be understood from the context, is not a sufficient reason for interfering with the Masoretic Text. The context of v. 9 suggests 'blasting' as a convincing translation.

v. 10: In the light of the psalm as a whole, a translation of the unaltered Masoretic Text with the words 'Confuse, my Lord, split their tongues' is reasonable. Why should the wish of destruction, spoken out in vv. 16 and 24, not erupt here and disturb the syntax? Psalms are poetic texts that do not develop their meaning in the order of the words and phrases but in 'simultaneous' reading which consciously registers links to what has been

continue to be made; some of the reasons given for such conjectural emendations involve the assessment of specific parts of the
text as 'senseless and distorted',[7] 'mutilated'[8] or 'unbearable'.[9]
Against these I would agree with Mitchell Dahood's opinion that
the consonantal text is generally sound and that its verses are
logically ordered.[10] A division of the psalm into two hymns
should be rejected on the ground that relationships between
keywords hold it together.[11] The decision for making as few as
possible text- and source-critical 'repairs' is based first and foremost upon a consideration of the available Hebrew text.[12] However, this decision is also based upon a fundamental principle
which should shape the approach to the text. This principle

read and what is to come. The disempowering of the enemies' language
and its violence is a central theme of this psalm.

v. 15: The meaning of the hapax legemenon רגש is unclear. Krieg suggests
a change to רגע ('a while'; Matthias Krieg, *Todesbilder im Alten Testament oder
'Wie die Alten den Tod gebildet'* [ATANT, 73; Zürich: Theologischer Verlag,
1988], p. 286 n. 117). Although this seems illuminating, I have chosen to
remain with the Masoretic Text and to translate 'in the crowd', following
Dahood (Mitchell Dahood, *Psalms* [AB; Garden City, NY: Doubleday, 1968],
p. 34). The precise meaning must remain open.

v. 16: I follow the *qere* and divide ישי[א]מות into two words: 'Let death fall
upon them'; cf. Ps. 89.23, and see Kraus, *Psalmen*, p. 560.

v. 18: The words of escape in vv. 18b, 19a and 20a are parallel and I have,
therefore, translated them similarly. These are expressions of escape which
include all times. As the expression of hope they shape and change the view
of both present and past.

v. 21: Literally, 'upon the state of peace'; בשלמו, 'upon those who are at
peace with him', makes more sense.

v. 23: The meaning of יהב is unclear. In the context of the lament psalms
the verb takes a range of meanings, from 'burden' to 'hope'. I have translated it with 'desire' to include both aspects.

7.   Kraus, *Psalmen*, p. 560.

8.   Hermann Gunkel, *Die Psalmen* (Göttingen: Vandenhoek & Ruprecht,
5th edn, 1968), p. 236.

9.   Bernhard Duhm, *Die Psalmen* (KAT, 14; Tübingen: J.C.B. Mohr, 2nd
edn, 1922), p. 153.

10.   Dahood, *Psalms*, p. 30.

11.   Gunkel, *Die Psalmen*, p. 238; Kraus, *Psalmen*, p. 561. Relationships
between keywords hold a psalm together and are unlikely to be coinciden-
tal. See Krieg, *Todesbilder im Alten Testament*, p. 287.

12.   That is, the Masoretic Text as it is found in the *BHS* (4th edn, 1990).

concerns the question, Whose interests are served by the production of a new text through conjectural emendations, textual alterations and omissions? The intention is to explore the different
strata and possibilities of interpretation that exist in a biblical
text, rather than seek to dominate the material by identifying it
as 'in need of repair'. As Jürgen Ebach has put it, 'We need to
learn to understand the biblical text as "satisfactory"'.[13] We
cannot, however, accept the text uncritically and without considering the context in which it is read. The questions and answers
of the past must be brought into a conversation with the questions and answers of the present. In this process it must be
remembered that, in general, the Psalms cannot be dated with
precision. Despite the efforts of historical criticism, it is only
rarely that a psalm can be assigned to a particular date. Psalms
are poetic texts, and it is impossible to make linear connections
from such texts back to the situation that gave rise to them.

The Topography of Violence

Reality as it *is* experienced is described by the Psalms metaphorically, as a reality which *can be* experienced. The Psalms offer the
reader the possibility of identification and connection with a
reality that the reader has experienced. They open up an imaginative space in which experiences can be located. Within this
imaginative space the Psalms express in words the experience of
violence. In Psalm 55 this constructed imaginative space, created
by language, may serve to locate a particular experience of violence. In this way it is possible to speak of a topography of
violence. This topography of (the experience of) violence is particularly and clearly placed in the city and in the desert.

The City as a Place of Violence

    10b. I see violence and strife in the city.
    11.   They surround it day and night on its walls,
          and trials and tribulations dwell at its heart.
    12.   Ruin dwells at its heart,
          oppression and deceit do not retreat from its market.

13. Jürgen Ebach, 'Interesse und Treue: Anmerkungen zu Exegese und
Hermeneutik', in Jürgen Ebach (ed.), *Biblische Erinnerungen: Theologische
Reden zur Zeit* (Bochum: SWI-Verlag, 1993), p. 42.

Verses 10b-12 portray a picture of a city, a city with walls and a market place. It is shown as a place of violence, although no concrete act of violence is named. Instead the city is populated with concepts which show a generally dreadful state of affairs: violence, strife, trials, tribulations, ruin, oppression and deceit. These concepts/words, which are the incorporation of violence, are personified as and act like people. Violence and strife surround the city on its walls; oppression and deceit do not retreat from its market place. Violence has entered the furthest corner of the city and is occupying it. Violence dominates both the walls and the central square. Together the verbs which express this domination, 'surround', 'not retreat', make up a circle and a point, movement and persistence. Violence is present not only in the spatial expanse but also in the movement within this space. It dominates time as well (v. 11). Time and space are subject to the effects of violence.

This portrayal of the city contradicts its true function, that of protection by means of its defences.[14] Because the city's wall distinguishes it clearly from what is outside, what lies within is supposedly protected. This distinction between within and without is attacked in Psalm 55: the wall no longer has a protective function. What lies within the city is, however, also wounded, as indicated by the double emphasis on 'at its heart'. It is apparent that the city, to which the connotation 'protection and safety' should be attributed, no longer offers a place of refuge; instead, it has become profoundly unsafe.

The city is not only a *place* of violence; it is also the *object* of violence. This can be seen from v. 11. Here the city is the object of those who dominate it. In those passages in the psalm where the 'I' speaks of itself (vv. 3-6), it speaks of itself as the object of violence. Associations of keywords produce a relationship between the 'I' and the city ('trials' in vv. 4 and 11, and 'at its heart' in vv. 5 and 11-12). There is, therefore, a relationship between the 'I' of the psalm, which expresses its own experiences of violence in words, and the defeated and occupied city. 'The humiliation of the individual can be seen to be internally related to the humiliation of the city.'[15] Both the city and the 'I' are objects of

---

14. E. Otto, 'עיר', *ThWAT*, VI, p. 61.
15. Krieg, *Todesbilder im Alten Testament*, p. 290.

violence. The city and the 'I' coincide in the extent of the violence
to which they are exposed. Like the city, the 'I' is both the place
and object of violence. If the verbs the 'I' uses to express its
experience in vv. 4b-6 are applied to the picture of the city, the
total domination of the city by violence becomes even clearer.
While the threatening movements in the image of the city are
horizontal, the trials which beset the 'I' move in vertical lines
('rain down upon', 'fall upon', 'overwhelm'). The resulting picture is that of a closed space from which it is impossible to
escape. The topography of violence dominates this space. In this
way the experience of violence is present on the surface level of
the text.

The Desert as Counter-space

> 7. So I said,
>   Had I the wings of a dove,
>   I wanted to fly away and have rest.
> 8. See,
>   I wanted to flee far off,
>   and settle in the wilderness,
> 9. to hurry to my refuge,
>   away from the blast of the wind, from the storm.

In vv. 7-9 the praying woman wishes that she could fly into the
desert, that she could escape from the enclosed space of violence.
The picture of the desert here offered is of a place of refuge; the
desert becomes a counter-space to the city. This is clear from the
verbs used. Here we find no verbs which 'encircle' and define a
space; instead, a cluster of verbs of movement ('fly', 'leave',
'retreat') and of stillness ('rest', 'settle') are related to the counter-
space of the desert.

The 'desert' has many and varied connotations in biblical texts.
It may be the place of death and chaos, frightening and full of
danger. 'Biblical people, used to village and city life, see the
desert as a yawning emptiness; no one lives there.'[16] Inasmuch as
the desert in Psalm 55 is conceived of as a counter-space to the
city's space of violence, the connotations here are reversed. The
city, generally representative of safe, habitable and cultivated

---

16. S. Talmon, 'מדבר', *ThWAT*, IV, p. 675.

land, has been transformed into a place of hopelessness, normally associated with the desert. The dangerous boundary between cultivated land and the desert has, in a sense, shrunk to the heart of the city. At the same time, the desert loses the connotation of death and becomes a place of refuge where violence no longer threatens. In this way another connotation of the desert is incorporated into the image. The desert offers 'asylum to outcasts and refugees'.[17] Hagar, Moses, David, Elijah and others fled into the desert. Here they were met by God or by God's messenger who gave them nourishment, strengthened and protected them. In contrast to them, the woman praying the psalm finds no shelter and meets no angel. The desert cannot offer even a transitional stage. The praying woman knows that flight is impossible. Her hope of rescue is, therefore, merely a wish; her place of refuge is a fictional place; it is a counter-space, but trapped— within the construction of the sentence—by the subjunctive of desire: 'Had I...' This is strengthened by the fact that there are no keyword connections between vv. 7-9 and the rest of the psalm. The flight remains text: it remains on the level of the 'I say' (v. 7)[18] which introduces the desert passage.

The praying woman's own strength is not enough to allow her to escape. In speech the 'I' turns itself into a dove and allows the bird to act as a kind of substitute and to do what the 'I' in this situation of violence is unable to do, namely, to find a means of escape and flight. This is equivalent to the dove's role in the flood story (Gen. 8). There the use of the dove represents an attempt 'to allow a bird in an emergency situation to bring about something that the people cannot do'.[19] The dove is often found in such desperate situations. Thus the cooing of a dove is also seen as representing lament (Isa. 38.14, 59.11; Nah. 2.8).

---

17. Talmon, 'מדבר', p. 678. See Erhard S. Gerstenberger, *Psalms. I. With an Introduction to Cultic Poetry* (FOTL, 14; Grand Rapids: Eerdmans, 1988), p. 224.

18. Against Kraus (*Psalmen*, p. 562), who views the 'So I said' simply as an easy transition that is metrically irrelevant.

19. Claus Westermann, 'Mensch, Tier und Pflanze in der Bibel', in Bernd Janowski, Ute Neumann-Gorsolke and Uwe Gleßmer (eds.), *Gefährten und Feinde des Menschen: Das Tier in der Lebenswelt des Alten Israel* (Neukirchen–Vluyn: Neukirchner Verlag, 1993), p. 93.

At the same time, the picture of the dove works on many levels. In the metaphor of the Song of Songs the dove functions as love's messenger.[20] It is possible that this area of meaning might also be evoked in Ps. 55.7. If that were so, the dove as the bearer of hope would stand in sharp contrast to the experience of violence. A topography of love would be projected against the topography of violence. And yet, this counter-projection would remain fictitious, incapable of realization in the all-dominating violence. The flight of the 'I' remains utopian and imaginary.

The Act and its Perpetrator

The perpetrator(s)[21] of this violence can be seen at various points in the psalm. It contains general statements which give no concrete indication of the nature of the act (v. 4: 'by the cries of the enemy, by the onslaughts of the wicked. They bring down trials upon me, and with anger they persecute me'; and v. 20b: 'they do not keep their word, and neither do they fear God'). It offers descriptions of violence personified in the image of the city (vv. 10b-11: 'I see violence and strife in the city. They surround it day and night on its walls, and trials and tribulations dwell at its heart'). It presents statements in the subjunctive which exclude certain types of perpetrator (v. 13: 'If an enemy had abused me I would have borne it. If a foe had set himself over me, I would have hidden myself from him'). It portrays the perpetrator's words and the way he says them (v. 22: 'His mouth flatters more smoothly than butter, but strife is in his heart; his words flow more gently than oil but they are daggers [drawn swords]'). It describes the perpetrator as known and trusted (vv. 14-15: 'But you: one of my own, my companion, my friend, with whom I

20. See Othmar Keel, 'Allgegenwärtige Tiere: Einige Weisen ihrer Wahrnehmung in der hebräischen Bibel', in Bernd Janowski, Ute Neumann-Gorsolke and Uwe Gleßmer (eds.), *Gefährten und Feinde des Menschen: Das Tier in der Lebenswelt des Alten Israels* (Neukirchen–Vluyn: Neukirchner Verlag, 1993), pp. 156-93, esp. pp. 168-69; also his *Deine Blicke sind Tauben: Zur Metaphorik des Hohen Liedes* (SBS, 114, 115; Stuttgart: Verlag Katholisches Bibelwerk, 1984), pp. 53-62.

21. The change between singular and plural is problematic. Perhaps it indicates the inseparable nature of structural violence and individual acts of violence.

enjoyed sweet fellowship, walked in the crowd in the house of our God'; and v. 21: 'He lays hands upon those who are at peace with him, he breaks his trust').

In my opinion v. 14, in which the perpetrator is addressed directly, is central to understanding the psalm. While in previous verses the praying woman seems to approach the act, speaking more of the structure of violence than of the violent act itself, here she breaks out of the former sentence structure and speaks directly to the perpetrator: 'But you: one of my own, my companion, my friend.' This evokes closeness, trust and shared experience. The naming of the perpetrator as someone who stood in a close relationship of trust to the praying woman encourages one to think of an abuse of this closeness. Verse 21 also suggests this, in as far as it speaks of breaking the trust, a trust which seems to have shaped a mutual relationship, something that is 'integrated, wholly human, encompassing mutual understanding and personal commitment'.[22] Against this background the designations of friendship become the designations of enmity;[23] the sudden change to the second person singular is thus a direct and merciless condemnation. The perpetrator is confronted with his action; in a way, he is openly named and unmasked. If one follows Sheppard in assuming that psalms were spoken aloud and intended to be overheard by both friends and enemies, then this observation can be formulated even more clearly. In Psalm 55 the man of trust is publicly declared to be a man who has in fact acted as an enemy.[24]

Both the perpetrator's words and the manner of his speech are unmasked too. Although it is not characterized as such, v. 23 offers a direct report of his speech. A comparison with Pss. 22.8-9 and 2.2-3 shows that a direct reporting verb need not be

22. Othmar Keel, *Feinde und Gottesleugner: Studien zum Image der Widersacher in den Individualpsalmen* (Stuttgart: Verlag Katholisches Bibelwerk, 1969), p. 134.

23. See Kraus, *Psalmen*, p. 563.

24. Gerald T. Sheppard, '"Enemies" and the Politics of Prayer in the Book of the Psalms', in David Jobling, Peggy L. Day and Gerald T. Sheppard (eds.), *The Bible and the Politics of Exegesis: Essays in Honor of Norman K. Gottwald on his Sixty-Fifth Birthday* (Cleveland, OH: The Pilgrim Press, 1991), p. 77.

present.[25] Statements by perpetrators are often cited in the Psalms (Pss. 3.3; 10.4,6; 12.5; 22.8-9; 35.21,25; 41.6; 42.11; 59.8; 64.6-7; 70.4; 71.11). With the help of v. 22, 'His mouth flatters more smoothly than butter, but strife is in his heart; his words flow more gently than oil but they are drawn swords', the perpetrator's statement in v. 23, 'Cast your desire upon Yahweh, and he, he will sustain you, he will not allow the righteous to stumble forever', can be viewed as mockery. These are the words which flow more gently than oil, but are intended to be deadly. The contrast between the words' content and their effect turns the comfort into mockery and lies. The praying woman experiences the perpetrator's words as violence, as weapon. Language is inseparably related to its effect; it has a performative character: it is 'a primary happening'.[26]

Language has extraordinary power; a power which can bring death in the same way as weapons and the tools of war, for 'the power to speak is directly related to the power to act'.[27] However, it would be too narrow to understand the psalm as the expression of violence in single words and phrases only. The point at issue is the connection between the structure of language and violence; that is, language as 'the place of conflict and of misrepresentation, as place of oppression and liberation'.[28] Ultimately, discourse and the establishment of reality are made

25. Against Kraus (*Psalmen*, p. 564), who sees v. 23 as encouragement and an oracle of salvation. I assume, with Keel (*Feinde und Gottesleugner*, pp. 143-44), that this verse is a quotation, although the reporting verb is missing.

26. Claus Westermann, 'Das gute Wort in den Sprüchen: Ein Beitrag zum Menschenverständnis der Spruchweisheit', in Frank Crüsemann, Christof Hardmeier and Rainer Kessler (eds.), *Was ist der Mensch...? Beiträge zur Anthropologie des Alten Testaments: Hans Walter Wolf zum 80. Geburtstag* (Munich: Chr. Kaiser Verlag, 1992), pp. 243-55. Cf. also Pss. 12.4-5, 52.6, 59.8, 64.4, 109.2-3,140–144; Jer. 54.17; Prov. 18.21; and the identification of the 'man of violence' with the 'man of lies' in Ps. 140.12.

27. Mieke Bal, *Death and Dissymetry: The Politics of Coherence in the Book of Judges* (Chicago: Chicago University Press, 1988) p. 245.

28. Gudrun-Axeli Knapp, 'Macht und Geschlecht: Neuere Entwicklungen in der feministischen Macht- und Herrschaftsdiskussion', in Gudrun-Axeli Knapp and Angelika Wetterer (eds.), *Traditionen Brüche: Entwicklungen feministischer Theorie* (Freiburg: Kore, 1992), pp. 287-325.

in and by language. Discourses are shaped by those things 'which are discussed in a society, which are dealt with as problems and as issues, and which contribute to the collective production of meaning'.[29] A distinction, though, must be made between dominant and marginal discourses. In the Hebrew Bible the discourse which defines the facts of rape as part of its meaning is the perpetrators' discourse. The victims' perspective is excluded and remains unspoken. This praxis of discourse is criticised in Psalm 55, in that the act and its perpetrator are named and the perpetrator's use of language is unmasked. In the perpetrator's discourse, rape has a particular meaning. It is labelled as a property crime. The violence which is done to a woman is thus denied and remains unspoken. To interpret the reality of a rape in terms different from these, and to express the experience of rape, is to interrupt the discourse of violence against women at one, albeit a minor, point. The naming of the act and of the perpetrator, and the unmasking of his language, allow Psalm 55 to offer an alternative to the discourse of violence. The psalm offers a discourse which is not a continuation of the denial and the violence, but which interrupts them.

The passages of the psalm in which the praying woman wishes death upon the perpetrators—'Let death fall upon them, let them go down alive to Sheol' (v. 16); 'God will hear and will humble them' (v. 20); 'But you, God, you will bring them down into the deepest pit, the men of blood and deceit will not achieve even half of their days' (v. 24)—reflect an attempt to break the perpetrators' power too. They express 'the wish that God would remove this injustice'.[30] Only death seems appropriate for bringing an end to violence, for only through death is reality reversed. Wishing evil for the enemy is an expression of the depth of the victim's despair, but it is also a means by which a promise is recalled to memory, the promise of help perverted in the perpetrator's mouth. Only the perpetrator's death makes it possible for the praying woman to speak the words in v. 23 as an expression

29. Ruth Seifert, 'Entwicklungslinien und Probleme der feministischen Theoriebildung: Warum an der Rationalität kein Weg vorbeiführt', in Knapp and Wetterer (eds.), *Traditionen Brüche*, pp. 255-85.

30. Jürgen Ebach, 'Der Gott des Alten Testaments—ein Gott der Rache?', in Jürgen Ebach (ed.), *Biblische Erinnerungen*, p. 89.

of the hope for help: 'Cast your desire upon GOD and he, he will sustain you, he will not allow the righteous to stumble forever.'

Like the violence itself, the end of violence is expressed in terms of a spatial metaphor: 'let them go down alive to Sheol' (v. 16) and 'into the deepest pit' (v. 24). Both these spaces border on and reach into death. The experience of violence to which the praying woman has been exposed is an experience of absolute powerlessness. It seems that from this perspective of powerlessness only the perpetrator's death can bring an end to the violence. The wish that God might make the perpetrators into objects in their turn is, in other words, a request to God that the dominant discourse of violence be perverted and thus made powerless. This request erupts into words in v. 10: 'Confuse, my Lord, split their tongues.' These words stand exactly between the pictures of city and the desert, thus preventing the collision of these two, diametrically opposed, conceptual spaces. The tongue symbolizes the human capability of speech, human language and thus human power. God is now required to confuse and split the tongues of those who threaten the woman by violence: it is necessary that God should destroy, thus disempower, the discourse of violence which silences the praying woman by ignoring her pain. This is a concrete expression of the praying woman's hope, a hope which she expresses when she articulates her pain in and through the words of the psalm. Her hope is that the discourse of violence will be interrupted, indeed demolished, and that another discourse will become possible—a discourse which will express her experience of violence verbally and will bring back her subjecthood, integrity and identity.

'But I': Trusting in God

2. O God, hear my prayer,
    and do not hide from my plea.
3. Attend to me and answer me.
17. For I, I call to God,
    and GOD will rescue me.
18. At evening, at morning, at midday I lament and moan,
    and he will hear my voice.
19. He will rescue my life for salvation
    from the quarrel against me

for they are too many about me.

24.   But I, I trust in you.

In Psalm 55 a movement can be seen, from the despairing cry in v. 2, via the speech in v. 17, to the end in v. 24: 'But I, I trust in you.' This trust in God makes it possible to name the action, to accuse the perpetrators and to hope for an end to the violence. At the same time—and this is the psalm's true achievement—the praying woman is able to turn her gaze away from the violence and discover herself as subject, able to define herself and to formulate a perspective on the future. What stands at the end of this psalm is not a humiliating shrinking of the self into the *status quo*, but an 'I' well on its way to rediscovering its identity. This identity is defined in relation to God, who is on the side of those suffering violence. In this way, the 'But I, I trust in God' is a call to God as the advocate of the dispossessed, as their deliverer and their refuge. 'And in as far as they trust themselves to this advocate, the dispossessed gain strength to resist. They repossess the identity which has been stolen from them.'[31] The ability to locate oneself in language, despite absolute powerlessness, can have a liberating effect, for it allows the silence about violence to be brought to an end so that the end of violence can begin. In Psalm 55 the bringing about of the end of violence through the perpetrator's death is not the last word. Through trust in God, a counter-discourse is brought into being. This counter-discourse enables the powerless object of violence to rediscover herself as a subject possessing her own identity.

A Hermeneutic Interlude

In Psalm 55 violence is articulated as a particular topography of violence. What kind of reading is necessary to locate women's specific experiences of violence in this 'landscape' and to see Psalm 55 as a text expressing women's particular experience of violence?[32] Which 'map' makes it possible to include violence

31. Raiser, 'Klage als Befreiung', p. 27.

32. Sheppard, ' "Enemies" and the Politics of Prayer', p. 81. See also Marie M. Fortune, ' "My God, My God, Why Have You Forsaken Me?"', in Marie M. Fortune (ed.), *Spinning a Sacred Yarn: Women from the Pulpit* (New York: The Pilgrim Press, 1982), pp. 65-71.

against women when reading Psalm 55?

An intertextual reading seems to me to be a promising model.[33] An exegetical method which uses intertextuality has the reading of the text as an 'act of creativity',[34] because the meaning comes into being only in the course of the reading process. In the process of reading any text is related to other texts for, intentionally or unintentionally, no text exists independently of its situation in a universe of other texts. It is only in the coming together of different texts, texts which respond to one another through time and space, that a text acquires meaning. Meaning can shift and is not trapped in the text itself. It takes its shape not only in relation to the texts which a particular text itself gives as references, but also in the connections brought by the 'simple coincidence of previous reading'.[35] Interpretation can also affect the synchronic weight of this text, in that the exegete decides for her- or himself to which, and to what type of, intertexts it is to be compared and which points (markings) are to be used for comparison. This is not an allowance for giving full rein to arbitrariness, but recognition that every interpretation (including traditional ones) reflects a particular interest. Each interpretation should make this interest clear as well as offer a reasonable account of the text. The specific allegiance of feminist interests which, in the present case, is concerned with the possibility of locating a particularly female experience of violence in the topography of violence found in Psalm 55 can thus be placed in the context of intertextual interpretation. A feminist-oriented intertextuality will make new connections between texts and will interweave the text with different texts. It will take seriously, and in a new way, the possibilities offered by textual breaks and

33. On intertextuality see Sipke Draisma, 'Introduction', in Sipke Draisma (ed.), *Intertextuality in Biblical Writings: Essays in Honour of Bas van Iersel* (Kampen: Kok, 1989), pp. 1-14; Karlheinz Stierle, 'Werk und Intertextualität', in Wolf Schmid and Wolf-Dieter Stempel (eds.), *Dialog der Texte: Hamburger Kolloquium zur Intertextualität* (Vienna: Wiener Slawistischer Almanach, 1983), pp. 7-26; Ulrich Broich and Manfred Pfister (eds.), *Intertextualität: Formen, Funktionen, anglistische Fallstudien* (Tübingen: Max Niemeyer Verlag, 1985).

34. Draisma, 'Introduction', p. 7.

35. Stierle, 'Werk und Intertextualität', p. 10.

tensions, themselves often intertextual markings.

The City as a Woman's Body

The violence to which the psalm's speaking 'I' is exposed is shown in the picture of the city which has been taken over. This is not a historically identifiable occupation of a historically identifiable city; rather, the image of the city is the part of the topography of violence, metaphorically expressed by means of the psalm's spatial structure.

In Hebrew, 'city' is a feminine noun and cities are often personified as women; here the grammatical feminine gender has a particular significance.[36] The city's feminine gender is explained through the function of the city as mother and feeder of its inhabitants.[37] However, although this association with 'the mother who protects and sustains life'[38] may play a role in the Hebrew Bible as a whole, in the case of Psalm 55 it does not, in my opinion, function as an intertextual marker. Here the linking of the 'city' with the verb 'surround' suggests a different connection. The verb 'surround' often appears in warlike, military contexts with the meaning 'surrounded by an enemy';[39] that is, it is often associated with the conquering of a city. In the psalms of lament this verb has negative connotations and is an expression of threat.[40] In Psalm 55 the action of the verb 'surround' is carried out in the city, or on its walls. The inner space of the city is thus affected. Violence has settled in the heart of the city and does not retreat from the market place (v. 12).

This marking can be linked to two Hebrew Bible stories, Judges 19 and Genesis 19. In each of these stories the location of violence is the heart of a city, the market place. Violence finds its beginning in a situation characterized by the verb 'surrounded';

36. John J. Schmitt, 'Israel and Zion—Two Gendered Images: Biblical Speech Traditions and Their Contemporary Neglect', *Horizons* 81.1 (1991), pp. 18-32, esp. p. 19 and pp. 27-29.

37. According to E. Otto, 'עיר', p. 61.

38. Odil Hannes Steck, 'Zion als Gelände und Gestalt: Überlegungen zur Wahrnehmung Jerusalems als Stadt und als Frau im Alten Testament', *ZTK* 86 (1989), p. 272.

39. García Lopez, 'סבב', *ThWAT* V, pp. 735-36.

40. Cf. Pss. 18.6; 17.11; 22.13, 17; 49.6; 109.3; 118.10-11.

a situation which results in rape or the threat of a rape. In Judges 19 a woman is raped all night long by men who surround the house. She dies early the next morning. If we relate Judges 19 and Psalm 55 to one another intertextually, reading them alongside one another, a parallel between the city and the woman's body presents itself. The violence to which the city is subjected in Psalm 55 represents the violence which destroys the woman in Judges 19. The conquering of the city represents the rape of the woman. As has already been shown, the 'I' in Psalm 55 locates herself in the image of the city, thus expressing her own experience of violence. Read as intertext, Judges 19 makes it clear that the praying woman in Psalm 55 is speaking out; she is making it clear that her own inner space, her own body, has been robbed of its integrity and security, just like the conquered city. This place, the city, is as accessible and vulnerable as a woman's body is. The limits of the city, like the limits of the body, have not been respected. Like the city, the body of a woman can be conquered, taken over, plundered and destroyed. There is a parallel between the military defeat of a city, and rape.

Psalm 55 portrays the closeness of the perpetrator to the victim, expressed in the words 'But you: one of my own, my companion, my friend.' This allows a further insight into the topography of the violence committed. This violence takes place in a space that is geographically and emotionally familiar. Emotional closeness should, however, exclude violence. The destruction of the psychological, emotional and physical integrity of the 'I' is even greater when such closeness is abused. The theory of intertextuality allows a person's experiences to be understood and read as text. The reader's 'experience text' is brought into relationship with the text under consideration and the two become connected.[41] If we read Psalm 55 from the perspective of the experiences of women who have been raped, a surprising parallel results. The psychological and emotional consequences of rape—such as depressive hopelessness, lack of self-confidence and damage to the identity, to name but a few[42]—closely match

41. James W. Volz, 'Multiple Signs and Double Texts: Elements of Intertextuality', in Draisma (ed.), *Intertextuality*, pp. 27-34.

42. Flohtmann and Dilling, *Vergewaltigung*, pp. 69-72; Feldmann, *Vergewaltigung und ihre psychischen Folgen*, pp. 30-32 and 50-53.

the feelings depicted in Psalm 55. Moreover, the topography of closeness is also to be found in most instances of rape. About half of all rapes are committed by men already known to the women attacked. Two-thirds of all rapes take place not outside but *in* the home. Indeed, 'the greatest threat is posed by a known perpetrator in a familiar environment'.[43]

Against this background, it is quite possible to read Psalm 55 as a lament over a rape and an accusation of the perpetrator. As has already been noted, this does not imply a reading which seeks to locate the psalm historically. Rather, it requires us to read Psalm 55 and the topography of violence it describes through the eyes of a praying woman. From a woman's perspective the structure of Psalm 55, and particularly its spatial structure, might reflect female experience of violence. The psalm allows an expression of this violence and the naming of its perpetrator; this brings about a rupture in the ruling discourse of violence. Thus the psalm offers to the raped woman a possibility of dealing with her experience.

From Speechless Powerlessness to the Finding of a New Identity

The praying woman turns to the collectively shaped linguistic form of the lament psalms in order to articulate her experience of violence. In a situation when her language has been silenced or when no one hears her crying, the Psalms offer her a chance to speak. The 'I' who has experienced herself as the object of sexual violence, whose identity and integrity have been destroyed, can find a new place for herself in the language space of the psalm. In this way she can become subject once more. If we assume that subjectivity is shaped by language, this is of the utmost importance.

However, Psalm 55 poses a problem here. The image which the praying woman uses to formulate her need, the analogy

43. Feldmann, *Vergewaltigung und ihre psychischen Folgen*, p. 17. See also M.C. Baurmann, *Sexualität, Gewalt und die Folgen für das Opfer: Zusammengefasste Ergebnisse aus einer Längsschnittuntersuchung bei Opfern von angezeigten Sexualkontakten* (Wiesbaden: Kriminalistisches Institut, 3rd edn, 1984), pp. 13-16. Feldmann speaks of 71 per cent (*Vergewaltigung und ihre psychischen Folgen*, p. 9).

between the conquered city and the raped body, is borrowed from a discourse which is structured by military categories. In this discourse of violence, cities are sexualized and the body of the woman is seen as equivalent to the city. Both are available; each can be occupied and owned by men. Within this discourse it seems that an end to violence is only possible through counter-violence. Only the death of the perpetrator brings his violence to an end. Only with his death do his victim's absolute powerlessness and closeness to death seem to be over. This should not be criticized; indeed, such an expression of anger can have a therapeutic effect for women who suffer from an inability to speak as a consequence of rape. Speaking with the help of this kind of discourse has an important liberating function in the process of coping with and working through such experiences.

Nevertheless, it is important to remember that the praying woman speaks here in terms of a discourse which can turn itself against her and within which she will tend to remain an object. This is a discourse which is focused more on the perpetrator than on the victim. Within it, it seems impossible for a woman to become an independent subject in her own right and by her own initiative. Violence is indeed radically named but, in the analogy between conquered city and raped woman's body, the woman tends to remain on the side of the victim. And within this discourse the end of violence is really and truly possible only through the death of the perpetrator.

But Psalm 55 does offer another way, a different sort of speaking. The image of the dove, although it allows the utopian dream of an escape which does not actually take place, indicates a different sort of speech. Verses 7-9 portray escape as an unrealizable possibility; the 'I' remains exposed as a victim. Nevertheless, this passage also reflects a survival strategy, namely, dissociation. The image of the dove which flies away into the desert in search of refuge stands isolated in the psalm. Terminologically it is not bound to the rest of the psalm in any way. The dove/desert image is in some way dissociated. Dissociation allows emotions to be split off and the body to be separated from the 'I' so that in situations of physical, emotional or psychological threat from which there is no escape a boundary can be imposed between the 'I' and the unbearable pain. This is an attempt to survive, 'the despairing attempt to rescue the "I" from disintegration and re-establish it'.[44] The imaginary flight of the dove into the desert also fulfils the function of preserving the 'I' from destruction at the deepest level of its being. In this sense it is irrelevant whether or not the dove's flight takes the grammatical form of the subjunctive of desire. By creating this image of the dove, the 'I' tries to achieve something which is not possible for the woman's body; it tries to bring the violence to an end by limiting its intrusion into her own inner space. With the help of this image, the 'I' seeks to set limits and to survive the overwhelming experiences of violence without losing herself.

The power to express new images and create new spaces in a situation of absolute powerlessness corresponds to the 'But I' at the end of Psalm 55. The possibility of finding a place of sanctuary, hinted at in vv. 7-9, here becomes a certainty. God is on the side of the praying woman who uses this psalm to articulate her experience of rape.

It can thus be seen that Psalm 55 is open to the particular experiences of violence suffered by women. The imaginative spaces of the 'desert' and 'city' offer the possibility of locating the pain and articulating the violence. When the psalms of lament are read in this way, the strategies by which violence against women is legitimated begin to crumble and a small space is opened up—a space called into being by the vocal, public lament of women. This can be the beginning of liberation.

---

44. Ursula Wirtz, *Seelenmord: Inzest und Therapie* (Stuttgart: Kreuz Verlag, 1992), p. 147; Feldmann, *Vergewaltigung und ihre psychischen Folgen*, pp. 52-53.

'UNDER THE SHADOW OF YOUR WINGS': THE METAPHOR OF
GOD'S WINGS IN THE PSALMS, EXODUS 19.4, DEUTERONOMY
32.11 AND MALACHI 3.20, AS SEEN THROUGH THE PERSPECTIVES
OF FEMINISM AND THE HISTORY OF RELIGION

Silvia Schroer[1]

The Wings of God in the Language of the First Testament

In the Psalms we find passages where those who offer prayer
express their longing for, or their confidence in, being able to
find shelter under the shadow of their God. How familiar these
passages are! Also familiar to all of us is an image, found in
Exod. 19.4 and Deut. 32.11, the image of God as a magnificent
bird. It is very likely the only metaphor of an animal still used in
the Christian tradition with direct reference to the first person of
the Trinity. We associate wings with the ability to fly, with speed
and, in certain instances, with heavenly beings. In addition the
Bible, as well as the whole Ancient Near East, associates wings
with both might or heightened power on the one hand, and with
protection and regeneration on the other hand. In the following
examples I want to show that feminist exegesis and theology,
helped by Ancient Near Eastern as well as Egyptian visual art,
can gain important religio-historical insights into how biblical
conceptions of God came into being.[2] The language of God's

1.   This paper is based on a lecture I delivered on 26 January 1996, at the
University of Bern, by invitation of its Protestant Faculty of Theology. It
was first published as 'Ihr Bäume alle, klatscht in die Hände', in R. Kessler
e.a. (ed.), *Festschrift für Erhard S. Gerstenberg* (Münster: LIT Verlag, 1997), pp.
296-316, translated by Barbara and Martin Rumscheidt.
2.   I leave aside the wings of the Cherubim and the wings of the storm
on which God swiftly rides (Pss. 18.10, 104.3; 2 Sam. 22.11), as well as the
winged Seraphim (Isa. 6) and the four-winged creatures of Ezek. 1 and 10. I

wings literally cries out for images; in ancient Israel and the cultures surrounding it, images abounded. I assume that Palestine shared in the symbols and images of the world of the Near East. For example, acquaintance with metaphors from the books of the dead and their vignettes is no more or no less astonishing than the acquaintance with the wisdom teachings of Amenemope (end of the New Kingdom) which can be shown to exist in Prov. 22.17–23.11, or the affinity of Psalm 104 with Egyptian hymns to the sun.

God's Sheltering Wings in the Psalms
The Psalms speak of God's sheltering wings in many places (17.7-8, 36.6c-8, 57.1, 61.4-5, 63.7-8, 91.1-4).

> Show your wonderful goodness [חסדיך], Saviour of those who entrust themselves into your right hand in face of their adversaries. Guard me like the apple of the eye, hide me in the shadow of your wings [בצל כנפיך] from the godless who despoil me, and my deadly foes who encircle me (Pss. 17.7-9).

> You, YHWH, give aid to humans and to animals! How precious is your goodness [חסדך], O God! In the shadow of your wings [בצל כנפיך] your human children take refuge. They feast on the abundance of your house and from the river of your delights you give them drink (Ps. 36.6c-8).

> Whoever dwells under the shelter [סתר] of the Most High, who reposes in the shadow [צל] of the Almighty, may say to YHWH: 'My refuge, my fortress, my God in whom I trust'. For God will rescue you from the slings of the hunter, from death and destruction. With God's pinions [אברתו] you will be covered, under His wings [תחת כנפיו] you shall find refuge. You need not be afraid...(Ps. 91.1-4).

In every one of these passages protection, refuge, security and rescue in the face of approaching danger are associated with God's wings. Again and again concepts like, צל, 'shadow'; חסה, 'to seek refuge' and the root סתר[נ], 'to take shelter', recur.[3] The

focus on the *protecting* wings and the metaphors around them. This restricts the discussion to texts that clearly speak of YHWH's wings, excluding the wings of beings or means of transportation around YHWH.

3.   Cf. Isa. 30.2-3 on the search for refuge with Pharoah and in the shadow of Egypt.

image of God in these verses includes goodness, mercy and caring through providing food and drink. When Boaz praises the Moabite woman Ruth, he makes use of the image of God who protects and shelters (Ruth 2.12).

It is not that these texts speak of a bird to which YHWH would be compared. Instead, they simply assume that the divinity has wings. Depending on their theological position, commentators on the Psalms have proposed quite different interpretations of those wings. In his exegesis of Ps. 17.8, in which he studied above all the metaphors of shelter and shadow, Hermann Gunkel thought of a bird protecting its brood. But he also referred to Isis, who is depicted in Egyptian pictures as protecting Osiris with her wings.[4] In his commentary on the Psalms Hans-Joachim Kraus relates the wings to the wings of the Cherubim in the Holy of Holies.[5] In their recent study, Frank-Lothar Hossfeld and Erich Zenger even offer *three* possible interpretations: the mother-bird, the wings of the Cherubim, and the Winged Sun.[6] But this speculative mixture of highly diverse images is somewhat overdrawn. I am inclined to rule out the second possibility, because the Cherubim are guardians more than anything else; they exercised their functions in the Temple of Jerusalem where, in addition, they were the monumental sculptures which formed the seat of the invisible God's throne. Neither in biblical texts nor in pictorial art are there any indications that people sought refuge under the wings of the Cherubim. And, YHWH is never identified with these hybrid creatures. It could be that the solar disk is behind the images of the Psalms.[7] But the sun is not particularly suited to offer

4. Cf. Hermann Gunkel, *Die Psalmen* (Göttingen: Vandenhoeck & Ruprecht, 5th edn, 1968), on this text.

5. Hans-Joachim Kraus, *Psalms* (2 vols.; Minneapolis: Augsburg–Fortress, 1988–89), on Ps. 17 and elsewhere.

6. Frank-Lothar Hossfeld and Erich Zenger, *Die Psalmen I* (NEB; Würzburg: Echter Verlag, 1993), p. 17. Both Erich Zenger, *Das Buch Rut* (ZBKAT, 8; Zürich: TVZ Verlag, 1986), p. 57; and Christian Frevel, *Das Buch Rut* (NSKAT, 6; Stuttgart: Verlag Katholisches Bibelwerk, 1992), p. 76, think here of the mother-bird and the Cherubim.

7. On the winged sun, cf. Otto Eissfeldt, 'Die Flügelsonne als künstlerisches Motiv und als religiöses Symbol', *Kleine Schriften* 2 (Tübingen: J.C.B. Mohr, 1963), pp. 416-19.

protection, especially shade. Furthermore, the Winged Sun is strongly associated with the king and the monarchy. If we assume that the winged disk represents the sky, not the sun, images of refuge under the protective sky make sense only if they are related to the winged suns found on the ceilings or entrances to the Temple, as we know from Egyptian temples. But we know of no such fittings in the Jerusalem Temple, and it is hard to match them with the idea of pinions giving cover. It is quite conceivable that, behind the metaphor of wings, there is an anthropomorphic understanding of God; in Isa. 49.2 it is said that YHWH, who called the servant even in the womb of his mother, 'hid me in the shadow of his hand' (cf. Isa. 51.16). However, it is also possible that here it is the bird's wings that give the image its meaningIn Egyptian art the king has long been portrayed as being protected by the wings of a god, be it the falcon-like god Horus (Fig. 1) or the winged goddess Maat (Fig. 2). Later the protection-giving goddesses with their wings, chiefly Isis and Nephthys, are found with the dead. An ivory piece from Samaria (Fig. 3) shows that Isis and Nephthys, who with their wings protected Osiris (shown here in the centre in the figure of the Djed-pillar), were known in Israel in the ninth to eighth centuries BCE.[8]

The Wings of the Vulture in Exodus 19.4 and Deuteronomy 32.11
A definitive picture of conceptions associated with the image of YHWH's protecting wings is not easily gained from the verses of the Psalms. Two passages seem clearer in their meaning: they are generally regarded as being of Deuteronomistic authorship, that is, from the sixth to fifth centuries BCE. Like the Psalms, they speak of God's saving actions on behalf of the people of Israel by leading them out of Egypt and through the desert. In Exod. 19.4

---

8.   Winged goddesses flanking a ruler appear in Syro-Levantine glyptic art as early as the Middle Bronze Age. (Cf. Beatrice Teissier, *Egyptian Iconography on Syro-Palestinian Cylinder Seals of the Middle Bronze Age* [OBO, Arch. Ser. 11), Freiburg: Universitätsverlag; Göttingen: Vandenhoeck & Ruprecht, 1986), from p. 54 and figs. 27-29. They are present, in other words, earlier than Isis and Nephthys in Egyptian art. This might suggest that the conception of winged protective goddesses was deeply rooted and held sway for a long time in the Levant.

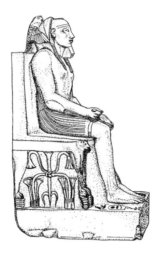

Figure 1. Diorite statue of King Chephren, Gisa, c. 2540–2505 BCE. Jean Leclant, *Egypt* (Geneva: Nagels Publishers, 1976), Fig. 182 (Drawing by Ms Ines Haselbach).

Figure 2. Counterweight of a pectoral from the treasure of Tutankhamon's tomb (1332–1323 BCE). Cyril Aldred, *Jewels of the Pharaohs: Egyptian Jewelry of the Dynastic Period* (London: Thames and Hudson, 1978), Fig. 100. (Drawing based on U. Winter, *Frau und Göttin: Exegetische und ikonographische Studien zum weiblichen Gottesbild im Alten Israel und in dessen Umwelt* [OBO, 53; Freiburg Schiseit Universitätsverlag; Göttingen: Vandenhoeck & Ruprecht, 1983], Fig. 516).

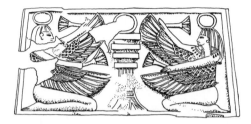

Figure 3. Ivory from Samaria (eighth century BCE). John Winter and Grace M. Crowfoot, *Early Ivories from Samaria (Samaria-Sebaste: Reports of the Work of the Joint Expedition in 1931–1933 and of the British Expedition, no. II)* (London: Palestine Exploration Fund, 1938), Pl. 3.1; Keel and Uehlinger, *Goddesses* Fig. 243.

YHWH has Moses instruct the Israelites gathered at Sinai:

> You yourself have seen what I did to the Egyptians and how I bore you on the wings of the vultures [כנפי נשרים] and brought you here to myself.

In the Song of Moses, Deut. 32.10-11, Moses reminds Israel how YHWH gathered His people in the desert: God found it in the desert land, in the howling waste of the wilderness. He surrounded it with protection, watched over it and guarded it like the apple of his eye.

> Like a vulture [כנשר] who protects its brood (its nest) and hovers [ירחף] over its young, so God spread out his wings [כנפיו], took this people and carried it on its pinions [אברתו].

Here, YHWH's watchful protection and care is compared to the behaviour of brooding birds. It is not eagles, as most translations put it, but goose-vultures of which the text speaks. As far as criteria can be established, נשר refers to the goose-vulture. It is spoken of in Job 39.27-30 and Prov. 30.17 as a creature feeding on carrion. This explains why in Lev. 11.13 and Deut. 14.12, together with other species of vultures, it is counted among the unclean animals. In Mic. 1.16 the daughter of Zion is bidden to make herself bald as the נשר. Such a bald head is characteristic of the goose-vulture.[9] Thus, in Deuteronomy 32 YHWH is explicitly compared to the vulture that cares for its young by hovering over and allegedly[10] carrying them on its pinions. What is described here is caring indeed, 'parent-like' behaviour.

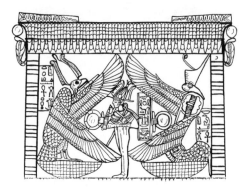

Figure 4. Pectoral from the treasure of Tutankhamon's tomb.
Aldred, *Jewels*, Fig. 96. (Drawing by Ms Ines Haselbach.)

9.   It is the wild bird that is most frequently spoken of in the Old Testament. The Septuagint already translated the word as ἀετός, given the Greek-Western admiration for the eagle and the concurrent loathing for the vulture. However, the eagle was paid no attention in Ancient Egypt and very little in many parts of the Ancient Near East. It is only on Ptolemaic coins that the eagle enters Palestine triumphantly as a symbol. Unlike our world, the world of the Ancient Near East held the vulture in great esteem. It was carefully recorded that these birds made their nests in rocky cliffs (Jer. 49.16), and how a large flock of vultures mysteriously gathered in a very short time around a carcass (Hab. 1.8; Job. 9.26, 39.29; 2 Sam. 1.23; cf. also Mt. 24.28, Lk. 17.37). We know today that vultures have a very efficient communication system. In connection with the vulture, cf. the relevant chapters in Othmar Keel, Max Küchler and Christoph Uehlinger, *Orte und Landschaften der Bibel: Ein Handbuch und Studienreiseführer*. I. *Geographisch-geschichtliche Landeskunde* (Zürich: Benziger; Göttingen: Vandenhoeck & Ruprecht, 1984), pp. 154-57.

10.   Research on these birds provides us with no evidence for that. On this misunderstanding, cf. H.G.L. Peels, 'On the Wings of the Eagle (Deut. 32:11)—An Old Misunderstanding', *ZAW* 106 (1994), pp. 300-303. The observations of lay people have been at odds with this scientific hypothesis for a long time.

In both the Near East and in Egypt the symbolism of the vulture is old. In both cultural spheres it is constantly associated with goddesses.[11] Pictorial findings from Catal Huyuk show that, as early as the Neolithic Age, people found comfort in the assurance that the Goddess not only gives birth to life but also devours it at the end when the dead are laid out for her—as was still done until recently in Iran, India and Nepal.[12] Thus, the vulture represents both becoming and passing away.

In Egypt Nekhbet, the tutelary goddess of Upper Egypt, is usually portrayed in the image of the goose-vulture. The name of the Goddess Mut, who wears only a vulture hood, was written using the picture of the goose-vulture. *Mwt* was an ideogram for motherhood.[13] In Egypt it was vulture-goddesses

11. On the relevant iconography cf. the extensive study by Silvia Schroer, 'Die Göttin und der Geier', *ZDPV* 3 (1995), pp. 60-80. The article failed to mention A. de Vries, *Dictionary of Symbols and Imagery* (Amsterdam: North-Holland, 1976). E. Winter is currently preparing a monograph on the vulture and the vulture-goddess in Egypt. W.W. Müller has shown that many inscriptions in Southern Arabia refer to vulture-deities: 'Adler und Geier als altarabische Gottheiten', in Ingo Kottsieper *et al.* (eds.), *'Wer ist wie du, Herr, unter den Göttern?' Studien zur Theologie und Religionsgeschichte Israels für O. Kaiser zum 70. Geburtstag* (Göttingen: Vandenhoeck & Ruprecht, 1994), pp. 91-107.

12. On the custom of ritual stripping of flesh, and on the so-called towers of silence onto which the bodies of the dead are laid for the birds to devour, cf. Joachim Bretschneider, *Architekturmodelle in Vorderasien und der östlichen Ägäis vom Neolithikum bis in das 1. Jahrtausend: Phänomeme in der Kleinkunst an Beispielen aus Mesopotamien, dem Iran, Anatolien, Syrien, der Levante und dem ägäischen Raum unter besonderer Berücksichtigung der bau- und religionsgeschichtlichen Aspekte* (AOAT, 229; Neukirchen–Vluyn: Neukirchener Verlag, 1991), pp. 33-37, tables 108-109 and Figs. 12-14.

13. The concepts formed with these letters refer to the physical mother, the mother of gods and kings and animals, the primordial and ancestral mother but also the womb and, interestingly, the coffin. At the same time, the goose-vulture stands also for *nrt* or *nrw*, terror—a persuasive illustration of the ambivalence of the *tremendum et fascinosum* of the holy. It is very likely the terror of death that is symbolically associated with the vulture, of which we read in Isa. 31.5: 'Like birds [כצפרים] hovering so YHWH Sabaoth will encircle Jerusalem, encircle and rob, flit around and embowel it.' (On this translation cf. Othmar Keel, 'Erwägungen zum Sitz im Leben des Pascha und zur Etymologie von פסח', *ZAW* 84 [1972], pp. 414-34, esp. pp. 430-31.) Cf. Silvia Schroer, *Die Göttin*, p. 67. There is an error in lines

granting protection, above all to the king whom they fed by letting him suck at their breasts. An adornment found on the body of King Tut-ankh-amon (see Fig. 4; also Fig. 3), shows the winged serpent Uto as the ruler of Lower Egypt, and the vulture-goddess as the ruler of Upper Egypt. They are both protecting the deceased, who is depicted in the figure of Osiris. But the accompanying inscription identifies Uto and Nekhbet as Isis and Nekhbet. Of primary significance is the aspect of protection, which is made apparent by means of the wings. The figure, whose work it is to grant protection, is quite secondary by comparison—be it a vulture-goddess, a serpent-goddess or any of the anthropomorphic goddesses of protection. It was not long before the protective power of these goddesses was called upon by large segments of the population. The goose-vulture and other apotropous creatures, such as frightful lions armed with knives, are portrayed on the so-called magic knives of the Middle Kingdom, i.e. large ivory amulets. They were meant to give protection against ill fortune to expectant mothers, to mothers and their children and to others under the care of these divinities. But they were also used in tombs as a means to protect the deceased. The motherly goddess is associated especially with birth and childbed, but also with death (a representation of her was placed into tombs). The numerous portrayals of vultures, found on the ceilings of tombs from the period of the Ramessids, indicate that—like her counterpart in Mesopotamia—this motherly goddess watched not only over the entry into life but also over the exit from it. Vulture-goddesses accompany the dead into the other world, being laid on their breasts on pectorals and amulets (Fig. 4) or painted on the papyri of the book of the dead placed into their graves. These goddesses are found also on many the of the sarcophagi that are highly decorated with paintings. The papyrus of the *Book of the Dead* belonging to a woman named Gaut-sushen, who had been a singer in a temple (Fig. 5) in the Twenty-first Dynasty, shows the dead woman in the figure of Osiris. Above her/him two goose-vultures flank a rising sun with the head of a falcon. In this way,

24-25 on that page, in connection with the writing of the name 'Mut'. The filth-vulture (the hieroglyphics of the vulture) has obviously nothing to do with the writing of that name; what is meant there is the goose-vulture.

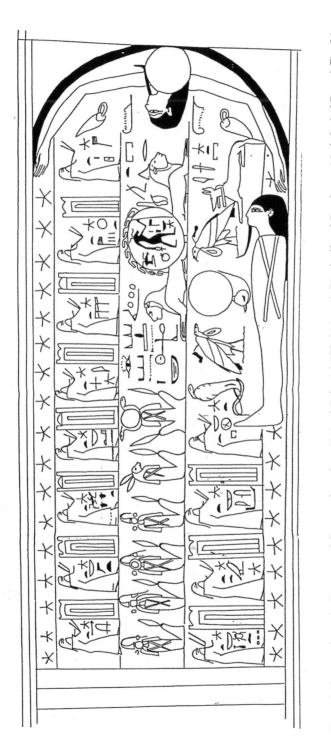

Figure 5. Excerpt from the Papyrus of Gaut-sushen, from Deir-el-Bahari (1075–944 BCE). Piankoff and Rambova, *Mythological Papyri*, Fig. 24 (Drawing by Ms Ines Haselbach).

intercession is offered by the vulture-goddess for the sun-like rebirth of the dead woman; in fact, the Goddess becomes a mid-wife for the woman's new life.[14]

Figure 6. Scarab from the Tell el-Aǧǧul (1750–1550 BCE).
After Keel and Uehlinger, *Goddesses* , fig. 4.

In Palestine the vulture is found chiefly on stamp seals from the Middle Bronze Age IIB (1750–1550 BCE), the formative period of Canaanite culture.[15] Those seals were primarily amulets, with protective powers, for guarding the living and the dead. Here we encounter once again the frightful lions and vultures with knives that appear on the magic knives of just about the same time. As in Egypt, these objects' duty probably was to protect mother and child. Other seals make the connection between Goddess, vulture and vegetation even more apparent. A scarab from Tell-el-Aǧǧul (Fig. 6) depicts a female ruler of animals kneeling over a lion. A goose-vulture sits opposite her with a twig in its talon. Twigs symbolize flourishing life and vitality. While the lion signals the wilder aspects of the Goddess, the vulture accentuates her motherly-regenerative powers. The symbolism of the vulture is present in the artwork of Palestinian miniatures as late as the Iron Age. A scarab from Meggido (Fig. 7),

14. Whenever the vulture-goddess is portrayed together with the life-giving sun in certain book-of-the-dead papyri, in the context of the judgment of the dead or the weighing of the hearts, she is depicted as a benevolent and protective ruler. Such portraits express the hope of the living and the dead for a merciful judgment. Cf. Alexandre Piankoff and Natasha Rambova, *Mythological Papyri: Egyptian Religious Texts and Representations III* (2 vols.; New York: Pantheon Books, 1954), I, p. 54, fig. 39.

15. On the vulture in Palestinian iconography and, in particular, in the artwork of seals, cf. S. Schroer, *Die Göttin*, pp. 62-66.

Figure 7. Scarab from Megiddo (seventh century BCE). After Keel and Uehlinger, *Goddesses* Fig. 318a.

from the seventh century BCE, shows a vulture in flight above a nursing goat or gazelle, the image of divine motherliness. Moreover, a twig is cut into the small surface of the seal.

Several biblical texts have preserved the notion of the vulture as a symbol of regeneration. In Ps. 103.3-5 the woman or man praying remembers God,

> [YHWH] who forgives all your iniquity and heals all your infirmities [תחלאיכי], who redeems your life from perdition and who crowns you with steadfast love and mercy [חסד ורחמים], who fulfils your longing with goodness so that your youth is renewed [תתחדש] like the vulture's [כנשר].

In Isa. 40.30-31 the image of the vulture is used also to describe the strength and vitality God gives:

> Youths faint and are weary, young men stumble and fall, but they who wait for YHWH ever renew their strength, so that like the vultures [כנשרים] they let their wings [אבר] grow [יעלו], they run and not grow weary, walk and not grow faint.

Forgiveness, healing and the verve of youth come from God, but the newly gained vitality is likened to the vulture. More often than not, this has caused commentators embarrassment. Because they did not know the symbolism that lies behind this picture, commentators were misled into making abstruse or meaningless explanations.[16] Here, it is true, regeneration and vitality do come

16. Claus Westermann, *Isaiah 40–66* (Philadelphia: Westminster Press, 1969), does not deal with the image in his commentary. Rudolph Kittel (*Die Psalmen* [Leipzig: A. Deichert, 1922], p. 332) and Bernard Duhm (*Die*

from a merciful, fatherly God (Ps. 103.8, 13). But חסד is the compassion that resides in the womb [רחם], originally associated
with motherly love and the mother-divinities.[17]

The Wings of the Sun in Malachi 3.20
The Book of Malachi comes from the early postexilic period.
Verse 3.20, which at first glance is quite enigmatic, tells of wings
that do not protect but heal. To the godless it prophesies the all-
destroying day of YHWH, whereas to those who fear YHWH it
promises a day of rejoicing:

> But for you who fear my name, the sun of righteousness [שמש
> צדקה] shall rise, and healing [מרפא] is in its wings [בכנפיה]. And
> you shall be born (anew) [ויצאתם] and leap with joy [ופשתם] like
> bull-calves let loose.

Here it is the sun that is portrayed with wings, like the wings of
the morning in Ps. 139.9. The verse does not speak of protection
under, but of the healing that is *in*, the wings. Several years ago
Hans-Peter Stahli made the case for relating the image of the
rising sun to YHWH.[18] Since then, the studies by Othmar Keel
and Christoph Uehlinger have bolstered the hypothesis that the
sun-god worshipped in Jerusalem was succeeded by YHWH,
who took on many of that god's attributes.[19] But why are the

Psalmen [KAT, 14; Tübingen: J.C.B. Mohr, 1922], pp. 368-69) assume that
legendary images are behind the text. Kraus (*Psalms*, II, p. 291) states, but
without further evidence, that the eagle is a symbol of youthful strength.

  17. Schroer, *Die Göttin*, p. 70, explores the possible connection of this
word-root to a species of vultures (i.e. the monk-vulture?), רחם/רחמה in
Lev. 11.18 and Deut. 14.17. On the biblical symbolism of the womb cf. Luise
Schottroff, Silvia Schroer and Marie-Theres Wacker, *Femnisticshe Exegese:
Forschungserträge zur Bibel aus der Perspektive von Frauen* (Darmstadt:
Wissenschaftliche Buchgesellschaft, 1995), esp. pp. 169-71 (ET *Feminist
Interpretation: The Bible in Women's Perspective* [Minneapolis: Fortress Press,
1998], pp. 173-75).

  18. Hans-Peter Stähli, *Solare Elemente im Jahweglauben des Alten Testaments* (OBO, 66; Freiburg: Universitätsverlag; Göttingen: Vandenhoeck &
Ruprecht, 1985), p. 35.

  19. Othmar Keel and Christoph Uehlinger, *Göttinnen, Götter und
Gottessymbole: Neue Erkenntnisse zur Religionsgeschichte Kanaans und Israels
aufgrund bislang unerschlossener ikonographischer Quellen* (QD, 134; Freiburg:
Herder, 3rd edn, 1995; ET *Goddesses, Gods, and God Symbols* [Minneapolis:

leaps of the righteous compared to the leaps of young cattle, and what is the point of 'healing in the wings?'

The key to the interpretation of this curious metaphor is provided by the decoration of Egyptian tombs from the Nineteenth and Twentieth Dynasties. In the tomb of Irinefer in Deir el-Medina (Fig. 8) we see the deceased standing before twin sycamores, between which the sun is rising. The sun is also portrayed as a small calf, for the sun's sphere is born of the heavenly cow, the Goddess Nut and, of course, the offspring of the heavenly cow is a calf. A similar depiction is found in the tomb of Sennedjem (Fig. 9). Chapter 109 in the *Book of the Dead* makes a connection between the sun-calf and the deceased's hope that he will be born anew like the sun:

Figure 8. Drawing from the tomb of Irinefer in Thebes (Twentieth Dynasty). After Othmar Keel, *Jahwe-Visionen und Siegelkunst: Eine neue Deutung der Majestätsschilderungen in Jes 6, Ez 1 und Sach 4* (SBS, 84-85; Stuttgart: Verlag Katholisches Bibelwerk, 1977), Fig. 233.

Fortress Press, 1998]); and 'Jahwe und die Sonnengottheit von Jerusalem', in Walter Dietrich and Martin Klopfenstein (eds.), *Ein Gott allein? YHWH-Verehrung und biblischer Monotheismus im Kontext der israelitischen und altorientalischen Religionsgeschichte* (OBO, 139; Freiburg/Göttingen: Universitätsverlag/Vandenhoeck & Ruprecht, 1994), pp. 269-306.

Figure 9. Drawing from the tomb of Sennedjem in Deir el-Medina (Nineteenth Dynasty). After Keel, *Jahwe-Visionen*, Fig. 232.

1.   I know the Eastern gate of heaven...
7.   I know those twin sycamores of turquoise
8.   between which Ra steps forth...
19. I know the powers of the East,
20. It is Herakhty, the sun-calf, the morning-star.[20]

When biblical texts speak of God's wings or the wings of the vulture, it is the symbolism of protection that governs them more than any other. Through the symbolism of the sun, the book of Malachi has kept alive the notion that wings also bring regeneration or 'healing', as the Bible calls it. This book promises the righteous, the people who believe in YHWH, nothing less than a new life, a new birth like the sun's, the calf of the heavenly cow. The meaning of the Malachi verses becomes transparent only against the background of pictorial art. The issue is not simply that the leaps of joy are arbitrarily likened to those of calves, so that their vitality may be fully grasped. (This is how all interpretations up to Herbert Niehr's put the matter.) The issue is the

20. As cited in Erik Hornung, *Das Totenbuch der Ägypter* (Zürich: Artemis, 1979).

new life made possible by faith.[21] Wilhelm Rudolph, and others with him, related the opaque phrase 'you shall rise' in his commentary[22] to 'the stall' of those calves. His intent was apologetic, albeit unarticulated, because he sensed that the formulation suggested something he would rather not bring out. But, correctly understood, 'you shall rise' [ויצאתם] actually means 'you shall be born' (as in Gen. 15.4, 17.6, 25.25 and elsewhere). Psalm 110 also speaks quite clearly about regeneration through a sun-like birth in its promise to the king:

> From the mother-womb of the dawn [מרחם משחר] will come to you the dew of your youth (Ps. 110.3b).

A similar idea is expressed in Trito-Isaiah. A promise is made to the righteous who keep a fast in accordance with God's will, namely by doing justice:

> Then shall your light break forth like the dawn [כשחר] and your healing [וארכתך] shall forthwith spring up [תצמח], your righteousness shall go before you and the glory of YHWH shall follow you (Isa. 58.8).

As in Malachi, in this text too those who fear God are promised an all-embracing regeneration. The notion of healing, springing up like a plant, may well be reminiscent of rites of the Osiris cult, since sprouting grain signalled the hope for a new life of the dead.[23]

An Assessment in Light of the History of Religion and Feminism

I believe that, from the perspective of systematic theology, it is useful to reconstruct a background from the history of religion

---

21. Cf. G. Johannes Botterweck, 'Die Sonne der Gerechtigkeit am Tage Jahwes: Auslegung von Malachias 3.13-21', in *Bild und Leben* (1960), pp. 235-237. Herbert Niehr, *Der höchste Gott: Alttestamentlicher YHWH-Glaube im Kontext syrisch-kanaanäischer Religionen des 1. Jahrtausends v. Chr.* (Berlin: W. de Gruyter, 1990), esp. pp. 141-63.

22. Wilhelm Rudolph, *Haggai-Sacharja-Maleachi Kommentar* (KAT, 13.4; Gütersloh: Gütersloher Verlagshaus Gerd Mohn, 1976), p. 289.

23. Note the connection between the much-increased light of the sun and YHWH's healing of the people's wounds in Isa. 30.26, a text which promises healing by the merciful God of justice.

and the pictorial symbolism behind biblical texts which speak of God's wings.

A strong connection was made in the Ancient Near East between the Mother-Goddess and the vulture, to which rich notions of protection and regeneration were attributed. Whenever there is mention of the protective wings of YHWH, the motherliness of YHWH is not particularly emphasized. Nevertheless, it is definitely present.[24] In this respect, YHWH is the successor of the Goddess. As late as Mt. 23.37 and Lk. 13.34, Jesus compares himself and his mission as God's wisdom to a mother-bird that wants to take her brood under her wings.

This confirms other observations, according to which the God of Israel was able to integrate—at times with apparent difficulty—the dimension of motherliness from the powers and qualities associated clearly with goddesses. Hosea 11 or Second and Third Isaiah may serve as examples of this claim. Female eroticism, however, was not integrated and, as current studies show, obvious difficulties arose also when the understanding of regeneration was portrayed in unambiguously female imagery. There is no longer any doubt that aspects of the Goddess were integrated only very deficiently into the development toward the monotheism that, itself, arose from a process of accumulating, eliminating and integrating divine aspects from highly diverse origins. This is characterized also by the disappearance of the concrete female way of looking at things. Thus already in the Psalms, when wings are mentioned, only God's wings are meant, and there is no reference to any figure. On the other hand, Egyptian painting shows that gynaikomorphous goddesses of protection and goddesses in the form of birds were readily interchangeable.[25] Today, the aspect of motherliness has to be reinstated in the Christian image of God. But we cannot

24. The fact that a brooding mother bird is inviolable (according to Deut. 22.6) is further evidence that she at least still reminds people of something holy. This is comparable to the prohibition against boiling a kid in its mother's milk (Exod. 23.19), because a suckling mother animal was held to be holy from time immemorial.

25. In Job 33.25 it is an angel who—in the end—assumes the role of a motherly regenerative goddess, allowing the person approaching death to regain the strength of youth.

stop at rediscovering God as a big brood-hen because, for too long, being a woman was reduced to motherliness as a matter of course. In this case, the pictures and texts discussed invite us to speak more regularly of God as one who heals and gives new strength and life (thereby offering an alternative to esoteric proposals of regeneration). In addition, within the context of gender research, these pictures and texts invite us to compare the current social construct of motherliness and the Ancient Near East's constructions of it. This allows us to discover that, far too inflexibly, we associate motherliness with protection and shelteredness. The Near East thought much more dynamically of 'being born anew', and about the new strength that results from protection and shelter.[26]

It is also in relation to hermeneutics that attention to biblical texts could be informative for feminist theologians. However diverse, the texts document a wisdom common to their different authors: new images of God do not come out of thin air but from pictures, conceptions and constellations already present. The vulture that had been so closely associated with the Goddess was not eliminated, which would have been a very simple thing to do. Instead, people returned to this symbol, let parts of it live on and carefully wove them into the language about the God of Israel. The wings of the divinity no longer protect only kings and the deceased, but also the living women and men who prayed the Psalms. The Egyptian notions of regeneration were not thrown out but integrated. Even if the consequences and the result of such intricate piece-work in theology annoys us feminists in some respects, in this case we must take up an apprenticeship with those who committed Israel's faith and theology to writing. Images of God are changeable; what needs to be learned here is that their change requires ingenuity and patience. There is no *tabula rasa*, no beginning from scratch. If it wishes to be conscious of history, concrete and non-elitist, feminist theology must openly face the power of existing images and the images that have developed over extensive historical stretches. Then can feminist theology form its utopias, in dialogue with such images.

26. This thought is present also in Isa. 66.13, which speaks of the divine-motherly comfort that brings about the renewal of one's youth.

This calls for patience in keeping present symbols, images and metaphors. And this also calls for courage and imagination in weaving something new from old cloth. A not insignificant aspect of all this is the confidence that under God's wings protection is found; and, in her wings, there is healing.

HEARING THE CRIES UNSPOKEN:
AN INTERTEXTUAL-FEMINIST READING OF PSALM 109

Beth LaNeel Tanner[1]

How are the Psalms read and interpreted? Certainly there are a multitude of ways. These poems can be seen as a liturgical guide to understanding the temple cult; as myth to investigate the religious beliefs of ancient Israel; as Scripture to tell the reader about God; or as devotional literature to engage the reader in a personal exploration of faith. In *Interpreting the Psalms*, Patrick Miller has observed that the Psalms function on all of these levels simultaneously. It is not a question of picking one interpretation over the other. Miller stresses that the language of the Psalms is 'open and metaphorical' and it 'invites, allows and calls for interpretation that looks and moves forward into the present and future as well as for interpretation that looks backward'.[2] The Psalms, then, engage both the ancient 'texts' of the Hebrew Bible and the 'texts' of the interpreter. This flexibility in the metaphorical language of the psalms should make them prime texts for a feminist interpretation. Historically, however, this has not been the case. Few feminist interpreters have given attention to the ways the psalms engage the lives of women. This presentation will begin a conversation that hopefully will invite a fruitful engagement of the Psalms by feminist scholars.

---

1.   This paper has undergone several revisions and therefore is also a 'community project'. Two groups have been especially helpful—the faculty and PhD students of the Bible department at Princeton Theological Seminary, and The Psalms Section Committee of the SBL. In addition, there are several scholars whose insights deserve a special mention—Drs Julie Duncan, Patrick Miller, Dennis Olson and Kathrine Sakenfeld, and Elna Solvang.

2.   P. Miller, *Interpreting the Psalms* (Philadelphia: Fortress Press, 1986), p. 51.

Preliminary Considerations: Intertextuality

This presentation will explore a feminist reading of the Psalms by using an intertextual methodology. Intertextuality has come to the forefront in literary circles in recent years and is a growing interest among Jewish and Christian biblical scholars.[3] But intertextuality is a multifaceted term: some scholars arguing for a philosophical understanding of the term, while others suggest it as a methodological process for critical inquiry.[4] Henrich Plett, for example, will not even speak of intertextuality but only of 'intertextualities':

> Currently, 'intertextuality' is a fashionable term, but almost everybody who uses it understands it somewhat differently. A host of publications has not succeeded in changing the situation. On the contrary: their increasing number has only added to the confusion.[5]

Based on this variety of meanings for intertextuality, it becomes clear that there is not *a* theory of intertextuality. It is impossible to detail the breadth of the intertextual discussion in a paper of this length, but in general terms intertextuality is a paradigm concerned with all of the other 'texts' that are imbedded explicitly or implicitly in the literary text under consideration. Roland Barthes explains, 'The text is a tissue of quotations drawn from

---

3. See, e.g., Daniel Boyarin, *Intertextuality and the Reading of Midrash* (Indianapolis: Indiana University Press, 1990); Dana Fewell (ed.), *Reading Between the Texts: Intertextuality and the Hebrew Bible* (Louisville, KY: Westminster/John Knox Press, 1992); or George Aichele and Gary Phillips (eds.), *Intertextuality and the Bible* (Semeia, 69/70; Atlanta: Scholars Press, 1995).

4. For a sampling of the variety of methods see Julia Kristeva, *Desire in Language: A Semiotic Approach to Literature and Art* (New York: Columbia University Press, 1980); or Harold Bloom, *The Anxiety of Influence* (New York: Oxford University Press, 1973); or Roland Barthes, *Image-Music-Text* (New York: Hill and Wang, 1977); or Michael Riffaterre, 'The Interpretant in Literary Semiotics', *American Journal of Semiotics* 3 (1985), pp. 41-55; or Jonathan Culler, 'Presupposition and Intertextuality', *Modern Language Notes* 91 (1976), pp. 1380-96.

5. Henrich Plett, 'Intertextualities', in H. Plett (ed.), *Intertextuality* (Berlin: W. de Gruyter, 1991), pp. 3-27 (3).

innumerable centers of culture.'[6] This definition indicates that an intertextual paradigm involves more than an influence study—it involves texts, cultures and the way these interact in the process of reading. My own particular intertextual-feminist paradigm will involve four methodological considerations.

The first consideration is 'the primary *who*' of the intertextual paradigm. Is the central focus on the author, the text, or the reader? In the intertextual reading proposed here, it is the reader who will be the central figure, because it is in her or his reading that intertextuality is created.[7] It is in her or his knowledge, life experience and hermeneutic of meaning that all intertextual traces are noted and their importance tracked down. Roland Barthes explains:

> A text is made up of multiple writings, drawn from many cultures and entering into mutual relations of dialogue, parody, contestation, but there is one place where this multiplicity is focused and that place is the reader, not as was hitherto said, the author. The reader is the space on which all the quotations that make up a writing are inscribed without any of them being lost; the text's unity lies not in its origin but in its destination.[8]

But even though the reader takes center stage, she or he is not there alone.[9] Yvonne Sherwood explains that despite Barthes's focus on the author, he must also share the limelight:

> Barthes, who envisions the author leaving stage-right, 'diminishing like a figurine at the far end of the literary stage' is haunted by the possibility of a final encore and finds it impossible to describe the act (or 'pleasure') of reading without appealing to the agency of the text. Paradoxically his writings seem to support the unlimited freedom of the reader *and* the limitations of that freedom by textual constraints ('the text dislocates the reader's historical, cultural, and psychological assumptions').[10]

6. Barthes, *Image-Music-Text*, p. 146.
7. This form of intertextuality, where the reader is central, is the method argued for by Roland Barthes, Michael Riffaterre and Günard Genette.
8. Barthes, *Image-Music-Text*, p. 160.
9. The central focus of an intertextual study is heavily debated. Kristeva and Bloom place the author as central. Riffaterre and Genette place the text in the primary position.
10. Yvonne Sherwood, *The Prostitute and the Prophet: Hosea's Marriage in*

Because the reader is the one where these intertextual traces are seen, it is imperative that the reader not be simply reduced to a single uniform entity—recall that Barthes's quotation concerning a text also applies to the reader as a 'text'. For example, the 'who' in this particular paradigm uses, of course, a decidedly feminist ideology[11] but, as Barthes reminds us, the reader is the center of a complex reading of many texts from a variety of sources.

The second methodological consideration is to explore the question touched on above, of *what* is a text. Julia Kristeva argues that a text is more than a literary document. She blurs the line between a 'sign' or 'word' and 'text', so that the base unit becomes a 'text' and subsequently everything is a text: a piece of paper with letters on it is a text but so, also, history as understood by the reader is a text, the reader's cultural ideologies is a text, and, even the reader is a text.[12] In addition, each of these major texts is also a mosaic of quotations. For example, the cultural text is made up of not only the reader's historical-cultural circumstance, but also of how the reader reads and understands all of the various bits of information concerning that culture. For this reason, the cultural, historical and psychological texts are reader specific. In addition, since each of the major texts is a mosaic of these other smaller texts, the amount of texts available for any one intertextual event is almost infinite.

The third consideration is to ask how the meaning of a text is produced *by the reader*. In an intertextual framework meaning is fluid, not static, because each text is itself a mosaic of quotations that can be read in different ways by different readers, or even in different ways by the same reader. The intertextual reader is

Literary-Theoretical Perspective (JSOTSup, 212; Sheffield: Sheffield Academic Press, 1996), pp. 26-27, citing (1) Roland Barthes, 'The Death of the Author', in *idem*, *Image-Music-Text*, p. 145; and (2) *The Pleasure of the Text* (New York: Hill and Wang, 1975), p. 14.

11. Ideology is not to be understood as a pejorative term, but as a lens or way of comprehending reality and the world.

12. For a good summary of Kristeva's definition of a text see Jay Clayton and Eric Rothstein, 'Figures in the Corpus: Theories of Influence and Intertextuality,' in J. Clayton and E. Rothstein (eds.), *Influence and Intertextuality in Literary History* (Madison, WI: University of Wisconsin Press, 1991), esp. pp. 17-21.

always searching for how a text refers to other texts, sometimes as a simile, sometimes as a parody, sometimes as a presupposition. This reader uses other texts in her or his information system to discover more than is apparent in the printed text—worlds are hidden in and between the lines and meanings are formed from a variety of spheres of influence. This freedom of reading is what allows the space for feminist readings in a field where for hundreds of years male privileged readings have been the fixed and only 'approved' understanding.

The fourth and final consideration is what Tim Beal has described as the *reader's strategy of containment*. This 'strategy of containment' is how the reader, with all of these hundreds of texts to read from (history, culture, personality, knowledge base), selects a way to understand the text in front of her or him.[13] This strategy represents a complex set of ideologies—understood as the lens or ways by which the reader sees meaning in a given text and selects the other texts that will enter into conversation with it. While this combination of texts and ideologies is unique for each reader, there are also general categories shared by an interpretive community.

In this particular paper the interpretive community is identified as biblical scholars. The primary texts of this community are the biblical text, the reconstructed history and culture of the biblical period, the studies of the academic literary community working in intertextuality, a particular religious ideology that reads the biblical material as sacred, and a feminist ideology that focuses on the recovery of the voices of women in the biblical text. In addition to these texts of the interpretive community, I also add 'texts' to the intertextual process pertaining to my own ideologies as a Caucasian woman in North American culture with academic training in biblical studies and with a personal interest in feminist methodology and psalms research.

This intertextual-feminist hermeneutic has challenged me to read the Psalms with new eyes and to forsake the cult-functional paradigm presented by Mowinkel and followed by traditional scholarship for almost 80 years. Instead, this article will adopt an

13. Tim Beal, 'Ideology and Intertextuality: Surplus of Meaning and Controlling the Means of Production', in Fewell (ed.), *Reading Between the Texts*, pp. 27-39 [36].

even older tradition that places a psalm in a specific historical context via a superscription. Examples of this tradition are seen in Psalms 51, 52, 56 and 57, where the superscriptions locate the psalm with a specific incident in the life of King David. This canonical tradition shows a way of reading particular psalms with narratives.

Based on this intertextual-feminist hermeneutic and the additional cue taken from psalm superscriptions, this study will focus, first, on reading the Leah and Rachel narrative of Genesis 29 and 30. This reading will highlight the story of the women and point out the gaps and ambiguity evident in the biblical text. In addition, this reading will also point out some ways used by traditional biblical scholars in attempts to fill in the gaps and smooth out the story's ambiguities.

Second, we will turn to Psalm 109. First, the traditional cult-functional and decisively masculine perspective of traditional psalms scholars will be reviewed. Then, instead of reading the psalm by using a law court as its reconstructed *Sitz im Leben*, it will be read using the Genesis story as its *Sitz im Leben*. This reading will in essence add a new superscription to the psalm, a superscription which reads: 'A Prayer for Leah and Rachel when their Father forced them to marry Jacob'. This intertextual process will illustrate how reading a psalm with a narrative concerning women can provide a new feminist reading of both texts; and highlight new images in the metaphorical poetry of the Psalms that are not dependent on the temple cult for an explanation.

Leah and Rachel: Their Story[14]

Who are these women characters and what has been said of them? A review of the interpretation of their story is not overly

14. For this presentation, Leah and Rachel are treated as full-fledged literary characters. This perspective does not imply a literal sense of historicity and takes no stand on the historical existence of these characters in particular or the patriarchs/matriarchs in general. For a discussion of the historical issues see, e.g., John Bright, *A History of Israel* (Philadelphia: Westminster Press, 3rd edn., 1981); J. Maxwell Miller and John H. Hayes, *A History of Ancient Israel and Judah* (Philadelphia: Westminster Press, 1986); and Thomas L. Thompson, *The Historicity of the Patriarchal Narratives: The Quest for the Historical Abraham* (BZAW, 133: Berlin: W. de Gruyter, 1972).

helpful. Von Rad (c. 1972) focused on the contest between Laban and Jacob, mentioning the women only as objects of the contest and vehicles of birthing. He credits the naming of the sons not to the women, but to a 'very free etymological game in which the narrator sparkles'.[15] His preoccupation with the narrator and the 'sources' prevents him from taking the characters of Leah and Rachel very seriously. Brueggemann suggested in his 1982 commentary that 'the story should be heard as a humorous narrative designed for entertainment'.[16] Brueggemann, while exploring one of the plots in this pericope, virtually ignores the women. His focus is on the plot of the trickster, Jacob, who is outdone by the even trickier Laban. By contrast, in Fretheim's 1994 Genesis we find a change in the direction of the interpretation. He writes, 'This section [Gen. 29.31–30.24] reads rather like a genealogy, but the conflict between Leah and Rachel and the divine response to the oppression of the women provide a basic story line.'[17] These interpretations serve as an example of the intertexual process. Three interpreters, reading the same text, have brought different 'texts' or ideologies to bear upon it. Von Rad's 'texts' were concerned with sources and the role of the narrator. Brueggemann's 'texts' are focused on the story of one-up-manship. Fretheim is concerned with at least three 'texts'—the story-genealogy genre, a focus on the women as characters, and a focus on the character of God. This presentation will take its cue from Fretheim and focus on the story of the women's interaction with each other, the men and God.

The pericope begins as Jacob, having run for his life from Esau, appears at the well and meets Rachel (Gen. 29.1-2). Soon the readers learn the complicating plot turns. Jacob decides on first look that he 'loves' Rachel (29.9-10, 20) and makes a deal for her, while she remains silent (29.15-19). Jacob, however, is not given his bride but rather he has to work to earn her price.[18] We also

15. Gerhard von Rad, *Genesis: A Commentary* (OTL; Philadelphia: Westminster Press, 1972), p. 294.

16. Walter Brueggemann, *Genesis* (Interpretation; Atlanta: John Knox Press, 1982), p. 250. Emphasis is mine.

17. Terence Fretheim, *Genesis* (Interpreter's Bible; Nashville: Abingdon Press, 1993), p. 554.

18. Probably because the escaping Jacob brought no bride price with

learn of an older sister, Leah, but she is introduced in uneventful fashion.[19] However, the introduction of the two sisters sets up the competition to come because even before the marriage deception, ambiguity is set before the reader—for seven long years we know whom Jacob loves and whom he does not, but we do not know why Jacob has made this choice.

The real tension begins after Leah is substituted for Rachel in vv. 21-27. As John Calvin so aptly stated, 'Laban, blinded by avarice, so sets his daughters together, that they spend their whole lives in mutual hostility.'[20] The voices of the women are unheard in the terseness of the narrative concerning Jacob and Laban's deal (vv. 15-27). The absence of the women's thoughts and feelings leaves the reader with questions such as: Does Rachel sob, or rejoice, when her sister is married to Jacob? Does Leah remain a silent co-conspirator because of a secret love for Jacob, or because she is afraid of her father? Does Leah's heavy veil hide a smile of triumph, or tears of devastation? What is the relationship of the sisters during the second seven-year period of Jacob's service? The women have yet to speak, and neither ever declares her love for Jacob. These gaps in our knowledge simply add to the ambiguity of the situation.[21] But despite the reader's

him, as his father's servant had done (Gen. 24.10 onwards).

19. Translators and interpreters have often attempted to 'justify' Jacob's actions by translating Gen. 29.17 as an indicator that there was something wrong with Leah. For example, the RSV reads 'Leah's eyes were weak but Rachel was beautiful and lovely'. The NRSV translators changed the word 'weak' to 'lovely', noting that the Hebrew meaning of רכות is uncertain. Von Rad, for an example of a commentator, reads this uncertain word as eyes that are weak, meaning they are pale or lack luster. But he is not even content leaving it there, writing: 'The Oriental likes a women's eyes to be lively and to glow...' (*Genesis*, p. 291), thus justifying Jacob's selection. This example shows how a desire to fill in the gaps in the narrative results in a translation that justifies Jacob's choice of the younger sister.

20. John Calvin, *Commentary on the Book of Genesis* (ET; Grand Rapids: Eerdmans, 1948), p. 133.

21. Commentators have filled in this gap in their own way. Von Rad focuses on how Laban has tricked his nephew, leaving the women as pawns in the treachery (*Genesis*, p. 291). Calvin does not backdrop the women, writing: 'he [Laban] obtrudes his daughter as an object of merchandise, thinking nothing of the disgrace of the illicit sale... He not only involves his nephew in polygamy, but pollutes both him and his own

lack of knowledge concerning the women's motivation, the narrator explains the reality of the situation in 29.31 as:

> When the Lord saw that Leah was unloved, he opened her womb; but Rachel was barren.

Pardes understands the story at this point to center on 'the struggle between the loved barren one and the less loved fertile co-wife'.[22] This impossible situation in which these two women must forever struggle illustrates the shame and terror of patriarchy. Two women—one barren but loved, the other unloved and fertile—must live in the same place with the same man, with no real alternative but to turn against each other.[23] It is not until they begin naming their children that we get any idea of their thoughts and feelings concerning their lives. Finally, Leah speaks.

Pardes notes, 'The split between the two sisters is fleshed out when the narrator at last gives us access to their feelings.'[24] Even here, however, the women do not speak to each other or to their husband or father directly. Feelings are expressed, instead, in the naming of the children. Brenner and van Dijk-Hemmes have suggested that these naming speeches are most often performed by women (27 times by women and 14 times by men) and that 'the giving of the name often tells us more about the giver of the name than about the one who receives it'.[25] This story of birthing and naming belongs to the women alone; Jacob is mentioned only secondarily and not by name. The ambiguities in the first part of the story deepen as Leah speaks the names of her children.

Beginning with the narrator's pronouncement in v. 31 that

daughters by incestuous nuptials' (*Genesis*, p. 133).

22. Ilana Pardes, *Countertraditions in the Bible: A Feminist Approach* (Cambridge, MA; Harvard University Press, 1992), p. 63.

23. The animosity between the sisters is not actually voiced until later in the narrative. The competition between two women in a similar situation is also is expressed by Sarah against Hagar (Gen. 16) and by the narrator in the Hannah and Peninnah pericope (1 Sam. 1).

24. Pardes, *Countertraditions*, p. 63.

25. Athalya Brenner and Fokkelein van Dijk-Hemmes, *On Gendering Texts: Female and Male Voices in the Hebrew Bible* (BIS, 1; Leiden: E.J. Brill, 1993), p. 98.

YHWH opened Leah's womb but that Rachel is barren, we then learn that

> Leah conceived and bore a son, and she named him Reuben; for she said, 'Because the Lord has looked on my affliction, surely now my husband will love me' (v. 32).

Interestingly, YHWH looks on affliction (עני) and takes action throughout the Hebrew Bible. The most monumental instance for Israel is in Exod. 3.17 (NRSV: 'misery'), but another women also cries to the Lord 'to look on the affliction (NRSV: 'misery') of your servant'.[26] The woman is Hannah and her prayer in 1 Sam. 1.10-11 is for a child. Is Leah's affliction the same? After all, she has been married to Jacob for at least seven years at the point of the pronouncement in v. 31. Was she also barren until 'God opened her womb?' As the narrative continues, it appears that Leah's current affliction is not the barren seven years but the pain of being the 'unloved' wife. In v. 31 the narrator tell us that 'The Lord saw that Leah was hated (NRSV: unloved)'. Then when Leah gives birth to her second son in v. 33, she names him Simeon,

> because the Lord has heard that I am hated, שנואה [Feminine singular Qal passive participle, as in v. 31].

This double pronouncement of Leah being hated appears to settle the matter of her affliction. But as above, the motivation for the hate is elusive. Is it Jacob's love for Rachel that causes him to be the one who hates Leah?[27] Or was it Leah's own actions in the marriage plot that has caused such animosity? Is it Jacob who hates her, or is the rest of the family and/or community involved? Again ambiguity has the upper hand, aided by the use of the participle form—Leah is hated, confirmed by the narrator and herself, but by whom and for what reason we do not know. As two more sons are born to Leah, we continue to learn about

---

26. See Miller, *Psalms*, p. 56, for the relationship between Hannah's cry for God to look upon her affliction and the prayers of the lamenters in the Psalms. The story of Hannah and Peninnah is the only other narrative in the Hebrew Bible where women talk of their affliction, and that affliction is related to YHWH's closing of a women's womb.

27. Jacob never indicates he hates Leah; but the narrator tells us that Jacob loves Rachel more than Leah in v. 30, ויאהב גם את רחל מלאה:

her—from wanting to be loved (v. 32) to praising the Lord (v. 35). The first two names are related to her affliction and her status as the unloved wife. The third and fourth have a triumphant quality. With Levi she claims her husband because of her fertility, and with Judah she praises the Lord. Has Leah come to an understanding of her own identity with the birth of the sons? Is she comfortable with her position or are the last two names intended to twist the knife a little more in her sister's heart?

Rachel remains silent and barren. When she does find her voice, the pain in her cry is obvious to all. Unable to speak through the action of naming a child, she instead sees her barrenness, envies her sister and cries to her husband, 'Give me children, or I will die!' (30.1) Pardes writes, 'Her desperate craving for offspring is inflamed by envy. In a few words she conveys the unbearable agony of being a barren women: childlessness means death.'[28] Her cry is also the cry of Sarah and Rebekah and Hannah. The pain of emptiness and social ridicule also echoes the pain of rejection and hate carried by her sister. The two sisters are trapped in a desperate cycle of hate and rejection. At a time when a sister should comfort the other's pain, these two inflict unspeakable pain on each other. But the ambiguity is more than between the human characters. Rachel's cry also introduces the question of theodicy. In 29.31 God saw (וירא) Leah's state and opened her womb, but in v. 30.1, it is Rachel that sees (ותרא) her barrenness and cries to her husband who immediately blames the problem on God (v. 2). Is God choosing the unloved one over the beautiful and loved Rachel? Is Leah more pious, naming her children for God's action toward her, or is she using the praise of God to make everyone aware of what she has that Rachel does not? Should Rachel have cried to God instead of Jacob? All of this still remains unresolved.

Like Sarah before her Rachel, the favored one, does not wait for God to act but gives Jacob her maid, who bears him two sons (30.6-8).[29] With her first naming speech Rachel deepens the

---

28. Pardes, *Countertraditions*, p. 64.

29. There is some question as to the 'legal ownership' of these children. It is not entirely clear that this was a surrogate situation, but this narrative certainly suggests as much. For further discussion on this topic see Fredrick

question of God's action in this contest saying, 'God has judged me, and has also heard my voice and given me a son' (v. 6). Her first naming indicates that her cry to Jacob was also, or in addition to, her cries to God. The second son's naming shows just how far the competition between her and Leah has gone, 'With mighty wrestlings I have wrestled with my sister, and have prevailed' (v. 8).

Leah has ceased to have children also (29.35). Has God's favor been removed? So she too gives her maid to Jacob and the maid bears two more sons. The sisters have forced two others into the intolerable situation. The victims become the victimizers. Do Bilhah and Zilpah cry out like Hagar? Do they feel the sting of their mistresses' contempt? Their silence in the narrative is deafening.

Direct dialogue between the sisters finally occurs over the prize Reuben brings to his mother Leah (30.14-17). Rachel seems to have learned well from her husband and her deal for the mandrakes, a symbol of fertility, is reminiscent of Jacob's deal with Esau. Leah, however, is not quite as gullible as Esau—her deal is for Jacob and Jacob willingly complies. He is reduced to part of the deal. What would possess a woman to strike a deal for sex with a husband who would prefer to be with her sister? Has jealousy so overwhelmed her that the desire for another child subsumes all else, or is her ability to bear children the only thing that forms her identity? The deal is successful and God is again credited with the results (v. 17). Then finally the story's ambiguity comes as another birthing. In another action devoid of a motivation, God remembers Rachel and opens her womb (v. 22). At the end as in the beginning, the motives of all involved remain elusive. But the striking parallel with the Jacob and Esau pericope, and the women's continuing animosity, show that the women have learned the unacceptable ways of the cheating men. It is here that patriarchy has triumphed—as John Calvin observed: the women have forever been set against each other by the men. The sisters have willingly practiced the iniquity of the fathers and husbands—injuring each other and victimizing their slaves, while all the while being victims themselves.

Knobloch, 'Adoption', *ABD*, I, pp. 76-79.

Hearing the Psalms with the Women

It is with the women's story in view that we now turn to the Psalter. How will their story influence the words and images that we hear? The Psalms contain humanity's cries to God—cries of praise and thanksgiving and the cries of lament and woe. The psalmic language and its interpretation, however, are primarily masculine; and the images are often ones of war, politics, courts of law and temple rituals—all associated with male patriarchal spaces. Can women find their voice here? Certainly it is not the faint-of-heart feminist that dares to tread here in the Psalms. Women are rarely mentioned specifically, and one reading of Psalm 45 could make women think the cause is hopeless. But how much of our reading of the Psalms comes from the texts, and how much has been formed by the 'texts' that our forefathers have brought to their readings of this poetry? When Mowinckel removed the Psalms from personal and home use and placed them in the temple cult, he also effectively removed them from the realm of women.[30] Certainly there are psalms that belong in the places of kings and courts, as for example Pss. 2, 45 and 72; and of temples and worship, as for example Pss. 93, 95 and 96. But as Patrick Miller's recent work illustrates, it is time to bring different 'texts' to psalm scholarship[31] and to ask, Is the language of the psalms 'open and metaphorical' enough to include Leah and Rachel too? Can Psalm 109 move from the law court to the home court?

Psalm 109 opens with these words:

> Do not be silent, O God of my praise.
> For wicked and deceitful mouths are opened against me,

30. For an interesting appraisal of the cost to women of the movement of Israel's religious center from the smaller home and cult to the central temple in Jerusalem see Carol Meyers, *Discovering Eve: Ancient Israelite Women in Context* (Oxford: Oxford University Press, 1988); or Erhard Gerstenberger, *Yahweh the Patriarch: Ancient Images of God and Feminist Theology* (trans. F. Gaiser; Minneapolis: Fortress Press, 1996).

31. Patrick Miller, 'Things too Wonderful: Prayers Women Prayed', in *They Cried to the Lord: The Form and Theology of Biblical Prayer* (Minneapolis: Fortress Press, 1994), pp. 233-43.

> Speaking against me with lying tongues,
> They beset me with words of hate and attack me without cause.
> In return for my love they accuse me even while I pray for them.
> So they reward me evil for good, and hatred for my love (vv. 1-5).

Traditionally, this opening has been read by interpreters as an indication that the one lamenting is in a court of law and unjustly accused of a crime. He—because, even today, most scholarship assumes that the one speaking is a he—is standing in a court of law, the place of the men at the city gate. Kraus intensifies the masculine imagery: 'as in war, he [the Psalmist] is encircled on all sides'.[32] Allen also sets the masculine stage and even adds YHWH to the masculine list of characters: 'The setting is then to be reconstructed as a religious court where the psalmist claimed his innocence before priestly judges as representatives of YHWH'.[33] Is this law court the only alternative, as many commentators have suggested? What if this psalm is read from the Leah-Rachel story just outlined? Then the psalm will be the voice of the silent ones. The psalms will fill some of the gaps in the narrative, but will also bring to light previously unrecognized gaps.

'God of my praise' (אלהי תהלתי, v. 1) opens the scene of the psalm and is reminiscent of the naming of Leah's fourth son, Judah.[34] Accompanied by the command 'do not be silent' (אל תחרש), we are reminded not of a court of law, but of the silence of the women as their fate was determined by the men in the early part of the Genesis narrative. The cry to God can been seen in light of the long silences, as the four women are given to others without any comment or choice on their part. The silence of

---

32. Hans-Joachim Kraus, *Psalms 60–150* (trans. H. Oswald; Minneapolis: Fortress Press, 1989), p. 339.

33. Leslie Allen, *Psalms 101–150* (WBC; Waco, TX: Word Books, 1983), p. 75.

34. The two words, ידה in Gen. 29.35 and הלל in Ps. 109.1 but are parallel not identical. These opening words are a good oppurtunity to point out that intertextuality involves more than influence on the author via an absolute process. In other words, it does not have to be exact words or obvious quotation of one story in another. Intertextuality is more open, involving the free interaction of texts to create different meanings. For further explanation see George Aichele and Gary Phillips, 'Introduction: Exegesis, Eisegesis, Intergesis', in *idem* (eds.), *Intertextuality and the Bible*, pp. 7-18.

patriarchy is contrasted with the plea to God to *not be silent* (אל
תחרש).[35]

The remainder of the opening verses is centered on the tension
between the 'love' (אהבה) of the one praying and 'hate' (שנאה)
that is returned. Walter Brueggemann sees in these verses not
necessarily a court of law, but 'a raw undisciplined song of hate
and wish for vengeance by someone who has suffered deep hurt
and humiliation'.[36] Here in the psalm we can hear the anguish of
rejection—of Leah as she cries at the naming of her first son,
'surely now my husband will love me' (Gen. 29.32); and at the
birth of her second son, 'that the Lord has heard that I am hated'
(v. 33). These opening words can easily be visualized as the
prayer of Leah.[37]

Yet the story of Leah and Rachel teaches us that life is not lived
in a vacuum. Rachel also cries out in her barrenness; and she,
too, may feel hate from the community, her sister or even from
God. Leah, the hated one, also shows contempt for her younger
sister. Jacob's relationship with Laban also seems on the verge of
hate (Gen. 31.4 onwards). The maids' silent voices bring to mind
echoes of the story of Sarah and Hagar (Gen. 16) and the hate
between slave and mistress. In other words, the meaning of the
psalm's opening words is seen differently when read against the
Genesis narrative. It is not just one of the characters that may cry
these words; rather, all share in this complicated tension of love
and hate.

A lengthy accusation or curse dominates the next section of the

35. This plea appears three times in the Psalms. In 35.22 and 109.1 the
lamenter is under great duress and needs God to speak for her or him. In
83.2 it is the community that is in dire straits—pressed by others. In each of
these instances the person/s cries/cry to God because they are in a position
of subordination. It is only God that can exercise more power than the
oppressors.

36. Walter Brueggemann, *The Message of the Psalms: A Theological Commentary* (Minneapolis: Augsburg Press, 1984), p. 83.

37. It is, indeed, this very connection that prompted the exploration of
reading these two texts together. Intertextuality begins when one text
engages another in the mind of the reader. For a more complete treatment
of this complex phenomenon see Leslie Ben-Porat, 'The Poetics of Literary
Allusion', *PTL: A Journal for Descriptive Poetics and Theory of Literature* 1
(1976), pp. 105-28.

psalm (vv. 6-19). Reading with the Genesis narrative as referent, the curse is uttered by the one who is hurt and broken.[38] It is a cry for justice. The traditional intertextual reading of a law court is focused on the beginning of the curse, vv. 6-7; but vv. 9-16 switch from legal language to the imagery of home—of 'children' and 'wives' (vv. 9-10), of 'second generations' (v. 13), of the 'father's iniquity' and the 'mother's sin' (v. 14), of the cursed one's 'memory being cut off from the earth' (v. 15). Reading the psalm against the complex relationships in the Leah and Rachel story can thus illustrate a different understanding of the relationship between the one lamenting and his or her accusers.

For example, the enemy in the Psalms is often contrasted as the binary opposite from the one lamenting. The enemy is the outsider, the foreigner, the Philistine or the Canaanite, the one that is totally evil and destructive. Yet, by juxtaposing the story of Leah and Rachel, the enemy is found in one's own house and is a member of one's own inner circle. The enemy is even the fathers and mothers of the house of Israel. The metaphorical language of the household take, on a different sense when read with the Genesis narrative.

Over against Mowinckel, who argues for the enemy as totally other,[39] Claus Westermann has suggested a different concept as a theory of understanding individual laments. As opposed to the enemy as other, Westermann has always maintained that the enemy is close at hand to the lamenter—sharing the same

38.   The identity of the one speaking in this section has been heavily debated. The group of accusers of vv. 1-5 changes without explanation to the singular of vv. 6-19. Allen, Kraus, Weiser (A. Weiser, *The Psalms* [OTL; trans. H. Hartwell; Philadelphia: Westminster, 1962]) and many other scholars have taken this to mean that the psalmist is now quoting the enemies and their curses. The NRSV even adds 'They said' at the beginning of v. 6. For a good review of the issue see Allen, *Psalms*, pp. 72-73. Others, such as Brueggemann, Kirkpatrick (A.F. Kirkpatrick, *The Book of Psalms with Introduction and Notes* [Cambridge: Cambridge University Press, 1902]) and Mays (J.L. Mays, *Psalms* [Interpretation; Louisville, KY: John Knox Press, 1994]), have argued that the psalmist has simply changed the focus from accusations against an entire group to a single accuser in that group.

39.   Sigmund Mowinckel, *The Psalms in Israel's Worship* (trans. D.R. Ap-Thomas; Sheffield: JSOT Press, 1962). See esp. pp. 225-46.

community.[40] He also argues that the pain is not metaphorical but a real and immediate threat to the one crying out.[41] Finally, Westermann argues that since the relationship with God is the foundation of the community in which both lamenter and enemy participate, there is a real question of theodicy evident in individual lament psalms. 'The evildoers (in the opinion of the lamenter) no longer take God seriously, and yet God does not condemn them. The lamenter takes God seriously, yet the enemy is able to mock with impunity.'[42] Taking Westermann's observations as a text for our reading, the Genesis story gives his reading a narrative context. This reading expands the psalm's meaning from a male patriarchal space to a space shared by women, men, slaves and children. This intertextual reading expands even further Westermann's idea of the relationship between the lamenter and the enemy in individual laments. It illustrates that the Psalms must not be read exclusively as the good against the bad, but can (and probably should) be read more in line with the Genesis narrative, where victims are also victimizers and the characters are neither wholly good nor wholly corrupt. The intertextual process has provided a feminist understanding for Psalm 109. Using this new reading, the text is 'freed' from the court of law so that we can hear other images in its metaphorical matrix.

An intertextual reading also provides a two-way reading. Just as the narrative can provide fresh insights on the psalm, the psalm can also influence the reading of the narrative. Dana Fewell explains, 'Texts talk to one another; they echo one another; they push one another; they war with one another. They are voices in chorus, in conflict and in competition.'[43] So, turning the focus in the opposite intertextual direction, the psalm gives us the opportunity to focus on gaps in the Genesis narrative that are previously unrecognized. Verses 9-14 of the psalm focus on the oppressor's children. The wish of the one praying the prayer

40. Claus Westermann, *Praise and Lament in the Psalms* (trans. K. Crim and R. Soulen; Atlanta: John Knox Press, 1981), p. 193.

41. Westermann, *Praise and Lament*, p. 193.

42. Westermann, *Praise and Lament*, p. 194.

43. Dana Nolan Fewell, 'Introduction: Writing, Reading, and Relating', in Dana Nolan Fewell (ed.), *Reading Between the Texts*, p. 12.

is that the oppressor's children be orphaned (v. 9); that they wander about and beg (v. 10); that no-one pity the orphan children (v. 12). What does the reader know of how these four Genesis women, living together under obvious duress, related to the children of this strange union? From the narrative we know virtually nothing about the children until they are much older. In Genesis 29 and 30 it is difficult to notice the children, but the psalm can remind us that they are affected by the situation too.

Was this one big happy family, or did the four women act in the same way as Sarah and Hagar (Gen. 16.49 and 20.8-10), or Peninnah and Hannah (1 Sam. 1.2-8)? It does not seem much of a stretch to imagine the women's antagonism extending to the children of the other—that the curses of Psalm 109 were prayed by Rachel on the children of Leah; or that Leah prayed like curses against the beloved Joseph.[44] We have already seen that the animosity set up by the deal made by Laban and Jacob was passed on to the mothers in their interactions with each other and with their father. The psalm, especially v. 14 of the curse, invites us to recall that the iniquity (עון) of the father and the sin (חטאת) of the mother was not blotted out and was also visited on the children. Brother did turn against brother and Joseph, the favorite one of the favorite wife, was sold into slavery by the brothers of the less-loved Leah and the two slaves. These children have learned well from the actions of their elders.

The last section of the psalm (vv. 20-31) is an appeal to God to remedy the cries of the ones oppressed and in distress. Keeping this in mind, the last section of this intertextual reading will show the synergy of the two texts. The Genesis narrative does not contain any words that the women lifted to YHWH in prayer. But first Leah (29.33) and then Rachel (30.6) declare that YHWH has heard (שמע) them. Their prayers of intercession may have been erased from the terse Hebrew narrative, but the remnant exists in the sisters' confessional naming of their children. The psalm, then, gives voice to both their pain and their prayers

44. There may be an indication of such a tension in the text. Reuben goes out and brings his mother mandrakes (Gen. 30.14). He did not bring them for the entire household. The only way that Rachel can get the mandrakes is to strike a deal for them. This may indicate that the household was divided along maternal loyalty lines.

of intercession. Then finally, just as the psalm moves from intercession to praise, Rachel and Leah are finally able to praise God 'in the midst of the throng' (v. 30), since the throng of their children became the representation of the people Israel. This 'throng', רבים, literally 'the many' of v. 30 in the psalm, gives one final intertextual connection. It shows that the promise of many descendants given to the patriarch Abraham in Gen. 17.3 can here be understood as a promise to these two matriarchs as well. The end of Leah and Rachel's story is found in the praise that their descendants lift to YHWH, who hears their cry of pain—be that the cry of victimized women in Genesis 29 and 30, or the cry of Israel from the victimization of slavery.

With this last section we complete the reading of these two texts and, hopefully, understand Psalm 109 in a new light. Instead of a patriarchal court of law, with the story of Leah and Rachel in mind the psalm takes on a new meaning. Walter Brueggemann writes in his reflection on this psalm:

> Whose psalm is this?... It could be the voice of a woman who is victimized by rape, who surely knows the kind of rage and indignation that does not need 'due process' to know the proper outcome. It could be the voice of a black in South Africa (or here?) who has yet again been brutalized or humiliated by the system. Or it could be a Palestinian peasant weary of war, resentful of displacement.[45]

Or it could be the cry of four women, trapped in a patriarchal system which denies them choice of circumstance or even a voice of objection, and turns them against the men and each other. Women who cry out in pain to the only one who sees beyond their patriarchal entrapment and provides blessing in the very midst of their suffering.

45. Brueggemann, *Message of the Psalms*, p. 87

BIBLIOGRAPHY

Aichele, George, and Gary Phillips, 'Introduction: Exegesis, Eisegesis, Intergesis', *Semeia* 69/70 (1995), pp. 7-18.

Albertz, Rainer, 'Der sozialgeschichtliche Hintergrund des Hiobbuches und der "Babylonischen Theodizee" ', in J. Jeremias and L. Perlitt (eds.), *Die Botschaft und die Boten: Festschrift H.W. Wolff* (Neukirchen–Vluyn: Neukirchener Verlag, 1981), pp. 349-72.

—*Religionsgeschichte Israels in alttestamentlicher Zeit*, II (Göttingen: Vandenhoeck & Ruprecht, 1992) ET: *History of Israelite Religion in the Old Testament Period*, II (OTL; London: SCM Press, 1994).

Allegro, John M., 'Qumran Cave 4 I (4Q158–4Q186)', in *Discoveries in the Judaean Desert of Jordan*, V (Oxford: Clarendon Press, 1968).

Allen, Leslie C., *Psalms 101–150* (WBC, 21; Waco, TX; Word Books, 1983).

Alter, R., *The Art of Biblical Poetry* (San Francisco: HarperCollins, 1985).

Anderson, B.W., *Creation in the Old Testment* (Issues in Religion and Theology, 6; Philadelphia: Fortress Press, 1981).

Anderson, William H.V., 'The Curse of Work in Qoheleth: An Exposé of Genesis 3:17-19 in Ecclesiastes', *EvQ* 70.2 (1998), pp. 99-113.

Anglo, Sydney, 'Evident Authority and Authoritative Evidence: The *Malleus Maleficarum*', in S. Anglo (ed.), *The Damned Art: Essays in the Literature of Witchcraft* (London: Routledge & Kegan Paul, 1977), pp. 1-31.

—'Reginald Scot's *Discoverie of Witchcraft: Scepticism and Sadduceeism*', in S. Anglo (ed.), *The Damned Art: Essays in the Literature of Witchcraft* (London: Routledge & Kegan Paul, 1977), pp. 106-39.

Assmann, J., 'Weisheit, Loyalismus und Frömmigkeit', in E. Hornung and O. Keel (eds.), *Studien zu altägyptischen Lebenslehren* (OBO, 28; Göttingen: Vandenhoeck & Ruprecht, 1979), pp. 11-72.

—*Ägypten: Theologie und Frömmigkeit einer frühen Hochkultur* (Stuttgart: Kohlhammer, 1984).

— *Ma'at: Gerechtigkeit und Unsterblichkeit im Alten Ägypten* (Munich: Beck, 1990).

— 'Weisheit, Schrift und Literatur im Alten Ägypten', in A. Assmann (ed.), *Weisheit: Archäologie der literarischen Kommunikation*, III (Munich: Fink, 1991), pp. 475-500.

Bail, Ulrike, 'Vernimm, Gott, mein Gebet': Ps 55 und Gewalt gegen Frauen', in Hedwig Jahnow (ed.), *Feministische Hermeneutik und Erstes Testament* (Kohlhammer: Stuttgart, 1994), pp. 67-84.

—*Gegen das Schweigen klagen: Eine intertextuelle Studie zu Ps 6, Ps 55, und 2. Sam 13.1-22* (Gütersloh: Gütersloher Verlagshaus, 1998).

Bal, Mieke, *Death and Dissymetry: The Politics of Coherence in the Book of Judges* (Chicago: Chicago University Press, 1988).

Baltzer, K., 'Women and War in Qohelet 7:23–8:1a', *HTR* 80.1 (1987), pp. 127-32.

Barstow, Anne Llewellyn, *Witchcraze: A New History of the European Witch Hunts* (San Francisco: Pandora/Harper Row, 1994).

Barthes, Roland, *Image-Music-Text* (New York: Hill and Wang, 1977).

Barton, G.A., *The Book of Ecclesiastes* (ICC; repr., Edinburgh: T. & T. Clark, 1959 [1908]).

Batiffol, P., 'Le Livre de la Prière d'Aseneth', *Studia patristica: Etudes d'ancienne littèrature chrétienne*, I-II (Paris: Leroux, 1889–90), pp. 1-115.

Baumann, Gerlinde, *Die Weisheitsgestalt in Proverbien 1–9: Traditionsgeschichtliche und theologische Studien* (FAT, 16; Tübingen: J.C.B. Mohr, 1996).

—' "Zukunft feministischer Spiritualität" oder "Werbefigur des Patriarchats"? Die Bedeutung der Weisheitsgestalt in Prov. 1–9 für die feministisch-theologische Diskussion', in L. Schottroff and M.-Th. Wacker (eds.), *Von der Wurzel getragen: Christlich-feministische Exegese in Auseinandersetzung mit Antijudaismus* (BIS, 17; Leiden: E.J. Brill, 1996), pp. 135-52.

Baumgarten, Joseph M., 'On the Nature of the Seductress in 4Q184', *RevQ* 15 (1991), pp. 133-43.

Baurmann, M.C., *Sexualität, Gewalt und die Folgen für das Opfer: Zusammengefasste Ergebnisse aus einer Längsschnittuntersuchung bei Opfern von angezeigten Sexualkontakten* (Wiesbaden: Kriminalistisches Institut Wiesbaden, 3rd edn, 1984).

Baxter, Christopher, 'Johann Weyer's *De Praestigliis Daemonum*: Unsystematic Psychopathology', in S. Anglo (ed.), *The Damned Art: Essays in the Literature of Witchcraft* (London: Routledge & Kegan Paul, 1977), pp. 53-76.

— 'Jean Bodin's *De la démonomanie des sorciers*: The Logic of Persecution', in S. Anglo (ed.), *The Damned Art: Essays in the Literature of Witchcraft* (London: Routledge & Kegan Paul, 1977), pp. 76-105.

Beal T., 'Ideology and Intertextuality: Surplus of Meaning and Controlling the Means of Production', in Nolan Fewell (ed.), *Reading Between the Texts*, pp. 27-39.

Bechtel, Lyn M., 'What If Dinah Is not Raped?', *JSOT* 62 (1994), pp. 19-36.

—'A Feminist Approach to the Book of Job', in A. Brenner (ed.), *A Feminist Companion to Wisdom Literature* (Sheffield: Sheffield Academic Press, 1995), pp. 222-52.

Becker, Joachim, *Wege der Psalmenexegese* (SBS, 78; Stuttgart: Verlag Katholisches Bibelwerk, 1975).

Ben-Porat, Leslie, 'The Poetics of Literary Allusion', *PTL: A Journal for Descriptive Poetics and Theory of Literature* 1 (1976), pp. 105-28.

Bergant, Dianne, ' "My Beloved is Mine and I Am His" (Song 2.16): The Song of Songs and Honor and Shame', *Semeia* 68 (1994), pp. 23-40.

Beuken, W.A.M., '1 Samuel 28: The Prophet as "Hammer of Witches" ', *JSOT* 6 (1978), pp. 3-17.

— *The Book of Job* (Leuven: Leuven University Press, 1994).

Bird, P., 'The Harlot as Heroine: Narrative Art and Social Presupposition in Three Old Testament Texts', *Semeia* 46 (1989), pp. 119-39.

—'To Play the Harlot: An Inquiry into an Old Testament Metaphor', in Peggy L. Day (ed.), *Gender and Difference in Ancient Israel* (Minneapolis: Fortress Press, 1989), pp. 75-94.

Blake, William, *Job, Invented and Engraved* (New York: United Book Guild, 1947).

Blamires, Alcuin (ed.), *Woman Defamed and Woman Defended: An Anthology of Medieval Texts* (Oxford: Clarendon Press, 1992).

Blenkinsopp, J., *Ezra-Nehemiah: A Commentary* (OTL; Philadelphia: Westminster Press, 1988).

— 'The Social Context of the "Outsider Woman" in Proverbs 1–9', *Bib* 42 (1991), pp. 457-73.

—'The Family in First Temple Israel' in Leo G. Perdue *et al.* (eds.), *Families in Ancient Israel* (Louisville, KY: Westminster/John Knox Press, 1997), pp. 51-57.

Bloch, R. Howard, *Medieval Misogyny and the Invention of Western Romantic Love* (Chicago: University of Chicago Press, 1991).

Bloom, Harold, *The Anxiety of Influence* (New York: Oxford University Press, 1973).

Boström, G., *Proverbiastudien: Die Weisheit und das fremde Weib in Spr. 1–9* (Lund: C.W.K. Gleerup, 1935).

Boström, L., *The God of the Sages: The Portrayal of God in the Book of Proverbs* (ConBOT, 29; Stockholm: Almqvist & Wiksell, 1990).

Botterweck, G. Johannes, 'Die Sonne der Gerechtigkeit am Tage Jahwes: Auslegung von Malachias 3.13-21', in *Bild und Leben* 1 (1960).

Boyarin, Daniel, *Intertextuality and the Reading of Midrash* (Indianapolis: Indiana University Press, 1990).

Braulik, Georg, 'Das Deuteronomium und die Bücher Ijob, Sprichwörter, Rut: Zur Frage früher Kanonizität des Deuteronomiums', in E. Zenger (ed.), *Die Tora als Kanon für Juden und Christen* (Freiburg: Herder, 1996), pp. 61-138.

Brenner, Athalya, 'God's Answer to Job', *VT* 31 (1981), pp. 129-37.

—'Job the Pious? The Characterization of Job in the Narrative Framework of the Book', *JSOT* 43 (1989), pp. 37-52.

— 'Some Observations on the Figurations of Woman in Wisdom Literature', in Heather A. McKay and David J.A. Clines (eds.), *Of Prophets' Visions and the Wisdom of Sages: Essays in Honour of R. Norman Whybray on his Seventieth Birthday* (JSOTSup, 162; Sheffield: Sheffield Academic Press, 1993), pp. 192-208.

—'M Text Authority in Biblical Love Lyrics: The Case of Qoheleth 3.1-9 and its Textual Relatives', in Brenner and van Dijk-Hemmes, *Gendering Texts*, pp. 133-63.

—*The Intercourse of Knowledge: On Gendering Desire and 'Sexuality' in the Hebrew Bible* (BIS, 26; Leiden: E.J. Brill, 1997).

Brenner, A. (ed.), *A Feminist Companion to Wisdom Literature* (FCB, 9; Sheffield: Sheffield Academic Press, 1995).

Brenner, A., and F. van Dijk-Hemmes, *On Gendering Texts: Female and Male Voices in the Hebrew Bible* (BIS, 1; Leiden: E.J. Brill, 1993).

Bretschneider, Joachim, *Architekturmodelle in Vorderasien und der östlichen Agäis vom Neolithikum bis in das 1. Jahrtausend: Phänomene in der Kleinkunst an Beispielen aus Mesopotamien, dem Iran, Anatolien, Syrien, der Levante und dem ägäischen Raum unter besonderer Berücksichtigung der bau- und religionsgeschichtlichen Aspekte* (AOAT, 229; Neukirchen–Vluyn: Neukirchener Verlag, 1991).

Bright, John, *A History of Israel* (Philadelphia: Westminster Press, 3rd edn, 1981).

Broich, Ulrich, and Manfred Pfister (eds.), *Intertextualität: Formen, Funktionen, anglistische Fallstudien* (Tübingen: Max Niemeyer Verlag, 1985).

Brooke, George, 'The Wisdom of Matthew's Beatitudes (4QBeat and Mt. 5.3-12)', *Scripture Bulletin* 19 (1988–1989), pp. 35-41.

Brosius, Maria, *Women in Ancient Persia: 559-331 BC* (Oxford: Clarendon Press, 1996).

Brownmiller, Susan, *Gegen unseren Willen: Vergewaltigung und Männerherrschaft* (Frankfurt: Fischer Verlag, 1980).

Brueggemann, Walter, *Genesis* (Interpretation; Atlanta: John Knox Press, 1982).

—*The Message of the Psalms: A Theological Commentary* (Minneapolis: Augsburg Press, 1984).

Brunner, H., 'Der freie Wille Gottes in der ägyptischen Weisheit', in *Les sagesses du proche-orient ancien: Colloque de Strasbourg 17-19 mai 1962* (Bibliothèque des centres d'études supérieures spécialisés. Travaux du centre d'études supérieures spécialisés d'histoire des religions de Strasbourg; Paris: Presses Universitaires de France, 1963), pp. 103-20.

—'Persönliche Frömmigkeit', *LÄ*, IV (1982), pp. 951-63.

Cady Stanton, Elizabeth, *The Woman's Bible* (2 vols.; Edinburgh: Polygon Books, 1985).

Cady, S., M. Ronan and H. Taussig, *Sophia: The Future of Feminist Spirituality* (San Francisco: Harper & Row, 1986).

—*Wisdom's Feast: Sophia in Study and Celebration* (San Francisco: Harper & Row, 1989).

Calvin, John, *Commentary on the Book of Genesis* (Grand Rapids: Eerdmans, 1948).

Camp, C.V., *Wisdom and the Feminine in the Book of Proverbs* (Bible and Literature, 11; Sheffield: Almond Press, 1985).

— 'Woman Wisdom as Root Metaphor: A Theological Consideration', in K.G. Hoglund *et al.* (eds.), *The Listening Heart: Essays in Wisdom and the Psalms in honor of R. E. Murphy* (JSOTSup, 58; Sheffield: JSOT Press, 1987).

—'Understanding a Patriarchy: Women in Second Century Jerusalem through the Eyes of Ben Sira', in A.-J. Levine (ed.), *'Women Like This': New Perspectives on Jewish Women in the Greco-Roman World* (SBL Early Judaism and its Literature, 1; Atlanta: Scholars Press, 1991), pp. 3-39.

— 'What's So Strange About the Strange Woman?', in David Jobling, Peggy L. Day and Gerald T. Sheppard (eds.), *The Bible and the Politics of Exegesis: Essays in Honor of Norman K. Gottwald on His Sixty-Fifth Birthday*, (Cleveland: Pilgrim Press, 1991), pp. 17-31.

—'Wise and "Strange": An Interpretation of the Female Imagery in Light of Trickster Mythology', in Brenner (ed.), *A Feminist Companion to Wisdom Literature*, pp. 131-56.

—'Honor and Shame in Ben Sira: Anthropological and Theological Reflections', paper read at First International Conference on Ben Sira, Soesterberg, the Netherlands, 28-31 July, 1996.

— 'Honor, Shame and the Hermeneutics of Ben Sira's Ms C', in Michael Barré (ed.), ' *Wisdom, You are My Sister!*'': *Studies in Honor of Roland E. Murphy, O. Carm., on the Occasion of his 80th Birthday* (CBQMS, 29; Washington: Catholic Biblical Association, 1997), pp. 157-71.

Camp, Claudia V., and Carole R. Fontaine, 'The Riddles of the Wise and their Riddles', in Susan Niditch (ed.), *Text and Tradition: The Hebrew Bible and Folklore* (Semeia Studies; Atlanta: Scholars Press, 1990), pp. 127-52.

Chedid, Andrée, *La femme de Job* (Paris: Editions Calmann-Lévy, 1993).

—*Die Frau des Ijob: Erzählung* (Limburg: Lahn Verlag, 1995).

Chesnutt, R., *From Death to Life: Conversion in Joseph and Aseneth* (JSPSup, 16; Sheffield: Sheffield Academic Press, 1995).

Christianson, E.S., *A Time to Tell: Narrative Strategies in Ecclesiastes* (JSOTSup, 280; Sheffield: Sheffield Academic Press, forthcoming).

Clark, Elizabeth A., *Women in the Early Church* (Message of the Fathers of the Church, 13; Wilmington, DE: Michael Glazier, 1983).

Clayton, Jay, and Eric Rothstein (eds.), *Influence and Intertextuality in Literary History* (Madison, WI: University of Wisconsin Press, 1991).

Clines, D.J.A., 'Nehemiah 10 as an Example of Early Jewish Biblical Exegesis', *JSOT* 21 (1981), pp. 111-17.

— *Job 1–20* (WBC, 17; Dallas, TX: Word Books, 1989).

— *Interested Parties: The Ideology of Writers and Readers of the Hebrew Bible* (JSOTSup, 205; Sheffield: Sheffield Academic Press, 1995).

Collins, John J., 'The Biblical Precedent for Natural Theology', *JAAR* 45.1 Supplement [March 1997], B, pp. 35-67.

Corley, Kathleen E., *Private Women, Public Meals: Social Conflict in the Synoptic Tradition* (Peabody, MA: Hendricksen, 1993).

Corrington, Gail Paterson, *Her Image of Salvation: Female Saviors and Formative Christianity* (Louisville, KY: Westminster Press, 1992).

Crenshaw, James L., *Old Testament Wisdom: An Introduction* (Atlanta: John Knox Press, 1981)

— *Ecclesiastes: A Commentary* (OTL; Philadelphia: Westminster Press, 1987).

—*Urgent Advice and Probing Questions: Collected Writings on Old Testament Wisdom* (Macon, GA: Mercer University Press, 1995).

Crüsemann, Frank, 'Hiob und Kohelet: Ein Beitrag zum Verständnis des Hiobbuches', in R. Albertz *et al.* (eds.), *Werden und Wirken des Alten Testäments, Festschriftch C. Westermann* (Göttingen: Vandenhoeck & Ruprecht; Neukirchen-Vluyn: Neukirchener Verlag, 1980), pp. 372-93.

—'Im Netz: Zur Frage nach der "eigentlichen Not" in den Klagen der Einzelnen', in Rainer Albertz *et al.* (eds.), *Schöpfung und Befreiung: Festschrift für Claus Westermann* (Stuttgart: Calwer-Verlag, 1989), pp. 139-48.

—*Die Tora: Theologie und Sozialgeschichte des alttestamentlichen Gesetzes* (Munich: Chr. Kaiser Verlag, 1992).

Culler, Jonathan, 'Presupposition and Intertextuality', *Modern Language Notes* 91 (1976), pp. 1380-96.

Dahood, Mitchell, *Psalms* (AB; Garden City, NY: Doubleday, 1968).

Day, Peggy L., *An Adversary in Heaven: Satan in the Hebrew Bible* (HSM, 43; Atlanta: Scholars Press, 1988).

Deninger-Polzer, Gertrude, 'Hiobs Frau: Leidtragende, nicht Randfigur', in K. Walter (ed.), *Zwischen Ohnmacht und Befreiung: Biblische Frauengestalten* (Freiburg: Herder, 1988), pp. 109-21.

Denis, Albert-Marie, *Concordance grecque des pseudépigraphes d'Ancient testament: Concordance, corpus des textes, indices* (Avec la collaboration d'Yvonne Janssens et le concours du CETEDOC; Louvain-la-Neuve: Université Catholique de Louvain, 1987).

Dentzer, J.-M., *Le motif du banquet couché dans le Proche-Orient et le monde grec du VIIe au IVe siécle avant J.-C.* (BEFAR, 246; Rome: Ecole française, 1982).

De Pury, A., 'Sagesse et révélation dans l'ancien testament', *RTP* 27 (1977), pp. 1-50.

Dietrich, Walter, *Ein Gott allein? YHWH-Verehrung und biblischer Monotheismus im Kontext der israelitischen und altorientalischen Religionsgeschichte* (OBO, 139; Freiburg: Universitätsverlag/Göttingen: Vandenhoeck & Ruprecht, 1994), pp. 269-306.

Dijk-Hemmes, Fokkelien van, 'Who Would Blame Her? The "Strange" Woman of Proverbs 7', in *Reflections on Theology and Gender* (Kampen: Kok, 1994), pp. 21-32.

Dijk-Hemmes, Fokkelien van, and Athalya Brenner (eds.), *Reflections on Theology and Gender* (Kampen: Kok, 1994).

Dobash, R. Emerson, and Russell Dobash, *Violence against Wives: A Case against the Patriachy* (New York: The Free Press, 1979).

Draisma, Sipke, 'Introduction', in Sipke Draisma (ed.), *Intertextuality in Biblical Writings: Essays in Honour of Bas van Iersel* (Kampen: Kok, 1989), pp. 1-14.

Duhm, Bernhard, *Die Psalmen* (KAT, 14; Tübingen: J.C.B. Mohr, 2nd edn, 1922).

Dussel, Enrique, *Herrschaft und Befreiung: Ansatz, Stationen und Themen einer lateinamerikanischen Theologie der Befreiung* (Friebourg: Edition Exodus, 1985).

Eaton, M., *Ecclesiastes* (TOTC; Downer's Grove, IL: InterVarsity Press, 1983).

Ebach, Jürgen, 'Hiob/Hiobbuch', *TRE* 15 (1986), pp. 360-90.

— 'Der Gott des Alten Testaments—ein Gott der Rache?', in Jürgen Ebach (ed.), *Biblische Erinnerungen: Theologische Reden zur Zeit* (Bochum: SWI-Verlag, 1993), pp. 81-93.

—'Interesse und Treue: Anmerkungen zu Exegese und Hermeneutik', in Jürgen Ebach (ed.), *Biblische Erinnerungen: Theologische Reden zur Zeit* (Bochum: SWI-Verlag, 1993), pp. 27-51.

—*Hiobs Post: Gesammelte Aufsätze zum Hiobbuch, zu Themen biblischer Theologie und zur Methodik der Exegese* (Neukirchen–Vluyn: Neukirchener Verlag, 1995).

— *Streiten mit Gott. Hiob. Teil 1: Hiob 1–20. Teil 2: Hiob 21–42* (Neukirchen–Vluyn: Neukirchener Verlag, 1996).

Eissfeldt, Otto, 'Die Flügelsonne als künstlerisches Motiv und als religiöses Symbol', in *Kleine Schriften*, II (Tübingen: J.C.B. Mohr, 1963), pp. 416-19.

Elliger, Karl, *Deuterojesaja* [BKAT 11.1; Neukirchen–Vluyn: Neukirchener Verlag, 1970-1978].

Ellul, J., *Reason for Being: A Meditation on Ecclesiastes* (trans. J.M. Hanks; Grand Rapids: Eerdmans, 1990).

Eskenazi, T.C., and E.P. Judd, 'Marriage to a Stranger in Ezra 9–10', in T.C. Eskenazi and K.H. Richards (eds.), *Second Temple Studies*, II (JSOTSup, 175; Sheffield: JSOT Press, 1994), pp. 266-85.

Eskenazi, T.C., 'Out from the Shadows: Biblical Women in the Postexilic Era', *JSOT* 54 (1992), pp. 25-43.

— 'Out from the Shadows: Biblical Women in the Post-Exilic Era', in Athalya Brenner (ed.), *A Feminist Companion to Samuel and Kings* (FCB, 5; Sheffield: Sheffield Academic Press, 1994), pp. 252-71.

Feldmann, Harald, *Vergewaltigung und ihre psychischen Folgen* (Forum der Psychiatrie, Neue Folge, 33; Stuttgart: Ferdinant Enke Verlag, 1992).

Fewell, Dana Nolan (ed.), *Reading Between the Texts: Intertextuality and the Hebrew Bible* (Louisville: Westminster/John Knox Press, 1992).

Flohtmann, Karin, and Jochen Dilling, *Vergewaltigung: Erfahrungen danach* (Frankfurt: Fischer Verlag, 1987).

Fohrer, G., 'Die Weisheit im Alten Testament', in G. Fohrer, *Studien zur alttestamentlichen Theologie und Geschichte (1949-1966)* (BZAW, 115; Berlin: W. de Gruyter, 1969), pp. 242-74.

Fontaine, Carole R., 'Folktale Structure in the Book of Job: A Formalist Reading', in E.R. Follis (ed.), *Directions in Biblical Hebrew Poetry* (JSOTSup, 40; Sheffield: Sheffield Academic Press, 1987), pp. 205-32.

—'Ecclesiastes', in C.A. Newsom and S.H. Ringe (eds.), *The Women's Bible Commentary* (Louisville, KY: Westminster/John Knox Press, 1992), pp. 153-55.

—'Proverbs', in Carol Newsom and Sharon Ringe (eds.), *The Women's Bible Commentary* (Louisville, KY: Westminster/John Knox, 1993), pp. 145-52.

—'Proverb Performance in the Hebrew Bible', reprinted in David J.A. Clines (ed.), *The Poetical Books: A Sheffield Reader* (The Biblical Seminar, 41; Sheffield: Sheffield Academic Press, 1997), pp. 316-32.

Fortune, Marie M., ' "My God, My God, Why Have You Forsaken Me?" ', in Marie M. Fortune (ed.), *Spinning a Sacred Yarn: Women from the Pulpit* (New York: The Pilgrim Press, 1982), pp. 65-71.

Fox, M.V., *Qohelet and his Contradictions* (JSOTSup, 71; Sheffield: Almond Press, 1989).

Fox, M.V., and B. Porten, 'Unsought Discoveries: Qohelet 7:23–8:1a', *HS* 9 (1978), pp. 26-38.

Frei, P., 'Zentralgewalt und Lokalautonomie im Achämeniden reich', in P. Frei and K. Koch, *Reichsidee und Reichsorganisation im Perserreich* (OBO, 55; Freiburg: Universitätsverlag; Göttingen: Vandenhoeck und Ruprecht, 1984), pp. 7-43.

Fretheim, Terence, *Genesis* (IB; Nashville: Abingdon Press, 1993).

Frevel, Christian, *Das Buch Rut* (NSKAT, 6; Stuttgart: Verlag Katholisches Bibelwerk, 1992).

Fuchs, Gisela, *Mythos und Hiobdichtung: Aufnahme und Umdeutung altorientalischer Vorstellungen* (Stuttgart: Kohlhammer, 1993).

Garrett, D.A., 'Ecclesiastes 7.25-29 and the Feminist Hermeneutic', *CTR* 2.2 (1988), pp. 309-21.

Geller Nathanson, H. Barbara, 'Reflections on the Silent Woman of Ancient Judaism and her Pagan Roman Counterpart', in Kenneth Hoglund *et al.* (eds.), *The Listening Heart: Essays in Wisdom and the Psalms in Honor of Roland E. Murphy, O. Carm.* (JSOTSup 58; Sheffield: Sheffield Academic Press, 1987), pp. 259-80

Geller, Stephan A., 'Where is Wisdom?: A Literary Study of Job 28 in its Settings', in J. Neusner, B.A. Levine and E.S. Frerichs (eds.), *Judaic Perspectives on Ancient Israel* (Philadelphia: Fortress Press, 1987), pp. 155-88.

Genette, Günard, *Palimpsestes: La littérature au second degré* (Paris: Seuil, 1982).

Gerstenberger, Erhard S., *Psalms: Part 1. With an Introduction to Cultic Poetry* (FOTL, 14; Grand Rapids: Eerdmans, 1988).

—*Yahweh the Patriarch: Ancient Images of God and Feminist Theology* (trans. F. Gaiser; Minneapolis: Fortress Press, 1996).

Gese, H., 'Die Weisheit, der Menschensohn und die Ursprünge der Christologie als konsequente Entfaltung der biblischen Theologie', *SEA* 44 (1979), pp. 77-114.

—'Wisdom, Son of Man, and the Origins of Christology: The Consistent Development of Biblical Theology', *Horizons in Biblical Theology* 3 (1981), pp. 23-57.

Gianni, Marta, 'Il "Malleus Maleficarum" e il "De Pythonicis Mulieribus": Due modi d'indendere la stregoneria sul finire del XV secolo', in G. Arnaldi *et al.* (eds.), *Studi sul medioevo cristiano offerti a Raffaello Morghen per il 90° anniversario dell'Istituto Storico Italiano* (1883-1973), I (Rome: Nella sede dell'istituto, 1974), pp. 407-26.

Ginsburg, C.D., *Coheleth (Commonly Called the Book of Ecclesiastes)* (repr., New York: Ktav, 1970 [1861]).

Goitein, S.D., 'Women as Creators of Biblical Genres', *Prooftexts* 8 (1988), pp. 1-33.

Gordis, R., *Koheleth—The Man and his World* (repr.; New York: Bloch Publishing, 1962 [1955]).

—*The Book of God and Man: A Study of Job* (Chicago: Chicago University Press, 1965).

—*Koheleth: The Man and his World* (New York: Schocken Books, 3rd edn, 1968).

Gruber M.I., 'The Hebrew *qĕdēšāh* and her Canaanite and Akkadian Cognates', in *The Motherhood and God and Other Studies* (Atlanta: Scholars Press, 1992), pp. 17-47.

Guest, Edgar, 'Home', in John Bartlett, *Bartlett's Familiar Quotations* (rev. by Emily Beck; Boston: Little, Brown & Company, 14th edn, 1968), p. 963.

Gunkel, Hermann, *Die Psalmen* (Göttingen: Vandenhoeck & Ruprecht, 5th edn, 1968).

Gurney, O.R. *The Hittites* (Harmondsworth: Penguin Books, rev. edn, 1981).

Gutiérrez, Gustavo, *Hablar de Dios desde el sufrimiento del inocente: Una reflexíon sobre el libro de Job* (Salamanca: Ed. Sigueme, 1986).

—*Von Gott sprechen in Unrecht und Leid—Ijob* (Munich: Kaiser Verlag; Mainz: Grünewald Verlag, 1988).

Habel, Norman, *The Book of Job: A Commentary* (OTL; Philadelphia: Westminster Press, 1985).

Hainthaler, Theresia, *'Von der Ausdauer Ijobs habt ihr gehört' (Jak 5,11): Zur Bedeutung des Buches Ijob im Neuen Testament* (Main: Peter Lang, 1988).

Hartley, John E., *The Book of Job* (NICOT, 18, Grand Rapids: Eerdmans, 1988).

Heijerman, M., 'Who Would Blame Her? The "Strange" Woman of Proverbs 7', in van Dijk-Hemmes and Brenner (eds.), *Reflections on Theology and Gender*, pp. 21-32.

Hermisson, Hans-Jürgen and Eduard Lohse, *Glauben* (Stuttgart: Kohlhammer, 1978).

Hog Doty, Susan Elizabeth, 'From Ivory Tower to City of Refuge: The Role and Function of the Protagonist in "Joseph and Aseneth" and Related Narrative' (PhD dissertation; The Iliff School of Theology and the University of Denver, 1989)

Hoglund, H.G., *Achaemenid Imperial Administration in Syria-Palestine and the Missions of Ezra and Nehemiah* (Atlanta: Scholars Press, 1992).

Hornung, Erik, *Das Totenbuch der Ägypter* (Zürich: Artemis, 1979).

Horst, Peter W. van der, 'The Role of Women in the Testament of Job', *Ned TTs* 40 (1986), pp. 273-89.

Hossfeld, Frank-Lothar, and Erich Zenger, *Die Psalmen*, I (NEB; Würzburg: Echter Verlag, 1993).

Huber, Paul, *Hiob—Dulder oder Rebell? Byzantinische Miniaturen zum Buch Hiob in Patmos, Rom, Venedig, Sinai, Jerusalem und Athos* (Düsseldorf: Patmos Verlag, 1986).

Jahnow, H. *Feministische Hermeneutik und Erstes Testament* (Kohlhammer: Stuttgart, 1994), pp. 67-84.

Janowski, B., 'Die Tat kehrt zum Täter zurück: Offene Fragen im Umkreis des "Tun-Ergehen-Zusammenhangs"', *ZTK* 91 (1994), pp. 247-71.

Kayatz, Chr., *Studien zu Prov. 1–9. Eine form- und motivgeschichtliche Untersuchung unter Einbeziehung ägyptischen Vergleichsmaterials* (WMANT, 22; Neukirchen-Vluyn: Neukirchener Verlag, 1966).

Keel, Othmar, *Feinde und Gottesleugner: Studien zum Image der Widersacher in den Individualpsalmen* (Stuttgart: Verlag Katholisches Bibelwerk, 1969).

— 'Erwägungen zum Sitz im Leben des Pascha und zur Etymologie von פסח', *ZAW* 84 (1972), pp. 414-34.

—*Jahwes Entgegnung an Ijob: Eine Deutung von Ijob 38-41 vor dem Hintergrund der zeitgenössischen Bildkunst* (Göttingen: Vandenhoeck & Ruprecht, 1978).

—*Deine Blicke sind Tauben: Zur Metaphorik des Hohen Liedes* (SBS, 114/115; Stuttgart: Verlag Katholisches Bibelwerk, 1984).

—'Allgegenwärtige Tiere: Einige Weisen ihrer Wahrnehmung in der hebräischen Bibel', in Bernd Janowski, Ute Neumann-Gorsolke and Uwe Gleßmer (eds.), *Gefährten und Feinde der Menschen: Das Tier in der Lebenswelt des Alten Israels* (Neukirchen-Vluyn: Neukirchener Verlag, 1993), pp. 156-93.

—'Jahre und die Sonnengottheit von Jerusalem', in Walter Dietrich and Martin Klopfenstein (eds.), *Ein Gott Allein? YWHW-Verehrung und biblischer Monotheismus im Kontext der israelitschen und altorientalischen Religionsgeschichte* (OBO, 139; Freiburg: Universitätsverlag; Göttingen: Vandenhoek & Ruprecht, 1994), pp. 269-306.

Keel, Othmar, and Christoph Uehlinger, *Göttinnen, Götter und Göttessymbole: Neue Erkenntnisse zur Religionsgeschichte Kanaans und Israels aufgrund bislang unerschlossener ikonographischer Quellen* (QD, 134; Freiburg: Herder, 3rd edn, 1995; ET *Goddesses, Gods, and God Symbols* [Minneapolis: Fortress Press, 1998]).

Keel, Othmar, Max Küchler and Christoph Uehlinger, *Orte und Landschaften der Bibel: Ein Handbuch und Studienreiseführer*. I. *Geographisch-geschichtliche Landeskunde* (Zürich: Benziger Verlag; Göttingen: Vandenhoeck & Ruprecht, 1984).

Kessler, Rainer, '"Ich weiß, daß mein Erlöser lebet": Sozialgeschichtlicher Hintergrund und theologische Bedeutung der Löser-Vorstellung in Hiob 19,25', *ZTK* 89 (1992), pp. 139-58.

Kirkpatrick, A.F., *The Book of Psalms with Introduction and Notes* (Cambridge: Cambridge University Press, 1902).

Kittel, Rudolph, *Die Psalmen* (Leipzig: A. Deichert, 1922).

Klein, Lillian R., 'Job and the Womb: Text about Men, Subtext about Women', in Brenner (ed.), *A Feminist Companion to Wisdom Literature*, pp. 186-200.

Knapp, Gudrun-Axeli, 'Macht und Geschlecht: Neuere Entwicklungen in der feministischen Macht- und Herrschaftsdiskussion', in Gudrun-Axeli Knapp and Angelika Wetterer (eds.), *Traditionen Brüche: Entwicklungen feministischer Theorie* (Freiburg: Kore, 1992), pp. 287-325.

Knauf, Ernst A., 'Ijobs Heimat', *WO* 19 (1988), pp. 65-83.

Knobel, Peter S., *The Targum of Qohelet, tr. with a Critical Introduction, Apparatus and Notes* (The Aramaic Bible, 15; Collegeville, MN: Liturgical Press, 1991).

Knobloch, Fredrick W., 'Adoption', *ABD*, I, pp. 76-79.

Koch, Klaus, 'Is there a Doctrine of Retribution in the Old Testament?', in J.L. Crenshaw (ed.), *Theodicy in the Old Testament* (Issues in Religion and Theology, 4; Philadelphia: Fortress Press, 1983), pp. 57-87.

Koch, K., *Die Profeten I: Assyrische Zeit* (Stuttgart: Kohlhammer, 3rd edn, 1995).

Kramer, Heinrich, and James Sprenger, *The Malleus Maleficarum* (trans. with an introduction, bibliography and notes by Montague Summers; New York: Dover Publications, 1971).

Kraus, Hans-Joachim, *Psalmen* (BKAT, 15; Neukirchen–Vluyn: Neukirchener Verlag, 5th edn, 1978).

—'Logos und Sophia', in *Karl Barths Lichterlehre* (TS, 123; Zürich: Theologischer Verlag, 1978).

— *Psalms* (2 vols.; Minneapolis: Augsburg Press, 1988–89).

— *Psalms 60-150* (trans. H. Oswald; Minneapolis: Fortress Press, 1989).

Krieg, Matthias, *Todesbilder im Alten Testament oder 'Wie die Alten den Tod gebildet'* (ATANT, 73; Zürich: Theologischer Verlag, 1988).

Krispenz, J., *Spruchkompositionen im Buch Proverbia* (EHS.T, 349; Frankfurt: Peter Lang, 1989).

Kristeva, Julia, *Desire in Language: A Semiotic Approach to Literature and Art* (New York: Columbia University Press, 1980).

Krüger, T., '"Frau Weisheit" in Koh 7,26?', *Bib* 73 (1992), pp. 394-403.

Kugel, James, *In Potiphar's House: The Interpretive Life of Biblical Texts* (San Francisco: HarperCollins, 1990; repr. Cambridge, MA: Harvard University Press, 1994).

Lambert, W.G., *Babylonian Wisdom Literature* (Oxford: Clarendon Press, 1960).

Lang, B., *Die weisheitliche Lehrrede: Eine Untersuchung von Sprüche 1-7* (SBS, 54; Stuttgart: Katholisches Bibelwerk, 1972).

—*Frau Weisheit: Deutung einer biblischen Gestalt* (Düsseldorf: Patmos, 1975).

—'Schule und Unterricht im alten Israel', in M. Gilbert (ed.), *La sagesse de l'Ancien Testament* (BETL, 51; Gembloux: Duculot, 1979), pp. 186-201.

—'Der monarchische Monotheismus und die Konstellation zweier Götter im Frühjudentum: Ein neuer Versuch über Menschensohn, Sophia und Christologie', in W. Dietrich and M.A. Klopfenstein (eds.), *Ein Gott allein? YHWH-Verehrung und biblischer Monotheismus im Kontext der israelitischen und altorientalischen Religionsgeschichte* (OBO, 139; Freiburg: Universitätsverlag; Göttingen: Vandenhoeck & Ruprecht, 1994), pp. 559-64.

—'Monotheismus', *NBL*, II, cols. 834-44.

Langenhorst, Georg, *Hiob unser Zeitgenosse: Die literarische Hiob-Rezeption im 20. Jahrhundert als theologische Herausforderung* (Mainz: Grünewald Verlag, 2nd edn, 1995).

Lesses, Rebecca, 'The Daughters of Job', in E. Schüssler Fiorenza (ed.), *Searching the Scriptures* (2 vols.; New York: Crossroad Publishing, 1994), II, pp. 139-49.

Levack, Brian P. (ed.), *Articles on Witchcraft, Magic and Demonology: A Twelve Volume Anthology of Scholarly Articles. X. Witchcraft, Women and Society* (New York: Garland Publishing, 1992).

Levine, A.-J., 'Second Temple Judaism, Jesus, and Women: *Yeast of Eden'*, in Athalya Brenner (ed.), *A Feminist Companion to the Hebrew Bible in the New Testament* (FCB, 10; Sheffield: Sheffield Academic Press, 1996), pp. 302-31.

Lewis, Claudia, 'Requiem for a Jew', *Tikkun* 11 (1996), pp. 76-80.

Leyerle, Blake, 'John Chrysostom On the Gaze', *Journal of Early Christian Studies* 12. 8 (1993), pp. 159-74.

Lichtheim, M., *Ancient Egyptian Literature: A Book of Readings* (3 vols.; Berkeley: University of California Press, 1973–1980).

—*Ancient Egyptian Literature: A Book of Readings*. I. *The Old and Middle Kingdoms* (3 vols.; Berkeley: University of California Press, 1975).

—*Ancient Egyptian Literature*. II. *The New Kingdom* (3 vols.; Berkeley: University of California Press, 1976).

—*Maat in Egyptian Autobiographies and Related Studies* (OBO, 120; Freiburg: Universitätsverlag; Göttingen: Vandenhoeck & Ruprecht, 1992).

Linafelt, Tod, 'The Undecidability of ברך in the Prologue of Job and Beyond', *BibInt* 4 (1996), pp. 154-72.

Link, C., *Welt als Gleichnis* (BevT, 73; Munich: Chr. Kaiser Verlag, 1976).

Liwak, R., '"Was wir gehört und kennengelernt und unsere Väter uns erzählt haben" (Ps 78,3): Überlegungen zum Schulbetrieb im Alten Israel', in E. Axmacher and K. Schwarzwäller (eds.), *Belehrter Glaube: Festschrift für J. Wirsching zum 65. Geb.* (Main: Peter Lang, 1994), pp. 175-93.

Lohfink, N., 'War Kohelet ein Frauenfeind? Ein Versuch, die Logik und den Gegenstand von Koh. 7:23–8.1a herauszufinden', in M. Gilbert (ed.), *La sagesse de l'Ancien Testament* (BETL, 51; Leuven: Leuven University Press, 1979), pp. 259-87.

Lopez, García, 'סבב', *ThWAT*, V, pp. 730-44.

Loretz, O., 'Poetry and Prose in the Book of Qohelet (1:1–3.22; 7:23–8.1)', in J. de Moor and W. Watson (eds.), *Verse in Ancient Near Eastern Prose* (Neukirchen–Vluyn: Neukirchener Verlag, 1993), pp. 155-89.

Maier, C., *Die 'fremde Frau' in Proverbien 1–9: Eine exegetische und sozialgeschichtliche Studie* (OBO, 144; Freiburg: Universitätsverlag; Göttingen: Vandenhoeck & Ruprecht, 1995).

—'"Begehre nicht ihre Schönheit in deinem Herzen" (Prov. 6.25): Eine Aktualisierung des Ehebruchsverbots aus persischer Zeit', *BibInt* 5 (1997), pp. 46-63.

Maillot A., *La contestation: Commentaire de l'Ecclésiaste* (Lyon: Cahiers de réveil, 1971).

Marböck, J., *Weisheit im Wandel* (BBB, 37: Bonn: Hanstein, 1997).

Martínez, Florentino García, *The Dead Sea Scrolls Translated: The Qumran Texts in English* (trans. Wilfred G.E. Watson; Leiden: E.J. Brill, 1994).

Matthews, Victor H., Don C. Benjamin and Claudia V. Camp (eds.), *Honor and Shame in the World of the Bible*, Semeia 68 (1994).

Mays, James L., *Psalms* (Interpretation; Louisville: John Knox Press, 1994).

McKane, William, *Proverbs: A New Approach* (London: SCM Press, 1970)

McKenzie, John L., S.J., 'Reflections on Wisdom', *JBL* 86 (1967), pp. 1-9.

Meier, Sam, 'Job I–II: A Reflection of Genesis I–III', *VT* 39 (1989), pp. 183-93.

Meinhold, A., 'Gott und Mensch in Proverbien iii', *VT* 37 (1987), pp. 468-77.

Meyers, Carol, *Discovering Eve: Ancient Israelite Women in Context* (Oxford: Oxford University Press, 1988).

Miller, Patrick, 'Things too Wonderful: Prayers Women Prayed', in *They Cried to the Lord: The Form and Theology of Biblical Prayer* (Minneapolis: Fortress Press, 1994), pp. 233-43.

Müller, W., 'Adler und Geier als altarabische Gottheiten', in Ingo Kottsieper *et al.* (eds.), *'Wer ist wie du, Herr, unter den Göttern?' Studien zur Theologie und Religionsgeschichte Israels für O. Kaiser zum 70. Geburtstag* (Göttingen: Vandenhoeck & Ruprecht, 1994), pp. 91-107.

Midelfort, H.C. Erik, 'Witchcraft and Religion in Sixteenth-Century Germany: The Formation and Consequences of an Orthodoxy', *Archiv für Reformationsgeschichte* 62 (1971), pp. 266-78.

Miller, J. Maxwell, and John H. Hayes, *A History of Ancient Israel and Judah* (Philadelphia: Westminster Press, 1986).

Miller, Patrick D., *Interpreting the Psalms* (Philadelphia: Fortress Press, 1986).

—'Things too Wonderful: Prayers Women Prayed', in *They Cried to the Lord: The Form and Theology of Biblical Prayer* (Minneapolis: Fortress Press, 1994), pp. xxx.

Moore, Rick D., ' "Personification of the Seduction of Evil: "The Wiles of the Wicked Woman" ', *RevQ* 10 (1979–81), pp. 505-19.

Mowinckel, Sigmund, *The Psalms in Israel's Worship* (trans. D.R. Ap-Thomas; Sheffield: JSOT Press, 1962).

Murphy, R.E., 'What and Where is Wisdom?', *Currents in Theology and Mission* 4 (1977), pp. 283-87.

—'Israel's Wisdom: A Biblical Model of Salvation', *Studa Missionalia* 30 (1981), pp. 1-33, esp. 39-42.

—*Ecclesiastes* (WBC, 23a; Dallas, TX: Word Books, 1992).

—'Recent Research on Proverbs and Qoheleth', *CR:BS* 1 (1993), pp. 119-40.

Nathanson, B.H.G., 'Reflections on the Silent Woman of Ancient Judaism and her Pagan Roman Counterpart', in Kenneth Hoglund *et al.* (eds.), *The Listening Heart: Essays in Wisdom and the Psalms in honor of Roland E. Murphy, O. Carm.* (JSOTSup, 58; Sheffield, England: Sheffield Academic Press, 1987), pp. 259-80.

Newsom, Carol A., 'Woman and the Discourse of Patriarchal Wisdom: A Study of Proverbs 1–9', in Peggy L. Day (ed.), *Gender and Difference in Ancient Israel* (Minneapolis: Fortress Press, 1989), pp. 142-60

—'Job', in C.A. Newsom and H. Ringe, (eds.), *The Women's Bible Commentary* (Louisville: Westminster/John Knox Press, 1992), pp. 130-36.

Newsom, Carol A., and Sharon Ringe (eds.), *Women's Bible Commentary* (London: SPCK; Louisville, KY: Westminster/John Knox Press, 1992).

Nickelsburg, George W.E., *Jewish Literature Between the Bible and the Mishnah* (Philadelphia: Fortress Press, 1981).

Niehr, Herbert, *Der höchste Gott: Alttestamentlicher JHWH-Glaube im Kontext syrisch-kanaanäischer Religionen des 1. Jahrtausends v. Chr.* (Berlin: W. de Gruyter, 1990).

Noth, M., 'Die Bewährung von Salomos "göttlicher Weisheit" ', in M. Noth and D.W. Thomas (eds.), *Wisdom in Israel and in the Ancient Near East* (VTSup, 3; Leiden: E.J. Brill, 1955), pp. 225-37.

O'Connor, Kathleen, *The Wisdom Literature* (The Message of Biblical Spirituality, 5; Wilmington, DE: Michael Glazier, 1988).

Oeming, Manfred, ' "Kannst du der Löwin ihren Raub zu jagen geben?" (Hi 38,39): Das Motiv des "Herrn der Tiere" und seine Bedeutung für die Theologie der

Gottesreden Hi 38–42', in M. Augustin and K.-D. Schunck (eds.), *Dort ziehen Schiffe dahin….* *Collected Communications to the XIVth Congress of the International Organization for the Study of the Old Testament, Paris 1992* (BEATAJ, 28; Frankfurt: Peter Lang, 1996), pp. 147-63.

Ogden, G., *Qoheleth* (Readings: Sheffield: JSOT Press, 1987).

Otto, E., 'עיר', *ThWAT* , VI, pp. 56-74.

Paley, Morton D., *William Blake* (New York: Greenwich House, 1983).

Pardes, Ilana, *Countertraditions in the Bible: A Feminist Approach* (Cambridge, MA: Harvard University Press, 1992).

Paret, Rudi, *Der Koran: Kommentar und Konkordanz* (Stuttgart: W. Kohlhammer, 2nd edn, 1980).

Peels, H.G.L., 'On the Wings of the Eagle (Deut. 32.11)—An Old Misunderstanding', *ZAW* 106 (1994), pp. 300-303.

Perdue, Leo G., *Wisdom and Cult: A Critical Analysis of the Views of Cult in the Wisdom Literature of Israel's Ancient Near East* (SBLDS, 30; Missoula, MT: Scholars Press, 1977).

—'The Israelite and Early Jewish Family', in Perdue *et al.*, *Families in Ancient Israel*, p. 175.

—'Household, Theology, and Contemporary Hermeneutics', in Perdue *et al.*, *Families in Ancient Israel*, pp. 237-39.

—*Wisdom and Cult: A Critical Analysis of the Views of Cult in the Wisdom Literature of Israel's Ancient Near East* (SBLDS, 30: Missoula, MT: Scholars Press, 1997).

Perdue, Leo G., Joseph Blenkinsopp, John J. Collins and Carol Meyers, *Families in Ancient Israel* (Louisville, KY: Westminster / John Knox Press, 1997).

Perry, T.A., *Dialogues with Koheleth: The Book of Ecclesiastes* (University Park, PA: Pennsylvania State University Press, 1993).

Perry-Lehmann, M. (ed.), *There Was a Man in the Land of Uz: William Blake's Illustrations to the Book of Job* (Jerusalem: The Israel Museum, 1992).

Phillips, John A., *Eve: The History of an Idea* (San Francisco: Harper & Row, 1984).

Piankoff, Alexandre, and Natasha Rambova, *Mythological Papyri* (2 vols.; Egyptian Religious Texts and Representations, 3 ; New York: Pantheon Books, 1954).

Philonenko, Marc, *Joseph et Aséneth: Introduction, texte critique, traduction et notes* (Studia Post-biblica; Leiden: E.J. Brill, 1968).

Plett, H., 'Intertextualities', in H. Plett (ed.), *Intertextuality* (Berlin: W. de Gruyter, 1991), pp. 3-27.

Pomeroy, Sarah B., *Goddesses, Whores, Wives, and Slaves: Women in Classical Antiquity* (New York: Schocken Books, 1975).

—*Women in Hellenistic Egypt from Alexander to Cleopatra* (New York: Schocken Books, 1984), pp. 26-38.

Pressler, Carolyn, *The View of Women Found in the Deuteronomic Laws* (BZAW, 216; Berlin: W. de Gruyter, 1993).

Puech, Emile, 'Un hymne essénien et les Béatitudes', *RevQ* 13 (1988), pp. 57-88.

—'The Collection of Beatitudes in Hebrew and in Greek (4Q525 1-4 and MT 5, 3-12)', in F. Manns and E. Alliata (eds.), *Early Christianity in Context: Monuments and Documents* (Studium Biblicum Franciscanum; Collectio Maior, 38; Jerusalem: Franciscan Printing Press, 1993), pp. 353-68.

Rad, Gerhard von, *Old Testament Theology* , I (New York: Harper and Row, 1962).

—*The Problem of the Hexateuch and Other Essays* (New York: McGraw–Hill, 1966).

—*Genesis: A Commentary* (OTL; Philadelphia: Westminster Press, 1972).

—*Wisdom in Israel* (Nashille: Abingdon Press, 1972).

—*Weisheit in Israel* (Neukirchen-Vluyn: Neukirchener Verlag, 3rd edn, 1985).

Rahner, K., *Foundations of Christian Faith* (New York: Seabury, 1978).

Raiser, Konrad, 'Klage als Befreiung', *Einwürfe* 5 (1988), pp. 13-27.

Raphael, M., *Thealogy and Embodiment: The Post-Patriarchal Reconstruction of Female Sacrality* (Sheffield: Sheffield Academic Press, 1996).

Rappoport, Angelo S., *Myth and Legend of Ancient Israel* (III New York: Ktav, 1966).

Reed, Esther D., 'Whither Postmodernism and Feminist Theology?', *FT* 6 (1994), pp. 15-29.

Rickenbacher, O., *Weisheitsperikopen bei Ben Sira* (OBO, 1; Freiburg: Universitätsverlag, 1973).

Riffaterre, Michael, 'The Interpretant in Literary Semiotics', *American Journal of Semiotics* 3 (1985), pp. 41-55.

Ringgren, H. 'אָב *'āḇ, ThWAT*, I, cols. 1-19 (from col. 7) .

Römheld, K.F.D., *Wege der Weisheit: Die Lehren Amenemopes und Proverbien 22,17-24,22* (BZAW, 184; Berlin: W. de Gruyter, 1989), pp. 151-81.

Roo, Jacqueline C.R. de, 'Is 4Q525 a Qumran Sectarian Document?', in Stanley E. Porter and Craig A. Evans (eds.), *The Scrolls and the Scriptures: Qumran Fifty Years After* (Sheffield: Sheffield Academic Press, 1997), pp. 338-67.

Rudman, Dominic, 'Woman as Divine Agent in Ecclesiastes', *JBL* 116 (1997), pp. 411-27.

Rudolph, Wilhelm, *Haggai-Sacharja-Maleachi-Kommentar* (KAT, 13.4; Gütersloh: Gütersloher Verlagshaus [Gerd Mohn], 1976).

Ruger, H.P., ' "Amôn-Pflegekind: Zur Auslegungsgeschichte von Prov. 8:30a', in *Übersetzung und Deutung: Studien zu dem AT und seiner Umwelt. A.R. Hulst gewidmet von Freunden und Kollegen* (Nijkerk: F. Callenbach, 1977), pp. 154-63.

Ruppert, Lothar, 'Klagelieder in Israel und Babylon: Verschiedene Deutungen der Gewalt', in Norbert Lohfink (ed.), *Gewalt und Gewaltlosigkeit im Alten Testament* (Freiburg: Herder, 1983), pp. 111-58.

Sandelin, Karl-Gustav, 'A Wisdom Meal in the Romance Joseph and Aseneth', in *Wisdom as Nourisher: A Study of the Old Testament Theme, its Development Within Early Judaism and its impact on Early Christianity* (Åbo: Åbo Akademi, 1986), pp. 151-57.

Sanders, Jack T., 'When Sacred Canopies Collide: The Reception of the Torah of Moses in the Wisdom Literature of the Second-Temple Period', paper read at the SBL Annual Meeting, 1996.

Schiele, Beatrix, 'Die Gewalt gegen Frauen als Herausforderung einer feministischen Ethik', *Schlangenbrut* 25 (1991), pp. 6-12.

Schmid, H., *Altorientalische Welt in der alttestamentlichen Theologie* (Zurich: Theologische Verlag, 1974).

Schmid, H.H., *Gerechtigkeit als Weltordnung: Hintergrund und Geschichte des alttestamentlichen Gerechtigkeitsbegriffes* (BHT, 40; Tübingen: J.C.B. Mohr, 1968).

Schmidt, H.H., *Wesen und Geschichte der Weisheit* (BZAW, 101: Berlin: Alfred Töpelmann, 1966).

Schmitt, John J., 'Israel and Zion—Two Gendered Images: Biblical Speech Traditions and Their Contemporary Neglect', *Horizons* 81.1 (1991), pp. 18-32.

Schottroff, Luise, *Lydia's Impatient Sisters: A Feminist Social History of Early Christianity* (trans. Barbara and Martin Rumscheidt; Louisville, KY: Westminster/John Knox Press, 1991).

Schottroff, Luise, Silvia Schroer and Marie-Theres Wacker, *Feministische Exegese: Forschungserträge zur Bibel aus der Perspektive von Frauen* (Darmstadt: Wissenschaftliche Buchgesellschaft, 1995; ET *Feminist Interpretation: The Bible in Women's Perspective* [Minneapolis: Fortress Press, 1998]).

Schottroff, Luise, and Marie-Theres Wacker (eds.), *Kompendium Feministiche Bibelauslegung* (Gütersloh: Gütersloher Verlag, 1998).

Schottroff, Willy, 'Zur Sozialgeschichte Israels in der Perserzeit', *Verkündigung und Forschung* 27 (1982), pp. 46-68.

Schreiner, Stefan, 'Der gottesfürchtige Rebell oder Wie die Rabbinen die Frömmigkeit Hiobs deuteten', *ZTK* 89 (1992), pp. 159-71.

Schroer, Silvia, 'Entstehungsgeschichtliche und gegenwärtige Situierungen des Hiob-Buches', in Ökumenischer Arbeitskreis für Bibelarbeit (ed.), *Hiob (Bibelarbeit in der Gemeinde)* (Basel: Reinhardt Verlag; Zürich: Benziger Verlag, 1989), pp. 35-62.

—'In die Enge getrieben—in die Weite geführt: Hiobs Klage und die erste Gottesrede (Hiob 3 und 38–39)', in Ökumenischer Arbeitskreis für Bibelarbeit (ed.), *Hiob*, pp. 128-60.

— 'Die göttliche Weisheit und der nachexilische Monotheismus', in M.-Th. Wacker and E. Zenger (eds.), *Der eine Gott und die Göttin: Gottesvorstellungen des biblischen Israel im Horizont feministischer Theologie* (QD, 135; Freiburg: Herder, 1991), pp. 151-82. Reprinted in S. Schroer, *Die Weisheit hat ihr Haus gebaut*, pp. 27-62.

— 'Die Göttin und der Geier', in *ZDPV* 3 (1995), pp. 60-80.

— *Die Weisheit hat ihr Haus gebaut: Studien zur Gestalt der Sophia in den biblichen Schriften* (Mainz: Grünewald, 1996).

—'Weise Frauen und Ratgeberinnen in Israel—literarische und historische Vorbilder der personifizierten Chokmah', *BN* 51 (1990), pp. 41-60 (reprinted in S. Schroer, *Die Weisheit hat ihr Haus gebaut: Studien zur Gestalt der Sophia in den biblischen Schriften* [Mainz: Grünewald, 1996], pp. 63-79).

Schuller, Eileen M., 'The Apocrypha' in Carol A. Newsom and Sharon H. Ringe (eds.), *The Women's Bible Commentary* (Louisville, KY: Westminster/John Knox Press, 1992), pp. 235-43.

Scot, Reginald, *The Discoverie of Witchcraft* (with introduction by H.R. Williamson; (Carbondale, IL: Southern Illinois University Press, 1964).

Scott, R.B.Y., *Proverbs and Ecclesiastes* (AB; Garden City, NY: Doubleday, 1965).

—'Priesthood, Prophecy, Wisdom, and the Knowledge of God', *JBL* 80 (1961), pp. 1-15.

Seidel, Hans, *Das Erlebnis der Einsamkeit im Alten Testament: Eine Untersuchung zum Menschenbild des Alten Testaments* (Berlin: Evangelische Verlagsanstalt, 1969).

Seifert, Ruth, 'Entwicklungslinien und Probleme der feministischen Theoriebildung: Warum an der Rationalität kein Weg vorbeiführt', in Gudrun-Axeli Knapp and Angelika Wetterer (eds.), *Traditionen Brüche: Entwicklungen feministischer Theorie* (Freiburg: Kore, 1992), pp. 255-85.

—'Krieg und Vergewaltigung: Ansätze zu einer Analyse', in Friedel Schreyögg (ed.), *Nirgends erwähnt—doch überall geschehen… Vergewaltigung im Krieg*

(Munich: Gleichstellungsstelle für Frauen, 1992), pp. 1-19.

Seybold, Klaus, *Das Gebet des Kranken im Alten Testament: Untersuchungen zur Bestimmung und Zuordnung der Krankheits—und Heilungspsalmen* (Stuttgart: W. Kohlhammer, 1973).

Skehan, P.W, 'Structures in Poems on Wisdom: Proverbs 8 and Sirach 24', *CBQ* 41 (1970), pp. 365-79.

Sheppard, Gerald T., ' "Enemies" and the Politics of Prayer in the Book of the Psalms', in David Jobling, Peggy L. Day and Gerald T. Sheppard (eds.), *The Bible and the Politics of Exegesis: Essays in Honor of Norman K. Gottwald on his Sixty-Fifth Birthday* (Cleveland, OH: The Pilgrim Press 1991), pp. 61-82.

Sherwood, Yvonne, *The Prostitute and the Prophet: Hosea's Marriage in Literary-Theoretical Perspective* (JSOTSup, 212; Sheffield: Sheffield Academic Press, 1996).

Shupak, N., *Where can Wisdom be Found? The Sage's Language in the Bible and in Ancient Egyptian Literature* (OBO, 130; Freiburg: Universitätsverlag / Göttingen: Vandenhoeck & Ruprecht, 1993).

Sitzler, Dorothea, *Vorwurf gegen Gott: Ein religiöses Motiv im Alten Orient (Ägypten und Mesopotamien)* (Studies in Oriental Religions, 32; Wiesbaden: Otto Harrassowitz, 1995).

Smalley, Beryl, *Medieval Exegesis of Wisdom Literature* (Atlanta: Scholars Press, 1986).

Snijders, L.A., 'The Meaning of זר in the Old Testament: An Exegetical Study', *OTS* 10 (1954), pp. 1-154.

—'זר / זור', *ThWAT*, II (1977), pp. 556-64.

Sparks, H.F.D., *The Apocryphal Old Testament* (Oxford: Clarendon Press, 1984).

Spieckermann, Hermann, 'Die Satanisierung Gottes: Zur inneren Konkordanz von Novelle, Dialog und Gottesreden im Hiobbuch', in I. Kottsieper *et al.* (eds.), *Wer ist wie du, HERR, unter den Göttern?: Studien zur Theologie und Religions-geschichte Israels für O. Kaiser zum 70. Geburtstag* (Göttingen: Vandenhoeck & Ruprecht, 1994), pp. 431-44.

Stähli, Hans-Peter, *Solare Elemente im Jahweglauben des Alten Testaments* (OBO, 66; Freiburg: Universitätsverlag; Göttingen: Vandenhoeck & Ruprecht, 1985).

Stanton, Elizabeth Cady, *The Woman's Bible* [2 vols.; Edinburgh: Polygon Books, 1985 [1898]), II, pp. 99-100.

Stardhartinger, Angela, *Das Frauenbild im Judentum der hellenistischen Zeit: Ein Beitrag anhand von Joseph und Aseneth* (AGJU; Leiden: E.J. Brill, 1995).

Steck, Odil Hannes, *Friedensvorstellungen im alten Israel: Psalmen. Jesaja. Deutero-jesaja* (Zürich: Theologischer Verlag, 1972).

—*World and Environment* (Nashville: Abingdon Press, 1978).

—'Zion als Gelände und Gestalt: Überlegungen zur Wahrnehmung Jerusalems als Stadt und als Frau im Alten Testament', *ZTK* 86 (1989), pp. 261-81.

Steiert, F.-J., *Die Weisheit Israels—ein Fremdkörper im Alten Testament? Eine Unter-suchung zum Buch der Sprüche auf dem Hintergrund der ägyptischen Weisheits-lehren* (FThSt, 143; Freiburg: Herder, 1990).

Sterring, Anki, 'The Will of the Daughters', in A. Brenner (ed.), *A Feminist Companion to Exodus to Deuteronomy* (FCB, 6; Sheffield: Sheffield Academic Press, 1994), pp. 88-99.

Stierle, Karlheinz, 'Werk und Intertextualität', in Wolf Schmid and Wolf-Dieter

Stempel (eds.), *Dialog der Texte: Hamburger Kolloquium zur Intertextualität* (Vienna: Wiener Slawistischer Almanach, 1983), pp. 7-26.

Strugnell, John, 'Notes en marge du volume V des "Discoveries in the Judaean Desert of Jordan"', *RevQ* 7 (1970), pp. 163-276.

Susman, Margarete, *Das Buch Hiob und das Schicksal des jüdischen Volkes* (Freiburg: Herder, [1968] 1946).

Sutter Rehmann, L. 'Das Testament Hiobs: Hiob, Dina und ihre Töchter', in L. Schotroff and M.-T. Wacker (eds.), *Kompendium feministische bibelauslegung* (Güterlöh: Gütersloher Verlag, 1998), pp. 465-73.

Talmon, S., 'מדבר', *ThWAT*, IV, pp. 660-95.

Teissier, Beatrice, *Egyptian Iconography on Syro-Palestinian Cylinder Seals of the Middle Bronze Age* (OBO, Arch. Ser. 11; Freiburg: Universitätsverlag; Göttingen: Vandenhoeck & Ruprecht, 1986).

Terrien, S., *The Elusive Presence* (New York: Harper & Row, 1978).

—'The Play of Wisdom: Turning Point in Biblical Theology', *Horizons in Biblical Theology* 3 (1981), pp. 125-53.

—*The Iconography of Job through the Centuries: Artists as Biblical Interpreters* (University Park, PA: Pennsylvania State University Press, 1996).

Thistlethwaite, Susan Brooks, '"You May Enjoy the Spoil of Your Enemies": Rape as a Biblical Metaphor for War', *Semeia* 61 (1993), pp. 59-78.

Thompson, Thomas L., *The Historicity of the Patriarchial Narratives: The Quest for the Historical Abraham* (BZAW, 133; Berlin: W. de Gruyter, 1974).

Thürmer-Rohr, C., 'Aus der Täuschung in die Ent-Täuschung: Zur Mittäterschaft von Frauen', in *idem*, *Vagabundinnen: Feministische Essays* (Berlin: Orlanda Frauenverlag, 1987), pp. 38-56.

Tobin, Thomas, '4Q185 and Jewish Wisdom Literature', in H. Attridge, J. Collins and T. Tobin (eds.), *Of Scribes and Scrolls* (College Theology Society Resources in Religion, 5; Maryland: University Press of America, 1990), pp. 145-52.

Tomaselli, Sylvana, and Roy Porter (eds.), *Rape* (Oxford: Basil Blackwell, 1986).

Toorn, K. van der, 'Female Prostitution in Payment of Vows in Ancient Israel', *JBL* 108 (1989), pp. 193-205.

Torjesen, Karen Jo., *When Women Were Priests: Women's Leadership in the Early Church and the Scandal of their Subordination in the Rise of Christianity* (San Francisco: Harper & Row, 1993).

Trenchard, Warren C., *Ben Sira's View of Women: A Literary Analysis* (BJS, 38; Chico, CA: Scholars Press, 1982).

Vall, G., 'The Enigma of Job 1,21a', *Bib* 76 (1995), pp. 325-42.

VanderKam, James C., *The Dead Sea Scrolls Today* (Grand Rapids: Eerdmans, 1994).

Vries, A. de, *Dictionary of Symbols and Imagery* (Amsterdam: North-Holland, 1976).

Volz, James W., 'Multiple Signs and Double Texts: Elements of Intertextuality', in Sipke Draisma (ed.), *Intertextuality in Biblical Writings: Essays in Honour of Bas van Iersel* (Kampen: Kok, 1989), pp. 27-34.

Washington, Harold C., 'The "Strange" Woman (נכרוה/אשה זרה) of Proverbs 1–9 and Post-Exilic Judaean Society', in Brenner (ed.), *A Feminist Companion to Wisdom Literature*, pp. 157-84.

Weinberg, J.P., *The Citizen-Temple-Community* (trans. D.L. Smith-Christopher; JSOTSup, 151; Sheffield: Sheffield Academic Press, 1992).

Weiser, A., *The Psalms* (OTL; trans. Herbert Hartwell; Philadelphia: Westminster, 1962).

Wertheimer, Solomon A. (ed.), *Battei Midrashot II* (Jerusalem: Mosad HaRav Quq, 2nd edn, 1968).

Westermann, Claus, *Isaiah 40–66* (Philadelphia: Westminster Press, 1969).

—*Praise and Lament in the Psalms* (trans. K. Crim and R. Soulen; Atlanta: John Knox Press, 1981).

—'Das gute Wort in den Sprüchen: Ein Beitrag zum Menschenverständnis der Spruchweisheit', in Frank Crüsemann, Christof Hardmeier and Rainer Kessler (eds.), *Was ist der Mensch....? Beiträge zur Anthropologie des Alten Testaments. Hans Walter Wolf zum 80. Geburtstag* (Munich: Chr. Kaiser Verlag, 1992), pp. 243-55.

—'Mensch, Tier und Pflanze in der Bibel', in Bernd Janowski, Ute Neumann-Gorsolke and Uwe Gleßmer (eds.), *Gefährten und Feinde des Menschen: Das Tier in der Lebenswelt des Alten Israel* (Neukirchen-Vluyn: Neukirchner Verlag, 1993), pp. 90-102.

Whybray, R.N., *Wisdom in Proverbs* (Studies in Biblical Theology; London: SCM Press, 1965).

— *Ecclesiastes* (OTG; Sheffield JSOT: Press, 1989).

— *Ecclesiastes* (NCB; Grand Rapids: Eerdmans; London: Marshall Morgan & Scott, 1989).

—*The Composition of the Book of Proverbs* (JSOTSup, 168; Sheffield: Sheffield Academic Press, 1994).

Wicksteed, John H., *Blake's Vision of the Book of Job* (London: J.M. Dent & Sons, 1910).

Wilckens, Robert (ed.), *Aspects of Wisdom in Judaism and Early Christianity* (Notre Dame: Notre Dame University, 1975).

Williams, Mary Newman, and Anne Echols, *Between the Pit and Pedestal: Women in the Middle Ages* (Princeton, N.J.: Markus Wiener Publishers, 1994).

Winston, David, *The Wisdom of Solomon* (AB, 43; Garden City: Doubleday, 1979).

Wirtz, Ursula, *Seelenmord: Inzest und Therapie* (Stuttgart: Kreuz Verlag, 1992).

Wolde, Ellen van, 'The Development of Job: Mrs Job as Catalyst', in Brenner (ed.), *A Feminist Companion to Wisdom Literature*, pp. 201-21.

Wright, G.E., *God Who Acts* (SET, 8; Chicago: Regnery, 1952).

Yee, Gale A., ' "I Have Perfumed my Bed with Myrrh": The Foreign Woman (*'iššâ zārâ*) in Proverbs 1–9', *JSOT* 43 (1989), pp. 53-68.

—'I Have Perfumed my Bed with Myrrh: The Foreign Woman (*'iššâ zārâ*) in Proverbs 1–9' in Brenner (ed.), *A Feminist Companion to Wisdom Literature*, pp. 110-26.

—'The Socio-Literary Production of the "Foreign Woman" in Proverbs', in Brenner (ed.), *A Feminist Companion to Wisdom Literature*, pp. 127-30.

Zenger, Erich, *Das Buch Rut* (ZBKAT, 8; Zürich: TVZ Verlag, 1986).

Zilboorg, Gregory, *The Medical Man and the Witch during the Renaissance* (The Hideyo Noguchi lectures; Publications of the Institute of the History of Medicine, 3.2; The Johns Hopkins University Press, 1935; New York: Cooper Square Publishers, 1969).

Zimmerli, W., 'The Place and the Limit of the Wisdom in the Framework of the Old Testament Theology', *SSJT* 17 (1964), pp. 146-58.

—*Old Testament Theology in Outline* (Atlanta: John Knox Press, 1978).

Zimmermann, F., *The Inner World of Qohelet* (New York: Ktav, 1973).

Zimmermann, Ruben, 'Homo Sapiens Ignorans: Hiob 28 als Bestandteil der ursprünglichen Hiobdichtung', *BN* 74 (1994), pp. 80-100.

INDEXES

INDEX OF REFERENCES

BIBLICAL BOOKS